KEY ISSUES IN AFRICAN DIPLOMACY

Developments and Achievements

Edited by
Sven Botha and Jo-Ansie van Wyk

First published in Great Britain in 2024 by

Bristol University Press
University of Bristol
1–9 Old Park Hill
Bristol
BS2 8BB
UK
t: +44 (0)117 374 6645
e: bup-info@bristol.ac.uk

Details of international sales and distribution partners are available at bristoluniversitypress.co.uk

© Bristol University Press 2024

British Library Cataloguing in Publication Data
A catalogue record for this book is available from the British Library

ISBN 978-1-5292-2257-9 hardcover
ISBN 978-1-5292-2258-6 ePub
ISBN 978-1-5292-2259-3 ePdf

The right of Sven Botha and Jo-Ansie van Wyk to be identified as editors of this work has been asserted by them in accordance with the Copyright, Designs and Patents Act 1988.

All rights reserved: no part of this publication may be reproduced, stored in a retrieval system, or transmitted in any form or by any means, electronic, mechanical, photocopying, recording, or otherwise without the prior permission of Bristol University Press.

Every reasonable effort has been made to obtain permission to reproduce copyrighted material. If, however, anyone knows of an oversight, please contact the publisher.

The statements and opinions contained within this publication are solely those of the editors and contributors and not of the University of Bristol or Bristol University Press. The University of Bristol and Bristol University Press disclaim responsibility for any injury to persons or property resulting from any material published in this publication.

Bristol University Press works to counter discrimination on grounds of gender, race, disability, age and sexuality.

Cover design: Hayes Design and Advertising
Front cover image: 123RF / michal812
Bristol University Press uses environmentally responsible print partners.
Printed and bound in Great Britain by CPI Group (UK) Ltd, Croydon, CR0 4YY

To our students: past, present and future

Contents

List of Figure and Tables		vii
List of Abbreviations		viii
Notes on Contributors		x
Acknowledgements		xiv
1	Introducing African Diplomacy as a Field of Study *Sven Botha and Jo-Ansie van Wyk*	1
2	An Overview of the Evolution of Diplomacy in Europe and Africa *François Theron*	11
3	Common African Positions as Diplomatic Instruments *Jo-Ansie van Wyk*	29
4	South Africa's Economic Diplomacy and the African Continental Free Trade Agreement: Challenges and Prospects *Sanusha Naidu, Faith Mabera and Arina Muresan*	42
5	Prospects for Smart Diplomacy and Its Use in the Foreign Policies of African Small Island Developing States *Suzanne Graham and Victoria Graham*	56
6	Maritime Diplomacy and the African Maritime Agenda *Francois Vreÿ*	71
7	Twitter/X Diplomacy and Its Use and Practice in Africa *Suzanne Graham and Victoria Graham*	88
8	The Quiet Diplomacy of the Chibok Abductions *Sven Botha*	105
9	A Diplomatic Conduit: The Role of Science Diplomacy in Africa *Lesley Masters*	121
10	Africa's Health Diplomacy *Jo-Ansie van Wyk*	137
11	Ghana's Cultural Diplomacy *Sandra Asafo-Adjei*	150
12	Morocco's Cultural Diplomacy with Africa *Faiza Koubi*	163

13	Understanding Knowledge Diplomacy in Africa *Jane Knight*	178
14	African Agency: The Case of Russian Nuclear Programmes in Egypt, Ghana, South Africa and Zambia *Dzvinka Kachur and Robyn Foley*	196
15	Challenges and Triumphs for Women Leaders in African Diplomacy *Jennifer Chiriga, Rudo Chitiga and Hesphina Rukato*	221
16	African Diplomacy: An Agenda for Practice and Research *Jo-Ansie van Wyk and Sven Botha*	236

Index   248

List of Figure and Tables

Figure

7.1	Social media in Africa (c March 2022)	93

Tables

7.1	Top 12 African countries in terms of internet penetration (c December 2020)	93
7.2	African regional bodies using Twitter/X (2024)	95
13.1	Conceptual framework for IHERI in a knowledge diplomacy relationship	182
13.2	The Pan-African University's application of key elements of knowledge diplomacy conceptual framework	191
14.1	Research reactors in Africa	198
14.2	Africa nuclear power programme status	199
14.3	Agreements between Russia (or Rosatom) and Zambia	212

List of Abbreviations

AfCFTA	African Continental Free Trade Area
ANC	African National Congress
APSA	African Peace and Security Architecture
AU	African Union
BRICS	Brazil, Russia, India, China and South Africa
CAP	common African position
CDC	Centres for Disease Control
DIRCO	Department of International Relations and Cooperation
ECOWAS	Economic Community of West African States
EU	European Union
FDI	foreign direct investment
FOCAC	Forum on China–Africa Cooperation
GDP	gross domestic product
ICRC	International Committee of the Red Cross
ICT	information and communications technology
IORA	Indian Ocean Rim Association
MDG	Millennium Development Goal
NATO	North Atlantic Treaty Organization
NEPAD	New Partnership for Africa's Development
NGOs	non-government organizations
OAU	Organization of African Unity
PAU	Pan-African University
PSC	Peace and Security Council
R2P	Responsibility to Protect
REC	regional economic community
SADC	Southern African Development Community
SDG	Sustainable Development Goal
SIDS	small island developing states
STI	science, technology and innovation
UN	United Nations
UNDP	United Nations Development Programme

LIST OF ABBREVIATIONS

UNESCO	United Nations Educational, Scientific and Cultural Organization
UNGA	United Nations General Assembly
UNSC	United Nations Security Council
WHO	World Health Organization
WTO	World Trade Organization

Notes on Contributors

Sandra Asafo-Adjei holds a MA in International Affairs from the Legon Centre for International Affairs and Diplomacy (LECIAD) and BA (Hons) English and French from the University of Ghana. Sandra's interests and expertise cover public policy, policy evaluation, cultural diplomacy and peace and security studies. Sandra aims to be part of the next generation of global female policy makers and thought leaders and to make an impact on global public policy formulation and analysis.

Sven Botha is Lecturer in the Department of Political Sciences at the University of Pretoria, South Africa. Sven has worked and published in the areas of responses to terrorism, gender, foreign policy and diplomacy.

Jennifer Chiriga is a policy expert and development practitioner with accumulated work experience in the private sector, civil society and government, as well as in intergovernmental organizations and institutions. She served as Chief of Staff at the African Union Commission and African Union Development Agency (AUDA-NEPAD). She is a member of the Southern African Development Community (SADC) Electoral Advisory Council (SEAC).

Rudo Chitiga is a senior diplomat and former Zimbabwean Ambassador to France, Portugal, Spain and the Vatican. She has held senior management and leadership positions in government, intergovernmental and civil society organizations at national, regional and international levels including Permanent Secretary in the Ministry of Women's Affairs Community Small and Medium Enterprises Development in Zimbabwe.

Robyn Foley is a researcher at the Centre for Sustainability Transitions, Stellenbosch University. Focusing on complexity in governance and the political economy, she co-edited *Anatomy of State Capture*, also contributing to 6 of the 19 chapters in the book. In 2019, Robyn attained her MPhil in Sustainable Development (cum laude) from Stellenbosch University. She also holds a BSc Physics (2007) and a BSc Honours in Technology Management (2008) from the University of Pretoria.

NOTES ON CONTRIBUTORS

Suzanne Graham is Professor in the Politics and International Relations Department and Senior Director: Academic Development and Support at the University of Johannesburg.

Victoria Graham is Associate Professor and Senior Director: Strategic Initiatives and Administration, University of Johannesburg. She holds a PhD in Political Studies from the University of Johannesburg. She is also a research associate in the Department of Political Sciences, University of Pretoria.

Dzvinka Kachur is a research fellow at the Centre for Sustainability Transitions, Stellenbosch University. Her research interests cover the topics of disinformation in South Africa and Russian influences in Sub-Saharan Africa. In her recent research, Dzvinka investigated the 2014 Russia–South Africa nuclear agreement and the Russian presence in Mozambique, Zimbabwe, Tanzania and Zambia. She holds degrees from the University of Oxford (MSc) and the National University of Kyiv-Mohyla Academy (MSc).

Faiza Koubi is a PhD candidate in International Relations at the University of Mohammed V of Rabat, Morocco. She received a Master's degree in Contemporary History from University Paris I Pantheon la Sorbonne, Paris, France, and another in International Studies from Mohammed V University. Faiza completed a diplomatic course at Ecole Nationale d'Administration of France and Morocco. Her work focuses on Moroccan mediation in neighbour conflicts. She is interested in diplomacy, conflict and peace studies, and transnational security issues.

Jane Knight is Professor at the University of Toronto and the University of Johannesburg. Her research focuses on the intersection of international relations and international higher education, research and innovation. Her numerous publications address issues of diplomacy, soft power, regionalization and internationalization. She is the recipient of several awards and two honorary doctorates in addition to her PhDs in Higher Education and Political Science.

Faith Mabera is Senior Researcher at the Institute for Global Dialogue, where she oversees the Foreign Policy Analysis programme. Her research interests include the Responsibility to Protect (R2P), African diplomacy, foreign policy analysis, African peace and security issues, norm dynamics in international relations, and global governance. She is also the co-editor of the book *Africa–China Cooperation towards an African Policy on China?* (Palgrave, 2020). Faith holds a PhD from the University of Pretoria.

Lesley Masters is Senior Lecturer at Nottingham Trent University and a senior research associate at the University of Johannesburg, South

African Research Chairs Initiative (SARChI) Chair in African Diplomacy and Foreign Policy. Before moving into academia, Lesley was a senior researcher at the Institute for Global Dialogue based in Pretoria, responsible for the management of projects on foreign policy and diplomacy. Her research continues to focus on foreign policy, global governance and international diplomacy.

Arina Muresan is a senior researcher at the Institute for Global Dialogue where she contributes to programmatic areas on foreign policy analysis, geopolitical dynamics and governance, and diplomacy. She leads the South Africa in the World project, which reflects on South African foreign policy and diplomacy and has a keen interest in economic and commercial diplomacy, China's engagement in Africa and leadership dynamics. She is part of an ongoing project, the African First Ladies Database, a research project analysing the political leadership, role and influence of the continent's post-colonial First Ladies.

Sanusha Naidu is a senior research associate based at the Institute of Global Dialogue. Her expertise is on South African foreign policy analysis, Africa's relations with actors from the Global South (China and India) and international development cooperation and democratization. Sanusha has published extensively, including two edited books on China–Africa relations and a special edition of the journal *Politikon* on Africa's relations with external powers.

Hesphina Rukato is the author of *Future Africa: Prospects for Democracy and Development under NEPAD* (Africa Research and Publications, 2010). An Africa development specialist, she is a former deputy chief executive at the New Partnership for Africa's Development (NEPAD) Secretariat and has served as deputy chief of staff at the African Union (AU) Commission and associate lecturer at the Thabo Mbeki Leadership Institute. She has served on several boards in the public and private sectors and is co-founder of two companies in the textile and food sector.

François Theron is a former South African diplomat who served in several European, African and Latin American posts. He was a member of the Policy Unit, of which he was briefly acting director prior to his retirement. He holds the BA and LLB degrees, a Master's degree in Diplomatic Studies and is an attorney of the High Court of South Africa.

Jo-Ansie van Wyk is Research Professor of International Politics in the Department of Political Sciences, University of South Africa, Pretoria, South Africa. She has a doctorate in international relations from the University of Pretoria, South Africa. She has published widely and is the co-editor of four volumes of the *South African Foreign Policy Review* (Human Sciences Research Council, 2012, 2015, 2019 and 2022).

Francois Vreÿ is Emeritus Professor in Military Science, Stellenbosch University. He currently serves as research coordinator for the Security Institute for Governance and Leadership in Africa (SIGLA) located within the Faculty of Military Science, Stellenbosch University. One of the research hubs he manages is that of maritime security governance off Africa, which forms part of the landward, cyber and maritime security focus areas of SIGLA

Acknowledgements

A research project is never undertaken in isolation and this book is no exception. There are several people who made this publication possible. First, we wish to thank Dr Philipa Grand, who initially commissioned this collection; your feedback on the draft proposal helped to inspire much of the book's structure. Second, we would like to thank Rebecca Tomlinson, Zoe Forbes, Stephen Wenham and the phenomenal team at Bristol University Press whose outstanding efforts have helped to make this publication a reality.

Next, we wish to thank all the authors who contributed to this volume. Your respective chapters have helped to fill a gaping hole in the literature on diplomatic practice in Africa. We sincerely hope that you have found this process as enlightening and rewarding as we have. It has been a pleasure and a privilege working with all of you. We sincerely hope your participation in this project will result in the emergence of a new research community consisting of scholars and practitioners dedicated to the advancement of insights on and the practice of African diplomacy.

1

Introducing African Diplomacy as a Field of Study

Sven Botha and Jo-Ansie van Wyk

Introduction

In the preface of her second volume of diplomatic theory and practice titled *Global South Perspectives of Diplomacy*, Yolanda Spies asserts that the rest of the world outside of the Global North 'is yet to make a definitive mark on diplomatic studies, and as a proud African and Global Southerner, I want to see this rectified' (Spies, 2019: ii). This book responds to, inter alia, Spies' call, and while it does not claim to rectify this shortfall in its entirety, it attempts to help readers understand how African states practise diplomacy. It is also worth noting that in attempting to map and arouse academic and practitioner interest in African diplomacy, this book does not aim to make contributions to diplomatic theory, despite a clear and ever-present intellectual gap that remains in this area (Sharp, 2009; Balzacq et al, 2020). The book is a first attempt in that process.

Before proceeding, some clarification of the concept 'African diplomacy' is required. African diplomacy, according to the editors, is the tool employed by African state, non-state and intergovernmental actors in their actions towards, interactions with, transactions with and responses to African and non-African players at the bi-, multi- and polylateral levels. Although Africa defies generalizations, the term Africa is used here, unless otherwise specified, as a reference to formal and official continental diplomacy by, for example, the African Union (AU), consisting of the continent's 55 states. A second reference to Africa entails the diplomacy of individual African states, which may be confusing as, for example, European diplomacy is not necessarily synonymous with French diplomacy. In this instance, Africa is referred to as the location of the actor but also in the context of the continent's shared intention and efforts relating to Pan-Africanism, unity and solidarity.

The editors of this volume believe that a thorough explanation of the circumstances of diplomatic functions and practice in Africa, focusing on lived realities and concepts, must first be presented before theoretical discourse can begin; this is a clear shortcoming of the volume and will be addressed in the concluding chapter.

This objective is achieved by presenting a collection of chapters from African and Afro-centric scholars and practitioners, with each chapter investigating a specific diplomatic typology or reality. Therefore, the typological approach is the dominant methodological tradition within this volume. This chapter is dedicated to charting a course for the reader and introducing the reader to African diplomacy as a sub-discipline of diplomatic studies and international relations. In doing so, African diplomacy is regarded as a sub-discipline owing to a unique context that requires increased scholarly attention. Spence, Yorke and Masser (2021: 222) note that 'more needs to be done to understand the different ways people view diplomacy and their role in it – how it has an impact on their lives, and what stories, assumptions and myths give meaning to the actions of the state'. They proceed to note that a better understanding of individual contexts 'will help governments to gain greater legitimacy in their foreign policy and helps publics make more informed decisions[s], which facilitates accountability and fosters more activities and engaged societies' (Spence et al, 2021: 222).

Following this introduction, the chapter proceeds to briefly unpack how the perceptions about Africa as an international actor have changed over time before explaining how the change in perception is inspired by African diplomacy. It is argued that African diplomatic practice is unique as it amplifies the need to expand our routine understanding of why and how diplomacy is practised. The chapter concludes by offering a brief overview of the chapters that follow.

Perceptions and the functions of (African) diplomacy

Perspectives and perceptions of Africa's place and influence as an actor on the international stage have differed over time. Concluding his assessment of Africa in 2001, former US Secretary of State Henry A. Kissinger (2001: 210), for example, noted that 'the continent [Africa] is a tragedy; it is also a challenge'. In 2018, Karabo and Murithi (2018: 4) argued that the continent's international relations had entered a state of 'flux'. This state of flux is caused by several radical changes occurring in the Global North at the time, including, but not limited, to the rise of the far right, the United Kingdom's exit from the European Union (EU) – or Brexit – and the emergence of anti-migrant sentiments in political and social circles. At the same time, non-Western powers such as Russia and China and a middle power such as India have targeted Africa as a geopolitical springboard.[1] These dual realities provided Africa with two options: as Karabo and Murithi (2018: 4) note, 'Africa therefore stands on the precipice of either allowing itself to once again become a neo-colonial carcass for … Eastern forces to feed off or becoming an autonomous agent of its own destiny and self-determination'. In 2020, Munyi, Mwambari and Ylönen (2020: 3) conceptualized three types of agency at play within the African context: agency as institutionalization, agency as creativity and initiative in international behaviour and norm development, and agency as influence. For Olonisakin and Tofa (2020: 18–25), African agency has largely gone unnoticed and is present within the Economic Community of West African States (ECOWAS) when intervening in Liberia and Sierra Leone, the AU and the Responsibility to Protect (R2P), and African youth migration.

Just as diplomacy can help us to manage perceptions of foreign publics of the sending state (Rhee et al, 2021: 683–703; Vibber and Lovari, 2022: 156–66), it is intended for this volume to provide a balanced picture of Africa's achievements as a diplomatic actor. Diplomacy serves at least four key functions:

- Representing a state and facilitating negotiation and dialogue aimed at identifying areas of agreement and disagreement between states to avert conflict.
- Gathering information targeted at better understanding the receiving state's foreign policy.
- The expansion of political, economic and cultural ties between states.
- The employment of diplomatic instruments to uphold international law (Anon, 2011).

These stated functions of diplomacy, while initially correct, discount and ignore the changing international dynamics, particularly in Africa and off its waters. Chief among these dynamics is, for example, changes in the continent's maritime domain (see Chapter 6), the influence of non-state actors (see Chapter 8) and technology (see Chapters 5, 7 and 9). International institutions, particularly international organizations, no longer solely serve as meeting points for mutual deliberation and debate. Instead, an international organization such as the United Nations (UN) and the AU as a regional organization are used as platforms to introduce and socialize the international community to African perspectives and interests (see Chapter 3), although the success of this introduction and socialization is debatable (see Chapters 4 and 6).

In response to Africa's position in international relations and its diplomatic role, it is proposed that the four functions of diplomacy referred to earlier are insufficient for the purpose of understanding African diplomatic practice and should therefore be expanded and redefined. To this end it is argued that (African) diplomacy has six functions. These functions are:

- Diplomacy functions as an instrument of communication and information gathering.
- Diplomacy functions as an instrument to gain, maintain and project status and influence.
- Diplomacy has a regulatory function in that its formal and legal conventions regulate state behaviour and practices.
- Diplomacy functions as a conflict prevention and resolution mechanism.
- Diplomacy has a normative function in that it socializes states regarding acceptable and unacceptable behaviour and practices.
- Diplomacy functions as an instrument of diversity and innovation as a universally accepted institution.

Throughout this volume, communication remains an essential part of diplomatic practice, whether formal or informal, on the bilateral or multilateral level, or by means of a state or non-state actor. The desire for and execution of influence is clearly demonstrated in energy diplomacy, for example, where African states such as Zambia, Egypt and Ghana have condoned Russia's invasion of Ukraine on 24 February 2022, which could most likely alter the dynamics of future nuclear cooperation. On the opposite end of the spectrum, as Chapter 15 reveals, the gender–diplomacy nexus still requires much progress as Africa's female diplomats are often required to find innovative ways of remaining natural, thus exerting influence, to ensure that their male colleagues are comfortable with a female superior.

The regulatory function of diplomacy is evident in Africa's diplomatic space. Diplomacy, as noted, is an international institution, with universally accepted practice-based shared values, customs and legal conventions such as international law. Therefore, diplomacy has a regulatory function that obliges states to, for example, accept certain universally agreed norms and to comply with the UN Charter. Besides ensuring compliance, the regulatory function of diplomacy enables states to express their sovereignty at international organizations such as the United Nations General Assembly (UNGA). This was illustrated by an earlier reference to African states' various and divergent positions in the UNGA regarding Russia's invasion of Ukraine in 2022. African states are keen to use international organizations, including the UN, to uphold international law but also to assert their own agency. While Africa has achieved many commendable successes, it is nevertheless plagued by war, being the only continent in the world to suffer an increase in the frequency of political violence and coups (Raleigh and Kishi, 2021). To this end, governments in Africa have had to call on non-state actors to aid in negations with other non-state actors such as terrorist groups. Chapter 8 of this volume shows how the International Committee of the Red Cross (ICRC), as an international non-state actor, played a critical role in, for example, securing the release of some of the Chibok girls. Continuing this theme, Chapter 9 argues that African states are becoming increasingly interested in the use of science diplomacy, but turning good intentions into tangible realities remains another matter, with the required financial resources not always forthcoming.

Common purpose and socialization are evident within African diplomatic practice. This theme is not only present within the discourse pertaining to common African positions (CAPs) within multilateral settings, but also with African states such as Ghana and Morocco that practise cultural diplomacy (see Chapters 11 and 12). Both cases, as set out in this volume, show how these states employ various mechanisms for the promotion of African culture and values. This practice shows that African states are aware that their culture can be an invaluable diplomatic tool when leveraged correctly.

Finally, African diplomatic practice deserves to be known for its diversity and innovation. This is in part due to the continent's cultural strength, but also the innovative spirit in science, technology and general diplomatic leverage. Luh and Baltag (2021: 12) argue that the European Union's health and/or vaccine diplomacy was lacking and that the COVID-19 pandemic was a wakeup call for the bloc to strengthen its cooperation on health. For its part, Africa was able to fall back on its past experiences with other diseases such as the Ebola and Zika viruses, which propelled the continent into action when COVID-19 emerged (see Chapters 9 and 10). On a similar front, the digital capabilities of the African state are also noteworthy. As Turianskyi and Wekesa (2021: 355) note, '[w]hile most African governments have yet to systematically deploy digital means of doing diplomacy in formal and structured ways, many have begun to practice it in a non-formalised and ad hoc manner'. This is particularly true of the African head of state vis-á-vis social media platforms such as Twitter, giving rise to Twitter diplomacy (see Chapter 5). Furthermore, Africa's small island developing states (SIDS) have employed the use of smart diplomacy[2] within their circles of diplomatic practice, which has resulted in states such as Mauritius and Seychelles investing heavily in their digital capabilities (see Chapter 5).

Structure of this volume

This volume unfolds in 16 chapters which are introduced here. In Chapter 2, François Theron commences with an introduction to the origins of diplomacy before proceeding to focus on the birth of the Westphalian state system. He continues with a discussion on the end of classical diplomacy and the events and developments associated with the advent of the modern global states system. He dates Africa's entry into the Westphalian state system as 1815, coinciding with the Concert of Europe. However, Theron is mindful of earlier and simultaneous diplomatic events and developments on the African continent and cites several examples of this. He proceeds to focus on post-colonial and post-independence African diplomacy, highlighting continental dynamics and linkages with other international developments. Theron comments on the Westphalian state system and, despite earlier and resurgent voices against it, the continent's adherence to the territorial state and colonially drawn borders. He observes: 'Whatever the initial intentions of the Pan-Africanists at the time of independence, Africa's political leaders soon accommodated themselves to a sovereigntist and classically Westphalian version of diplomacy' (see Chapter 2). Despite rhetoric against the Westphalian state system and its idealism, African leaders have consolidated and, in some instances, entrenched their political power and rule, using the colonial territorial state as a point of departure. However, it remains to be seen to what extent the territorial state will be eroded or endure as the continent moves towards the operationalization of its integration project through, for example, the African Continental Free Trade Area (AfCFTA), which promotes open borders and the free movement of goods, people and services (see Chapter 4). Theron concludes that African diplomacy has failed in many instances as much as it has achieved successes, as outlined in the remainder of the volume. Theron finally concludes: 'The future of African foreign policy and diplomacy remains challenging.'

In Chapter 3, Jo-Ansie van Wyk focuses on common African positions (CAPs) as one of the practices of African diplomacy, especially at AU level. Although Africa's adoption of common positions is not unique (the EU, for example, also practises this), the AU (unlike the EU) does not have a legal regime regarding CAPs. CAPs emerge seemingly on an ad hoc basis or in preparation for major multilateral conferences; be that as it may, CAPs, as a diplomatic practice, have regained their status since the establishment of the AU, being one of the objectives of the AU Constitutive Act. Furthermore, it is consistent with African desires to unite the continent, promote and realize Pan-Africanism, and demonstrate solidarity with like-minded governments and individuals both inside and outside of Africa. More importantly, CAPs have advanced the continent's collective bargaining power at international negotiations and remains an expression of the normative aspirations of the continent. However, one of the challenges to CAPs links to Chapter 2's reference to the tendency of African states to advance national, rather than continental, interests at times.

In their contribution, Sanusha Naidu, Faith Mabera and Arina Muresan (Chapter 4) continue with collective diplomatic action on the continent. Their specific focus is one of the continent's most recent diplomatic achievements: the establishment of the AfCFTA. Ambitious as it is, the AfCFTA exemplifies economic diplomacy as a diplomatic practice using

South Africa as an illustrative case study. They refer to South Africa's foreign policy focus on Africa in the context of the country's economic diplomacy. The authors position this vis-à-vis the AfCFTA but caution against, for example, South Africa walking a tightrope between its national interests and those of the continent.

Whereas Chapter 4 focuses on one of Africa's more powerful states, Chapter 5 by Suzanne Graham and Victoria Graham shifts the focus to the diplomatic practices of Africa's six SIDS, namely Cabo Verde, Comoros, Guinea-Bissau, Mauritius, São Tomé and Príncipe, and Seychelles. They consider whether smart diplomacy can be adopted and practised by these states. The authors define smart diplomacy in the context of smart power. They posit that this requires SIDS to meet certain criteria. Chapter 4 concludes that smart diplomacy offers significant prospects for African SIDS and that:

> what should be emphasized is that these small states have used their own African agency to project a niche diplomacy in the global arena, such as advocating for the blue economy, leading on maritime diplomacy efforts, and using location as a geostrategic tool to leverage bilateral and multilateral deals and benefit their own economies.

Africa's littoral states are a unique category of states due to, for example, their geographical location, maritime jurisdiction and the challenges associated with piracy at sea, illegal and unreported fishing, and the impact of climate change on the world's oceans. In Chapter 6, Francois Vreÿ explores Africa's maritime agenda and maritime diplomacy as a specialized diplomatic practice. The author provides conceptual clarification regarding maritime diplomacy while also providing empirical evidence of the continent's diplomatic interactions in this regard, but posits that the expansion of cooperative practices and the institutionalization of maritime cooperation is required.

Chapter 7 continues to address the uses and implications technology has for African diplomacy. Attention is given to the rise of Twitter diplomacy as a typology and practice taking hold within the African context. Here, Suzanne Graham and Victoria Graham explore the concept and practice of Twitter diplomacy and offer empirical evidence of its prevalence in Africa, as well as the advantages and disadvantages of this emerging practice of African diplomacy.

Chapter 8 turns our attention to the need to expand the African discourse on quiet diplomacy by looking beyond the state-to-state nature of such diplomacy. Using the Chibok abductions of April 2014 as a case study, Botha applies the conceptual characteristics of quiet diplomacy, thereby illustrating that (violent) non-state actors play a vital role in facilitating quiet diplomacy on the continent. Additionally, Botha finds that social media platforms, such as Twitter, can undermine diplomatic practices.

The volume's ninth chapter on the interplay between science, technology and diplomacy is contributed by Lesley Masters. She outlines the conceptual parameters of science, technology and innovation (STI) and takes stock of its status in Africa and within African diplomacy. Masters highlights that the continent's STI bases remain scarce and underdeveloped but shows the advances resulting from successful science diplomacy.

The following chapter maintains the attention on science but specifically in the context of the continent's health diplomacy. In Chapter 10, Jo-Ansie van Wyk discusses how the COVID-19 pandemic has sharpened the focus on health globally and continentally. African health diplomacy is addressed in terms of the status of health on the continent and the existing diplomatic architecture to improve Africans' health, especially as it is a major focus of the UN Sustainable Development Goals (SDGs) and the AU's development blueprint, Agenda 2063. The chapter also addresses African diplomacy in the context of its response to the global COVID-19 pandemic.

The next two chapters introduce cultural diplomacy as a concept and practice of African diplomacy, focusing on Ghana (Chapter 11) and Morocco (Chapter 12). Both chapters underline the diplomatic mobilization of culture, and its benefits and potential. In the case of Ghana, one of the targets of the country's cultural diplomacy remains the African diaspora, particularly descendants of the global slave trade. In Morocco, as Faiza Koubi outlines, the country's cultural diplomacy has involved instruments such as religion, science and education.

The volume continues with a chapter on knowledge diplomacy (Chapter 13) by Jane Knight. Although previous chapters have referred to digital diplomacy and STI, Knight focuses on the agential power of knowledge in diplomacy. Besides exploring the concept and practice of knowledge diplomacy, Knight narrows her focus to highlight the significance of the establishment of the Pan-African University (PAU) by the AU as an instance of the continent's knowledge diplomacy, a practice which she distinguishes from both cultural and educational diplomacy.

African agency in the context of the continent's energy diplomacy is presented in Chapter 14. Focusing on African diplomatic engagements with a global superpower, Russia, Dzvinka Kachur and Robyn Foley examine Egypt, Ghana, South Africa and Zambia's relations with Russia in the context of nuclear energy expansion. Although the authors highlight each state's unique interactions with Russia's Rosatom, their diplomatic relations and practices converge in the context of Russia's geostrategic ambitions, Africa's energy needs and energy diplomacy as a diplomatic practice.

Jennifer Chiriga, Rudo Chitiga and Hesphina Rukato are the authors of the volume's penultimate chapter (Chapter 15). Focusing on the challenges and triumphs of women in African diplomacy, these authors reiterate the agency of women in African diplomacy, especially in Track II diplomacy.

The chapter outlines the AU's normative framework for gender equality, and the authors' involvement in some of the AU's processes pertaining to gender. They conclude with challenges to diplomatic leadership and practical lessons learnt from African diplomacy regarding the continent's women, peace and security agenda.

The final chapter of the volume (Chapter 16) returns to the analytical framework presented earlier in this introductory chapter to determine the functions and practice of African diplomacy deduced from the conceptual, empirical, theoretical, methodological and practical contributions of each author, and the implications. The editors conclude the volume by offering an agenda for the practice of and research on African diplomacy.

Notes

1. A middle power is typically defined as a state that cannot be classified as a great power but seeks to bring about cohesion and stability within the international community. From this perspective, a state is usually classified as a 'middle power' based on its behaviour within the international system (see Jordaan, 2003; Spies, 2019).
2. While a definition follows in Chapter 5, smart diplomacy occurs when a state opts to combine its digital capabilities with partnerships on the public and private sectors to strengthen its diplomatic practice.

References

Anon (2011) 'The functions of diplomacy', *E-International Relations*, [online] 20 July, Available from: www.e-ir.info/2011/07/20/the-functions-of-diplomacy/ [Accessed 15 December 2021].

Balzacq, T., Charillon, F. and Ramel, F. (2020) 'Introduction: history and theories of diplomacy', in T. Balzacq, F. Charillon and F. Ramel (eds) *Global Diplomacy: An Introduction to Theory and Practice*, Cham: Palgrave Macmillan, pp 1–16.

Jordaan, E. (2003) 'The concept of a middle power in international relations: distinguishing between emerging and traditional middle powers', *Politikon: South African Journal of Political Studies*, 30(1): 165–81.

Karabo, T. and Muruthi, T. (2018) 'The African Union: a decade and a half later', in T. Karabo and T. Muruthi (eds) *The African Union: Autocracy, Diplomacy and Peacebuilding in Africa*, London: I.B. Tauris, pp 1–11.

Kissinger, H. (2001) *Does America Need a Foreign Policy? Towards a Diplomacy for the 21st Century*, New York: Simon and Schuster.

Luh, S. and Baltag, D. (2021) 'The role of EU health attachés for global health diplomacy in times of COVID-19', *Global Affairs*, 7(6): 903–20.

Munyi, E.N., Mwambambari, D. and Ylönen, A. (2020) 'Conceptualising agency and influence in African international relations', in E.N. Munyi, D. Mwambari and A. Ylönen (eds) *Beyond History: African Agency in Development, Diplomacy, and Conflict Resolution*, London: Rowman and Littlefield, pp 3–11.

Olonisakin, F. and Tofa, M. (2020) 'Approaching African agency in international relations', in E.N. Munyi, D. Mwambari and A. Ylönen (eds) *Beyond History: African Agency in Development, Diplomacy, and Conflict Resolution*, London: Rowman and Littlefield, pp 13–31.

Raleigh, C. and Kishi, R. (2021) 'Africa: the only continent where political violence increased in 2020', *Mail and Guardian*, [online] 1 February, Available from: https://mg.co.za/africa/2021-02-01-africa-the-only-continent-where-political-violence-increased-in-2020/#:~:text=In%202020%2C%20Africa%20was%20the,9%20000%20more%20reported%20fatalities [Accessed 12 July 2022].

Rhee, K., Crabtree, C. and Horiuchi, Y. (2024) 'Perceived motives of public diplomacy influence foreign public opinion', *Political Behavior*, 46(1): 683–703.

Sharp, P. (2009) *Diplomatic Theory of International Relations*, Cambridge: Cambridge University Press.

Spencer, J., Yorke, C. and Masser, A. (2021) 'Conclusion', in J. Spencer, C. Yorke and A. Masser (eds) *New Perspectives on Diplomacy: Contemporary Diplomacy in Action*, London: I.B. Tauris, pp 219–23.

Spies, Y.K. (2019) *Global South Perspectives on Diplomacy*, Cham: Palgrave Macmillan.

Turianskyi, Y. and Wekesa, B. (2021) 'African digital diplomacy: emergence, evolution, and the future', *South African Journal of International Affairs*, 23(3): 341–59.

Vibber, K. and Lovari, A. (2022) 'The overlooked public: examining citizens' perceptions of and perceived role in hosting mega-events', *Place Branding and Public Diplomacy*, 18(2): 156–68.

2

An Overview of the Evolution of Diplomacy in Europe and Africa

François Theron

The origins of diplomacy

In his classic though outdated definition of diplomacy, Sir Ernest Satow (1973: 1) describes diplomacy as the intelligent, tactful and peaceful conduct of official relations between the governments of independent states. To this Sir Harold Nicolson (1963: 15) added that diplomacy was the management and adjustment by ambassadors and envoys of international relations through negotiation. After dismissing the 16th century theory that 'the first diplomatists were angels' serving as messengers between heaven and earth, Nicolson (1939: 17) suggested that at some stage humanity must have realized that negotiation was essential between groups of humans if only to indicate that they had enough of battle and would like it to end. It must have become apparent that nothing would be achieved if the emissaries or messengers were killed and eaten before having delivered their message. Following this, as Hamilton and Langhorne (2011: 7) suggest, there would 'have to be rules which assure the safety of the messenger'. Even if the practice of diplomacy varied from region to region, because its origin is based on communication and protection of the messenger, it was inevitable that there would be significant similarities of method and style.

The first known peace treaty was signed about 2300 BC between a king of Ebla in present-day Syria and a king of Assyria (Nigro, 2008: 195). In describing these early forms of diplomatic interaction, Berridge and Lloyd (2012: 88) refer to the diplomatic system practised by the kingdoms of the Near East from about 2500 to 500 BC as 'cuneiform diplomacy' because of the exchange of messages written in cuneiform characters on stone tablets. This reveals a system with a common language, with its own law, customs and protocol. This was undoubtedly a sophisticated system at the time, and the authors note that 'in its essentials, modern diplomacy can be seen as expressing the same needs and practices as the ancient cuneiform system' (Berridge and Lloyd, 2012: 88).

In 432 BC, the basic rules and conduct of diplomacy were adopted by the ancient Greeks at the Congress of Sparta. These became a template for much of the diplomacy of the next 22 centuries until the aftermath of the Battle of Waterloo in 1815 (Fletcher, 2016: 28). During the period of their city-state's imperial expansion (509 BCE–14 CE), the Romans could not ignore diplomacy as a tool of statecraft. However, under the rule of the emperors, diplomacy became increasingly irrelevant as it was by force of arms that the *Pax Romana* was established over what became a world empire. As former United Nations Secretary-General Boutros Boutros-Ghali said, 'the Roman Empire had no need for diplomacy' (Spies, 2019: 57). Yet Rome made major contributions to what in future would become international law by incorporating into Roman law some of the laws and customs of the peoples of non-Roman origin living within the empire. This came to be known as the *ius gentium*, or law of nations which, along with the *ius naturale*, played an important part in the development of international law by Grotius (Wanlass, 1970: 82).

The fall of the Roman Empire in 476 CE was followed by the Dark Ages and it is not possible to speak of an international system during this time and the early Medieval period. The Roman Catholic Church, for example, survived the Roman Empire and began to operate both as an international organization and through the Papacy as a suzerain over the peoples of Europe, in both spiritual and temporal senses. It sought to influence rulers and dictate the evolution of societies throughout Europe, albeit a Europe consisting of a hotchpotch of thousands of autonomous jurisdictions. As Nigro (2008: 196) explains:

> The focus of political authority was personal, feudal, and local. The idea that political rule was strictly linked to control of territory rather than to other sources of authority was largely absent, so that rulers were not geographically sovereign in the sense of exerting supreme and monopolistic authority over and within a given territory and population.

Against the background of this historical introduction to contextualize the origins of diplomacy, the chapter describes the origins of the modern states system before proceeding to outline the start of the global states system. Following this predominantly European focus, the chapter then turns to Africa and positions the continent as a diplomatic actor.

The birth of the modern system of states

The evolution of diplomacy, after what Coolsaet (1998: 5) describes as 'the termination of the normative chaos of the late Middle Ages, the political chaos of the religious wars and the economic particularism of medieval society', can be seen in several following transformative stages. First, the growth of powerful and relatively centralized kingdoms, such as England, France and Aragon, Second, the development of the modern system of states in Renaissance Italy, at first in the form of competing city-states. A significant innovation here was the institution of the resident ambassador, which meant that diplomacy became a full-time profession even if initially staffed by noblemen or intimates of the sovereign. This contributed to the centralization of the administration of diplomacy into state ministries dedicated to 'foreign affairs' (Coolsaet, 1998: 3). The 'Italian system' was exported to the rest of Europe when France under Charles VIII invaded the Italian peninsula in 1494. Cardinal Richelieu of France is generally credited with establishing the first foreign ministry, in 1624.

The Protestant Reformation that commenced in October 1517 set in train a long series of religious wars such as the Eighty Years' War (1568–1648) and the Thirty Years' War (1618–48) that ravaged most of Europe. These wars were ended by the Peace of Westphalia in 1648, which 'is nowadays generally considered to be the moment of birth of the modern territorial state, and with it the modern state system and modern diplomacy' (Coolsaet, 1998: 3). Westphalia transformed diplomacy in that it strengthened the evolving non-feudal and secular political authorities, such as the increasingly 'national' kingdoms and other types of monarchical states of the European world, effectively ratifying the concept of the nation state, 'still a key component' of international life in the 21st century 'but by no means the only one' (Heine, 2006: 4). For Coolsaet (1998: 5), 'This [was] the classical period of diplomacy, because, between 1650 and 1850, European states were of the "perfect kind"'. Ruler owed no allegiance upward nor downward. They were absolute in their power to conduct foreign policy. The diplomatic elites were moreover often interrelated and shared at least common values'.

The period from 1648 to the French Revolution in 1789 saw diplomacy becoming increasingly professionalized. Several theorists wrote about diplomacy and concepts such as the balance of power and negotiation. The most well-known was François de Callières' *On the Manner of Negotiating with Sovereign Princes* (1716), which became a classic (and still useful) textbook on diplomatic practice. Another significant milestone in diplomatic history was the Anglo-Spanish Treaty signed in July 1713, as part of the Peace of Utrecht ending the War of the Spanish Succession (1701–14), which in its Preamble explicitly reflected and referred to the doctrine of balance of power as a means of securing and consolidating peace in Europe. This was the first such avowal in so important an international instrument. Besides these events, the 18th century was also disturbed by several wars triggered by the hegemonic ambitions of France and Prussia, which, in turn, were countered by a determination by other powers to reassert the balance of power. These were effectively 'world wars' and included the Nine Years' War (1689–97), the War of the Spanish Succession (1702–14), the War of the Austrian Succession (1739–48), the Seven Years' War (1756–63) and the American War of Independence (1775–83). No permanent international organizations existed to keep or to make peace. Yet, despite this vacuum:

> The growth of a generally accepted body of diplomatic practice and tradition and its gradual extension to cover the whole of Europe clearly had a stabilising and unifying effect … Both the theory of the balance of power and the practice of inter-state diplomacy were within their own limits, a civilising influence … Without them Europe would have been a more unstable, more anarchic, more dangerous place in whose history violence and destruction would have bulked larger. (Anderson, 1993: 292–3)

The French Revolution (1789–99) and the subsequent Napoleonic Wars (1799–1815) ended the Westphalian period of interstate relations. Diplomacy was replaced by warfare. France's quest for hegemonic power in Europe was resisted and ultimately defeated by a coalition of allies led by Britain, Austria, Russia and Prussia. From 1814 to 1815 Europe's leading statesmen met at the Congress of Vienna to reconstruct the European states system and to avoid future French aggression and indeed the breakout of any future war. Europe's frontiers were redrawn to reflect an elaborate balance of power, but the statesmen also realized that more was required than the redistribution of territory to keep the peace. For this reason, in November 1815, Austria, Britain, Prussia and Russia formed the Quadruple Alliance, and in October 1818, by the Treaty of Aix-la-Chapelle, France was invited to join the alliance, which now became the Quintuple Alliance. It was particularly agreed that frequent talks were required to address any difficulties that could develop, and therefore undermine peace. This conference system came to be known as the Congress System or Concert of Europe. Statesmen and diplomats of the time understood that the French Revolution and the ensuing period of warfare had unleashed the forces of liberalism and nationalism, which, unless monitored and kept in bounds, could destabilize the continent.

Except for limited wars such as the wars of German and Italian unification and the Crimean War, which, despite being fought on the periphery of Europe, had political consequences that would increasingly poison international politics, the Congress of Vienna provided Europe with a century of peace until 1914. Starting with Vienna in 1814–15, there were at least 26 congresses (attended at head of state or foreign minister level) and conferences (attended at ambassador level) right up to the London Conference of 1912–13 on the crises in the Balkans (Lascurettes, 2017: 23–5).

In the view of the British diplomat Tom Fletcher (2016: 47), 'the hundred years that followed the Congress of Vienna of 1815, while ending in diplomatic failure that led to the First World War, were European diplomacy's finest century'. The Congress of Vienna also endeavoured to bring some order to the diplomatic profession through its *Règlement de Vienne*, which in many respects was confirmed by the Vienna Convention on Diplomatic Relations of 18 April 1961. Diplomacy was to be a profession 'distinct from politics and statecraft' (Fletcher, 2016: 50). The profession, however, continued to be dominated by the aristocracy and upper classes of Europe, who shared many of the same values, and they tended to speak the same language, French, until at least the Second World War.

Despite these developments regarding diplomacy as a practice, profession and conflict resolution mechanism, 'European diplomacy's finest century' (Fletcher, 2016: 47) was merely a precursor to more challenges to diplomacy and state relations.

The end of classical diplomacy and the advent of the global states system

Inevitably, the upheavals and wars in 19th century Europe, as mentioned earlier, made the task of diplomats much more difficult as domestic politics and public opinion intruded more and more into foreign policy. Indeed, Lascurettes (2017: 15) points to the liberal wave of revolutions across Europe in 1848 and the Crimean War (1853–56), which left behind resentment and distrust between the great powers, as major causes of the eventual demise of the Concert of Europe. Among the causes of the First World War was the disintegration of shared values as interstate relations became much more competitive and tense, as well as the absence of great diplomatic practitioners such as assembled at Vienna in 1814 (Kissinger, 1994: 194).

The classical period of European diplomacy ended with the First World War (1914–18). Until then, diplomacy as practised by the great powers had been primarily Eurocentric. Even the colonial empires were viewed as extensions of Europe – 'our ancestors the Gauls' is what children were taught throughout the French colonies (Grant, 1972: 13). The cataclysm of the First World War and the inability of the powers to reach a durable settlement at the Paris Peace Conference in 1919 heralded the 'end of the European state system and the beginning of the global state system of the 20th and 21st centuries' (Nigro, 2008: 206). Through imperialism and colonialism, as well as by European military and technological superiority, the European or Vienna system of diplomacy was imposed across the world as the template for global diplomacy and as it is still practised in the 21st century.

Despite the failure of diplomacy to prevent the outbreak of the First and Second World Wars, the 20th century also witnessed several diplomatic innovations. Multilateralism as a diplomatic practice increased significantly with, inter alia, the creation of the League of Nations in 1920 and of the United Nations in 1945, following the two world wars. Another, if not very novel, trend was the increased regularity with which heads of state and government attended to diplomatic business.

A major development of the 20th century state system and international politics was decolonization in Africa and elsewhere from European powers, which greatly increased the number of states in the international system. Bilateral diplomacy grew as new states were keen to assert their sovereignty and establish their national embassies in the capitals of the major powers. In the last quarter of the 20th century, globalization became increasingly pronounced as nation states were linked through trade, finance, technology and human mobility. More contact produced both opportunities to address common concerns but also challenges as, for example, financial crises became increasingly globalized.

The decolonization process that unfolded after the Second World War saw the emergence of new sovereign states in Africa. However, Africa's presence and role in international diplomacy predates the 20th century, as the next section outlines.

At Vienna in 1815, Africa enters the centre stage

At the Congress of Vienna in 1815, Africa received the belated collective attention of Europe's statesmen. Until the 19th century, Britain and the other European powers had confined their imperial ambitions in Africa to the odd coastal outpost from which they could exert their economic and military influence. Until the 1870s, only 10 per cent of the continent was under direct European control, with Algeria held by France, the Cape Colony and Natal by Britain and Angola by Portugal. British activity on the West African coast was centred around the lucrative slave trade (David, 2011).

For Africa, the transatlantic slave trade was 'particularly cataclysmic' (Spies, 2019: 82). The very nature of the slave trade intensified warfare in Africa due to the economic benefits accrued from capturing and selling slaves. Concomitantly, this fuelled a significant arms trade that involved Europeans exchanging arms for slaves. In the 18th century alone about 6 million African slaves were shipped across the Atlantic, which added to other transfers and trafficking of human beings over the centuries and, including the trans-Sahara trade, means that, according to Acemoglu and Robinson (2010: 29), more than 10 million Africans were shipped out of the continent as slaves, imposing 'a perverse effect on political and economic institutions in Africa'.

At the insistence of Britain, the Congress of Vienna in its Final Act of 9 June 1815 (incorporating Act XV of 8 February 1815) declared the international slave trade to be 'repugnant to the principles of humanity and universal morality' and that 'the public voice, in all civilized countries, calls aloud for its prompt suppression' (Congress of Vienna, 2015). Britain's aim had been the total abolition of the slave trade. Faced with the toothless nature of Act XV of the Final Act, British Foreign Secretary Lord Castlereagh was obliged to negotiate 'direct treaties' with relevant states (Nicolson, 1947: 211–13). Britain's efforts in this regard led to the emergence of two new diplomatic instruments. One was a form of economic sanction against countries or colonies which refused to abolish the slave trade and the other was the institution of a conference of ambassadors meeting at the Foreign Office, with Lord Castlereagh as chairperson, to monitor the execution of the various agreements eventually reached concerning abolition. As Nicolson (1947: 216) says, 'the constitution of such a "watching committee" on the part of the great powers was at the time a startling innovation and provided a useful precedent for the future'.

Whereas the early part of the 19th century saw efforts to disentangle the slave trade that empowered Europe and the Americas, the latter part of the century saw a return to Africa by these powers. Instead of trafficking Africans out of the continent, the Scramble for Africa in the late 19th century would see the entire continent subjected to external occupation. The 19th century Scramble for Africa, which lasted until the outbreak of the First World War in 1914, coincided with the decline of the European Congress System as a peacekeeping system and increasing rivalry and growing enmity among European powers. In this environment, European powers saw colonial acquisitions as potentially increasing their military power and as sources of raw materials to drive an industrial and military complex. The desire on the part of some Christians to evangelize Africa was another factor. However, competition for African territories exacerbated international rivalries and for this reason German Chancellor Otto von Bismarck hosted the Berlin Conference of 1884–85 to determine and agree on the rules of conduct of African colonization and to divide the continent – in other words, to agree as to who should obtain what. The conference hastened the dash to colonize Africa and a reason for this was the principle of effectivity contained in the conference's General Act. This stated that colonizing countries could hold colonies only if they possessed and administered them, failing which another country could assert a claim to the territories concerned. Consequently, in Central Africa, for example, expeditions were dispatched to coerce traditional rulers into signing treaties, using force if necessary.

The legacy of the Berlin Conference for Africa's well-being and governance was most unfortunate as the plenipotentiaries demonstrated scant regard for the interests of the African peoples. As was noted by the Independent High-Level Panel of the African Union (AU) in its Audit of the African Union in 2007, the colonizers ignored or swept aside the fact that:

> State and nation-building preceded the arrival of the first Europeans in Africa. The forms of state and nation-building were based on the centrality of community, solidarity and inclusion of populations around emerging territorial spaces. Boundaries, such as they existed, were not necessarily conceived as sacrosanct and immutable walls of division and separation. They also served as transactional spaces for mediating various social, economic, political and cultural flows. Instead, Africa was partitioned into a host of small politico-administrative units on the basis of the Westphalian concept of the nation-state. (AU, 2007: 1)

The Berlin Conference failed to secure peace in Europe and Africa as Bismarck had intended. This was due to the erratic diplomacy of Germany's Kaiser Wilhelm II and his *Weltpolitik*. By provoking the Moroccan crises of 1905–6 and 1911, the Kaiser succeeded only in turning the Scramble for Africa into one of the triggers of the First World War in 1914.

Meanwhile, as indicated in the AU Audit of 2007, colonization imposed on Africa Eurocentric systems of governance, but also airbrushed out of history indigenous traditions and customs, substituting settler activities as 'African' history. The result was the destruction of Africa's often sophisticated and rules-bound systems of governance and of diplomacy, which also explains today's dearth of knowledge about pre-colonial Africa. For Adegbulu (2011: 170):

> The fact is that in the 19th Century when Europe occupied Africa, her scholars did not attempt to study and understand or to build on the historical traditions in existence there; they sought instead to challenge and to supplant them. The history of European traders, missionaries, explorers, conquerors and rulers constituted, in their own view, the sum total of African history.

Some of Africa's diplomatic traditions dated from ancient times. As Mohammed (2015: 95–6) notes, 'the ancient Egyptian and the Aksum civilization were believed to have been pioneers in practicing the early African diplomacy with the outside world. In East Africa, the Aksum Dynasty of Ethiopia maintained diplomatic relations with Europe since the 4th century'. Mohammed adds that West African kingdoms like Kanem Bornu, Dahomey and Oyo appointed 'a professional diplomatic staff to carry out the diplomatic missions'.

Irwin (1975: 81–2) describes the historical context: if diplomacy is indeed, as Satow famously defined it, 'the conduct of business between states by peaceful means … then precolonial Africa was no stranger to diplomacy or the diplomatic arts'. For, as he elaborates, 'official contact between these [pre-colonial] states seem to have been maintained by methods and procedures which historians of the non-African world describe as diplomatic' (Irwin, 1975: 81–2). Early African diplomacy concerned the negotiation of treaties, the delimitation of frontiers, dispute resolution, crisis management, an exchange of representatives and the establishment of permanent or temporary missions. Diplomatic gifts were often exchanged, and the principle of diplomatic immunity was widely recognized.

Evidence suggests the existence of formal relations at the highest governmental levels between the peoples of, for example, West Africa in the pre-colonial era, and of the existence of an interstate system (Smith, 1973: 599–600). Seemingly, interstate relations in this African region were governed by a system of customary law which 'provided a bond between the different states and peoples of West Africa, and a form of international law by which their relations with each other could be regulated' (Smith, 1973: 599–600). Customary law was said to govern the 'treatment of strangers, the duties of hosts to guests, the protection that should be extended to foreign traders and the like to a degree that makes it possible to speak of a system of African customary international law' (Irwin, 1975: 82). Adegbulu (2011: 171–3) adds that 'diplomacy was being carried on in West Africa in a very decent and dignifying manner', and the exchange of ambassadors and 'diplomatic marriages' were common in pre-colonial West Africa. Many of the African states were 'loosely formed empires' with porous boundaries and time-consuming communications due to distance and customs which generally was not conducive to the establishment of permanent institutions (Adegbulu, 2011: 171–3). Irwin (1975: 82) mentions that pre-colonial African diplomacy has been likened to the conditions prevalent in medieval Europe. 'The two regions were similar in that neither had developed the modern concept of an international society composed of entities called states, all supposed to be equal, sovereign, and completely independent.'

The advent of Islam in pre-colonial West Africa was significant (Adegbulu, 2011: 171); for example, it was accompanied by the introduction of literacy, which enabled written records to be kept and this in turn enabled the development of diplomacy. Adegbulu (2011: 172) adds that the introduction of Arabic writing into the Sudan 'enabled Songhai to exchange diplomatic letters with Morocco and Kanem Bornu with Tunis, Tripoli and even with the Turkish Emperor at Istanbul'.

Smith (1973: 612) notes that the introduction of Islamic doctrine and Islamic law into West Africa and then much of Africa, especially the forest states, from the 11th century onwards, 'seems to have been carefully accommodated to the fundamental precepts of the customary law, and with customary law it served to foster unity among the different peoples.' Smith (1973: 612) notes also that these 'external influences' facilitated 'the development of a written record and a permanent diplomacy.' These were 'important criteria for the emergence of a diplomacy fitted to contend with the political problems of the age immediately preceding the colonial age, problems already exacerbated by improved communications and more efficient weapons.'

Mansa Kankan Musa, the King of Mali from 1307 to 1332, left a significant mark on West African politics and diplomatic interactions. During his reign, his empire building increased the size of the Kingdom of Mali to include present-day Senegal, Mauritania, Mali, Burkina Faso, Niger, The Gambia, Guinea-Bissau, Guinea and Côte d'Ivoire. Mansa Musa dispatched several diplomatic missions to the Middle East. His famous pilgrimage to the Middle East was itself a major diplomatic event when, in July 1324, he met the Mamluk Sultan of Egypt, Al-Nasir Muhammad, in a formal summit meeting. Smith (1973: 602–3) also mentions that 'occasionally some of the West African sovereigns sent their representatives to reside abroad, rather than merely on visiting embassies, the earliest known example occurring in the late 17th century'. In the early 19th century, and 'mainly in order to keep in touch with the British traders[,] ... the Ashanti ... stationed a representative at Cape Coast' (Smith, 1973: 602–3). Another form of continuous diplomacy prevalent in West Africa and of indigenous origin was the 'representation of a state or community abroad by chiefs or officials of the foreign state', a system resembling modern honorary consuls (Smith, 1973: 618).

Pre-colonial West African diplomats often carried credentials, badges of office, or diplomatic uniforms (Adegbulu, 2011: 175). Smith (1973: 605) also notes that 'African hospitality and the honour done to strangers were remarked upon by most of the early European travellers'. Protocol and etiquette played an important role in the diplomacy of pre-colonial West Africa and negotiators were employed who were skilled in foreign tongues. Finally, treaties in West Africa were regarded as sacrosanct (*pacta sunt servanda*).

Irwin (1975: 86–90), in his study of Asante diplomacy and diplomatic practice (1816–20), identifies a consistent pattern of diplomatic behaviour and gives detailed descriptions of the elaborate but also very time-consuming customs and rituals associated with the reception as well as the departure of foreign envoys. Every effort was made to impress the visitors with the power and magnificence of the Asante state. The Asante diplomatic style demonstrated many overlaps with European diplomacy. According to contemporary reports, Asante foreign policy 'was decided by the king and his advisers, subject to a veto by the aristocracy' (Irwin, 1975: 86). In conclusion, Smith (1973: 619) argues that 'the practice of diplomacy was almost always associated with states whose governments possessed at least some elements of central power'. And with reference to its relevance to contemporary 20th and 21st century African diplomacy, Smith (1973: 620) provides the following summing up of pre-colonial diplomacy in West Africa:

[T]he West African system was usually able to meet what was required of it … The conquests of the Muslim Holy War and the European partition were to be made possible not so much by the diplomatic inadequacy as by the military incapacity of the African resistance. Finally, though the development of the indigenous forms of international relations was broken with the establishment of European colonies, these forms can still provide a tradition for the governments, foreign offices and foreign services of modern West Africa.

African diplomacy after independence

The period of colonization by foreign European powers hampered the development of African diplomacy, but the memory of linkage and cooperation for mutual benefit was not forgotten and, almost simultaneously with the process of decolonization starting in the 1950s and early 1960s, African leaders saw the benefits of Pan-Africanism and of cooperation in foreign policy, as well as acting as a bloc at the UN, where they could also count on the support of Asian states (Akpan, 1976: 11–14).

Contemporary African diplomacy and its objectives are deeply rooted in the history of African nationalism, which, in turn, is intimately connected to the founding figures of African independence and nationalism. On 6 March 1957, Ghana became the first Sub-Saharan African country to obtain independence. Kwame Nkrumah proclaimed that Ghana's independence would be meaningless unless it was linked to the total liberation of Africa. This was the start of a chain reaction leading to the successive independence of all African countries, a process which culminated in the 1994 democratic elections in South Africa. By 27 April 1994, Africa was rid of the direct colonial political domination that flowed from the Berlin Conference of 1884–85. As the 2007 Audit of the African Union proclaimed: 'From Cape to Cairo, Nouakchott to Lagos, Praia to Port Louis, Africa was free: free, free at last' (AU, 2007: 3).

Yet despite this yearning for unity, Pan-Africanism 'also fed into one of the most divisive discourses in African diplomacy, namely the post-colonial political integration of the continent' (Spies, 2016: 44). At the outset there were two groups representing African nationalism at continental level. The Casablanca Group advocated the rapid unification of African states under a central government 'to reverse the colonial legacy of artificial boundaries' (AU, 2007: 4). A former secretary-general of the Commonwealth, Chief Emeka Anyaoku (1999), called this group the 'enthusiastic school of African nationalism', which included Kwame Nkrumah (Ghana) and Julius Nyerere (Tanzania).

The other group was the Monrovia Group, which accepted the 'Berlin frontiers' and that continental unity would be achieved gradually, starting with 'economic and political cooperation arrangements' (AU, 2007: 4). Chief Anyaoku (1999) described the Monrovia Group, which included Léopold Senghor (Senegal) and Félix Houphouët-Boigny (Côte d'Ivoire), as 'markedly subdued'. Initially, this group favoured 'greater participation in the political process of a French Union or Community of which Africa would be a constituent part', rather than outright independence (Anyaoku, 1999). The Ghana–Guinea Union formed in 1958 and aligned with the Casablanca Group was later expanded to include Mali, forming the Union of African States (UAS). In 1961, the UAS was enlarged to include Libya, Egypt, Morocco and the Algerian Front for National Liberation (FLN). The UAS was disbanded in 1963 and the gradualist Monrovia Group prevailed, but both the Monrovian and Casablanca Groups were invited to Addis Ababa by Emperor Haile Selassie I of Ethiopia, and the fruit of their compromise was the Organization of African Unity (OAU), founded in 1963 (Anyaoku, 1999).

As well as promoting African unity, the OAU established a Liberation Committee to provide assistance to the liberation movements and coordinate the liberation struggle in Southern Africa. By 1994, with South Africa's democratic transition, Africa was finally liberated as the founders of the OAU envisaged. However, as Chief Anyaoku (1999) lamented, 'the route to unity still remains largely uncharted' and the legacy of the OAU rather mixed: 'The Francophone and Anglophone groupings of African states competed to control African diplomacy. In many of the OAU meetings, these groups openly opposed each other, and [the] OAU often faced problems in reaching consensus' (Mohammed, 2015: 102). An illustrative example of this was when a South African candidate, Dr Nkosazana Dlamini-Zuma, campaigned to become chairperson of the AU Commission. Her candidature was resisted by the Francophone countries. It took two AU summits (January and July 2012) to overcome the deadlock and for Dlamini-Zuma to secure election as the first ever anglophone and female chairperson of the AU Commission.

Among the failures of the OAU was its inability to prevent some 26 coup d'états during the late 1960s and 1970s, this notwithstanding its objection to the transfer of power by force (Mohammed, 2015: 102). In 1986, Yoweri Museveni, later President of Uganda, called the OAU 'a trade union of dictators' (Zhuwakinyu, 2020). Unfortunately, as Gwaambuka (2016) contends, Museveni became 'an ardent member of the same trade union he used to malign back when he rode the moral high wave'. Several of Africa's dictators managed to stay in power by choosing ideological sides during the Cold War (Spies, 2018: 5).

Despite the failures of the OAU, several achievements can rightfully be attributed to African diplomacy. These include treaties to facilitate African regional economic integration. A significant African contribution at both the UN and OAU–AU levels had been the 'Diplomacy of Development', namely the United Nations General Assembly's unanimous adoption of the Millennium Development Goals (MDGs), which was reiterated in 2015 when the UN adopted the Sustainable Development Goals (SDGs) (Spies, 2018: 9–12). The AU approved the New Partnership for Africa's Development (NEPAD) in 2001 as a plan to promote economic growth in Africa. The principal drivers of this ambitious programme were the South African, Nigerian and Algerian presidents, Thabo Mbeki, Olusegun Obasanjo and Abdelaziz Bouteflika, and President Abdoulaye Wade of Senegal, whose own plan was merged with NEPAD.

A significant accomplishment was the establishment of the AU with its Constitutive Act in 2002, which provides for the Union's right to intervene in a member state, and for the right of a member state to request such intervention, in 'respect of grave circumstances, namely: war crimes, genocide and crimes against humanity' (Article 4 (h)), and 'the right of Member States to request intervention from the Union in order to restore peace and security' (Article 4 (j)) (AU, 2002). In this regard, an important step was the elaboration of Africa's new peace and security architecture (APSA) as the OAU had proven inadequate in preventing, for example, the Rwandan genocide in 1994. Included in this architecture are the AU Peace and Security Council and the African Standby Force.

The idealism that seemed to accompany the launching of the AU now seems a distant memory and at times the AU rather resembles its predecessor, the OAU. The AU has not prevented or resolved conflicts and war on the continent, or ended the prevalence of coups or improved continental development. In 2017, for example, the AU called for the withdrawal of member states from the International Criminal Court (ICC), although the resolution was non-binding and opposed by significant states such as Nigeria and Senegal. At the time only South Africa and Burundi had decided to withdraw from the ICC on the grounds that it undermined 'their sovereignty and [was] unfairly targeting Africans' (Igunza, 2017). However, South Africa subsequently retracted its intention to withdraw from the ICC (Borger, 2023).

Spies (2018: 1) suggested that African diplomacy presents a distinct form or style of diplomacy. The appeal to Pan-Africanism (Akpan, 1976: 11–14) and the yearning for traditional 'authentic' pre-colonial African diplomacy (Smith, 1973: 620) certainly added a difference to post-colonial African diplomacy with its aversion to interstate rivalry and Nkrumah's insistence that the way forward was in unity. However, African diplomacy quickly adapted to the Westphalian sovereigntist approach to statecraft. Although the OAU symbolized the call to unity, the norm of Westphalian sovereignty was enshrined in the policies and practices of the OAU and its successor, the AU. Retaining the colonial borders, and consolidating their sovereignty, became a hallmark of African international relations. In the early days of independence, African leaders sought to 'thwart any move towards supranationality'

(Nwekwo, 2015: 15). The AU, notwithstanding the provisions of Article 4 of its Constitutive Act and the APSA, cannot be compared to the European Union, for example, in which member states have relinquished substantial parts of their sovereignty. Nor does the establishment of the Pan-African Parliament (PAP) change this analysis as African governments 'are averse to giving the PAP legislative powers' (Louw-Vaudran, 2021).

Besides these internal African challenges, the continent must also contend with the broader international community and the hierarchy of states. The idea of international society with its emphasis on constructive social relations remains contested as states vie for power and the achievement of their national interests (Spies, 2016: 39–41). A related question, therefore, is whether Africa and African diplomacy fit in the existing Eurocentric or American-centric, liberal international order? This is far from just an academic question. For example, Ndumiso Ntshinga, a former South African Ambassador to the AU, commented on the undemocratic and alienating nature of the international system (Zhang, 2013: 90–91). According to Faleye (2014: 158–9), the Westphalian order's Eurocentric mentality was 'planted around the world through colonialism' but it does not fit Africa because the new states were never nation states with boundaries cutting across 'transnational kinships'. This dissatisfaction with the current international order explains, for example, South Africa's decision during Jacob Zuma's presidency to join the Brazil, Russia, India, China (BRIC) forum to form BRICS, the conviction being that the global future lies 'in the East' (Marthoz, 2012: 3).

Outside the Euro/Western-centric view of the international system, China has created an alternative discourse designed to appeal to Africa (Zhang, 2013: 2–3). Beijing's messaging promotes two contradictory conceptions of democracy. The first is that 'Africa should have its own style of democracy rather than copying a Western political system'. The second is to apply the Western concept of democracy to the international system to ensure 'an equal say for both China and Africa' (Zhang, 2013: 18–19). China is here lining up 'with African countries by expressing camaraderie with the "victimised"', according to Zhang (2013: 28). This may be the message, but the opposite may be true, for, in the view of Laïdi (2012: 621), 'China is one of the states most hostile to' democratizing the international system. For example, it opposes enlarging the Security Council. China's motives need to be analysed in terms of great power competition, bearing in mind that Beijing has moved on from the 'harmonious world' concept to the 'Community of Common Destiny' which has as its 'vehicle' the 'Belt and Road Initiative' (Tobin, 2020).

Conclusion

Historically, diplomacy has undergone significant changes. Modern diplomacy as defined in the context of the Westphalian notion of statehood, sovereignty and state-to-state relations has set new challenges to this foreign policy instrument. Diplomacy has been forged and shaped as much by war as by peace. The European states system that followed the Peace of Westphalia of 1648 had consequences not only for Europe. As much as the Peace of Westphalia set the course for Europe it also set the course for Africa as, over time, ambitious European states expanded their reach and colonial assets and dominance in Africa.

The chapter outlined the origins of diplomacy over several major developments. Historical African examples of diplomacy were offered with a particular emphasis on West Africa as an illustrative example of African diplomacy. The region offers a unique insight into the origins and development of diplomacy on the continent, and the continent's position in international relations. Rooted in cultural norms and customary practices, historical African diplomacy evolved into an institution to enable representation in and communication between communities and empires.

The chapter also focused on the birth of the modern states system after the Peace of Westphalia until the French Revolution. The latter's significance is, inter alia, that it brought an ambitious Napoleon to power who disrupted the relative peace on the European continent. Napoleon ended the Westphalian era of diplomacy and replaced it with warfare. The Congress of Vienna convened in 1815 aimed to return to diplomacy as a practice of interstate relations. The Congress era lasted for almost a century, a period during which the prevalence and practice of diplomacy changed. It was also the era during which Africa became increasingly significant. The Congress era ended the global slave trade; the continent became the focus of European powers, and the Berlin Conference of 1884–85 decided the colonial fate of many Africans.

The First World War (1914–19) ended the century of Congress diplomacy. It also ended the life of empires and states, contributing factors that led to the Second World War (1939–45). The end of the Second World War paved the way for the decolonization process in, for example, Africa. As European powers broke up and others could not fight the call for independence, a new African state system emerged, adding new sovereign states and UN members. The continent remains a significant actor in global politics and has crafted a unique diplomatic presence and practice. Whatever the initial intentions of the Pan-Africanists at the time of independence, Africa's political leaders very quickly retreated into the Westphalian mode of sovereignty and statecraft. In Africa, diplomatic developments included the establishment of the OAU, replaced by the AU in 2002. Both organizations accepted and maintained the Westphalian mode.

References

Acemoglu, D. and Robinson, J.A. (2010) 'Why is Africa poor?', *Economic History of Developing Regions*, 25(1): 21–50.

Adegbulu, F. (2011) 'Pre-colonial West African diplomacy: its nature and impact', *Journal of International Social Research*, 4(18): 170–82.

Akokpari, J. (2016) The Challenges of Diplomatic Practice in Africa, *Journal for Contemporary History*, 41(1), June, Available from: https://open.uct.ac.za› Akokpari_Article_2016 [Accessed 22 October 2021].

AU (African Union) (2002) *Constitutive Act of the African Union* [online], Available from: https://au.int/sites/default/files/pages/34873-file-constitutiveact_en.pdf [Accessed 22 November 2023].

AU (African Union) (2007) *Audit of the African Union* [online], 18 December 2007, Available from: www.securitycouncilreport.org [Accessed 18 October 2021].

Akpan, M.E. (1976) *African Goals and Diplomatic Strategies in the United Nations. An In-Depth Analysis of African Diplomacy*, North Quincy, MA: Christopher Publishing House.

Anderson, M.S. (1993) *The Rise of Modern Diplomacy 1450–1919*, London: Routledge.

Anyaoku, E. (1999) *Lessons from over Four Decades of African Diplomacy*, Address to the Conference on African Diplomacy in the 21st Century, London, 24 March.

Berridge, G.R. and Lloyd, L. (2012) *The Palgrave Macmillan Dictionary of Diplomacy* (3rd edn), London: Palgrave Macmillan.

Borger, J. (2023) 'South Africa's President and ANC Sow Confusion over Leaving ICC', *The Guardian* [online], 25 April, Available from: www.theguardian.com/world/2023/apr/25/south-africas-president-and-party-sow-confusion-over-leaving-icc [Accessed 15 April 2024].

Congress of Vienna (2015) *Final Act of the Congress of Vienna*, 9 June 1815, *Act No. XV – Declaration of the Powers, on the Abolition of the Slave Trade* [online], 8 February 1815, Available from: www.hlrn.org/img/documents/final_congress_viennageneral_treaty1815.pdf [Accessed 17 July 2022].

Coolsaet, R. (1998) 'The transformation of diplomacy at the threshold of the new millennium', *Discussion Papers*, No. 48 [online], Leicester: Leicester Diplomatic Studies Programme, Available from: https://rikcoolsaet.be/files/1998/01/wzin04-thetransformationofdiplomacyatthethresholdofthenewmillenium-rikcoolsaet-be.pdf [Accessed 22 November 2023].

David, S. (2011) 'Slavery and the "Scramble for Africa"', *BBC* [online], 17 February, Available from: www.bbc.co.uk/history/british/abolition/scramble_for_africa_article_01.shtml [Accessed 17 July 2022].

Faleye, O.A. (2014) 'Africa and international relations theory: acquiescence and responses', *Globalistics and Globalization Studies*, 28(1): 154–63.

Fletcher, T. (2016) *Naked Diplomacy. Power and Statecraft in the Digital Age*, London: William Collins.

Grant, S.J. (1972) *A Case Study of a Model Teacher Training Course in Ivory Coast Student Characteristics and Participatory Behaviour*, PhD dissertation, University of Massachusetts Amherst [online], June, Available from: https://scholarworks.umass.edu/cgi/viewcontent.cgi?article=3159&context=dissertations_1 [Accessed 12 October 2021].

Gwaambuka, T. (2016) 'Is the African Union a Dictators' Talking Club?', *The African Exponent* [online], extract carried on *Muck Rack, Articles by Tatenda Gwaambuka*, Available from: https://muckrack.com/tatenda-gwaambuka/articles [Accessed 21 March 2024].

Hamilton, K. and Langhorne, R. (2011) *The Practice of Diplomacy: Its Evolution, Theory and Administration*, London: Routledge.

Heine, J. (2006) 'On the manner of practising the new diplomacy', *Centre for International Governance Innovation Working Paper No 11* [online], October, Available from: www.files.ethz.ch/isn/25748/Paper11_Jorge_Heine_web.pdf [Accessed 17 July 2022].

Igunza, E. (2017) 'African Union backs mass withdrawal from ICC', *BBC* [online], 1 February, Available from: www.bbc.com/news/world-africa-38826073 [Accessed 17 July 2022].

Irwin, G.H. (1975) 'Precolonial African diplomacy: the example of Asante', *International Journal of African Historical Studies*, 8(1): 81–96.

Kissinger, H.A. (1994) *Diplomacy*, New York: Simon & Schuster.

Laïdi, Z. (2012) 'BRICS: sovereignty power and weakness', *International Politics*, 49(5): 614–63.

Lascurettes, K. (2017) *The Concert of Europe and Great-Power Governance Today*, Rand Corporation [online], Available from: www.rand.org/content/dam/rand/pubs/perspectives/PE200/PE226/RAND_PE226.pdf [Accessed 17 July 2022].

Louw-Vaudran, L. (2021) 'Pan-African parliament's woes reflect a crisis in leadership', *Institute of Security Studies (ISS) Today* [online], 10 June, Available from: https://issafrica.org/iss-today/pan-african-parliaments-woes-reflect-a-crisis-in-leadership [Accessed 17 July 2022].

Marthoz, J. (2012) *The Challenges and Ambiguities of South Africa's Foreign Policy*, Norwegian Peacebuilding Resource Centre (NOREF) Report [online], September, Available from: www.files.ethz.ch/isn/153069/1d25c90556f0a6f66548551220c882e8.pdf [Accessed 17 July 2022].

Mohammed, S.A. (2015) 'Organization of African Unity and the African diplomacy', *Izmir Review of Social Sciences*, 3(1): 95–108.

Nicolson, H. (1939) *Diplomacy*, Oxford: Oxford University Press.

Nicolson, H. (1947) *The Congress of Vienna: A Study in Allied Unity: 1812–1822*, London: Constable & Co.

Nigro, L.J. (2008) 'Theory and practice of modern diplomacy: origins and development to 1914', in J. Boone Bartholomees (ed) *The US Army War College Guide to National Security Issues, Volume 1, Theory of War and Strategy* (3rd edn) [online], Available from: www.jstor.org/stable/resrep12025.19 [Accessed 17 July 2022].

Nwekwo, T. (2015) 'Pre-colonial and post-colonial African diplomacy and the influence of the African Union in Africa's diplomatic history', unpublished paper [online], Available from: www.researchgate.net/publication/281320392_PRE-COLONIAL_AND_POST-COLONIAL_AFRICAN_DIPLOMACY_AND_THE_INFLUENCE_OF_THE_AFRICAN_UNION_IN_AFRICA'S_DIPLOMATIC_HISTORY [Accessed 17 July 2022].

Satow, E. (1973) *A Guide to Diplomatic Practice* (4th edn), London: Longman.

Smith, R. (1973) 'Peace and palaver: international relations in pre-colonial West Africa', *Journal of African History*, 14(4): 599–621.

Spies, Y.K. (2016) 'Africa and the idea of international society', *Journal for Contemporary History*, 41(1): 38–56.

Spies, Y.K. (2018) 'African diplomacy', in G. Martel (ed) *The Encyclopedia of Diplomacy*, London: John Wiley, pp 1–14.

Spies, Y.K. (2019) *Global Diplomacy and International Society*, London: Palgrave Macmillan.

Tobin, D. (2020) *How Xi Jinping's 'New Era' Should Have Ended U.S. Debate on Beijing's Ambitions*, Centre for Strategic and International Studies Report [online], 8 May, Available from: www.csis.org/analysis/how-xi-jinpings-new-era-should-have-ended-us-debate-beijings-ambitions [Accessed 17 July 2022].

Wanlass, L.C. (1970) *Gettell's History of Political Thought*, New York: George Allen and Unwin.

Zhang, X. (2013) 'How ready is China for a China-style world order? China's state media discourse under construction', *Ecquid Novi: African Journalism Studies*, 34(3): 79–101.

Zhuwakinyu, M. (2020) 'Shame on you, AU and SADC', *Engineering News* [online], 21 February, Available from: www.engineeringnews.co.za/print-version/shame-on-you-au-and-sadc-2020-02-21 [Accessed 17 July 2022].

3

Common African Positions as Diplomatic Instruments

Jo-Ansie van Wyk

Introduction

The objectives of the African Union (AU) are outlined in Article 3 of its Constitutive Act and include, inter alia, to 'promote and defend African common positions on issues of interest to the continent and its peoples' (AU, 2002). Since the establishment in 1963 of the Organization of African Unity (OAU), the AU's predecessor, the continent has been steadfast in promoting African unity and solidarity while also attempting to prevent Africa's marginalization from the international arena. These efforts have produced mixed results but since the establishment of the AU in 2002, the continent has refined its diplomatic efforts and practices in the context of the Constitutive Act. One such practice has been the increased adoption of common African positions (CAPs) on areas of common African concern as well as on broader international matters.

Historically, Africa has, under the OAU, adopted several CAPs. In 1987, for example, it adopted a common position on Africa's external debt, followed, in 1994, by a CAP on human and social development. Thereafter, several other common positions were adopted and covered a variety of issues, such as food security (1996), biodiversity (1997), weapons proliferation and trafficking (2000), digital inclusion (2001) and the future of children (2001) (Adeoye, 2020: 5). However, the idea of CAPs has gained more traction since the OAU transformed into the AU in 2002 and the subsequent adoption of a plethora of CAPs: UN reform (2005), crime prevention and criminal justice (2005), the Millennium Declaration and the Millennium Development Goals (2005), youth (2006), migration and development (2006), mining (2009), youth development (2010), development effectiveness (2011), the post-2015 development agenda (2014), data (2014), development finance (2015), ending child marriage in Africa (2015), climate change (2015), UN review of peace operations (2015), sustainable development and poverty eradication (2015), controlled substances and access to pain management drugs (2016), the world drug problem (2016), humanitarian effectiveness (2016), silencing the guns (2016), migration (2017), international plant treaty (2017), asset recovery (2020), food systems (2021), disaster risk reduction (2022), neglected tropical diseases (2022), energy access and just energy transition (2022) and cyber security (2023).

Africa is not unique in employing common positions as diplomatic instruments. The European Union (EU), for example, often uses common positions at multilateral fora to promote its interests and within the EU to achieve internal cohesion. CAPs are distinct from EU common positions in terms of the process resulting in the crafting and adoption of a common position. Unlike EU common positions, CAPs are seemingly often the result of a less formal process, but, like the EU process, also highly political.

The aim of the chapter is to analyse CAPs as an African diplomatic instrument. It unfolds in five sections. The first section presents a conceptual analysis of common positions as a diplomatic instrument. Thereafter the chapter focuses on the elements, nature and objectives of CAPs. It then proceeds to outline the diplomatic path leading to the crafting and adoption of a CAP before exploring the notion of commonality in the context of CAPs. A discussion on African states' universal application, promotion and implementation of CAPs follows. The final part of the chapter contains the conclusion of the study.

Defining common positions

No single definition of a common position exists. Hence, this chapter defines it as the result of a diplomatic process among members of an international intergovernmental actor resulting in a decision on the actor's diagnosis of an issue, often including an actor's demands and recommendations for addressing the matter. Besides the underlying principle of unity, a common position is also a reflection of an actor's interests, expectations and negotiating strategy regarding an issue. Typically, a common position contains normative, instructive and performative elements.

As a diplomatic instrument, common positions are utilized in various ways. First, they are the result of an internal decision-making process that reflects the commitments of member states of a multilateral organization. In this instance, common positions are sometimes for internal use of an organization or in some instances adopted to be taken to other multilateral organizations such as the UN. Second, common positions are adopted to present the views and promote the interests of an organization. In the third instance, common positions are used as a negotiating strategy to achieve an objective. Fourth, a common position is sometimes utilized as a conciliation and conflict resolution mechanism to accommodate divergent views. Five, in some instances common positions aim to harmonize an organization's internal procedures. In 2008, for example, the EU adopted a common position that defines common rules for its members to govern the control of exports of military technology and equipment. Finally, common positions are adopted for symbolic purposes such as to express an organization's views or solidarity with an actor or regarding a matter of significance.

Some of the normative elements of a common position include reference to an actor's foundational values and principles and justify an actor's engagement on the issue. Instructive elements often include an actor's demands and recommendations for remedial action regarding an issue. It thus instructs a state party to a common position how and what to negotiate to achieve the purpose of the common position, which is however ultimately the objectives of an actor. The performative elements of a common position refer to how it performs and is practised as a diplomatic instrument. In other words, what does an actor achieve with the adoption of and adherence to a common position?

Common African positions

The AU has provided insights into the elements, nature and diplomatic objectives of common positions. In constructivist terminology, CAPs represent and reflect African states' identity, interests and aspirations. Moreover, intersubjectivity is enhanced by a continuous socialization process and thus the institutionalization and routinization of the crafting and adoption of a CAP as a diplomatic practice. This is diplomatically beneficial as it increases the confidence, status and independence of an actor, or a collective of actors such as the AU.

The Ezulwini Consensus, the CAP on United Nations (UN) reform, is a significant illustration of the objectives and power of a CAP. The reform of the UN and its organs to improve the representation of, for example, African states has been ongoing for decades. Since 1945, when the UN was established, the number of African states has increased, a reality which is not reflected in organizations such as the United Nations Security Council (UNSC). UN Secretary General Kofi Annan's tenure paid renewed attention to UN reform. Annan was Ghanaian by birth, and his efforts were received positively by African states. One of the first major common positions adopted by the AU since its establishment was the CAP on the Proposed Reform of the United Nations of 2005, the so-called Ezulwini Consensus, in response to the Report of the High-Level Panel on Threats, Challenges and Change (AU, 2015a). The Ezulwini Consensus, besides endorsing the Responsibility to Protect norm and others, called for 11 additional members of the UNSC, thus expanding its members from 15 to 26. Moreover, Africa wanted two permanent and five non-permanent seats on the UNSC (AU, 2015a).

The origins of the Ezulwini Consensus lie in the AU summit meeting in Nigeria in January 2005. One of the outcomes of the summit was the establishment of the Committee of Ten (C-10) AU member states to draft an African position on UN reform. African foreign ministers met two months later (March 2005) in Ezulwini, Swaziland, during the 7th Extraordinary Summit of the AU and formulated a common African position. Subsequently, the AU Executive Committee adopted what became known as the Ezulwini Consensus as the continent's official position on UN reform. As a common position, the Ezulwini Consensus has been regarded as a break from the past in Africa, where individual state interests and sovereignty have often superseded continental common interests.

The AU CAP on Humanitarian Effectiveness, adopted in 2016, is another illustrative example of the elements, nature and objectives of a CAP. In this CAP, the normative elements of a common position are clear, with the emphasis on humanitarian effectiveness, inclusivity, Pan-Africanism, 'solidarity, cooperation and mutual accountability' (AU, 2016b: 3). Moreover, the AU also reiterated that the CAP is 'an expression of Africa's core values and the essence of being African and extends to the ethos of what Africa is thinking and positioning itself, for its people as well as its commitment to humanitarian effectiveness on the continent' (AU, 2016b: 8).

Moreover, the AU included the slogan 'One Africa, One Voice, One Message', reiterating the collective and undivided nature of the continent's common positions. It outlines the CAP as a 'consolidation' of African aspirations regarding humanitarian effectiveness but also regarding reform of the global humanitarian architecture (AU, 2016b: 3). Besides this, the AU explained that the CAP is Africa's 'contribution in shaping future humanitarian architecture' and its intention to resolve the root causes of the humanitarian crisis on the continent (AU, 2016b: 3, 5).

Adopting a common position presupposes the existence of an audience or opponent for or against whom the common position is adopted. This audience or opponents could be external and/or internal. The CAP on Humanitarian Effectiveness refers to this aspect: 'The CAP is commended for the attention of all Member States, Regional Economic Communities, civil society and the Diaspora, African Union Partners and African people and the global humanitarian community at large to improve humanitarian effectiveness on the continent' (AU, 2016b: 6).

With the establishment of the AU, the continent's new political architecture galvanized support for engagement with the international community and created greater awareness of common – rather than individual – African interests. Emphasis was specifically placed on the need for collective African efforts to have one voice (that is, a common position) at international and multilateral negotiations and deliberations. Hence, these diplomatic instruments have continued as instruments of Pan-Africanism and agency for the continent. The AU has also emphasized the principles of inclusivity, transparency, recognition and integration (AU, 2014).

A subsequent example of and commitment to promoting the continent's common interests includes the developmental blueprint *Agenda 2063: The Africa We Want*, adopted in 2015 (AU, 2015b). Therein, the AU reiterated its intention to reduce the continent's global marginalization and enhance internal unity and its influence in global affairs (AU, 2015b). Agenda 2063, read with the Constitutive Act, expresses Africa's collective aspirations to end global inequality and achieve equity. Aspiration 7 ('Africa as a strong, united, resilient and influential global player and partner') of Agenda 2063 formulates this as:

> improving Africa's place in the global governance system (UNSC, financial institutions, global commons such as outer space); improving Africa's partnerships and refocusing them more strategically to respond to African priorities for growth and transformation; and ensuring that the continent has the right strategies to finance its own development and reducing aid dependency. (AU, 2015b)

Diplomatic path to a common African position

The formulation of common positions is often a tough political negotiation process. The diplomatic path to a CAP is frequently arduous and often the result of the continent's long engagement with a question or challenge. The EU, for example, has formalized the process to arrive at a common position, whereas the AU seems to be taking a less formal approach, albeit within the bureaucratic, institutional and legal confines of the AU.

The EU Council has also formalized the adoption of common positions in cases when the EU Council does not agree with decision of the European Parliament. The adoption of a common position is prepared by so-called working parties and the Committee of Permanent Representatives (COREPER, consisting of the permanent representatives of member states). In the next phase of the process, the EU Council negotiates a so-called political agreement outlining the proposed common position. The working party finalizes the details of the document and then refers it to the EU Council of Ministers to be adopted as a common position. The EU Council occasionally reached an agreement in principle (called a General Approach) prior to the EU Parliament's delivery of its position (European Commission, 2012).

In the context of the EU, the adoption of common positions occurs with or without debates. A qualified majority is required to adopt a common position and there is no time limit prescribed. Once a common position is adopted, the EU Council explains its position and the reasons therefor to the EU Parliament. Once the EU Parliament receives this communication, it has three months to deliberate on the Commission's common position. If the Parliament disagrees with it, a compromise must be reached in parliamentary committees followed by a third reading. Proposed amendments are put to vote in the relevant parliamentary committee(s), which are decided by a simple majority. Once adopted, the document is referred to a Parliamentary Plenary where the common position must be adopted by an absolute majority (European Commission, 2012).

This section explores at least four paths to CAPs: the consolidation of a historical position on an issue; the appointment of an ad hoc high-level committee to develop a draft CAP for adoption; an initiative of the AU Commission or a specific AU commissioner; a consultative process resulting in a CAP prior to a multilateral conference or negotiations, or as a reaction to such events. An example of the latter includes the adoption of a CAP in preparation for a multilateral conference or session such as the CAPs adopted prior to the UN General Assembly Session on the World Drug Problem that took place in April 2016, and the 63rd session of the Commission on the Status of Women (2019) (AU, 2016a).

The adoption of the CAP on the Global Compact on Safe, Orderly and Regular Migration is an example of the diplomatic path of a common position. The CAP's genealogy includes a series of AU decisions, declarations, roadmaps and initiatives on migration and the free movement of people, including the AU Commission Initiative against Trafficking (AU.COMMIT), AU, COMMIT, the AU–Horn of Africa Initiative on Human Trafficking and Smuggling of Migrants and the implementation of the 2006 Ouagadougou Plan of Action in the Prevention of Smuggling and Trafficking of Persons, especially Women and Children in Africa. Moreover, this particular CAP is a consolidation of earlier AU documents and positions such as the AU Constitutive Act, Agenda 2063, the Kampala Convention for the Protection and Assistance of Internally Displaced Persons, the Niamey Convention on Cross-Border Cooperation, the Maputo Protocol, the Revised Migration Policy Framework for Africa, the African Common Position on Migration and Development, the AU Border Governance Strategy and other similar AU instruments and initiatives such as the African Peace and Security Architecture (APSA), the African Governance Architecture, the African Remittances Institute, the Joint Migration Programme, the Minimum Integration Plan, the Free Trade Agreement, the Comprehensive Africa Agriculture Development Programme and the Programme for Infrastructure Development in Africa (AU, 2019).

A second path involves an AU Assembly of Heads of State and Government appointment of an ad hoc high-level committee, as happened in the context of the CAP on the post-2015 Development Agenda. In the formulation and adoption of this CAP, the AU High-Level Committee was supported by the AU Commission, the New Partnership for Africa's Development (NEPAD) Agency, the African Development Bank (ADB), the UN Economic Commission for Africa (UNECA), the United Nations Development Programme (UNDP) Regional Bureau for Africa and the United Nations Population Fund (AU, 2014: 8).

The diplomatic path to the adoption of a CAP could also be initiated by the AU Commission and/or the AU commissioner responsible for the relevant portfolio. In April 2021, for example, the AU commissioner for infrastructure and energy convened an extraordinary meeting of African ministers of air transport and stakeholders to present a proposed CAP on the issue of a vaccine passport developed by the AU Commission, and its implication for international travel, to deliberate on the proposed CAP and to adopt it. The extraordinary meeting was also attended by high-level representatives of air transport institutions, regional economic communities (RECs) and industry partners from East African Commission (EAC), UNECA, the group of African ambassadors at the Council of International Civil Aviation Organization (ICAO), other ICAO Comprehensive Regional Implementation Plan for Aviation Safety in Africa (AFI) group members and ICAO regional directors, the secretary general of the African Civil Aviation Commission, the secretary general of the African Airlines Association, the regional vice president for Africa and the Middle East at the International Air Transport Association and the director of the Africa Centres for Disease Control (CDC) attended the meeting (AU, 2021).

Another path to the adoption of a CAP has been evident in, for example, the development of a CAP on food systems. During this process, the AU Commission and the AU Development Agency collaborated with UNECA, which hosted a regional dialogue on African food systems in the context of the Africa Regional Forum on Sustainable Development from March to July 2021 (UNECA, 2021). After the regional dialogue, the CAP was adopted in preparation of the UN Food Systems Summit of September 2021.

Compared to multilateral fora such as the UN and EU, the AU has paid significantly more attention to the impact of climate change on peace and security. As early as 2004, barely two years into its existence, the AU adopted declarations and resolutions on the impact of climate change on the continent's future. Following the Sirte Declaration, the Algiers Declaration on Climate Change in 2009 formed the basis of Africa's position in subsequent climate change negotiations (Scholtz, 2010: 3–29). In May 2018, the AU Commission requested the appointment of an AU envoy for climate change. This request was repeated by the Peace and Security Council

(PSC) in 2020 when it called for the adoption on a CAP on climate change and the establishment of an AU Special Fund for Climate Change (AUPSC, 2021a). In 2021, for example, the AU Peace and Security Council issued two communiques to this effect: Sustainable Peace in Africa: Climate Change and Its Effects on Peace and Security in the Continent (March 2021) and Climate Change and Peace and Security: The Need for an Informed Climate–Security–Development Nexus for Africa (November 2021) (AUPSC, 2021a, 2021b). These communiques are important milestones in the development of the continent's common position on climate change and security it hoped to adopt prior to Egypt's hosting of the UN Framework Convention on Climate Change Conference of the Parties in November 2022.

These examples are by no means the only diplomatic paths to the adoption of a CAP, but they provide insights into diplomatic initiatives, agency and response to international events. CAPs are presented internally and towards the international community as a reflection of African unity, solidarity and Pan-Africanism, a situation that warrants further exploration in the next section.

Commonality and compromise

One can question the extent and scope of commonality in CAPs: is a CAP a real reflection of the position of all AU members? CAPs are often the result of compromise between divergent continental positions during the drafting phase. An example of this includes the CAP on climate change, and the initial divergent positions by South Africa, Kenya and Ethiopia (Mudimeli, 2020: 58–76). Moreover, larger African states and better functioning RECs are often more diplomatically astute and proactively promote their interests.

The CAP on Migration and Development provides some insights into the question of commonality. In January 2006, the AU Executive Council mandated the AU Commission to convene an experts' meeting on migration and development, which took place in April 2006. This diplomatic process was swift and was not attended by all AU states. According to the AU, 'over 42 states' (that is, not all AU members), RECs, non-government organizations (NGOs) and international government organizations attended the meeting. The meeting adopted a Draft African Common Position on Migration and Development which was adopted by the AU Executive Council (EX.CL/Dec.305 (IX)) in July 2006.

Various themes emerge from a reading of CAPs. First, African states' shared colonial experience, marginalization and weak agential power in the maelstrom of international politics. Second, a more confident Africa is evident since the establishment of the AU has resulted in CAPs focusing on common African values and African agency vis-à-vis international governance. However, despite these shared experiences, values and aspirations, a CAP is not always reflective of a common African position. The process that results in the adoption of a CAP is often complex and, to counter divergence, the AU, unlike its predecessor, has invested more in consultative processes regarding the crafting and adoption of CAPs. Increasingly, a wide variety of international, regional and national stakeholders has become involved in the process of adopting a CAP. An example is the CAP on Humanitarian Effectiveness, where the AU mandated a high-level committee to develop a common position. The committee subsequently followed a participatory process, engaging national, regional and continental public and civil society stakeholders and organizations, and parliamentarians (AU, 2014). The process involved consultation with the Permanent Representatives Committee Sub-Committee on Refugees, Returnees and Internally Displaced Persons, the AU's Commissioner for Political Affairs, with technical support from the High-Level Advisory Group, the Norwegian Refugee Council, UN agencies, AU member states, RECs, regional mechanisms, the International Committee of the Red Cross (ICRC), the International Federation of the Red Cross and Red Crescent Societies, and national, regional and continental public and civil society stakeholders, civil society organizations, women and youth associations, academia and the diaspora (AU, 2016b: 10). What also distinguishes this CAP is its detailed recommendations to individual states, the continent and the international community (AU, 2006).

The principles of inclusivity and consultation have been reiterated in the final text of CAPs. In the case of the CAP on Humanitarian Effectiveness, the final text reads: 'The CAP was formulated through an inclusive consultative political process and received input from Member States, Regional Economic Communities, Institutions and Organs of the African Union, a wide range of stakeholders among them public and private sectors, parliamentarians, civil society, the Diaspora, and the youth' (AU, 2016b: 7).

This, however, begs the question whether the continent and individual AU members universally apply, promote and uphold CAPs.

Applying and upholding CAPs

Besides reflecting Africa's normative commitments, a CAP also strives to advance African interests, improve unity and enhance the role and impact of the continent to actively participate in global affairs. CAPs reiterate a position seemingly more important than commonality: Africa's representation, recognition and agency 'to enable Africa to ensure that its concerns are properly reflected at the Africa/Europe dialogue and other international fora' (AU, 2006).

Besides the outward projection and objectives of a CAP, it also speaks to an internal audience (that is, African member states). In the context of the CAP on Humanitarian Effectiveness, for example, the internal audience (governments) are addressed and implored to implement the CAP at national and regional level (AU, 2016b: 21). This begs the question whether individual AU members have been successful in applying, promoting and upholding CAPs. Here, mixed results are evident, seemingly due to member states' focus on national rather than continental interests (Smith, 2016). National leaders are keen to stay in power at home. AU events and decisions are often supported to enhance national governments' standing and status. Smaller, less powerful and influential African states seem to benefit from the adoption of a CAP as less resources are required to develop a diplomatic position from a national perspective. In some instances, individual African states' agential influence has been neutralized by the efforts of major powers and/or former colonial powers to achieve the latter's objectives and advance their interests at the negotiating table. Despite this, various sources seem to suggest that CAPs have predominantly trumped national positions in international fora and negotiations, but they have produced mixed results (Zondi, 2012; Cornelissen et al, 2014; Murithi, 2014; Gwatiwa, 2022).

Conclusion

Two decades after the establishment of the AU in 2002, it is increasingly institutionalizing and routinizing the adoption of CAPs, as required by its Constitutive Act. Underlying this diplomatic practice is the continent's aspiration to counter African marginalization, promote African unity and Pan-Africanism, have its voice heard, and establish an equitable international arena.

Various diplomatic paths lead to the crafting and adoption of a CAP. These are cumbersome and time-consuming processes that are expected to be improved once the AU's institutional transformation in terms of the Kagame Report has been implemented and completed (Kagame, 2017). CAPs have become an integral part of the AU's diplomatic practice and an enabler of, among others, African unity and agency in recent decades. By adopting and implementing CAPs, the AU has achieved at least six objectives. First, it has enabled its members to participate in continental decision making. Despite its laborious nature, the process to adopt a CAP is beneficial in terms of its consultative nature and decision making through consensus building. Hence, continental approval and adoption of a CAP enjoys legitimacy and buy-in.

Second, CAPs have strengthened regional integration and RECs. Regional consultation and deliberation on an issue identified for the development of a CAP is imperative for consensus building as RECs form the building blocks of the AU. Hence, regional trust building and cooperation is required, an aspect that strengthens regional integration and cooperation.

Third, CAPs mean that Africa's scarce diplomatic resources can be pooled. Individual African states often lack the resources and adaptive capacity to determine the outcome of international negotiations. Adopting a CAP provides a point of departure for African states' bilateral and multilateral engagements.

Fourth, CAPs are increasingly terminating the continent's international marginalization and improving its status and influence. Article 3 of the Constitutive Act of the AU is clear on the role of CAPs in enhancing the continent's international position to achieve global equity and continental development. Hence, the promotion and defence of common African positions is a legal instruction to and an obligation of AU members.

Fifth, CAPs have improved Africa's collective bargaining power in multilateral fora. A CAP is endorsed by 55 African states, a significant voting bloc in any multilateral organization. In the context of the UN, for example, Africa represents almost a quarter of the members. An AU mantra in most CAPs refers to the AU's emphasis on African representation and participation, and that the continent's 'voice is heard and is fully integrated into the global debate … [and] to speak with one voice and to act in unity' (AU, 2016a).

Last, the international community is increasingly socialized regarding its relations with the continent. This is evident in the increased country to continent (for example, the regular New Africa–France summits, Forum on China–Africa Cooperation (FOCAC) meetings and the Russia–Africa summits), continent to continent (for example, EU–AU summits), UN–AU engagements (for example, UN–AU Annual Conference) and solidarity engagements such as the Joint Africa–Arab Heads of State and Government Summit. These engagements take place against the background of CAPs in these settings and elsewhere enabling and advancing multilateralism and forming a basis for negotiations to realize the aspirations of all actors. These developments and partnerships reflect the continent's agency due to, inter alia, its adoption and promotion of CAPs as obliged by the AU Constitutive Act.

References

Adeoye, B. (2020) 'Common African positions on global issues: achievements and realities', *Institute for Security Studies Africa Report 30* [online], December, Available from: https://media.africaportal.org/documents/ar-30-2.pdf [Accessed 10 July 2022].

AU (African Union) (2002) *Constitutive Act of the African Union* [online], Available from: https://au.int/sites/default/files/pages/34873-file-constitutiveact_en.pdf [Accessed 7 July 2022].

AU (African Union) (2006) *African Common Position on Migration and Development*, EX.CL/277 (IX) [online], Available from: www.unhcr.org/protection/migration/4d5257e09/african-common-position-migration-development.html [Accessed 10 July 2022].

AU (African Union) (2014) *Common African Position on the Post 2015 Development Agenda* [online], March, Available from: https://au.int/sites/default/files/documents/32848-doc-common_african_position.pdf [Accessed 11 July 2022].

AU (African Union) (2015a) *The Common African Position on the Proposed Reform of the United Nations*, Ext/EX.CL/2 (VII) [online], Available from: https://old.centerforunreform.org/sites/default/files/Ezulwini%20Consensus.pdf [Accessed 5 March 2005].

AU (African Union) (2015b) *Agenda 2063: The Africa We Want. Framework Document* [online], Available from: https://au.int/sites/default/files/documents/33126-doc-framework_document_book.pdf [Accessed 12 July 2022].

AU (African Union) (2016a) *Common African Position for the UN General Assembly Session on the World Drug Problem*, STC/EXP/DC/3(I) [online], 19–21 April, Available from: https://au.int/sites/default/files/pages/32900-file-common_african_position_for_ungass_draft_6_-_english.pdf [Accessed 11 July 2022].

AU (African Union) (2016b) *Common African Position on Humanitarian Effectiveness* [online], Available from: www.tralac.org/images/docs/9719/common-african-position-cap-on-humanitarian-effectiveness-may-2016.pdf [Accessed 11 July 2022].

AU (African Union) (2019) *Common African Position on the Global Compact for Safe, Orderly and Regulatory Migration*, AU/STC/MRIDP/4(11) [online], Available from: www.giz.de/en/downloads/2019%20Common%20African%20Position%20on%20GCM%20ENG.pdf [Accessed 11 July 2022].

AU (African Union) (2021) 'African ministers of air transport adopt common position regarding international travel', Press statement [online], 15 April, Available from: https://au.int/en/pressreleases/20210415/african-ministers-air-transport-adopt-common-position-regarding-international [Accessed 11 July 2022].

AUPSC (African Union Peace and Security Council) (2021a) *Communique on the 1051st Meeting Held on Climate Change and Peace and Security: The Need for an Informed Climate–Security–Development Nexus for Africa*, PSC/PR/COMM.1051 [online], 26 November, Available from: www.peaceau.org/uploads/eng-final-communique-of-the-1051st-psc-meeting-held-on-26-november-2021-copy.pdf [Accessed 10 July 2022].

AUPSC (African Union Peace and Security Council) (2021b) *Communique on the 984th Meeting of the AUPSC at the Level of Heads of State and Government on Sustainable Peace in Africa: Climate Change and Its Effects on Peace and Security in the Continent*, PSC/AHG/COMM.1 (CMLXXXIV) [online], 9 March, Available from: https://reliefweb.int/sites/reliefweb.int/files/resources/eng-final-communique-for-the-984th-psc-meeting-sustainable-peace-climate-change-9-march-2021-final.pdf [Accessed 11 July 2022].

Cornelissen, C., Cheru, F. and Shaw, T. (eds) (2014) *Africa and International Relations in the 21st Century*, London: Palgrave Macmillan.

European Commission (2012) *Rules of Procedure of the European Parliament* [online], Available from: www.europarl.europa.eu/sides/getDoc.do?pubRef=-//EP//TEXT+RULES-EP+20120417+RULE-043+DOC+XML+V0//EN&language=EN&navigationBar=YES [Accessed 26 July 2019].

Gwatiwa, T. (2022) *The African Union and African Agency in International Politics*, Cham: Springer Nature.

Kagame, P. (2017) *The Imperative to Strengthen Our Union. Report of the Proposed Recommendations for the Institutional Reform of the African Union* [online], Available from: https://au.int/sites/default/files/pages/34915-file-report-20institutional20reform20of20the20au-2.pdf [Accessed 11 July 2022].

Mudimeli, U. (2020) *The Common African Position on Climate Change: A Critical Analysis*, Master in Diplomatic Studies dissertation, University of Pretoria.

Murithi, T. (2014) 'Introduction. The evolution of Africa's international relations', in T. Murithi (ed) *Handbook of Africa's International Relations*, New York: Routledge, pp 1–8.

Scholtz, W. (2010) 'The promotion of regional environmental security and Africa's common position on climate change', *African Human Rights Journal*, 10(1): 3–29.

Smith, K. (2016) 'Africa as an agent of international relations knowledge', in C. Cornelissen, F. Cheru and T. Shaw (eds) *Africa and International Relations in the 21st Century*, London: Palgrave Macmillan, pp 21–34.

UNECA (United Nations Economic Commission for Africa) (2021) 'African countries to speak with one voice at UN food summit' [online], 7 September, Available from: www.uneca.org/?q=stories/african-countries-to-speak-in-one-voice-at-un-food-summit [Accessed 11 July 2022].

Zondi, S. (2012) 'Common positions as African agency in international negotiations. An appraisal', in W. Brown and S. Harman (eds) *African Agency in International Relations*, London: Routledge, pp 19–32.

4

South Africa's Economic Diplomacy and the African Continental Free Trade Agreement: Challenges and Prospects

Sanusha Naidu, Faith Mabera and Arina Muresan

Introduction

Economic diplomacy has been the foundation of the international system whether we are examining the transnational value of the Old Silk Road, the rise of the Roman Empire, or the transactional diplomacy of colonialism, the cold war and the post-cold war historical epochs. Within this context of diplomatic affairs, the typology of economic diplomacy is not insulated from other forms of diplomatic engagements. If anything, it is a symbiotic relationship that economic diplomacy shares with the political, social, cultural, technological and environmental dimensions prevalent in the global landscape.

Not only does this define the way economic diplomacy should be interpreted but it also expands how the concept should be measured, especially regarding its implementation and the way it supports the strategic value of a country's foreign policy. Based on that short narrative, this chapter examines an understanding of economic diplomacy in policy decisions and implementation relating to South Africa's foreign policy behaviour. The chapter argues that South Africa's perspective of how economic diplomacy is determined in practice is linked to how its trade policy is defined. In this regard, the chapter explores to what extent the lines of commercial diplomacy are blurred with economic diplomacy and what fundamentally informs the country's engagements in foreign economic relations. To this end, the alignment and practice in terms of Pretoria's African policy, and the context of the African Continental Free Trade Area (AfCFTA), either as an expression of the country's formal economic diplomacy policy or its significance as only part of the tool in Pretoria's economic calculus is deemed important in disaggregating the way economic diplomacy is perceived.

The chapter is divided into three sections. The first focuses on the way economic diplomacy fits into the framework of South Africa's foreign policy orientation. Here, the authors explore the dynamics of Pretoria's conceptual understanding and distinguish between economic diplomacy being more than just about commercial and trade dynamics but also encompassing the way the economic rules are set in terms of the commercial and trade regime. In other words, the authors reflect on economic diplomacy as an encompassing framework. This section also examines how economic diplomacy aligns and synchronizes with other aspects of diplomacy such as peace and stability that remain a key driver in underpinning the way economic diplomacy is approached and viewed.

The second section builds on the first by exploring the practice of economic diplomacy from a continental perspective by assessing what it means, how it has been applied in terms of the state's capacity and drivers, especially regarding what has been constitutes as its trade policy with that of economic diplomacy.

The final section examines the AfCFTA as a case study, examining how it fits into an economic diplomacy framework, especially relating to the notions of continental economic cooperation. In this regard, consideration is given to the dynamics of regional economic integration trajectories as well as the overlaps and synergies with bilateral economic/trade frameworks. The latter expands on the challenges posed to the AfCFTA where the focus may remain only on the technicalities of trade. To this end, the conclusion of the chapter provides insights into the prospects of the AfCFTA having the potential of becoming a significant outlier of an inclusive continental economic diplomacy framework that needs to develop a broader diplomatic agenda for it to be successfully implemented.

Imperatives of South Africa's post-apartheid foreign policy

After its democratic transition, South Africa's foreign policy identity became a focus of debate and competing interpretations regarding the way Pretoria would position itself in regional, continental and global affairs. The discussion centred around how the Mandela presidency would articulate its distinctiveness in balancing what was characterized as a human rights-centric approach aligned to the moral efficacy of the anti-apartheid struggle with a pragmatic independent foreign policy orientation that was driven by the country's interests. Such propositions on what would constitute Pretoria's personality in global affairs soon became an overarching test of how South Africa defined its values in the expression of its foreign policy engagements.

The question of South Africa's relations with the People's Republic of China (Taiwan) and the Republic of China (China) became one of the first tests of the post-apartheid foreign policy. China demanded its allies' acceptance of its One China Policy rather than a dual approach by maintaining relations with both China and Taiwan. For South Africa, this challenged Pretoria's foreign policy position versus its economic interests. The ultimate question for the Mandela administration became whether South Africa could afford to continue to recognize Taiwan and compromise its global economic relations with Beijing, which was undoubtedly becoming a world economic powerhouse. Or could Mandela's stature as a global human rights icon leverage Taiwan to do the impossible and grant South Africa diplomatic relations with both Taipei and Beijing. Of course, not even Mandela's charm could extend that far. And so eventually the Mandela government had to concede that the political dynamics of a principled foreign policy approach could not assuage its commercial and trade-related expectations and interests. The Hong Kong factor is important, as the island served as an important transit hub for South African goods entering Asian markets. And with Hong Kong returning to Chinese rule in 1997, it was a consideration that had strategic implications for Pretoria's trade with Asia.

The One China question illustrates how South African foreign policy has been through various iterations in terms of what constitutes political diplomacy versus economic diplomacy. In many ways the conceptualization of South Africa's diplomatic overtures relating to its foreign policy stance has been aligned to President Thabo Mbeki's (2002) notion of 'islands of wealth, surrounded by a sea of poverty'. This notion that South Africa's foreign policy was and still is inextricably linked to the development of the African continent has remained complex and often an ambiguous identity for Pretoria. Is South Africa pursuing its economic relations for precisely its own national interests? Or is every global political and economic transaction more about the implications this has for the post-apartheid state being labelled as like its apartheid predecessor: selfish behaviour with narrow interests and extractive intentions? And herein lies the dilemma for South Africa's interpretation of economic diplomacy. Therefore, the essential issue to be addressed is whether South Africa sees its understanding of economic diplomacy to be more than how it pursues a commercial/trade strategy.

In its articulation of what are considered the key imperatives in South Africa's foreign economic trajectory, the issue of commercial diplomacy became more central as economic diplomacy is operationalized and built around trade, investment and branding the country as a destination for doing business. This demonstrates a more traditional sense of diplomacy underpinned by trade and a market-centric approach. From this perspective, economic diplomacy is determined to be about aligning to the macroeconomic policy of an export growth model that is linked to how missions and the bureaucracy help shape and deliver on such outcomes.

Where this becomes interesting is how the view of economic diplomacy intertwines with setting the rules of the game aimed at reforming the global economic order towards a just and fair international trade regime. Within this context, South Africa's agenda-setting abilities reveal the construct of a value proposition that suggest South Africa's national interests are not just about its own developmental agenda but are intrinsically linked to Africa's economic development. Mbeki's notion of an African Renaissance symbolized the rebirth of the continent's political, economic and social affairs and was an expression of how Pretoria could justify the pursuit of its economic interests in Africa. This is examined further in the following section.

Africa in South Africa's foreign policy orientation

Drawing on the African agenda as a key priority of its foreign policy, South Africa has engaged its economic diplomacy, alongside other instruments, as an essential and complementary tool of statecraft in pursuit of foreign policy goals. The strategic importance of the African continent, and specifically the Southern African sub-region, is a cross-cutting theme in its foreign policy agenda, underpinning its engagement in peace and security matters, provision of development assistance and the promotion of multilateralism at the regional and global levels. While South Africa's democratic transition and its post-1994 foreign policy orientation have formed a strong basis for its profile as a middle power, prevailing contradictions in implementation and the subsequent decline of its diplomatic and moral capital over the past decade have given rise to hard questions about the applicability of the middle power label.

Nearly three decades after the end of apartheid, the positive economic outlook during the first years of the democratic transition has given way to grim economic realities characterized by slow growth, pervasive inequality and higher levels of structural unemployment. Compared to an average growth of 4.3 per cent between 2001 and 2007 (IDC, 2013), the South African economy saw a sharp decline between 2018 and 2020, with the worst decline on record of 8.5 per cent in 2020, as a result of the compounding effects of the global pandemic, falling commodity prices and structural constraints such as electricity shortages and rising debt-servicing costs (World Bank, 2021). In addition to economic stagnation, South Africa has also been plagued by high levels of inequality, reaching 0.67 on the Gini index. The richest 10 per cent of the population holds almost 81 per cent of the wealth (Sulla et al, 2022: 1–2). The negative macroeconomic trends and structural constraints on the economy stand in stark contrast to the image of South Africa as an economic giant on the continent (ranked third largest in Africa based on nominal GDP), with the lion's share of intra-regional exports into the continent (24 per cent) and competitive advantage in mining, manufacturing, agriculture and financial services (TRALAC, 2023).

The vicious cycle of low growth and persistent socio-economic challenges have underscored the imperative for policy reforms and frameworks such as the 2020 Economic Reconstruction and Recovery Plan (ERRP), aimed at, for example, economic recovery, reform, infrastructure investment, job creation and inclusion. Complementary to broader fiscal and macroeconomic policy reforms to promote industrialization and build investor confidence, the ERRP acknowledges the centrality of economic diplomacy for resource mobilization and expansion of the market base for South African products across the continent and beyond (The Presidency, 2020). The need to ensure normative consistency between foreign policy objectives and domestic priorities by leveraging economic diplomacy was also outlined in the government's Economic Diplomacy Strategic Framework (EDSF), formulated in 2010 by the Department of International Relations and Cooperation (DIRCO), closely linked to other policy documents such as the South African Trade Policy and Strategic Framework (2010) and the National Development Plan (2012). The EDSF, for example, was envisaged as a pivotal framework to:

- direct the conceptualization and implementation of South Africa's economic diplomacy;
- strengthen the link between foreign policy and domestic policy; and
- delineate the economic and commercial dimensions of South Africa's foreign policy (DIRCO, 2012).

Moreover, the EDSF clarified the role of various departments and agencies in pursuit of economic interests and highlighted the need for coherence across bilateral and multilateral economic diplomacy engagements. A coordinated and targeted approach to economic diplomacy also prioritized South Africa's diplomatic missions and consulates abroad by providing training to diplomats, with an emphasis on identified core priorities and the interface with the African agenda. Accordingly, DIRCO's Economic Diplomacy Toolkit is premised on a three-pronged approach focusing on an effective, efficient and capable diplomatic corps, a close working relationship with corporate and private sectors, and synergy across government departments and entities (DIRCO, 2012).

The Ramaphosa administration has highlighted economic diplomacy and regional integration as a major enabler of the ERRP. It is also expected that this will enable South Africa to benefit from the AfCFTA while also expanding markets elsewhere. Within the Southern African Development Community (SADC), the focus on integration and growth targeted value chains in key sectors such as energy, agro-processing, mining, industrialization, infrastructure development and manufacturing (The Presidency, 2020). At a strategic level, the calibration of South Africa's economic diplomacy has drawn on the complex interdependence and shared fate between South Africa and the rest of the continent regarding peace, security, sustainable development and prosperity. In practice, however, harsh domestic realities and a global geopolitical and geo-economic context in flux have exposed mismatches between rhetoric and implementation. For instance, South African firms such as Woolworths, Massmart and the City Lodge Hotel Group have experienced challenges in venturing into new African markets. These challenges included abrupt changes in regulatory and fiscal frameworks, currency volatility, poor understanding of local consumer profiles and geography, and inappropriate marketing strategies. Apart from difficulties at the operational and regulatory levels, the pullback of South African firms from key African markets underscores the importance of an economic diplomacy strategy attuned to broader sectoral macroeconomic trends, as well as political and infrastructural realities (Phillip, 2021). In meeting the twin priorities of foreign direct investment (FDI) mobilization and investment promotion, South Africa's economic diplomacy should evolve from what Rana (2007: 214) has termed 'economic salesmanship' to a more dynamic role of 'regulatory management and resource mobilization', premised on the harmonization of bilateral and multilateral economic diplomacy. Such an approach also calls for a dynamic management strategy and adeptness in navigating the intricacies of global economic governance and participation in institutions such as the World Trade Organization (WTO) and the Group of 20 (G20), a grouping of states that includes the 20 largest economies in the world. For instance, while the principle of multilateralism and the championing of the developmental agenda have been set out as key drivers of South Africa's engagement in platforms such as the WTO and the G20, the links between its foreign policy goals and its domestic economic interests have remained poorly defined and articulated (Qobo, 2012).

While foreign policy objectives such as promoting multilateralism, advancing the African agenda and promoting regional integration are clearly laid out, the open question is whether South Africa can harness the potential of economic diplomacy as one of the instruments to achieve strategic goals. The AfCFTA may provide impetus for the development integration approach that has informed South Africa's regional economic strategy, but this needs to be supported by the coordination of promotion peace, cultural and developmental diplomacy across the continent (Vickers, 2012). Closer to home, there is a need for deeper reflection of how economic diplomacy can serve as a catalyst for domestic economic reforms by ensuring a better strategic fit between the external and domestic environment and enhancing negotiating strategies to advance national economic interests. Apart from their representational role, diplomats can also act as facilitators, advisors and promoters in shaping the messages and narratives surrounding perceptions and drawing on feedback mechanisms to positively influence policy making.

Inner workings of the bureaucratic machinery

South African policy makers and politicians seem to be riding an extended wave of hubris from the early years of post-apartheid South Africa, when the world welcomed a newly democratic country devoted to liberal democratic norms and open to a globalized economy. By highlighting its potential as a gateway into Africa, bridge builder and liberal darling of the African continent that had achieved a peaceful transition, much institutional and operational improvement was overlooked to the point where South African policy makers were unable to ensure that South African institutions maintained the high standards they had promised.

While gross domestic product (GDP) performance lags, another international benchmark that is used to compare South Africa's economic and commercial resilience is the World Economic Forum's (WEF) Global Competitiveness Report. In 2019, for example, South Africa's score was 62.4, a slight improvement from the previous year. However, in 2020 the WEF changed its evaluation and oriented towards economic performance and the ability to innovate and transform to a pandemic-centric reality, which included available incentives, competition and the ability to mobilize value chains and create new markets that are supported by strong public infrastructure, institutions, education and health, as well as progressive tax policy and social protection (Schwab, 2019; Schwab and Zahidi, 2020). With mounting concerns expressed by the Judicial Commission of Inquiry into Allegations of State Capture, Corruption and Fraud in the Public Sector including Organs of State (2022), South African institutions are relying on their former reputations as well as working hard to quell the additional impact of distrust, which also takes a toll on the morale of public servants. Against this background, South African policy makers have positioned themselves proactively, with President Cyril Ramaphosa spearheading economic reforms such as Operation Vulindlela, the ERRP and the National Infrastructure Plan 2050 that complement the National Development Plan of 2012. South Africa's ability to craft appropriate policy makes significant promises to observers, but its implementation and operationalization hit significant institutional barriers.

DIRCO has attempt to streamline institutional barriers through, for example, the Foreign Service Act, Act 26 of 2019, and aims to play the guiding role in 'conducting and coordinating the international relations and cooperation of the Republic at bilateral, regional and multilateral levels through the Foreign Service abroad and through interactions with foreign representatives in the Republic, in accordance with the foreign policy of the Republic' (Republic of South Africa, 2019). The Act does not explicitly explore the roles of other departments, but it is unclear if DIRCO has the resources to either manage or support the operationalization of economic diplomacy. Pockets of excellence within the civil and foreign service are frequently lauded. However, the scarcity of bureaucratic resources and the need to build bureaucratic competencies impact the ability of government departments to follow up effectively on their economic diplomacy activities (Muresan, 2020).

The Department of Trade, Investment and Competition (DTIC) is another significant player in the operationalization of South Africa's economic and commercial diplomacy. Although its performance is specifically based in driving economic and industrial policy oriented to employment, a general criticism is that government departments tend to operate in silos rather than coordinate initiatives with other departments. In terms of responsibilities, DIRCO drives the foreign policy and economic diplomacy process whereas the DTIC promotes trade and development and negotiates trade agreements. There is a degree of overlap in the use of some resources and coordination between DIRCO and the DTIC (Grant Makokera, 2015: 3), but some clarity in departmental roles and responsibilities is needed. Despite this, some innovation has occurred. The DTIC, for example, is designated as the focal point for foreign investors. Therefore, the department oversees the Invest SA One-Stop-Shop launched in 2016 as a key point of reference that communicates and facilitates engagement with other government entities, and clarifies regulations, registration, permits and licensing. Projects like Invest SA should impact positively on the concerns of governance structures but parliament, for example, has criticized the siloed approach and procedures regarding investment. Parliament has reiterated the urgent need to improve South Africa's competitiveness and the ease of doing business in the country (DTI, 2016).

The existence of multiple policy documents does not provide realistic clarity for the functioning of the relevant organizations. The broader concerns of utilizing human capital strategically are still to be addressed. Moreover, civil servant fatigue is not handled effectively, and therefore decisions are referred to pockets of excellence or escalated to more senior management or ministerial positions.

Proponents for operationalization: state actors

South African state-owned enterprises (SOEs) can contribute to promote economic salesmanship, regulatory management and resource mobilization.

Moreover, larger SOEs such as the energy utility Eskom, and the transport and infrastructure utilities such as the Passenger Rail Agency of South Africa, Transnet or the Airports Company South Africa can be instrumental to achieving national development goals. A supporting SOE, Brand South Africa (Brand SA), was established in 2002 to promote South African businesses, attract FDI and support image branding of the country. However, in 2020 it transpired that Brand SA came under immense strain due to, among other factors, a lack of executive leadership, allegations of corruption and maladministration, and poor governance that undermined its functioning. Brand SA's poor performance was also ascribed to the delays caused by the passing in 2021 of Jackson Mthembu, minister in the Presidency, who was involved in the reorganization of Brand SA (Fengu, 2020, 2021). Ironically, it has been the country's nation-branding institution that has caused additional reputational damage to South Africa. The once positively held attributes of a Rainbow Nation have been replaced by international perceptions of crime, corruption, civil unrest, xenophobic violence and public sector ineptitude.

Despite earlier setbacks, Brand SA still holds immense value as an additional avenue to attract foreign investment to South Africa. The SOE seems to be in better shape recently and is managed from the Presidency. However, while it is aware of issues such as energy insecurity, high crime rates and unemployment that undermine the brand, it remains to be seen whether the official South African branding agency will significantly contribute to achieving the objectives of the government's economic diplomacy agenda.

Engaging South African business

African businesses face political, social and economic risks to varying degrees. In addition, many businesses have different levels of complexities and access. South Africa's corporate landscape remains involved in undoing the legacy of apartheid, as prescribed by broad-based black economic empowerment legislation, but the structure of corporate South Africa does not reflect this reality and therefore a racial bias may persist. For South Africa, achieving the objectives of its economic diplomacy faces two principal challenges:

- improving South African corporate relations;
- integrating previously disadvantaged persons into meaningful and formalized economic contributions.

In this environment, the National Economic Development and Labour Council (NEDLAC) is the operational mechanism that facilitates discussions between business and government, including actors from labour and civil society. NEDLAC's Trade and Industry Chamber addresses practical issues such as digitization, infrastructure agencies, the Industrial Policy Action

Plan and the Black Industrialists Programme, the designation of products, beneficiation, incentives, customs and illicit imports. The Chamber is supported by the Technical Sectoral Liaison Committee sub-chamber that reviews South Africa's trade agreements and specifically focuses on non-agricultural market access and non-tariff barriers. The success of NEDLAC and this specific chamber depends on domestic exigencies as well as the bridge between government, the African National Congress (ANC) and its other alliance partners. This was evident during the Jacob Zuma presidency when meetings between government and NEDLAC were reduced to ad hoc engagements (Grant Makokera, 2015: 5).

The AfCFTA and South Africa's economic diplomacy

The key issue that underpins South Africa's ratification of the AfCFTA is how it will advance the country's trade with the continent. If South Africa expects the AfCFTA to establish trade corridors to stimulate South African investment in and market access to Africa, then South Africa's ability to offer reciprocal opportunities for African investors and businesses comes into question. One aspect that illustrates the complexity of South Africa's ability to reciprocate is the insulation of the South African economy due to existing tariff and non-tariff barriers. This is one example of the challenges to South Africa's Africa agenda. Another challenge to South Africa's economic diplomacy with the rest of the continent is the amendment to the Customs and Excise Duty Act in January 2021, which limits preferential duties on imports into the South African market to Egypt and São Tomé and Príncipe. This has complications for members of the Southern African Customs Union, which may not enjoy the same preferential duty on goods into the South African market. Moreover, if each AfCFTA member adopts a similar process, Africa's internal trade environment would fast become heavily bureaucratized with inadequate human capital supporting institutions.

Another aspect that affects the place of the AfCFTA in South Africa's economic diplomacy is the country's trade with the rest of the continent. While it is not disputed that South Africa is a major trading partner of the rest of Africa, concerns regarding the rules of origin persist. One example is the re-export of machinery and other capital goods via South African ports of entry into other African states. In terms of the rules of origin, one can question whether South Africa is merely a transit hub for the rest of the continent, or whether South Africa's interpretation of these rules effectively serves as an economic multiplier for the country's trade with the continent. Therefore, in the absence of clarity on the rules of origin, the issue is likely to remain on the negotiation agenda of AfCFTA states.

Besides reciprocity and rules of origin, the third issue affecting the link between South Africa's economic diplomacy and the benefits of the

AfCFTA is South Africa's approach to trade facilitation. This relates to the harmonization, standardization, ease of access to and implementation of processes, including procedures that enable businesses to integrate their products into value chains to achieve desired outcomes such as market access and profit. President Ramaphosa, who established a Red Tape Reduction Team in his office, has emphasized that South Africa is restructuring its trade facilitation architecture by minimizing bureaucratic procedures and requirements for doing business in the country (The Presidency, 2022). As much as this is a critical feature of attracting and enhancing investment in advancing the industrial and manufacturing sectors of the economy, especially in localizing economic development and stimulating growth for employment, the difficulty remains domestic legislation that hampers economic policy certainty. Changes to legislation on employment, skilled migration, labour and security, for example, are likely to deter investors from Africa and elsewhere.

Finally, consideration should be given to the mobility of people and goods under the AfCFTA. This is vital to free trade. The micro-economy in South Africa plays a pivotal role in the cross-border movement of people in trade and services, especially where it contributes to household income in regional economies. While the pandemic disrupted cross-border mobility and trade, traders in the cross-border economy are also caught up in the web of parochial immigration and migrant issues related to border management, corruption, inefficient bureaucracy and xenophobia. Given its emphasis on the African agenda, Pretoria struggles to rationalize the treatment of foreign economic migrants in some sectors of society. This makes it more difficult for the democratic post-apartheid state to overcome obstacles to its credibility – for example, whether engendering a legitimate engagement on the AfCFTA at the microeconomic level can be perceived as a genuine partnership with African countries at the macroeconomic level. It is also worth noting that these inherent contradictions in South Africa's body politic in reference to the African Union's (AU) development blueprint Agenda 2063, a veritable regional integration programme, and espousing a coherent and inclusive transformation agenda remains compromised by the way Africa is perceived in the domestic political, economic and social landscape, where prejudices towards African states north of the Limpopo are difficult to contain. Indeed, these underlying issues will continue to be important in how South Africa navigates its commercial and economic diplomacy, as they can contribute to the kind of anti-South African attitude that has occurred in the past.

Conclusion

South Africa's economic diplomacy aims to deepen its commercial and trade interests globally and continentally. Like all countries, South Africa views its economic diplomacy as an extension of its developmental agenda linked to national economic interests. As the South African minister of trade, investment and competition, Ebrahim Patel, has noted on numerous occasions, the intersection between the country's masterplans in key sectors including the automotive industry, steel, minerals and resources, poultry, tourism, agriculture and agro-processing, clothing and textiles, and forestry aims to revitalize the country's industrialization. Therefore, the country's economic diplomacy is intended to achieve economic transformation, broadening economic participation, employment, economic growth and development through an export-led strategy. While these masterplans are deemed important incubators for incentivizing engagement in the economy, it remains uncertain how such masterplans align to the integration of the AfCFTA into South Africa's economic diplomacy. South Africa's positioning of Africa in its foreign policy has created expectations that will not be achieved. Moreover, South Africa's involvement in the AfCFTA has to be reciprocal for the continental project to succeed and the country's intentions on the continent to be deemed non-threatening. The peace–stability–development construct in South Africa's Africa agenda will remain fragile as trade and broader economic tensions that have characterized Pretoria's political and economic identity continue. Issues such as migration and skills policy and tariff and non-tariff barriers will be seen as blockages to the liberalization of the South African market. Africa's trade imbalance with Pretoria will have to be justified because South Africa's two major commercial partners, the EU and China, are located outside the continent.

Economic diplomacy is based on the coordination of national interests to secure the country's trade and commercial gains. South Africa has an opportunity to do this by making the AfCFTA more than a supplement to its macroeconomic policies. The AfCFTA must be interpreted as achieving what South Africa sees as its value proposition in its Africa policy: advancing a just, equitable and sustainable partnership of inclusive development. This is probably where Pretoria must be clear that its economic diplomacy and trade relationships with African countries are as much about South Africa deepening its commercial interests as it is about ensuring reciprocity and strengthening the continent's trade architecture.

References

DIRCO (Department of International Relations and Cooperation) (2012) *Economic Diplomacy Strategic Framework*, Presentation to the National Council of Provinces Committee on Trade & Industry, Economic Development, Small Business, Tourism, Employment & Labour [online], 19 September, Available from: https://pmg.org.za/committee-meeting/14911/ [Accessed 23 November 2023].

DTI (Department of Trade and Industry) (2016) *Invest SA One-Stop Shop*, Briefing to the Portfolio Committee on Depart Trade and Industry [online], 20 April, Available from: https://pmg.org.za/committee-meeting/22411/ [Accessed 17 July 2022].

Fengu, M. (2020) 'Brand SA: former trustees slam Makhubela over "defamatory" allegations', *City Press* [online], 16 August, Available from: www.news24.com/citypress/news/brand-sa-former-trustees-slam-makhubela-over-defamatory-allegations-20200816 [Accessed 1 July 2022].

Fengu, M. (2021) 'Brand SA is a disaster', *City Press* [online], 18 April, Available from: www.news24.com/citypress/news/brand-sa-is-a-disaster-20210417 [Accessed 7 July 2022].

Grant Makokera, C. (2015) 'South African economic diplomacy: engaging the private sector and parastatals', *Institute for Security Studies Paper 280* [online], Available from: https://issafrica.s3.amazonaws.com/site/uploads/Paper280.pdf [Accessed 17 July 2022].

IDC (Industrial Development Cooperation) (2013) 'South African economy: an overview of key trends since 1994', IDC Paper [online], December, Available from: www.idc.co.za/wp-content/uploads/2018/11/IDC-RI-publication-Overview-of-key-trends-in-SA-economy-since-1994.pdf [Accessed 17 July 2022].

Judicial Commission of Inquiry into Allegations of State Capture, Corruption and Fraud in the Public Sector including Organs of State (2022) *Vol 4: All the Recommendations* [online], Available from: www.statecapture.org.za/site/files/announcements/672/OCR_version_-_State_Capture_Commission_Report_Part_VI_Vol_IV_-_Recommendations.pdf [Accessed 23 November 2023].

Mbeki, T. (2002) *Address at the Opening of the World Summit for Sustainable Development*, Johannesburg [online], 26 August, Available from: www.sahistory.org.za/archive/address-thabo-mbeki-opening-world-summit-sustainable-development-johannesburg-26-august [Accessed 17 July 2022].

Muresan, A. (2020) *South Africa in the World 2020: Pragmatism versus Ideology. Dialogue Report*, Institute for Global Dialogue [online], Available from: www.igd.org.za/publications/igd-reports/send/21-igd-reports/745-south-africa-in-the-world-2020-pragmatism-versus-ideology [Accessed 17 July 2022].

Phillip, X. (2021) 'South Africa: Shoprite's exit from rest of Africa points to cautionary "chasing the cycle" strategy', *The Africa Report* [online], 20 September, Available from: www.theafricareport.com/128425/south-african-retailers-mass-exit-from-rest-of-africa-is-a-cautionary-tale-of-chasing-boom-and-bust-cycle/ [Accessed 17 July 2022].

Qobo, M. (2012) 'Chasing after shadows or strategic integration? South Africa and global economic governance', in C. Landsberg and J. van Wyk (eds) *South African Foreign Policy Review*, Pretoria: Africa Institute of South Africa (AISA), pp 257–73.

Rana, K.S. (2007) 'Economic diplomacy: the experience of developing countries', in N. Bayne and S. Woolcock (eds) *The New Economic Diplomacy: Decision Making and Negotiations in International Relations*, London: Ashgate, pp 201–20.

Republic of South Africa (2019) *Foreign Service Act 26 of 2019* [online], Available from: https://www.gov.za/sites/default/files/gcis_document/202006/43403gon642.pdf [Accessed 19 February 2024].

Schwab, K. (2019) *Global Competitiveness Report, 2019*, World Economic Forum [online], Available from: www3.weforum.org/docs/WEF_TheGlobalCompetitivenessReport2019.pdf [Accessed 17 July 2022].

Schwab, K. and Zahidi, S. (2020) *Global Competitiveness Report, 2020*, World Economic Forum [online], Available from: www.weforum.org/reports/the-global-competitiveness-report-2020 [Accessed 17 July 2022].

Sulla, V., Zikhali, P. and Cuevas, P. (2022) *Inequality in Southern Africa: An Assessment of the Southern African Customs Union (English)*, Washington, DC: World Bank Group [online], Available from: http://documents.worldbank.org/curated/en/099125303072236903/P1649270c02a1f06b0a3ae02e57eadd7a82 [Accessed 23 November 2023].

The Presidency (Republic of South Africa) (2020) *The South African Economic Reconstruction and Recovery Plan* [online], Available from: www.gov.za/sites/default/files/gcis_document/202010/south-african-economic-reconstruction-and-recovery-plan.pdf [Accessed 17 July 2022].

The Presidency (Republic of South Africa) (2022) *Red Tape Reduction*, Presentation to the Portfolio Committee on Small Business Development [online], 16 November, Available from: https://pmg.org.za/committee-meeting/36039/ [Accessed 23 November 2023].

TRALAC (Trade Law Centre) (2023) *South Africa: intra-African trade and tariff profile 2022*, 1 September, Available from: https://www.tralac.org/resources/infographic/15181-south-africa-intra-africa-trade-and-tariff-profile.html [Accessed 19 February 2024].

Vickers, B. (2012) 'South Africa's economic diplomacy in a changing global order', in C. Landsberg and J. van Wyk (eds) *South African Foreign Policy Review*, Pretoria: Africa Institute of South Africa (AISA), pp 112–37.

World Bank (2021) 'Overview: South Africa' [online], 18 March, Available from: www.worldbank.org/en/country/southafrica/overview#1 [Accessed 17 July 2022].

5

Prospects for Smart Diplomacy and Its Use in the Foreign Policies of African Small Island Developing States

Suzanne Graham and Victoria Graham

Introduction

There are six African small island developing states (SIDS): Cabo Verde, Comoros, Guinea-Bissau, Mauritius, São Tomé and Príncipe and Seychelles. As a grouping, they are an underexplored area of study in small state literature (notable exceptions include Baldacchino and Milne, 2000; Thorhallsson, 2000, 2006, 2012, 2018; Srebrnik, 2004; Cooper and Shaw, 2009; Prasad, 2009; Sutton, 2011; Graham and Graham, 2016, 2019; Rana, n.d.; Sanches et al, 2022). This is slowly being remedied, as evidenced by Cheeseman (2021), Graham and Graham (2016, 2019), Johnson (2019), Sanches and colleagues (2022) and Veenendaal and Corbett (2015). This chapter aims to contribute to that process through its analysis of African SIDS and the prospects for usage of smart diplomacy as a tool in their foreign policies. A 2017 study of Southern African small states, including Comoros, Mauritius and Seychelles, found that although size is important in shaping foreign policy, it is 'not mutually exclusive from other typical domestic and international determinants that play a role in conditioning most states' foreign policies. Moreover, defence of national interest features as a common and undeniable primary foreign policy objective of these states' (Graham, 2017: 133). Therefore, although small island states face unique challenges and vulnerabilities daily, what drives the foreign policies of African SIDS is ultimately not dissimilar from those drivers in other states. As an instrument of foreign policy, what then is the role played by diplomacy, and in particular smart diplomacy, in the African

SIDS' ability to maximize their influence on the global stage? What are the strengths and limitations of smart diplomacy for them?

Defining foreign policy, smart power and smart diplomacy

A state's foreign policy reflects the 'sum total of its approaches toward and interactions with the world beyond its borders' (Breuning, 2007: 5). States conduct foreign policy to the benefit of their national interests and these interests are usually framed by their citizens' needs, national values and political, economic, social and cultural goals. Foreign policy indicates what is sought by a state. Diplomacy is a tool of foreign policy, and its success relies on skills and resources as well as on people, and is 'thus shaped by a country's culture, experience and history' (Bueger and Wivel, 2018: 11). It reflects the *how* in the conduct of foreign policy. States' domestic and international affairs are inextricably linked, even more so for small island states whose very existence depends on their ability to leverage global support. This could be in the form of economic support such as aid, investment, infrastructural development and championing tourism. It could also refer to political and cultural support, such as visits by heads of state for visibility and providing platforms for islands to showcase their circumstances in multilateral arenas or offering solidarity and kinship through cultural or language groupings such as the Lusophone Commonwealth or Community of Portuguese Language Countries (in the case of Cabo Verde and Guinea-Bissau). In Seychelles, for example, the historical combination of cultures populating the islands characterizes the country as a unique Creole mix, penned in poetry by the country's first president, James Mancham, and reflecting a melting pot of 'Ambassador of all cultures' (in Bueger and Wivels, 2018: 11).

In a world that remains dominated by states, governments rely on hard, soft, or smart power to leverage influence on the global stage. Smart power is a concept most often linked to Joseph Nye (2009: 160–63) and his reference to a combination of hard and soft power tactics in obtaining foreign policy goals. Nye (in Pitsuwan, 2014), a well-known American political scientist, also offers five questions as guidelines for an effective smart power strategy:

- What are the preferred goals or outcomes?
- What resources are available and in what contexts?
- What are the positions or preferences of the targets of influence?
- What forms of power behaviour are more likely to succeed?
- What is the probability of success?

American President Barack Obama and his Secretary of State at the time, Hillary Clinton, referred to this concept in their speeches as America's preferred foreign policy approach (Gallarotti, 2015), lending weight to the term. Effective smart power would entail making the best use of those foreign policy tools at a state's disposal that match the current global circumstance in play. States must develop smart power to implement smart diplomacy. Smart diplomacy refers to 'the art of realising national interests without hurting anyone or any country, a capacity to navigate through complex geopolitics and the power to attract and persuade others' (Khmer Times, 2016).

The argument exists that small island states are somehow weaker, especially those that fall into the least developed category, and that their isolation and associated vulnerabilities mean a lack of influence. But is this necessarily true, when small island states begin to make use of smart diplomacy strategies in their international relations? As Heng and Ad'ha Aljunied (2015: 436) contend, contrary to smallness indicating weakness, 'several methods are available to such states, from adopting "small but smart strategies" to the use of "resilient diplomacy"'.

Smart diplomacy is defined by the Global Diplomatic Forum as the 'practice of smart power beyond traditional diplomacy, with the employment of new technologies, public and private partnerships, as well as diaspora networks at the center of diplomacy' (GDF, 2024). The Forum identifies three pillars for effective smart diplomacy: digital capabilities, stakeholder diplomacy and feminist diplomacy (GDF, 2024). According to this definition, these pillars are essential in a state's transformation of smart power into effective leverage within bilateral and multilateral relations.

The African SIDS share similar histories, challenges and social contexts but differ in relation to stages of development and democratic consolidation. A few questions emerge in relation to their use of smart diplomacy. How do the African SIDS measure in relation to the three pillars defined by the Global Diplomatic Forum? To what extent are these states able to transform potential smart power characteristics into effective leverage in their international relations? Are individual African SIDS more able to do this than others? Is there room for another pillar that is more specific to the context of these small states and the power they may harness in 21st century statecraft? This final question drives the narrative of what African states themselves purport smart diplomacy to be in relation to supporting their own national interests.

In a rapidly advancing technological world, digital capabilities are becoming more prominent in statecraft. As Ghazi (2015) asserts, 'Governments and their affiliates can use online platforms not only to reach audiences for their cultural and trade offerings, but also to detect security threats, as digital capabilities prepare nations to protect their economic and military resources against cyber attacks'.

Moreover, it is cheaper and a time-saver to host diplomatic dialogues online, not to mention the benefits for the environment without the pollution caused by air travel. Building comprehensive digital foreign policy strategies is fast becoming an emerging trend globally as states recognize the benefits gained from online platforms. However, debates are also featuring worldwide around unequal digital access and that 'it is crucial to "leave no one offline". Further, we need to recognise that developing and least developed countries will be affected differently from developed countries' (Zhao in DiploFoundation, 2021).

Stakeholder diplomacy refers to the engagement with multiple actors within a system, other than but often including the state, that can effectively exercise leverage in the foreign relations of a state. Specifically, this type of diplomacy occurs in the context where actors that are emerging as independent influencers display a form of entrepreneurialism in their global engagements leading their countries to increased opportunities (Ghazi, 2015).

Feminist foreign policy, a concept that was spearheaded publicly by Swedish Foreign Minister Margot Wallström in 2014, moves foreign policy into the 21st century by acknowledging the need to strive towards gender equality in this field of governance, not only as a goal in itself, but also as 'a precondition for achieving ... wider foreign, development and security policy objectives' (Wallström in Rupert, 2015). Van Wyk (2007: 18) previously reported on an improvement in the role of women in African political leadership spaces thanks to African states' adoption of the 2003 Protocol to the African Charter on Human and People's Rights on the Rights of Women in Africa, which seeks 'to improve the status of women, gender equality and ending gender-based discrimination'. An example of this improvement is Ellen Johnson Sirleaf, also known as 'Africa's Iron Lady', becoming the first female president in Africa (Liberia) in 2006 and governing until 2018. Over the last 20 years, growing numbers of women have entered the field of diplomacy at ambassadorial level and a larger share in lower-ranking diplomatic posts. Some scholars contend that 'women are assumed to be efficient diplomats and negotiators, particularly in the "soft" humanitarian spheres of foreign policy' (Aggestam and Towns, 2018: 6). Whether this assumption is accurate or not, it is important that at least 49.58 per cent of the world's population is represented in international relations between sovereign states.

Smart diplomacy prospects in the African SIDS

More broadly, SIDS are referenced by 'their smallness, remoteness, oceanic nature, insularity, and small population size, among other defining traits' (Wong, 2011: 2). However, growing literature tends to focus on how small states may be able to use their 'smallness' to their advantage in international politics (Aiyar, 2008; Sanchez et al, 2022). This is so because all states, regardless of size, tend to have a policy outlining their view of the world beyond their borders and their goals and position within it (Graham, 2017) and act upon this in the multilateral arena in whatever ways they can. Sahib-Kaudeer, Jhummun and Gobin-Rahimbux (2016: 1) argue that the 'challenges faced by SIDS are not comparable to those of developed and developing countries'. They contend that 'the differences in geographic location, the availability of resources, the social and economic landscape and the environmental factors are significant and thus play a determining role in creating smart islands' (Sahib-Kaudeer et al, 2016: 1). In a world where the terms 'smart' power and 'smart' diplomacy are bandied about, African SIDS must take ownership of what 'smart' means in their circumstances and how to make their definition of 'smart diplomacy' work for them (Browning, 2006). Bueger and Wivels (2018) suggest how small island states can maximize their foreign policy influence. They identify three sources of small state influence: capability and location, political culture and institutional design, and political strategy. In terms of political strategy, Bueger and Wivels (2018: 1) argue that small states need to be 'smart' by 'setting the agenda, to frame international issues, propose rules and norms, and to provide expertise and problem-solving knowledge'. Using Seychelles as their case study, they find that ocean diplomacy, also referred to as blue diplomacy, is a valued instrument of Seychelles as an African small island state. Indeed, Seychelles is widely acknowledged to be at the forefront in the advocacy of the blue economy, but also as a key player in the field of maritime security. For example, the country volunteered to chair the Contact Group on Piracy off the Coast of Somalia, thereby demonstrating its own agency in international relations. As a result, its status as an:

> important voice in maritime security affairs was reaffirmed and in turn country representatives were invited to speak as experts on the subject at core international diplomatic events, such as the 2015 and 2017 G7 High Level Meetings on Maritime Security, and the 2017 international Our Oceans conference organized by the EU. (Bueger and Wivels, 2018: 9)

Africa's soft power is growing (Tella, 2021), and its diplomatic and economic successes afford the description of a hopeful 'Africa Rising' (The Economist, 2011). However, even then, scholars tend to ignore the soft power of Africa's island states (Johnson, 2019). They may not physically be part of the continent (excluding Guinea-Bissau), but they are African nonetheless. Moreover, in terms of good governance, the Mo Ibrahim Index (2020), for example, ranks Mauritius first out of 54 states, followed by Cabo Verde and Seychelles in third place with São Tomé and Príncipe tied in fifth place (Mo Ibrahim Foundation, 2023: 21). This means that despite their unique challenges and vulnerabilities, two-thirds of the African SIDS feature in the top five in terms of good governance in Africa. This is an important factor for African SIDS in leveraging their soft power internationally

Digital capabilities

In the United Nations (UN) E-Government Survey 2022, which tracks the progress of e-government development via the UN E-Government Development Index (EGDI), Mauritius is ranked highly in the country groupings with a high online services index (OSI) (UN, 2022: 62). The EGDI is a useful measure for government officers, policy makers and decision makers to gain a better 'understanding of the relative position of a country in utilizing e-government for the delivery of public services' (EGDI, 2022: 6). Cabo Verde improved in its rankings, moving into the middle high OSI grouping in recognition of its human capacity, online services and telecommunication infrastructure (EGDI, 2022: 6). Cabo Verde is ranked 110 in the world, São Tomé and Príncipe is 155, the Comoros is 177 and Guinea-Bissau is 186. Four countries in Africa are leading the region in terms of e-government development, and, perhaps surprisingly for some, Mauritius (63) and Seychelles (76) head this group, followed by South Africa (78 in the world) and Tunisia (91) (Department of Economic and Social Affairs, 2020: xx).

Mauritius has invested heavily in its Digital Mauritius 2030 Strategic Plan, which aims to transform the country into a high-income and inclusive economy. The government of Mauritius also supports the idea of Smart Cities or Towns, for example the Smart City Scheme, as well as accompanying legislation, the Investment Promotion (Smart City Scheme) Regulations 2015, to give its citizens the option of living in sustainable urban contexts (Sahib-Kaudeer et al, 2016). The Seychellois government is equally committed to improving its services through enhanced digital means, to deal with a limited workforce availability among other challenges. Cabo Verde has great ambitions to 'transform itself into a mid-Atlantic technology hub that will not only produce digital products but also serve as a centre for digital innovation in the ECOWAS [Economic Community of West African States] region' (International Trade Administration, 2021). Consequently, Cabo Verde has invested heavily in leveraging digital technologies and this is outlined in the 2018–30 Strategic Plan for Sustainable Development (PEDS in its Portuguese acronym) (Ministry of Finance, 2020).

Guinea-Bissau has had less success in the digital realm but recent support from the United Nations Development Programme (UNDP) may improve circumstances for this small West African state which is part of the mainland of Africa but with low-lying land and the Bijagos Archipelago included in its territory. The UNDP has:

initiated a project to support the Ministry of Foreign Affairs in expanding its digital presence and tapping into the potential of technology to improve the way it functions by connecting the diplomatic and consular corps and its delivery of services to promote the country's visibility and image all over the world. (UNDP, 2021)

The Comoros has three major islands, known as Grande Comore (Ngazidja), Mohéli (Mwali) and Anjouan (Ndzuani). The Union of Comoros also lays claim to a fourth island, Mayotte (Maore), presently administered by an overseas department of the French government. A recent project saw a high-speed broadband undersea cable (FLY-LION3) being laid linking the Comoros with Mayotte and Madagascar. This is an important boost for digital enhancement in the region, as well as creating 'resilience in a region of the world where cables are affected by undersea volcanic activity' (Kelly, 2016). A similar submarine cable has also enabled São Tomé and Príncipe to enhance its information and communications technology (ICT) sector (ITU, 2018).

Stakeholder diplomacy

Despite Mauritius' cultural relations with India, China and its fellow Commonwealth members, these relations can be significantly expanded. There are opportunities for domestic stakeholders to promote cultural diplomacy. As Pudaruth (2017: 6) asserts, Mauritius is a multicultural and 'multi-musical' country and 'has a lot to offer to the world in terms of its cultural diversity', especially in the promotion of music and dance as sources of soft power for the country's global image. The Comoros also has a rich cultural and natural heritage, which has a role to play in forging the development of sustainable tourism. Although the Comorian tourism industry is not as strong as in the other Indian Ocean African SIDS, it nevertheless contributes significantly to the Comorian economy. Mainly wealthy Europeans and Americans visit the Comoros for its marine attractions, beaches, unique bird species and mountain sceneries. As an external stakeholder, the United Nations Educational, Scientific and Cultural Organization (UNESCO) is working on a project with participants in the Comoros entitled, Capacity Building in Sustainable Tourism Development and Management for World Heritage in Comoros. The project, launched in 2020, is financed by Netherlands Funds-in-Trust and aims to:

> strengthen the capacities of key stakeholders in Comoros, including the national team in charge of preparing the UNESCO World Heritage nomination file for the Historic Sultanates of Comoros, to develop a sustainable tourism management plan and implementation strategy for the promotion of the cultural sector in Comoros using the

UNESCO sustainable tourism toolkit, expertise and other resources of the UNESCO Sustainable Tourism Programme, and to implement a training activity for local tour guides in the Historic Sultanates of Comoros. (UNESCO, 2020)

An important part of Cabo Verde's sustained diplomatic efforts lies in fostering solidarity among its diaspora stakeholders. This is because there are more people today with origins in Cabo Verde who live outside the country than inside it and the 'money that they send home brings in much-needed foreign currency' (BBC News, 2021). During the late colonial period the Portuguese African SIDS were tied together in many ways, one of which included many Cabo Verdean workers and administrators living and working in Guinea-Bissau to train colonial administrators. As such, there were many Cabo Verdeans who formed part of the core of the Guinea-Bissau independence movement (SAHO, 2021). Today, despite the country's lack of natural resources and limited arable land, the Cabo Verde islands have nevertheless won a global reputation for achieving stability. Key to enhancing this reputation is the initiation, by the government of Cabo Verde, of a digital project in which multiple stakeholders are engaged. These include, for example, the University of Cape Verde, non-governmental organizations and the World Bank (Ministry of Finance, 2020).

São Tomé and Príncipe has external stakeholders in the form of states such as the US and regional bodies such as the Economic Community of Central African States (ECCAS). The strategic location of São Tomé and Príncipe, in the Gulf of Guinea, has increased interest in the number of maritime regional security initiatives. It has played a role in ECCAS's Zone D maritime security exercises and is a participant in the US Navy's Africa Partnership Station ship visits to Gulf of Guinea countries. The Voice of America also broadcasts to large parts of Africa from a relay transmitter station in São Tomé (US Department of State, 2019).

Feminist foreign policy

The Seychelles Constitution makes no provision for quotas to advance the representation of women in government. Equally, in São Tomé and Príncipe, the Comoros, Guinea-Bissau and Mauritius there is no quota for gendered representation in parliament (Ramtohul, 2019; Morna et al, 2021). Agnes Monique Ohsan Bellepeau served as the acting president of Mauritius twice, initially from 31 March 2012 to 21 July 2012 and again from 29 May 2015 to 5 June 2015 (Watkins, 2021). Thereafter, Bibi Ameenah Firdaus Gurib-Fakim served as the sixth president of Mauritius from 2015 to 2018. Despite these successes, 'little space is made for women in the political field' (Ramtohul, 2019). Mauritian society remains largely patriarchal and conservative, with examples of women politicians being belittled in the media for casting a negative light on their family's reputation by taking up politics instead of the more respected housewife mantle. For example, new to parliament, a pregnant Joanna Berenger was described in a popular newspaper as having a 'ek zak dan tant', a Creole expression translated as a 'jackfruit in the basket' (Ramtohul, 2019). In Cabo Verde, 28 of 72 (39 per cent) seats in the National Assembly are held by women (International IDEA, 2024). There is also an active Network of Women Parliamentarians in Cabo Verde (Rede de Mulheres Parlamentares de Cabo Verde), who meet with government departments on issues of advancing gender equality in the country.

Similarly, in Guinea-Bissau, in August 2018, a law was adopted aimed at ensuring at least 36 per cent representation of women in elections or appointments to the National People's Congress (UNIOGBS, 2020: 106). Gender inequality remains problematic in the Comoros. At present, the only standing female member of parliament (MP), and second-ever female MP, is Hadjira Oumouri (UNFPA, 2018).

As a result of recent elections, held in 2020, 17 per cent of seats in the Comoros parliament are held by women, compared with 8 per cent in São Tomé and Príncipe, 14 per cent in Guinea-Bissau, 20 per cent in Mauritius, 23 per cent in Seychelles and 25 per cent in Cabo Verde (Morna et al, 2021). Some African SIDS have better gender representation than others, but it is nevertheless encouraging to see, even in more patriarchal societies, women taking on these leadership roles.

Niche diplomacy: what is 'smart' for the African SIDS?

Niche diplomacy exploits a speciality or interest that a state has (Rana, nd). As alluded to earlier in this chapter with the example of Seychelles, Mauritius also remains a unique blend of many cultures and has a Creole identity. Despite its small island status, 'its remoteness, and lack of natural resources have compelled it to be perpetually aware of what goes on at the regional and international levels and position itself in the limelight of international debates' (Makhan in Pudaruth, 2017: 5). It is referred to as Africa's success story (Ramtohul, 2019) and uses this in its global branding. Moreover, Mauritius is a geostrategic hotspot in the Indian Ocean. India, for example, has started to build a naval base on the remote Mauritian island of North Agalega and this boosts bilateral relations between the two states which already existed in the form of 'high-level diplomatic visits, several lines of credit for infrastructure projects, as well as joint patrol and surveillance operations' (Diwakar, 2021). Therefore, by virtue of its location, among other reasons, Mauritius is important to India as India needs Mauritius to offset growing Chinese influence in the Indian Ocean. China has been making 'strong overtures' to Indian Ocean island states, such as Seychelles, 'as it looks to secure key trade routes with its String of Pearls strategy – a line of cooperation agreements and military bases stretching from Hong Kong to Port Sudan' (Economist Intelligence Unit, 2012).

Seychelles is a leader in blue economy advocacy and is sought after in relation to maritime security. Seychelles, Mauritius and the Comoros are all members of the Indian Ocean Rim Association (IORA), an international organization set up to bolster trade and investment ties between coastal states bordering the Indian Ocean. The Comoros had requested membership of the IORA in 2012 in a strategic move 'towards countries where it enjoys a … favourable reception' and which may be willing to provide aid or investment (Economist Intelligence Unit, 2012). The Union of Comoros has subsequently joined IORA as a member. The Comoros is known to have an open-door foreign policy agenda (especially with Middle Eastern and emerging Asian states) and if it can be of strategic value to other global players in return for support, it is likely to do so.

Unfortunately, location is also detrimental to some African SIDS. Guinea-Bissau, for example, has become a well-known narco-state, a label given by the UN and US authorities a decade ago and the only African state to have the title. The country is characterized by some as a hub in the transportation of cocaine and heroin, from mostly Latin American markets to European markets (The Point, 2021). Others contend, however, that Guinea-Bissau is trying to shed this negative reputation, arguing that there are also 'quite courageous elements within the judicial police and within the political system who have stood up to drug trafficking' (Shaw in BBC News, 2020). Either way, this development has attracted more of the world's attention, and counter-narcotic support from various bodies including the United Nations Office on Drugs and Crime, to this small island than ever before. Guinea-Bissau could leverage this attention to its advantage.

Conclusion

Ghazi's (2015) projections of a smart diplomacy of the future entails digital capabilities, stakeholder diplomacy and feminist diplomacy, as discussed earlier, and these do have a place as instruments in the African SIDS' current and future foreign policy making. Indeed, great digital strides have been made, or are in the making, in all the African SIDS; these states have always relied on inner and outer stakeholder investments as a matter of survival, and feminist diplomacy, although less significant in some, is building in others in encouraging ways. However, what should be emphasized is that these small states have used their own African agency to project a niche diplomacy in the global arena, such as advocating for the blue economy, leading on maritime diplomacy efforts and using location as a geostrategic tool to leverage bilateral and multilateral deals and benefit their own economies. The chapter has illustrated the potential for smart diplomacy. Building networks and linkages among small states communities is another way to do this. As some island nations are submerging – the Maldives, for example – some African SIDS are on the rise and should model themselves as go-to locations not just for beautiful beaches but also as exemplar states on how to survive in global relations. That would be the smart thing to do.

References

Aiyar, S.S.A. (2008) 'Small states: not handicapped and under-aided, but advantaged and over-aided', *Cato Journal*, 28(3): 449–78.

Aggestam, K. and Towns, A. (eds) (2018) *Gendering Diplomacy and International Negotiation*, Basingstoke: Palgrave Macmillan.

Baldacchino, G. and Milne, D. (2000) *Lessons from the Political Economy of Small Islands*, Houndmills: Macmillan Press.

BBC News (2020) 'Cocaine and Guinea-Bissau: how Africa's "narco-state" is trying to kick its habit' [online], Available from: www.bbc.com/news/world-africa-52569130 [Accessed 26 November 2021].

BBC News (2021) 'Cape Verde country profile' [online], Available from: www.bbc.com/news/world-africa-13148486 [Accessed 25 November 2021].

Breuning, M. (2007) *Foreign Policy Analysis: A Comparative Introduction*, New York: Palgrave Macmillan.

Browning, C.S. (2006) 'Small, smart and salient? Rethinking identity in the small states literature', *Cambridge Review of International Affairs*, 19(4): 669–84.

Bueger, C. and Wivel, A. (2018) 'How do small island states maximize influence? Creole diplomacy and the smart state foreign policy of the Seychelles', *Journal of the Indian Ocean Region*, 14(2): 170–88.

Cheeseman, N. (2021) 'Smaller is beautiful: smaller African states do not necessarily make better democracies', *The Africa Report* [online], Available from: www.theafricareport.com/98933/smaller-african-states-do-not-necessarily-make-better-democracies/ [Accessed 27 November 2021].

Cooper, A.F. and Shaw, T.M. (eds) (2009) *The Diplomacies of Small States*, London: Palgrave Macmillan.

Department of Economic and Social Affairs (2020) 'United Nations E-Government Survey 2020' [online], Available from: www-un-org.ujlink.uj.ac.za/development/desa/publications/publication/2020-united-nations-e-government-survey [Accessed 1 December 2021].

DiploFoundation (2021) 'Report: 2021: the emergence of digital foreign policy' [online], Available from: https://meetings.diplomacy.edu/report/report-2021-the-emergence-of-digital-foreign-policy/ [Accessed 15 November 2021].

Diwakar, A. (2021) 'Why India views Mauritius as a strategic outpost in the Indian Ocean', *Turkish Radio and Television Corporation (TRT) World* [online], 5 August, Available from: www.trtworld.com/magazine/why-india-views-mauritius-as-a-strategic-outpost-in-the-indian-ocean-48945 [Accessed 12 December 2021].

Economist Intelligence Unit (2012) 'Comoros is admitted to the Indian Ocean Rim Association' [online], Available from: http://country.eiu.com/article.aspx?articleid=149805799&Country=Comoros&topic=Politics&subtopic=Forecast&subsubtopic=International+relations [Accessed 9 December 2021].

Gallarotti, G.M. (2015) 'Smart power: definitions, importance, and effectiveness', *Journal of Strategic Studies,* 38(3): 245–81.

Ghazi, Y.E. (2015) 'Smart diplomacy and the future of diplomatic undertaking', *Georgetown Journal of International Affairs* [online], Available from: www.georgetownjournalofinternationalaffairs.org/online-edition/smart-diplomacy-and-the-future-of-diplomatic-undertaking [Accessed 6 July 2021].

GDF (Global Diplomatic Forum) (2024) *Smart Diplomacy Principles*, [online], Available from: https://www.gdforum.org/smart-diplomacy-principles [Accessed 19 February 2024].

Graham, S. (2017) 'Drivers of the foreign policies of Southern African small states', *Politikon*, 44(1): 133–55.

Graham, S. and Graham, V. (2016) 'The quality of elections in African small island developing states', *Journal of Comparative Politics*, 14(1): 37–57.

Graham, S. and Graham, V. (2019) 'Quality political participation and the SDGs in African small island developing states', *Regions & Cohesion*, 9(2): 1–30.

Heng, Y.-K. and Ad'ha Aljunied, S.M. (2015) 'Can small states be more than price takers in global governance?', *Global Governance*, 21(3): 435–54.

International IDEA (2024). 'Gender Quotas Database' [online], Available from: https://www.idea.int/data-tools/data/gender-quotas-database/country?country=41 [Accessed 5 March 2024].

ITU (International Telecommunications Union) (2018) 'São Tomé and Príncipe' [online], Available from: www.itu.int/en/ITU-D/LDCs/Documents/2017/Country%20Profiles/Country%20Profile_Sao-Tome-and-Principe.pdf [Accessed 27 November 2021].

Johnson, T. (2019) 'Small states matter: an African perspective' [online], Available from: https://smallwarsjournal.com/jrnl/art/small-states-matter-african-perspective [Accessed 3 December 2021].

Kelly, T. (2016) 'How the WDR16 policy framework is applied in the Union of Comoros', *World Bank Blog* [online], Available from: https://blogs.worldbank.org/digital-development/how-wdr16-policy-framework-applied-union-comoros [Accessed 27 November 2021].

Khmer Times (2016) 'Smart diplomacy needed' [online], Available from: www.khmertimeskh.com/26298/smart-diplomacy-needed/ [Accessed 8 August 2012].

Ministry of Finance (2020) 'Digital Cabo Verde Project, digital – stakeholder engagement plan' [online], Available from: https://0-documents1-worldbank-org.ujlink.uj.ac.za/curated/ar/514671587067174761/pdf/Stakeholder-Engagement-Plan-SEP-Digital-Cabo-Verde-P171099.pdf [Accessed 13 December 2021].

Mo Ibrahim Foundation (2023) *2022 Ibrahim Index of African Governance.* [online], Available from: https://assets.iiag.online/2022/2022-Index-Report.pdf [Accessed 20 February 2024].

Morna, C.L., Tolmay, S. and Makaya, M. (2021) 'Women's political participation – Africa Barometer 2021', *International IDEA* [online], Available from: www.idea.int/sites/default/files/publications/womens-political-participation-africa-barometer-2021.pdf [Accessed 10 December 2021].

Nye, J. (2009) 'Get smart: combining hard and soft power', *Foreign Affairs*, 88(4): 160–63.

Pitsuwan, F. (2014) 'Smart power strategy: recalibrating Indonesian foreign policy', *Asian Politics & Policy,* 6(2): 237–66.

Prasad, N. (2009) 'Small but smart: small states in the global system', in A.F. Cooper and T.M. Shaw (eds) *The Diplomacies of Small States,* London: Palgrave Macmillan, pp 41–64.

Pudaruth, S.K. (2017) 'Nation rebranding through a new approach to cultural diplomacy: a case study of Mauritius', *SAGE Open*, 7(2): 1–13.

Ramtohul, R. (2019) 'Why very few women go into politics in Mauritius', *The Conversation* [online], 30 December, Available from: https://theconversation.com/why-very-few-women-go-into-politics-in-mauritius-128579 [Accessed 5 December 2021].

Rana, K.S. (nd) 'The diplomacy of small states' [online], Available from: https://learn.diplomacy.edu/pool/fileInline.php?&id=20937 [Accessed 5 March 2024].

Rupert, J. (2015) 'Sweden's foreign minister explains feminist foreign policy: Margot Wallström and colleagues face "the giggling factor"', United States Institute for Peace [online], Available from: www.usip.org/publications/2015/02/swedens-foreign-minister-explains-feminist-foreign-policy [Accessed 29 September 2021].

SAHO (South Africa History Online) (2021) 'Cabo Verde' [online], Available from: www.sahistory.org.za/place/cabo-verde [Accessed 12 December 2021].

Sahib-Kaudeer, N.G., Jhummun, D.S. and Gobin-Rahimbux, B. (2016) 'What is "smart" for small island developing states?', *IEEE International Conference on Emerging Technologies and Innovative Business Practices for the Transformation of Societies (EmergiTech)* [online], Available from: https://ieeexplore.ieee.org/document/7737303 [Accessed 18 July 2022].

Sanches, E.R., Cheeseman, N., Veenendaal, W. and Corbett, J. (2022) 'African exceptions: democratic development in small island states', *Journal of International Relations and Development*, 25: 210–34.

Srebrnik, H.F. (2004) 'Small island nations and democratic values', *World Development*, 32(2): 329–41.

Sutton, P. (2011) 'The concept of small states in the international political economy', *The Round Table*, 100(413): 141–53.

The Economist (2011) 'The hopeful continent' [online], 3 December, Available from: www.economist.com/leaders/2011/12/03/africa-rising [Accessed 11 December 2021].

The Point (2021) 'West Africa: understanding the nature and threats of drug trafficking to national and regional security in West Africa' [online], 11 May, Available from: https://thepoint.gm/africa/gambia/editorial/understanding-the-nature-and-threats-of-drug-trafficking-to-national-and-regional-security-in-west-africa [Accessed 18 July 2022].

Thorhallsson, B. (2000) *The Role of Small States in the European Union*, Aldershot: Ashgate.

Thorhallsson, B. (2006) 'The role of small states in the European Union', in C. Ingebritsen, I. Neumann, S. Gstohl and J. Beyer (eds) *Small States in International Relations*, Seattle: University of Washington Press, pp 3–36.

Thorhallsson, B. (2012) 'Small states in the UN Security Council: means of influence?', *Hague Journal of Diplomacy*, 7: 135–60.

Thorhallsson, B. (2018) 'Studying small states: a review', *Small States & Territories*, 1(1): 17–34.

UN (United Nations) (2022) *E-Government Survey 2022. The Future of Digital Government.* [online], Available from: https://desapublications.un.org/sites/default/files/publications/2022-09/Report%20without%20annexes.pdf [Accessed 20 February 2024].

UNDP (United Nations Development Programme) (2021). 'Harnessing digital transformation through e-Governance innovation' [online], Available from: www.gw.undp.org/content/guinea_bissau/en/home/news-centre/harnessing-digital-transformation-through-e-governance-innovatio.html [Accessed 10 December 2021].

UNESCO (United Nations Educational, Scientific and Cultural Organization) (2020) 'Comoros focuses on sustainable tourism management' [online], Available from: https://en.unesco.org/news/comoros-focuses-sustainable-tourism-management [Accessed 10 December 2021].

UNFPA (United Nations Population Fund) (2018) 'From midwife to MP – advancing the rights of women in the Comoros' [online], Available from: www.unfpa.org/news/midwife-mp-advancing-rights-women-comoros [Accessed 10 December 2021].

UNIOGBS (United Nations Integrated Peacebuilding Office in Guinea-Bissau) (2020) Together, we build peace. UNIOGBS Legacy Book, p 106 [online], Available from: https://uniogbis.unmissions.org/sites/default/files/legacy_book_uniogbis.pdf [Accessed 5 March 2024].

US Department of State (2019) 'U.S. relations with São Tomé and Príncipe' [online], Available from: www.state.gov/u-s-relations-with-sao-tome-and-principe/ [Accessed 10 December 2021].

Van Wyk, J. (2007) 'Political leaders in Africa: presidents, patrons or profiteers?', *The African Centre for the Constructive Resolution of Disputes (ACCORD) Occasional Paper*, 2(1): 1–38.

Veenendaal, W.P. and Corbett, J. (2015) 'Why small states offer important answers to large questions', *Comparative Political Studies*, 48(4): 527–49.

Watkins, J. (2021) 'List of female African presidents – updated July 2021', African Faith and Justice Network [online], Available from: https://afjn.org/list-of-female-africa-presidents-updated-july-2021/ [Accessed 10 December 2021].

Wong, P.P. (2011) 'Small island developing states', *WIREs Wiley Interdisciplinary Reviews: WIREs Climate Change*, 2(1): 1–6.

6

Maritime Diplomacy and the African Maritime Agenda

Francois Vreÿ

Introduction

Diplomacy is an enduring state practice, and maritime diplomacy through navies developed alongside the different domains of diplomatic practice that took shape over time. Contemporary diplomacy has many facets, covering the ever-expanding matters that states wish to address in pursuit of their national interests. The actors, modes, tools and issue areas depicted on the contents page of *The Oxford Handbook of Modern Diplomacy* (Cooper et al, 2013) attest to the widening scope of what modern-day diplomacy entails. This expanding sphere of diplomatic interests continues to redefine the ambit of diplomatic practices that diplomatic actors are expected to master and extends to maritime interests as well.

Maritime diplomacy is a unique type of diplomacy directed at pursuit of maritime state interests and operates in parallel with and as a particular adjunct to the general practice of diplomacy. One tendency is to group maritime diplomacy under defence diplomacy as the naval overlap is seen as a convenient maritime nexus within the historic diplomacy–defence connection (Cooper et al, 2013: 369). In retrospect, the politico-defence nexus serves some diplomatic purpose of states, but present-day international developments are forging a complex international environment requiring diplomatic practices to remain in step. Not only the domains but also actor proliferation and shifting priorities impact how and why states practise diplomacy, and this proliferation includes the rise of maritime interests and security on state agendas (Bueger and Edmunds, 2021: 180).

For coastal states the rise of a more urgent maritime agenda stimulated a rethink as to what maritime diplomacy entails in the 21st century and to consider it as a political instrument requiring attention. The political, economic and social aspects of maritime interests overlap with the scope of new diplomacy to include more than strict political and military interests. For Africa, maritime diplomacy is on the radar as well in the pursuit of 'maritime interests, usually by combining and/or applying the instruments of state power' (van Nieuwkerk and Manganyi, 2019: 2).

The chapter first demarcates and describes maritime diplomacy and then turns to the African maritime agenda and interests in the early 21st century. It covers three broad topics to define maritime diplomacy and to highlight Africa's maritime debate and the continent's maritime diplomacy. The next section delimits diplomacy as a practice before outlining the exercise of defence, naval and maritime diplomacy. The third section covers Africa's maritime debate, threats and vulnerabilities before offering illustrative examples of maritime diplomacy from African actors, and instances of external maritime diplomacy directed towards the continent.

Diplomacy, defence diplomacy and maritime diplomacy

Berridge and James (2003: 70) define diplomacy as 'the principal means by which states communicate with each other, enabling them to have regular and complex relations'. Bull (in Sofer, 1988: 196) expanded this with a view of 'the conduct of relations between states and other entities with standing in world politics by official agents and peaceful means'. In addition, Sofer (1988: 196) points out two important trends. First, that diplomacy attempts to implement foreign policy through negotiation, and to foster understanding and acceptance by other nations. Second, that methods of implementing diplomacy may change as well. Diplomacy during the cold war (circa 1945–89) had a strong coercive/force backdrop. Later literature on diplomacy accounts for international changes, including globalization, which drives an expansion of the modes and focal points of diplomacy in keeping with the view that diplomacy is in a constant state of flux (Sofer, 1988: 205). As a result, the dynamic state of international relations acted as a catalyst for a range of professionals and non-professionals to enter the diplomatic field as globalization and interdependencies grew and to allow diverse actor groupings to cooperate and liaise more closely.

Representation and governance have become two primary functions or outputs of diplomacy and bring an overlap between the core function and diplomatic practices. In addition, representation and governance bring newer demands and practices, as well as non-state actors and their skill sets, into the diplomatic ambit alongside the traditional state-on-state norm (Sending et al, 2011: 530). Such actor and issue proliferation serves as a catalyst to push diplomacy to address more non-traditional needs.

Defence diplomacy

Du Plessis (2008: 89) highlights the neglect of defence diplomacy despite its importance. He underlines the lack of understanding regarding its utility when restricted to the defence military ambit. Of importance is that Du Plessis frames the lack of insight into how defence diplomacy strengthens overall diplomacy in support of foreign policy. In essence, his critique outlines the lack of understanding that defence diplomacy is a pathway to also cover non-military matters in the overall national interests of a country without resorting to military coercion. In keeping with this view, du Plessis (2008: 94) describes naval diplomacy as the use of naval forces to pursue political objectives in a political rather than a militarily coercive way as navies operating in a diplomatic role have cooperative as well as coercive value. Du Plessis argues for using the potential of defence and naval diplomacy beyond their military coercion settings to contribute to outcomes.

The drive to exploit the broader cooperative potential lurking in the defence–naval–political triad holds the possibility to find expression through maritime diplomacy. Given that there are several types of diplomacy on the politico-military spectrum in the pursuit of foreign policy and national objectives, the emphasis is also to function more efficiently in the non-military and less coercive domains. This shift spills into the utility of soft and smart diplomacy debates on the usefulness of less coercion or a pragmatic mix of instruments and modes, as well as actors.

Hard, soft and smart diplomacy

Soft diplomacy refers to understanding and employing the non-coercive and threatening elements of policy for their maximum effect. This functions as an input (non-coercive and persuasive instruments) as well as an output seen as shaping the preferences of others (Nye, 2008: 94–5). Politics, economics and information are important domains harbouring soft power while new diplomacy also reflects the continuous broadening of diplomatic sectors and actors within the conduct of diplomacy (Sending et al, 2011: 533). Governments are not always able to adapt timeously to more efficient and more influential diplomatic instruments and thus often continue to use traditional diplomatic instruments. This soft-traditional disconnect underpins the necessity to expand the actors conducting diplomacy to harness scarce skills and more legitimacy as well as expertise to bring previously neglected domains into the modern diplomatic agenda and practices (Nye, 2008: 105).

The expansion of actors and power assets for better diplomatic strategies holds value for the maritime focus. Maritime diplomacy offers more than the avenues of naval and defence coercion given the rapidly expanding maritime security debate with its array of sectors demanding attention from governments and other actors with specialized expertise (Narula, 2015: 69–70). This raises the question: who brings what to the table of maritime diplomacy in response to the burgeoning issue areas to keep oceans safe, clean and productive?

Maritime diplomacy

Although maritime diplomacy does not appear in, for example, *A Dictionary of Diplomacy* (Berridge and James, 2003) as a form of diplomacy or in *The Oxford Handbook of Modern Diplomacy* (Cooper et al, 2013), Le Mière (2014: 7) wrote extensively on the topic and defines maritime diplomacy as 'the management of international relations through the maritime domain'. In executing maritime diplomacy, cooperative, persuasive and coercive maritime diplomacy are pathways to bring hard, soft and smart power to bear (Le Mière, 2014: 8). While Le Mière tends to view maritime diplomacy as close to the naval ambit and naval coercion, he also sees the naval nexus becoming less accentuated to accommodate international developments that call for more persuasion and cooperation.

Utility of maritime diplomacy

Maritime diplomacy holds most potential during peacetime to deal with rising complexity and to counter 'sea blindness' (the inability to see and/or understand maritime threats and security issues) as a debilitating phenomenon (Feldt, 2016: 11). One reason for this is a growing array of norms, conventions, popular resistance and ethical opposition as well as media exposure combined with the swift distribution of news to limit the use of coercion and military (including naval) force. Collectively, barriers to the use of coercion compel rulers to turn to more efficient ways and means to achieve diplomatic goals, with maritime diplomacy having avenues to signal intent and capabilities (le Mière, 2014: 70). The utility resides in the suitability of maritime forces, as noted by Till (2018), to serve diplomatic purposes through different activities, but that is but one way to conduct this form of diplomacy.

Constraints on naval forces often compel states to assume a diplomatic role (Till, 2018: 367). Through naval diplomacy, the military role of naval forces has been extensively used and analysed. However, softer and more pragmatic ways and means of maritime diplomacy by employing a wider spectrum of actors are less discussed, even though more suited to maritime diplomacy that seeks to exclude or lower the coercive or military imperative (le Mière, 2014: 83). While navies can play the coercive and cooperative game, they have limits regarding the latter, which allows for non-military actors and specialists with expertise, understanding and skills to work in sectors less amenable to naval force or coercion on its own or in combination with land and air power.

Viewing maritime diplomacy through the lens of contemporary developments in the international system, persuasive and cooperative maritime diplomacy has a growing applicability. Nationalism supported by gunboat diplomacy holds costs. However, avoiding violence, building capacity in weaker nations and fostering multilateral relationships with partner countries and membership of international organizations expand and emphasize the scope for cooperative maritime diplomacy (le Mière, 2014: 85). Add to this the codification of international law that further regulates and often restricts nations to use military coercion in furthering their interests at sea, and the logic of using more soft and smart power becomes apparent. International law has played its part to highlight non-coercive maritime diplomacy by defining more rigidly the rights and limitations of states operating at sea and so shrink the grey areas where the use of coercive naval action due to misunderstanding is higher. In Africa, these diplomatic shifts, options and preferences play out, offering room for coercive, persuasive and cooperative maritime diplomacy.

Africa's maritime interests and agendas

Maritime diplomacy discussions hardly cover practices emanating from the African continent. While le Mière (2014: 93) refers to the growth in developing countries using maritime diplomacy, none of his examples point to Africa. By the second decade of the 21st century Africa was high on the maritime security agenda, with opportunities and capacity to counter maritime threats and vulnerabilities, strengthen responses and mitigate the rise of disorder at sea off the vast African coastline. Le Mière (2014: 96) nonetheless refers to the maritime interests of developing countries to secure their interests in alignment with the growing debate emphasizing the importance of the oceans for future wealth, growth, prosperity of society and the environment. It is therefore prudent to view Africa and the use of maritime diplomacy within a changing diplomatic landscape. Africa's maritime agenda and interests rest upon a lesser emphasis on the roles of naval forces and the stark naval, foreign policy and national interest triad. New diplomacy, representation and governance priorities in diplomatic activities require a more critical focus when the use of maritime diplomacy and Africa with its 38 coastal states, vast oceans and weak naval and other maritime capabilities come into play. All this culminates in African littoral states possibly being less able to participate in the naval coercive club, but rather can build capacity in the persuasive and cooperative ambit of maritime diplomacy (Sending et al, 2011: 529).

Africa's maritime agenda is encapsulated in Africa's Integrated Maritime Strategy (AIMS-2050) (AU, 2012). Overall, AIMS-2050 is a blueprint to develop, harness and secure African maritime territories for the benefit of developing the African continent and its people. AIMS-2050 aligns with the Sustainable Development Goals (SDGs) of the United Nations (UN) through Agenda 2063 of the African Union (AU) to secure Africa's oceans and harness marine resources in pursuit of the continent's blue economy ambitions (AU, 2015). Both AIMS-2050 and Agenda 2063 call upon African governments to cooperate bilaterally and regionally to pursue Africa's ambition of becoming a recognized maritime player in the international maritime landscape (AU, 2015: 3). This is a significant ambition given the general critique of sea blindness levelled towards the continent and the failure to comprehend and exploit the opportunities residing in its maritime landscapes (Potgieter, 2021). As for maritime diplomacy, eradicating sea blindness to raise Africa's maritime profile as a secure and productive maritime player in the blue economy sector points to the importance of assisting African countries to function effectively in maritime diplomacy and use coercion, suasion and cooperation where and when necessary for good maritime governance.

Africa's maritime agenda on growing a productive blue economy embedded in safe and secure oceans is subject to dangerous non-traditional maritime security threats. While threats are a given, the range of threats and the required response pattern embedded in cooperation, partnerships and collaboration must be addressed. This connects to multiple African actors, maritime diplomacy and the conduits it offers to convey messages and promote action towards cooperation (Voyer et al, 2018). Success is embedded in building partnerships and growing capacity, improving regional cooperation and using existing continental frameworks for communicating explicitly and acting on selected continental maritime matters. While in general the African maritime agenda is embedded in peace, development and growth, maritime security is of particular significance and serves as a blue security bedrock for the pursuit of a thriving and uninterrupted blue economy (Bueger et al, 2020: 230–31). One important aspect for Africa is capacity building that feeds into new regional maritime arrangements, maritime security networks and better maritime governance, which hold relevance for maritime diplomacy through the smart use of coercion, persuasion and cooperation.

From debates to maritime diplomacy in Africa

The Gulf of Guinea, Gulf of Aden along the Horn of Africa, the waters off northern Mozambique in the southwestern Indian Ocean and the Mediterranean Sea bordering Libya's coast are current hubs of maritime insecurity calling for ways and means to safely exploit the flow and stock potential of Africa's oceans. The vast but productive Gulf of Guinea off West Africa is regularly red flagged as Africa's most insecure maritime area, drawing political and naval attention (Yücel, 2021). The Gulf of Aden and Red Sea remain the focus of international attention sparked by sea piracy and until recently had the largest concentrations of foreign naval vessels, a phenomenon slowly shifting to the Gulf of Guinea. Simultaneous armed conflict in Somalia, Yemen and Ethiopia along the strategic sea route to and from the Suez Canal reinforces perceptions about threats and vulnerabilities stemming from multiple state and non-state sources in the immediate region (Yohannes and Gebresenbet, 2018: 93–5).

In the south-western Indian Ocean, the radicalized insurgency in the northern coastal province of Mozambique raises the spectre of armed threats spilling offshore as these insurgents have already attacked coastal infrastructure critical to the emerging gas industry in the adjacent Ravuma Basin in the Mozambique Canal. These attacks drew in international and African military responses to shore up the country's security sector (Darden and Estelle, 2021: 438).

A fourth maritime insecurity hub with a stark humanitarian aspect exists off Libya in North Africa, where persistent refugee flows towards southern Europe are facilitated by criminal syndicates residing in Libya and to a lesser extent in neighbouring countries. This is a complicated soft security threat playing out on land and at sea and requiring a maritime response at the political and diplomatic levels as naval responses have limited utility to deal with the humanitarian basis of the threat (Zichi, 2018: 140–41). Collectively, maritime insecurity in these African waters draw attention to African maritime interests and a blend of coercive, persuasive and cooperative maritime diplomacy actions.

Any views on the pursuit of Africa's maritime interests by way of maritime diplomacy must account for the following. First, the extent to which African and international navies are present and able to play prominent roles within maritime diplomacy while noting that no common African navy exists. Some African coastal states, most notably Egypt, Algeria, Nigeria and South Africa, possess small navies, while other African states have only small coastguard-style agencies (Seychelles and Mauritius) or a collapsed navy (Mozambique, Somalia and Ethiopia). A second aspect relates to Africa being a large continent with 38 coastal states and several island states, with a 26,000 nautical mile coastline and 13 million square kilometre Exclusive Economic Zone (Surbun, 2021: 3). Maritime diplomacy for the continent takes place at the national level and includes a mix of national, regional and continental positions, interests and agendas. A third matter rests upon the high prevalence of non-traditional maritime security threats off Africa's coast and the African reality of small or weak navies having a limited role to play (Alsawalqa and Venter, 2021: 4). Finally, to deal with maritime interconnectedness, liminality and interdependence of events, African state and non-state maritime actors must build multilevel partnerships at regional, multilateral and bilateral levels to address its layered maritime interests by employing the different instruments (coastguards), modes (persuasion) and activities (capacity-building programmes) on offer (Bueger and Edmunds, 2021: 9–14). Maritime objectives pursued through maritime diplomacy have their own dynamic calling for maritime as well as diplomatic skills to deal with national and wider interests. African maritime interests are also subject to both continental and national interests, while the desired outcome is dependent on assistance as smart maritime diplomacy is conducted through cooperation and persuasion.

Africa's maritime agenda is connected to the international oceans agenda that strives to keep the oceans clean, productive and secure for current and future generations. This lofty ideal is unfortunately challenged by the prevalence of traditional and non-traditional maritime threats. Speller (2014), Bueger and Edmunds (2021) and Till (2018), for example, demarcate threats to good order at sea and flag the need for African maritime nations to master ways and means to mitigate insecurity and to use the oceans as a safe and productive stock and flow resource, and so realize its potential as best as possible. In the case of Africa, however, the dearth of information on African navies and their roles implies that the coercive mode of maritime diplomacy is less present while avenues such as persuasion and cooperation are possibly more in step with what AIMS-2050 envisages, labelled as cooperation, collaboration and capacity building (AU, 2012: 14).

The AU AIMS-2050, however, also calls for the establishment of African navies and coastguards in pursuit of interagency and transnational cooperation on maritime safety and security. Unfortunately, African navies remain marginal, with only Algeria, Egypt and South Africa possessing navies able to play some role in the maritime diplomacy domain when blue water capabilities are required. The Nigerian, Moroccan, Tunisian and Equatorial Guinean navies can conduct operations in their regional seas. As brown water navies, Angola, Tanzania, Sudan, Kenya, Ghana and Cameroon can conduct some littoral operations while maritime police forces such as Senegal, Gabon, Mauritius and Togo can conduct maritime law enforcement around harbours and seaports (Lionel, 2022).

African countries nonetheless use their very limited naval assets in several ways. The most recent African coercive naval deployment is the South African navy operating in support of the Southern African Development Community (SADC) Mission in Mozambique (SAMIM). This deployment is preventive and aims to interdict any seaward threat. Regarding coercive maritime diplomacy, three lessons stem from this deployment. First, in the absence of a credible Mozambican naval capability, external dependence involving extensive diplomacy emerged given Mozambique's inability to respond to armed threats in its own waters. Second, no other SADC coastal state was willing or able to support the SAMIM with a naval capability to deter insurgent support from the sea. Third, South Africa's own naval capability allowed for one temporary small patrol vessel that had to be withdrawn due to technical reasons and replaced at some future point by a South African navy frigate. Such limited naval capabilities do little to support regional and international diplomatic efforts. Moreover, it flags the lack of naval capabilities in the region's six coastal states and thus the limits of maritime diplomacy in the region.

A coercive naval deployment by Nigerian naval vessels to support the Economic Community of West African States Monitoring Group forces in Liberia and Sierra Leone unfolded over the period 1990–99 (Sule, 2013: 10). This largely Nigerian naval operation is perhaps the most coercive deployment of an African navy in recent times. It included naval fire support, troop landings, blockading maritime routes and logistical support as well as a clear diplomatic message to opposition forces. In 2011, the Kenyan navy's operations against Al-Shabaab resulted in the capture of the Port Kismayo in southern Somalia. The operation aimed to prevent spillovers of terror attacks into Kenya across the Somali–Kenya border (Olsen, 2018: 44). In this manner the AU Mission in Somalia received naval support in combatting Al-Shabaab, although the Kenyan naval mission was obviously a coercive Kenyan diplomatic message not to threaten Kenyan national interests and territorial sovereignty.

Egypt's response to Turkey's drive into Africa is perhaps best understood as a diplomacy of persuasion that includes a maritime dimension. In response to Turkey's employment of hard power elements into the eastern Mediterranean, Egypt participated in naval exercises with France and Greece in the same waters. Egypt thus plays along in a larger diplomatic game through naval posturing in the eastern Mediterranean. This posturing aims to offset the growing Turkish drive into Africa and so protect Egypt's energy interests in its Exclusive Economic Zone and shore up its maritime boundaries in the eastern Mediterranean against Turkish advances (Tanchum, 2021: 12–13). This is ongoing posturing in the Mediterranean with the Red Sea as a second theatre for maritime diplomacy as Turkey seeks more port facilities further south.

Since 2011, Operation Copper, a small maritime-based regional initiative off the northern coast of Mozambique in the south-western Indian Ocean, has been deployed. This operation entails counter-piracy operations portrayed as an African parallel to the international naval deployments since 2010 off the Horn of Africa that represent its own maritime diplomacy opportunities for African governments (Willett, 2011: 24). Operation Copper aligns with AIMS-2050 to curb piracy off the African coast. South Africa labelled Operation Copper a SADC operation together with Tanzania and Mozambique, but the bulk of the resources and platforms is provided by the South African navy (van Nieuwkerk and Manganyi, 2019: 7; defenceWeb,

2023). Seen through the lens of maritime diplomacy, Operation Copper positions the SADC within the continental anti-piracy ambit, an independent African contribution to promote maritime security and safeguard SADC waters and to prevent piracy further north from threatening a maritime flow resource critical to maritime trade with SADC countries (Sisulu, 2011). Operation Copper is ongoing, although South Africa is currently the sole participating SADC member maintaining a very limited and intermittent naval presence (defenceWeb, 2020, 2023). Although Operation Copper is relatively small compared to other anti-piracy missions in Africa, it is significant to South Africa, which, under the SADC banner, continues to cooperate to counter an international maritime threat and remains aligned with the AU and UN resolutions on maritime security.

Expanding on cooperative practices and institutionalizing maritime cooperation

One African maritime region where maritime exercises offer a continuing opportunity to engage in maritime diplomacy by way of cooperation is the Gulf of Guinea off West and Central Africa. Regional cooperation and international collaboration represent two major pathways for naval and wider maritime cooperation in the Gulf of Guinea. The regional organization for West and Central African states liaise and pool their naval and other maritime resources to counter threats in the region by way of the Yaoundé Code of Conduct (YCC) (Herpolsheimer, 2018: 69). The YCC is primarily directed at fostering cooperation between its 16 coastal countries by drawing in the right partners to promote a common strategy and foster regional cooperation against non-traditional maritime threats in the Gulf of Guinea (Herpolsheimer, 2018: 70). Here, the strand of diplomacy centres on improving cooperation to bring together many regional and national actors including states/navies and other agencies, as well as dedicated institutions and even landlocked countries to pursue the overall goal of the YCC: to pool resources and promote information sharing to achieve coordinated responses (Bell, 2021: 3). These outcomes are sought by way of government expenditures, naval and other platform acquisitions, legal training and coordinating cooperation of regional information sharing centres within the Yaoundé Architecture for Maritime Security (Bell, 2021: 13). The fundamental basis of this enterprise relies on maritime cooperation and promoting such cooperation regionally and among the multiple coastal states, a matter falling squarely into the realm of cooperative maritime diplomacy.

A second diplomatic initiative is vested in the extensive international collaboration between West African and other international navies and maritime agencies. Corymbe since 1990, Grand African Nemo (with France) and the Open Sea Initiative (with Portugal) are some examples.

The United States-sponsored Obangame Express, in operation since 2011, has the largest number of participating countries. In 2019, 31 North and South American, African and European states participated and cooperated to fight maritime crime, but the annual international exercise also offers wide opportunities to conduct maritime diplomacy to enhance cooperation and showcase commitments, skills and naval capacity, as well as other systems and platforms (Guedes, 2020: 14–15). The 31 countries bringing their maritime capabilities to such a large gathering of governments, navies and maritime agencies obviously see and use opportunities to promote their own national maritime interests. The annual cycle over the last decade demonstrates the national commitments in the region to cooperate, acquire the necessary platforms and build partnerships to expand their maritime capacity on several levels in response to the threats in the region's waters (Bell, 2021: 16–19).

South Africa also engages in naval exercises. Although some exercises take place in cooperation with the US, Russia, China and Germany, these activities have faded in the last few years. However, India and Brazil remain in the picture within the India–Brazil–South Africa Dialogue Forum, with an explicit maritime cooperation element (IBSAMAR). For South Africa, IBSAMAR is an instrument to strengthen south–south relations (DIRCO, 2021: 34). The same goes for South Africa's membership of the Indian Ocean Rim Association (IORA) as a platform for economic diplomacy and foreign policy through multilateralism but has no naval profile. In both cases, South Africa pursues its national interests by way of maritime conduits, with IBSAMAR reflecting a naval diplomacy opportunity and IORA offering a multilateral platform comprising 23 countries bordering the Indian Ocean and nine IORA Dialogue Partners having maritime interests in the Indian Ocean. This wide reach on maritime matters with no leeway for coercion was beneficial when South Africa chaired IORA (2017–19) to set the overall agenda for the wider Indian Ocean and Africa in particular.

IORA offers opportunities to engage in maritime diplomacy through cooperation with other member states as all African countries and island states bordering the western Indian Ocean (Comoros, Kenya, Madagascar, Mauritius, Mozambique, Seychelles, Somalia, South Africa, Tanzania) hold full IORA membership and thus a seat at the table for its annual meetings to set agendas on the Indian Ocean region through focus areas such as maritime safety and security, trade and investment, fisheries management, disaster risk management, tourism and culture, academic science and technology cooperation, the blue economy and women's economic empowerment (IORA, n.d.).

Maritime diplomacy towards Africa

Vessel acquisitions by West African navies since 2012 for Angola, Benin, Cameroon, Côte d'Ivoire, Equatorial Guinea, Gabon, Ghana, São Tomé and

Príncipe, and Togo have been from multiple provider countries like France, Germany, Israel, Italy and Turkey (Bell, 2021: 16–18). Arab countries to the north (Tunisia, Algeria and Egypt in particular) received German and French vessels, with Egypt leading with two helicopter-carrying landing vessels, four corvettes from France and four German attack submarines on order (Abrams, 2017: 3–4). Naval acquisitions are probably the hard power outcome of maritime diplomacy efforts, but not the only one, and even less so for African coastal states.

Other explicit examples of maritime diplomacy towards African coastal states stem from visits by naval and other agencies to African ports. In 2013 an Italian naval group led by an aircraft carrier visited 20 African countries on a diplomatic, military and humanitarian mission that included showcasing business entities on the aircraft carrier (Wingrin, 2014). In similar vein, a Turkish navy task force visited 28 African ports in 2014, partaking in several exercises and serving as a platform to showcase Turkish defence products and pave the way for other Turkish business interests to contact African partners (defenceWeb, 2024). On soft diplomacy, the Chinese naval hospital ship *Peace Ark* toured African countries on a humanitarian mission that included Djibouti, Gabon, Sierra Leone, the Democratic Republic of the Congo (DRC), Tanzania and Mozambique to offer free medical services during its stopovers (Xinhua, 2017). This is probably most clearly soft maritime diplomacy outreach aimed at cooperation and influence. Finally, China's Maritime Silk Road initiative targets several African countries facing the western Indian Ocean and it remains to be seen what exactly are the maritime implications of this vast economic outreach backed by hard naval power (Chang, 2018: 150).

African coastal countries' plans to grow their blue economies by opening maritime space and trade hubs for the global maritime supply system also depend on their navies' capabilities. The absence of credible naval capabilities suggests that other elements of maritime diplomacy and power must be employed in smarter ways to showcase what governments and their public and private agencies bring to the maritime domain. This is a field where maritime diplomacy holds good potential to fill the voids left by weak or absent African navies and the waning utility of the coercive maritime diplomacy element (Interview, 2022).

For African coastal states, this brings into play persuasion and cooperation in maritime diplomacy alongside other issues and instruments in the diplomacy toolbox to give expression to the objectives of Agenda 2063, AIMS-2050 and regional and national agendas on maritime security (le Mière, 2014: 100). This approach aligns with maritime diplomacy during times of peace where the focus is more on the elements of persuasion and cooperation. Persuasion and cooperation are probably better suited to support and secure the global maritime system with its different facets where small or absent navies and their diplomatic value are limited (le Mière, 2014: 66).

The overall idea of instruments and networking to harness more knowledge hubs to address issue proliferation also apply to the maritime domain and in turn call for more modes of practice and tools to address maritime agendas unique to Africa (Heine, 2013: 56).

Conclusion

Within the broader ambit of state diplomacy, maritime diplomacy serves two purposes. It covers the maritime domain beyond the coercive focus of navies and ties in with the shift to diplomacy that accommodates more actors to address issue areas that governments wish to tackle through diplomacy. Maritime diplomacy also aligns better with the expanding areas of concern in the widening oceans debate that hold the potential for interstate conflict if persuasion and cooperation on maritime matters fail to augment or replace the naval coercion route.

Maritime diplomacy in Africa and with Africa must be aligned with the continent's maritime agenda in pursuit of development and prosperity. African coastal states unfortunately harbour small and often weak navies and coastguard services that are ill suited or outdated for modern-day coercive maritime diplomacy. Although small naval deployments do take place, much of Africa's maritime diplomacy calls for and reflects preferences for cooperation even in deployments such as Operation Copper and naval support to the SADC mission in Mozambique.

Ideally, Africa's maritime diplomacy must underpin the continental maritime agenda that suggests cooperation and calls for regional and national entities to comply. Although, for example, regions bordering the Gulf of Guinea seem to be in step with AIMS-2050, more work needs to be done to build up the cooperative mode of maritime diplomacy as hardly any African coastal country faces naval threats. On the back of widespread non-traditional maritime security threats in African waters demanding maritime domain awareness and good governance, shifting the cooperative imperative to actions that impact maritime interests require much more attention from the continent's decision makers.

References

Abrams, E. (2017) 'United States assistance for Egypt', Council on Foreign Relations Testimony to the Senate Committee on Appropriations, Subcommittee on State, Foreign Operations, and Related Programs, United States Senate [online], 25 April, Available from: https://cdn.cfr.org/sites/default/files/report_pdf/Abrams%20Testimony%204.25.17.pdf [Accessed 18 July 2022].

Alsawalqa, R.O. and Venter, D. (2021) 'Piracy and maritime security in the north-western Indian Ocean: from the Gulf of Oman to the waters off the Somali coast', *Insight on Africa*, 14(1): 88–103.

AU (African Union) (2012) *2050 Africa's Integrated Maritime Strategy* [online], Available from: https://wedocs.unep.org/bitstream/handle/20.500.11822/11151/2050_aims_srategy.pdf [Accessed 18 July 2022].

AU (African Union) (2015) *Agenda 2063: The Africa We Want* [online], Available from: https://au.int/sites/default/files/documents/36204-doc-agenda2063_popular_version_en.pdf [Accessed 18 July 2022].

Bell, C. (2021) 'Pirates of the Gulf of Guinea: a cost analysis for coastal states', Stable Seas Report [online], November, Available from: www.stableseas.org/post/pirates-of-the-gulf-of-guinea-a-cost-analysis-for-coastal-states [Accessed 18 July 2022].

Berridge, G.R. and James, A. (2003) *A Dictionary of Diplomacy* (2nd edn), London: Palgrave Macmillan.

Bueger, C. and Edmunds, T. (2021) 'Pragmatic ordering: informality, experimentation, and the maritime security agenda', *Review of International Studies*, 47(2): 171–91.

Bueger, C., Edmunds, T. and McCabe, R. (2020) 'Into the sea: capacity-building innovations and the maritime security challenge', *Third World Quarterly*, 41(2): 228–46.

Chang, Y.C. (2018) 'The "21st century maritime Silk Road initiative" and naval diplomacy in China', *Ocean & Coastal Management*, 153: 148–56.

Cooper, A.F., Heine, J. and Thakur, R. (eds) (2013) *The Oxford Handbook of Modern Diplomacy*, Oxford: Oxford University Press.

Darden, J.T. and Estelle, E. (2021) 'Confronting Islamist insurgencies in Africa: the case of the Islamic State in Mozambique', *Orbis*, 65(3): 432–47.

defenceWeb (2020) 'Operation Copper extension to cost R154 million', [online] 6 May, Available from: www.defenceweb.co.za/featured/operation-copper-extension-to-cost-r154-million/ [Accessed 10 January 2022].

defenceWeb (2023) 'Extension of SANDF deployments in Mozambique and DRC to cost R2 billion' [online], 18 April, Available from: www.defenceweb.co.za/featured/extension-of-sandf-deployments-in-mozambique-and-drc-to-cost-r2-billion/ [Accessed 12 December 2023].

defenceWeb (2024) 'Turkish Navy task force en route to Africa' [online], 25 March, Available from: www.defenceweb.co.za/sea/sea-sea/turkish-navy-task-force-en-route-to-africa/ [Accessed 29 April 2024].

DIRCO (Department of International Relations and Cooperation) (2021) *Annual Report 2020/21* [online], Available from: www.dirco.gov.za [Accessed 18 July 2022].

Du Plessis, A. (2008) 'Defence diplomacy: conceptual and practical dimensions with specific reference to South Africa', *Strategic Review for Southern Africa*, 30(2): 87–119.

Feldt, L. (2016) 'The complex nature of today's maritime security issues: a European perspective', in J. Krause and S. Bruns (eds) *Routledge Handbook of Naval Strategy and Security*, Abingdon: Routledge, pp 35–50.

Guedes, H.P. (2020) 'Maritime piracy in the Gulf of Guinea', *Atlantic Centre Policy Brief Issue 04* [online], October, Available from: www.defesa.gov.pt/pt/pdefesa/ac/pub/acpubs/Documents/Atlantic-Centre_PB_04.pdf [Accessed 18 July 2022].

Heine, J. (2013) 'From club to network diplomacy', in A.F. Cooper, J. Heine and R. Thakur (eds) *The Oxford Handbook of Modern Diplomacy*, Oxford: Oxford University Press, pp 54–69.

Herpolsheimer, J. (2018) 'Transregional conflicts and the re-spatialization of regions "at sea": the Yaoundé process in the Gulf of Guinea', *Comparativ*, 28(6): 68–89.

IORA (Indian Ocean Rim Association) (n.d) 'What we do – priority areas' [online], Available from: www.iora.int/maritime-safety-security [Accessed 13 April 2023].

IORA (Indian Ocean Rim Association) (2019) 'Priorities and focus areas' [online], Available from: www.iora.int/en/priorities-focus-areas/overview [Accessed 18 July 2022].

Interview with member of the shipping industry in South Africa, 12 January 2022.

Le Mière, C. (2014) *Maritime Diplomacy in the 21st Century: Drivers and Challenges*, Abingdon: Routledge.

Lionel, E. (2022) 'The best navy in Africa', *Military Africa* [online], 10 March, Available from: www.military.africa/2018/01/the-top-10-best-and-strongest-navy-in-africa-2019/ [Accessed 18 July 2022].

Narula, K. (2015) 'Ensuring sustainable oceans', *Maritime Affairs: Journal of the National Maritime Foundation of India*, 11(1): 66–83.

Nye, J.S. (2008) 'Public diplomacy and soft power', *Annals of the American Academy of Political and Social Science*, 616(1): 94–109.

Olsen, G.R. (2018) 'The October 2011 Kenyan invasion of Somalia: fighting al-Shabaab or defending institutional interests?', *Journal of Contemporary African Studies*, 36(1): 39–53.

Potgieter, T. (2021) 'Culture, communities and society', in D.L. Sparks (ed) *The Blue Economy in Sub-Saharan Africa* (1st edn), Abingdon: Routledge, pp 11–34.

Sending, O.J., Pouliot, V. and Neumann, I.B. (2011) 'The future of diplomacy. Changing practices, evolving relationships', *International Journal*, 66(3): 527–42.

Sisulu, L.N. (2011) *Address by L.N. Sisulu, MP, Minister of Defence and Military Veterans at the SADC Extraordinary Meeting on Regional Antipiracy Strategy* [online], 25 July, Available from: www.gov.za/address-l-n-sisulu-mp-minister-defence-and-military-veterans-sadc-extraordinary-meeting-regional [Accessed 10 January 2022].

Sofer, S. (1988) 'Old and new diplomacy: a debate revisited', *Review of International Studies*, 14(3): 195–211.

Speller, I. (2014) *Understanding Naval Warfare*, Abingdon: Routledge.

Sule, A.M. (2013) *Nigeria's Participation in Peacekeeping Operations*, Thesis completed in partial fulfilment of the Certificate of Training in United Nations Peace Support Operations, Peace Operations Training Institute [online], Available from: https://cdn.peaceopstraining.org/theses/sule.pdf [Accessed 18 July 2022].

Surbun, V. (2021) 'Africa's combined exclusive maritime zone concept', *Institute for Security Studies Africa Report*, 32 [online], Available from: https://issafrica.s3.amazonaws.com/site/uploads/ar-32.pdf [Accessed 18 July 2022].

Tanchum, M. (2021) 'The geopolitics of the Mediterranean crisis. A regional perspective on the Mediterranean's new great game', in M. Tanchum (ed) *Eastern Mediterranean in Unchartered Waters: Perspectives on Emerging Geopolitical Realities*, Ankara: Konrad Adenauer Stiftung [online], Available from: www.kas.de/documents/283907/10938219/Eastern+Mediterranean+in+Uncharted+Waters_KAS+TurkeyA.pdf/6f554da1-93ac-bba6-6fd0-3c8738244d4b?version=1.0&t=1607590823989 [Accessed 18 July 2022].

Till, G. (2018) *Seapower: A Guide for the Twenty-First Century* (4th edn), Abingdon: Routledge.

Van Nieuwkerk, A. and Manganyi, C. (2019) 'South Africa's maritime foreign policy: a conceptual framework', *Scientia Militaria: South African Journal of Military Studies*, 47(2): 3–17.

Voyer, M., Schofield, C., Azmi, K., Warner, R., McIlgorm, A. and Quirk, G. (2018) 'Maritime security and the blue economy: intersections and interdependencies in the Indian Ocean', *Journal of the Indian Ocean Region*, 14(1): 28–48.

Willett, L. (2011) 'Pirates and power politics: naval presence and grand strategy in the Horn of Africa', *Royal United Services Institute Journal*, 156(6): 20–25.

Wingrin, D. (2014) 'Italian carrier group arrives in Cape Town', *DefenceWeb* [online], 6 February, Available from: www.defenceweb.co.za/sea/sea-sea/italian-carrier-group-arrives-in-cape-town/ [Accessed on 12 January 2019].

Xinhua (2017) 'Chinese naval hospital ship Peace Ark arrives in Tanzania' [online], 20 November, Available from: www.mfa.gov.cn/ce/cezanew/eng/znjl/t1514256.htm [Accessed on 12 January 2022].

Yohannes, D. and Gebresenbet, F. (2018) 'Transregional conflict crossing the Red Sea: the horn of Africa', *Comparativ*, 26(8): 90–108.

Yücel, H. (2021) 'Sovereignty and transnational cooperation in the Gulf of Guinea: how a network approach can strengthen the Yaoundé Architecture', *Scandinavian Journal of Military Studies*, 4(1): 146–57.

Zichi, G.L. (2018) 'A European fleet to address the migration challenge in the Mediterranean? The EUNAVFOR MED/Sophia between lights and shadows', *Athens Journal of Mediterranean Studies*, 4(2): 137–56.

7

Twitter/X Diplomacy and Its Use and Practice in Africa[1]

Suzanne Graham and Victoria Graham

Introduction

> A Swedish diplomat once asked me how one can reduce the complexities of international diplomacy to a 140-character tweet. I responded by saying that Twiplomacy must be regarded as an art form, one that uses the language of Twitter to condense foreign policy initiatives or official statements into short bursts of diplomacy.
>
> Manor, 2014

Twitter/X diplomacy (or hashtag diplomacy), sometimes referred to as Twiplomacy, is an emerging tool used by international policy actors, such as heads of state and diplomats, to conduct public diplomacy and to reach out to worldwide audiences. X is a social media tool that allows all registered users with access to the internet to send short messages, or 'tweets' of up to 280 characters in length (originally 140 characters, which is still the length for some languages). Users can also receive messages, attach web links or other resources and can 'follow' other Twitter/X users via this platform. Hashtags refer to identifiers, or labels, for specific content posted in tweets. This tool allows users to remain aware of the latest news and events worldwide, and to draw attention to specific statements or images or events quickly through retweeting, and all thanks to the relative convenience of a smart-enabled cellular phone or similar device. A 2020 study of government Twitter/X users around the world revealed that governments and leaders of 189 countries had an official presence on Twitter/X, with 163 accounts identified as

---

[1] Parts of this chapter were published originally in *Studia Europaea* (2, 2020), pp 133–56.

belonging to state leaders and 132 to foreign ministries. Therefore, close to 100 per cent of United Nations (UN) member states (193 members) consider Twitter/X to be a valid enough tool to employ it on a frequent basis. These users have a combined audience of more than 620 million followers (Burson Cohn & Wolfe, 2020).

If this is an accurate reflection of the perceived significance of Twitter/X to African governments, then it must be considered of value for individual diplomats, foreign ministries and heads of state and government in Africa. However, can this tool be of real use in the management and implementation of public diplomacy on a continent where internet penetration is 43 per cent of the combined population and, if so, what are these foreign policy makers using it for?

This chapter intends to address these questions by exploring the use of hashtag diplomacy in Africa in reference to select examples. It will begin by situating this type of diplomacy under the umbrella of public diplomacy and it will then move on to consider the viability and reach of this social media platform in Africa.

Diplomacy and the emergence of digital and Twitter/X diplomacy

Diplomacy involves the management of interstate relations and relations between states and other actors (Barston, 2013). It encompasses institutionalized, agential, routinized and regulated communication with public and state actors. 'Digital' diplomacy translates this concept through digital tools such as Twitter/X. Twitter/X diplomacy brings traditional and digital diplomacy and Twitter/X together. The emergence of the COVID-19 pandemic in 2020 moved diplomacy, and its related communication methods, online overnight. Digital platforms became the necessary means by which diplomats could safely continue to perform their roles and act upon their mandates. Of course, the use of digital communication tools had already been in place prior to the pandemic, with government officials making use of social media platforms in their diplomatic efforts. Although questions around the risks of using social media as a communication tool of diplomacy abound, in an increasingly digital world, it cannot be discounted. And it is within this digital debate that public diplomacy is most often emphasized.

Public diplomacy refers to that mechanism by which the government of a state promotes its foreign policy goals by communicating its foreign policy to international audiences, not only foreign governments but foreign publics too. It can, therefore, be regarded as an overarching concept encompassing cultural diplomacy, public affairs and propaganda (Hocking and Melissen, 2015). Cowan and Arsenault (2008) refer to three layers of public diplomacy. The first is one-way communication to a foreign audience (monologic), for example through a speech. The second is two-way or multidirectional communication (dialogue), for example discussions between two heads of state. The third refers to initiatives where people 'work together on a joint venture or project' (collaboration). It is important to consider in what ways hashtag diplomacy might be a useful tool for foreign policy practitioners. It may be that all three layers of public diplomacy referred to can be facilitated through Twitter/X. In December 2019 and January 2020 @Paul Kagame (Rwanda's President Paul Kagame) tweeted a confirmation of the positive bilateral relations shared between Rwanda and the United Arab Emirates while referencing its political leader @MohamedBinZayed, and congratulated his 'brother & friend' @hagegeingob (President Hage Geingob) on his re-election in Namibia and on the growing relationship between Rwanda and Namibia (Burson Cohn & Wolf, 2020). In another example, in December 2021, Zambian President Hakainde Hichilema (@HHichilema) marked the occasion of receiving credentials from the newly appointed Malawian high commissioner to Zambia, Maria Margaret Kamoto, and the Dutch ambassador to Zimbabwe, Zambia and Malawi, Dr Margaret Verwijk, tweeting that 'Economic diplomacy is at core of our regional & international relations. #Zambia is open for trade (Twitter.com)'.

While traditional diplomatic tools such as embassies, media appearances and cultural exchanges remain important, it is increasingly apparent that *digital* diplomacy is starting to occupy a more central role in public diplomacy (Collins et al, 2019). Unlike the formality that accompanies traditional diplomacy, Twitter/X allows government officials to broadcast their views without the need for formal diplomatic channels and the usual diplomatic jargon. Twitter/X diplomacy is, therefore, more accessible for interested publics and it encourages grassroots engagement as opposed to a top-down bureaucratic approach, for example when it comes to negotiation and dissemination of information. Via this platform, the public can become content producers of foreign policy agendas, not helpless consumers of it (Zaharna, 2015). Public choice has also expanded. Publics can choose 'to follow' state leaders they are interested in on Twitter/X. Governments have become increasingly aware of this and as a result public diplomacy literature has become peppered with phrases such as 'partnerships', 'mutuality', 'social networks' and 'relationship building'. Moreover, Twiplomacy can give legitimacy to informal exchanges between governments and among governments and citizens (with the adverse effect of perhaps delegitimizing the formal channels of communication, since these take longer) (Chhabra, 2020; Duncombe, 2018).

As Burson-Marsteller (2017) notes, 'digital diplomacy has gone from being an afterthought to being the very first thought of world leaders and governments across the globe, as audiences flock to their Twitter/X newsfeeds for the latest news and statements'. Rana (2011: 207) contends that 'public diplomacy as it takes place now could not be conducted without the

ICT revolution' and that due to evolving technologies, 'communication with publics is transformed'. However, Ciolek (in Ittefaq, 2019) asserts that while the mode of delivery is changing, the purpose of public diplomacy remains unchanged. After all, information and communications technology (ICT) is 'not a magic bullet', it is a 'tool', much as any type of diplomacy is a tool, and cannot substitute for foreign policy making or policy implementation (Rana, 2011: 207). It is true that 'Twitter has taken on diverse and occasional roles in diplomatic communications, from cordial announcements of bi-lateral cooperation to terse exchanges and diplomatic jabs, as well as more casual posts' (Chavan, 2019). Manor (2016) argues that 'understanding hashtags, or hashtag literacy, is now an acceptable form of communication for all those following diplomatic institutions be it scholars, journalists, citizens or even other diplomats'. He goes on to state that on occasion hashtags can indicate countries' entire foreign policy initiatives and they offer global followers the chance to understand how countries promote themselves around the world.

Twitter/X is appealing because it is quick and by nature enforces succinct short text messages. Public figures, like heads of state, enjoy this advantage as it also accommodates dynamic political situations requiring Twitter/X storms of information, advice, opinion and responses. Users can also search for specific hashtags and subjects can trend, which draws global attention to them. For example, when it became evident that the wearing of face masks and staying at home during the COVID-19 pandemic were necessary preventative measures, African leaders used Twitter/X to reach a wide audience and convey a unified response to dealing with the pandemic. The government of Botswana, for example, launched the #BWMaskChallenge, asking followers to share a selfie wearing a mask (@BWGovernment, 5 May 2020) and in South Africa, the Presidency encouraged followers to show their support for the lockdown measures by downloading and displaying a Twibbon on their social media profiles encouraging citizens to #StayHome and #StaySafe. Other African leaders also took to Twitter/X to educate audiences (local and foreign) on the importance of washing hands. In 2020, Presidents Paul Kagame (Rwanda), Macky Sall (Senegal), Abiy Ahmed Ali (Ethiopia), Mokgweetsi Masisi (Burundi) and Kassory Fofana (Guinea) released tweets demonstrating their participation in the 'safe hands challenge'. They called on fellow African leaders to record videos of themselves washing their hands – to set an example and slow the spread of the virus (Twiplomacy, 2020).

A consequence of Twiplomacy is the birth of a 'new' cult of personality in public diplomacy (Uysal and Schroeder, 2019). It made news headlines when former US President Donald Trump allegedly referred to some African countries as in 'very bad shape' and used offensive language to describe them, and @NAkufoAddo (President Nana Akufo-Addo of Ghana) responded on Twitter/X: 'we will not accept such insults, even from a leader of a friendly country, no matter how powerful' (Twitter.com). In another example, within a few hours of South Africa's former President Jacob Zuma joining Twitter/X in late 2018, his followers swelled from a few hundred to tens of thousands and four years later he had 616,000 followers (both fans and haters) (Twitter.com).

Mainstream news houses are relying increasingly on social media as a news source (O'Boyle, 2019). This is an important factor for foreign policy practitioners to consider, as social media can, through dialogue and engagement, assist states in building a positive image globally (Ittefaq, 2019).

Twitter/X diplomacy in Africa

It is interesting to note that the South African Presidency (@PresidencyZA) is among the top five most active Twitter/X accounts in Sub-Saharan Africa, according to the 2020 Twitter/X study, and has 2.1 million followers (Twitter.com). The hashtags #Rwanda and #Kagame are among the most frequently used, most especially because the President of Rwanda, Paul Kagame, consistently refers to these labels in his own tweets. President Kagame appears to value Twitter/X. He takes the time to respond to his followers and conversations in his Twitter/X feed, which would require a great deal of time as he has 2.6 million followers (Twitter.com). Nearly all of his tweets are responses to other Twitter/X users. Before he deactivated his Twitter/X account in 2019 due to 'constant insults and name-calling' (Kejitan, 2020), President Uhuru Kenyatta of Kenya had around 3.62 million followers on Twitter/X, the most in Africa at the time.

As of January 2022, the most followed African politicians on Twitter/X are Egyptian President Abdul Fattah Al-Sisi (5.5 million), followed by Kenyan Vice President William Ruto (4.4 million). Nigerian President Muhammadu Buhari (4 million) comes next and then Rwandese President Paul Kagame (2.5 million), followed by Uganda's Yoweri Museveni (2.4 million), Ghana's Nana Ajuko-Addo (2.1 million), South Africa's Cyril Ramaphosa (2.1 million), Senegal's Macky Sall (1.8 million), Ethiopia's Abiy Ahmed Ali (1.1 million) and Tanzania's President Suluhu Hassan (almost hitting 1 million).

Table 7.1 offers a possible explanation for why Kenya's president had the most followers in Africa at one time. Kenya has the largest percentage of population with access to the internet. Despite this, almost 840 million people (61 per cent of the African population) are yet to come online across Africa (Kemp, 2022). Digital inequality therefore remains a challenge for 'Twitter diplomats' on the continent, particularly if they are trying to sell their foreign policy to the African people.

Interestingly, as Figure 7.1 shows, of those who are online in Africa, far more use Facebook (82 per cent) than Twitter/X (4 per cent), which suggests that governments might need to diversify their social media presence more if they want to use these platforms to reach people for diplomatic purposes.

Table 7.1: Top 12 African countries in terms of internet penetration (c December 2020)

Country and rank	Population with access to internet (%)
1. Kenya	85
2. Libya	84
3. Nigeria	83
4. Mauritius	72.2
5. Seychelles	72.1
6. Morocco	68.5
7. Tunisia	68.4
8. Reunion	67.4
9. Cabo Verde	62.7
10. Gabon	60
11. South Africa	57.7
12. Egypt	57.3

Source: Internet World Stats (2022).

Figure 7.1: Social media in Africa (c March 2022)

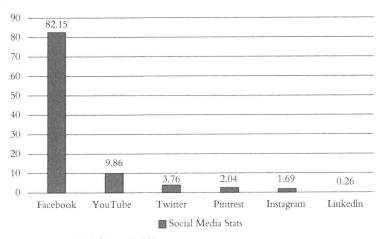

Source: Statcounter Global Stats (2022).

Manor (2016) contends that the value of Twitter/X, and other social media platforms, as diplomatic channels for African countries lies in three parts: diaspora diplomacy, networked diplomacy and nation branding. African countries can bolster trade and cultural links with global diasporas by investing in tweets about embassy activities, events, historical connections and common thoughts on economic and political issues. For example, in the United Kingdom the Ethiopian embassy has 7,000 followers on Twitter/X and the Ethiopian foreign ministry has an active Twitter/X presence in important expatriate locations including Canada, Israel, Lebanon, Saudi Arabia, the US and the UK. Examples such as these reflect the value of using Twitter/X for diaspora diplomacy. In relation to networked diplomacy, Manor (2016) found that when Amina Mohamed was the Cabinet Secretary for Foreign Affairs for Kenya, she was able to serve as a hub of information linking ministers who did not follow each other directly on Twitter/X. At the time, she performed the role of 'an information junction … attracting attention from her peers around the globe' (Manor, 2016). This reflects a type of social media mobility which small countries may also make use of to elevate their global diplomatic positions.

When it became clear in early 2020 that an international pandemic had begun, and global lockdowns (as well as limited travel and closed airports) were inevitable, regional and international bodies began to embrace Zoom and other online and teleconferencing platforms to conduct meetings. For example, despite the pandemic, African governments and regional organizations like the African Union (AU) held several virtual peace and security conferences, bringing together thousands of African stakeholders. At this point, it is important to note that African regional bodies had a Twitter/X presence prior to the global COVID-19 pandemic (see Table 7.2 for Twitter/X joining dates and followers), although some have a great deal more followers than others. Soon it became commonplace to see shared pictures of participants on their video screens as well as to hear meeting chairs reminding participants to 'please, mute your microphones' or the opposite when the chance to speak arose: 'You are still on mute!' The increased sharing of screen grabs and pictures of their online meetings by state leaders prompted Israeli diplomat Joshua Brook to coin the term 'Zoomplomacy' in mid-May of 2020.

South African President Cyril Ramaphosa, AU chairman in 2020, moved all AU meetings online when the pandemic struck. In May 2020, the AU successfully hosted a 'Silencing the Guns' online, hybrid conference, with some participants attending physically and others virtually. The advantages of online diplomacy here included reduced costs of connecting key stakeholders, as well as quicker turnaround time on decision making due to the increased availability of more members (Adesina, 2022: 94–5).

In terms of nation branding, governments can make use of Twitter/X to flex any soft power they may have, manage their international reputation and attract investors. In July 2015, US President Barack Obama visited Kenya as part of the Global Entrepreneurial Summit. This visit drew a lot of media attention and Kenyan authorities made use of this attention to boost its brand internationally via Twitter/X and other media. It marketed

Table 7.2: African regional bodies using Twitter/X (2024)

Regional organization	Date joined	Number of followers
African Union	May 2010	1 million
Southern African Development Community Secretariat	August 2016	97.8K
East African Community	May 2009	150K
Economic Community of West Africa	November 2014	181.6K
Arab Maghreb Union	July 2017	15
Economic Community of Central African States	September 2014	3562
Common Market for Eastern and Southern Africa Secretariat	January 2010	14.2K
Community of Sahel-Saharan States Secretariat Executive	July 2020	230
Intergovernmental Authority on Development Secretariat	March 2010	62.7K
African Continental Free Trade Area Secretariat	July 2019	56.6K
Pan-African Parliament	January 2013	48.2K

Source: Twitter.com (2021).

itself to close on 2 million people as a rising economic power with growth opportunities for international investors. This was done using the Obama hashtag alongside #chooseKenya as well as Kenya's ministry of foreign affairs, Kenyan President Uhuru Kenyatta's personal Twitter/X handle and the president's official channel. When the American news network CNN made a serious error in labelling Kenya a 'hotbed of terror' prior to Obama's visit, Kenya's active Twitter/X community criticized the network, setting it right, using the hashtag #someonetellcnn, which trended for several days (Mutiga, 2015).

To tweet or not to tweet?

Twitter/X diplomacy has implications for international relations. Dee (in Graham, 2020: 137) suggests that:

> Whilst Twitter has become a major component of diplomatic life, with diplomats themselves frequently tweeting position updates and news from negotiations, it does also present a major challenge for diplomacy. If diplomacy is best achieved where trust is developed quietly and away from the public eye, Twitter can provide the medium for removing

that trust between diplomats as any statement, off-hand comment, or 'red-line' presented can be tweeted and showcased to the world. Worse still, it raises serious concerns where diplomats' own politicians can broadcast statements which either contradict or undermine the position they are presenting or even attack the other party with whom the diplomats are seeking to build rapport and trust.

Another emerging trend has been the 'politicization' of Twitter/X. More and more state actors, and citizens too, are using Twitter/X to launch political attacks. In 2015, for example, a Twitter/X war ('Twar') broke out when the 'active community of Kenyans on Twitter' (KOT for short) responded to a remark that former Zimbabwean President Robert Mugabe supposedly made about Kenyans being 'good at stealing'. KOT led a barrage of verbal attacks on Twitter/X against Zimbabweans using the tag 'Kenyans vs Zimbabweans'. It was tweeted and re-tweeted over 9,000 times (BBC News, 2015). In this case, no evidence was found that Mugabe said anything of the sort, but this incident highlights the erroneous nature of fake news and what this could provoke in diplomatic channels through the platform of Twitter/X.

Although some would suggest that social media platforms like Twitter/X should be thought of as 'the world's largest cocktail parties, where everyone is invited and guests kindle conversations and relationships, just as in real life' (Elhai, 2019), others would suggest that Twitter/X diplomacy has potentially disastrous consequences for diplomatic relations. The fast-paced, relatively uncensored nature of Twitter/X means that diplomats can tweet anything and, even if well-meant, the slightest misreading of it could have serious consequences for all actors involved. Traditional diplomatic controls or risk assessments via bureaucratic processes can be bypassed with the use of this social media platform. Heads of state can tweet foreign policy positions without consulting cabinets and often these become formal policy, setting back government strategists. This relatively unfiltered expression of opinion or emotion of state leaders can also prove very telling for interested observers. The risk of different publics having access to a type of 'insider' knowledge of what drives a world leader could be useful for allies and adversaries alike. For example:

> African governments still dwell on the traditional form of diplomacy and are yet to embrace the Twittersphere as a reciprocal discursive and democratic space. They ought to harness the soft power capability of social media platforms like Twitter to further diplomatic relations and initiate dialogue between citizens and diplomats in a constructive, democratic manner. However, countries must prioritise infrastructure development for internet connectivity and ensure affordable data

pricing in order to make participation in digital diplomacy truly inclusive. (Shumba, 2020)

In Africa, Algeria is a good example of a country using Twitter/X for political ends. Domestic and foreign crises are highlighted in various tweets by Algerian citizens and officials. In response. Moroccan activists have created their own hashtag referencing Moroccan Sahara. Algerian 'foreign-oriented' tweets focused on Iran in 2017 after the announcement that Iranian President Hassan Rouhani would be visiting Algeria. Activists launched a Twitter/X campaign, for example #(No to Rouhani in Algeria) and #(Algerians against Iran) to condemn the visit for fear that Iran might try to interfere in the Algerian domestic situation. President Rouhani's visit was postponed as a result.

A study conducted by communications firm Portland (2016), entitled 'How Africa Tweets', found that political hashtags made up close to 9 per cent of all hashtags in Africa. This was an interesting finding, especially since this percentage was comparatively higher than those in the UK, the US, France or Canada, where data and social media platforms are largely more accessible. This study suggests that conventional channels for freedom of expression are limited, encouraging users to go online to express their opinions. A main finding of this study was that 'Twitter is a valuable tool for engaging a population around an issue or an election' (Manor, 2016).

This is an important point for policy makers and advisors in cabinets to reflect upon as social media can become an important government communication tool. In 2015, for example, Egypt had the most tweets in Africa with 456 million, followed by Nigeria (347 million), South Africa (323 million), Kenya (76 million) and Ghana (65 million) (Portland, 2016). It is also important to note that although Twitter/X may not always be effective as a protest or campaign tool, the #Kony2012 movement ended in failure as the leader of the Ugandan Lord's Resistance Army, Joseph Kony, eluded capture despite the world's focus; in some instances, if enough people 'speak' through platforms such as these, governments start to pay attention.

In April 2014, over 200 girls were abducted from their schools in Nigeria by Boko Haram, a radical Islamic group. The vice president of the World Bank for Africa, Oby Ezekwesili openly called on the Nigerian government to 'bring back our girls' (Mark, 2014). Thereafter, Twitter/X users across Nigeria began using the hashtag #BringBackOurGirls and very soon over a million tweets included this hashtag worldwide. The hashtag #BringBackOurGirls movement became a global campaign that drew attention from around the world, endorsed by Michelle Obama, US First Lady at the time, and highlighted the plight of ordinary citizens in Nigeria's north-east at the mercy of Boko Haram's activities. However, the initial global attention began to fade and two years later some girls were released. One hundred and twelve girls remain missing.

Ministries of foreign affairs in Africa are using tweets to advertise important milestones in bilateral relations, to express messages of condemnation, condolence, or congratulations, to declare solidarity and support by retweeting, and to relay information. For example, in August 2019, Chad's ministry of foreign affairs, @ChadianMFA, retweeted the call by Moussa Faki Mahamat, the chairperson of the AU Commission, for a new multilateral world order post-G7 summit. This tweet declared that Africa knows what it wants: all its partners to adapt by responding to #Agenda2063 for #TheAfricaWeWant. In October 2019 @ChadianMFA reported a meeting between Chad's foreign minister, Cherif Mahamat Zene and United Kingdom ambassador to Chad, Rowan Laxton. They met to talk over strengthening bilateral and business relations between the two countries. The ministry also congratulated Ethiopian Prime Minister Abiy Ahmed Ali on his Nobel Peace Prize win in 2019. @ChadianMFA tweeted: 'You have inspired Africa and the whole world for signing a peace deal with Eritrea and ending two decades of hostilities. Well-deserved award' (Twitter.com). In November 2019, @ChadianMFA tweeted Chad's condemnation of 'terrorist' attacks in Mali and Burkina Faso respectively and reached out to the people and governments of both countries to offer Chad's support. For public diplomacy purposes it is important for Twitter/X followers to be given some insight into what is being tweeted.

South Africa's Department of International Relations and Cooperation (DIRCO) tweeting simply that the president of the Central African Republic (CAR), Faustin-Archange Touadera, was received by the minister of international relations and cooperation, Dr Naledi Pandor, at a South African airport in March 2020 was a missed opportunity. What is it about South Africa–CAR relations that the public should be made aware of or should care about? What is the purpose of the tweet? If the tweet offers essentials, then it remains an information-relaying tool only. To broadcast the South African government's intent to serve the people of Africa, the deputy minister of international affairs and cooperation, Candith Mashego-Dlamini, was quoted in a March 2020 @DIRCO_ZA tweet as saying: 'African continent is less about its political leadership and more about its people – Africa's greatest asset.' South Africa took on the chair of the AU for 2020. @DIRCO_ZA, which has about 51,000 followers, has also retweeted posts that mention DIRCO in a positive light. In early March 2020, @DIRCO_ZA retweeted Georgian Ambassador Beka Dvali (@BekaDvali1), who expressed his 'utmost pleasure & honour, in my capacity of Dean of European Group of Ambassadors to South Africa, meeting Ambassador Maud Dlomo, Deputy Director General for #Europe & #Americas at DIRCO'.

Twitter/X accounts may be used by international organizations to draw media attention to smaller, more under-resourced states. Three of the six African small island developing states (SIDS) feature in the top ten African countries in terms of internet penetration (see Table 7.1): Seychelles; Mauritius and Cabo Verde.

In an example of self-promotion on Twitter/X, the Republic of Seychelles' department of foreign affairs (@SeychellesDFA) drew attention to Seychellois Ambassador Barry Faure, secretary of state for foreign affairs and blue economy, who presented at two high-level panels on human rights promotion and protection at Human Rights Council talks in Geneva, Switzerland in February 2020. States and international actors can boost each other through social media platforms. For example, Seychelles and the United Nations Development Programme (UNDP) refer to each other's handles via Twitter/X. Amanda Serumaga (@ASerumaga), who is the new UNDP resident representative to Seychelles, tweeted: 'Thank you to Ambassador Barry Faure @BarryFaure @SeychellesDFA for an excellent discussion on all things #SIDS! @UNDPSeychelles commits to continuing our support to #ClimateChange mitigation #BlueEconomy and the push to listen to SIDs voices!' (Twitter.com).

Mauritius has numerous Twitter/X channels: @GovMauritius; @MFA_MU, which is the official account of the ministry of foreign affairs; @MauritiusPM; @Diplomacy_MU. In March 2019, @Diplomacy_MU retweeted Mauritius' national birthday congratulations from India and Israel's diplomacy Twitter/X channels. It also retweeted the Ukrainian ministry of foreign affairs (@MFA_Ukraine), which celebrated the anniversary of Mauritius' Independence Day. Ukraine's ministry also stated that the country considers Mauritius to be an important partner in Africa and that it continues to count on the Republic for further support of Ukraine's territorial integrity. The prime minister of Mauritius, Pravind Jugnauth, used his Twitter/X handle @PKJugnauth to reach out to Mauritian diasporas, wishing all his compatriots at home and abroad a happy Independence Day.

In February 2020, the president of Cabo Verde used his Twitter/X handle (@PresidenciaCV) to announce the visit of a Luxembourgish delegation to the African state. Luxembourg is paying for a solar photovoltaic production system for Cabo Verde's parliament, with an expectation of up to 30 per cent reduced electricity usage. The president of the country's National Assembly, Jorge Santos, the minister of foreign affairs and communities of Cabo Verde, Luís Filipe Tavares, and the Luxembourgish minister for cooperation and humanitarian action, Frantz Fayot, participated in these talks. Luxemburg and Cabo Verde have a longstanding relationship of cooperation programmes, the current round of which started in 2021 and will last until 2024 with an increased investment from €45 million to around €60 million (Macauhub, 2020).

Cowan and Arsenault's (2008: 11) position that regardless of the public diplomacy initiative or tool, the most effective outcome is the intent behind the initiative and that intent is designed 'with an eye for the best means of engaging with and building credibility among foreign publics. This credibility may be based on manipulation'. In some cases, as Donaldson (2016) notes, 'regimes may even use social media to allow people opportunities to air grievances and create an illusion of free expression, whilst themselves diverting or subverting debate'.

Finally, it is also worth noting that Twitter/X can only operate freely in countries where the government allows it to do so. In June 2021, Twitter/X deleted a tweet by Nigerian President Buhari which threatened secessionist groups in the south-east. The government suspended Twitter/X thereafter, calling the platform 'very, very suspect' (Maclean, 2021). In January 2022, this ban was lifted after an agreement was reached that would allow Twitter/X to restore operations in Nigeria. The Nigerian government commented at the time that the agreement 'opens a new chapter in global digital diplomacy' (Akinwotu, 2022).

Conclusion

This chapter briefly explored the nature and value of Twitter/X or hashtag diplomacy and its use and practice in Africa, with reference to a few examples. It began by outlining where Twitter/X diplomacy fits within the umbrella of diplomacy and especially public diplomacy. Although traditional tools of diplomacy remain intact, the evolving nature of technology demands that to stay relevant, state leaders and other foreign policy makers must acknowledge the potential impact of using social media networks as a diplomatic tool and decide how best to reduce its risks and exploit its advantages. Social media is fast and effective. However, it can also be home to Twitter/X wars and the possibility of misinterpretation or insults that traditional bureaucratic modes of diplomacy, by their very nature of being thought-through and methodical, strive to avoid. This chapter referred to the point that only 43 per cent of Africa has internet penetration, which means that for African leaders to reach out to foreign publics using Twitter/X, in other African countries for example, they will be reaching out to a relatively few with access to the internet. Despite this, African countries acknowledge the power of this medium and some governments have taken stringent measures, especially during elections, to prevent the public from accessing Twitter/X. Moreover, there are examples of African leaders, such as Rwanda's Paul Kagame, and African ministries of foreign affairs making frequent use of the platform, and this would suggest some belief in its necessity.

It is evident that African ministries of foreign affairs and state leaders are using tweets to advertise important milestones in bilateral relations, to express messages of condemnation, condolence or congratulations, to declare solidarity and support by retweeting, and to relay information. In addition, as Manor (2016) contends, 'digital diplomacy holds the potential to increase the effectiveness of African diplomacy in diverse areas'. This includes governments reaching out to diaspora communities, using soft power boosts through nation branding and self-promotion, and becoming active hubs in growing networks connecting leaders and policy makers with common goals and challenges. The public, as agents and part of the public diplomacy process, can draw global attention to issues that affect them, such as climate change. This platform also affords communities considered to be outside the realm of usual actors in the political world the opportunity to have a voice, such as the youth. Social media sites like Twitter/X can also be used by small island developing states to project onto a global platform their relevance and needs. Used properly, digital diplomacy can, in conjunction with traditional diplomacy, be an effective platform for policy makers and state leaders in 21st century diplomatic activities.

References

Adesina, O.S. (2022) 'Africa and the future of digital diplomacy', in A. Uche Ordu (ed) *Foresight Africa. Top Priorities for the Continent in 2022*, Washington, DC: Brookings [online], Available from: www.brookings.edu/wp-content/uploads/2022/01/foresightafrica2022_fullreport.pdf [Accessed 18 July 2022].

Akinwotu, E. (2022) 'Nigeria lifts Twitter ban seven months after site deleted president's post', *The Guardian* [online], 13 January, Available from: www.theguardian.com/world/2022/jan/13/nigeria-lifts-twitter-ban-seven-months-after-site-deleted-presidents-post [Accessed 20 February 2022].

Barston, R.P. (2013) *Modern Diplomacy* (4th edn), London: Routledge.

BBC News (2015).' The Kenyans who attacked Robert Mugabe on Twitter' [online], 6 November, Available from: www.bbc.com/news/blogs-trending-34735212 [Accessed 20 February 2022].

Burson Cohn & Wolfe (2020) *Twiplomacy Study 2020* [online], Available from: https://www.twiplomacy.com/twiplomacy-study-2020 [Accessed 5 March 2024].

Burson-Marsteller (2017) *Twiplomacy Study 2017* [online], Available from: https://www.twiplomacy.com/_files/ugd/5835d4_0fcb735c94eb4647a0105bcab85f7f5d.xlsx?dn=Twiplomacy-2017-Master-Data-File-1.xlsx http://twiplomacy.com/blog/twiplomacy-study-2017/ [Accessed 5 March 2024].

Chavan, D.D. (2019) 'Twitter diplomacy' [online], Available from: https://abhipedia.abhimanu.com/Article/IAS/MTE4OTU0/Twitter-Diplomacy-India-and-the-world-IAS [Accessed 15 February 2020].

Chhabra, R. (2020). 'Twitter diplomacy: a brief analysis', *Observer Research Foundation Issue Brief*, No 335 [online], Available from: https://policycommons.net/artifacts/1351583/twitter-diplomacy/1963741/ [Accessed 18 July 2022].

Collins, S.D., DeWitt, J.R. and LeFebvre, R.K. (2019) 'Hashtag diplomacy: Twitter as a tool for engaging in public diplomacy and promoting US foreign policy', *Place Branding and Public Diplomacy*, 15: 78–96.

Cowan, G. and Arsenault, A. (2008) 'Moving from monologue to dialogue to collaboration: the three layers of public diplomacy', *ANNALS of the American Academy of Political and Social Science*, 616(1): 10–30.

Donaldson, A. (2016) 'The soft power of Twitter', *The British Council* [online], January, Available from: www.britishcouncil.org/research-policy-insight/insight-articles/soft-power-twitter [Accessed 18 July 2022].

Duncombe, C. (2018) 'Twitter and the Challenges of Digital Diplomacy', *SAIS Review of International Affairs*, 38(2): 91–100.

Elhai, W. (2019) 'Twitter is a cocktail party, not a press conference (or, social media for reporting officers)', *Foreign Service Journal* [online], December, Available from: https://afsa.org/twitter-cocktail-party-not-press-conference-or-social-media-reporting-officers [Accessed 27 February 2020].

Graham, S. (2020) 'Hashtag diplomacy and its use in Africa', *Studia Europeana*, 2: 133–55.

Hocking, B. and Melissen, J. (2015) *Diplomacy in the Digital Age*, Clingendael: Netherlands Institute of International Relations.

Internet World Stats (2022) 'Internet penetration in Africa' [online], Available from: www.internetworldstats.com/stats1.htm [Accessed 20 February 2022].

Ittefaq, M. (2019) 'Digital diplomacy via social networks: a cross-national analysis of governmental usage of Facebook and Twitter for digital engagement', *Journal of Contemporary Eastern Asia*, 18(1): 49–69.

Kejitan, V. (2020) 'Uhuru: why I deactivated my Twitter account', *The Standard* [online], 25 November, Available from: www.standardmedia.co.ke/kenya/article/2001395176/uhuru-why-i-deactivated-my-twitter-account [Accessed 20 February 2022].

Kemp, S. (2022) 'Digital 2022: global overview report', DataReportal [online], 22 January, Available from: https://datareportal.com/reports/digital-2022-global-overview-report [Accessed 20 March 2022].

Macauhub (2020) 'Luxembourg finances solar energy project of the Cabo Verde parliament' [online], 19 February, Available from: https://macauhub.com.mo/2020/02/19/pt-luxemburgo-financia-projecto-de-energia-solar-do-parlamento-de-cabo-verde/ [Accessed 20 July 2020].

Maclean, R. (2021) 'Nigeria bans Twitter after president's tweet is deleted', *The New York Times* [online], 5 June, Available from www.nytimes.com/2021/06/05/world/africa/nigeria-twitter-president.html [Accessed 25 March 2022].

Manor, I. (2014) 'Exploring the use of hashtags', *Exploring Digital Diplomacy* [online], 30 September, Available from: https://digdipblog.com/2014/09/30/hashtags/ [Accessed 20 February 2020].

Manor, I. (2016) 'Digital diplomacy in Africa: a research agenda', *University of Southern California Center on Public Diplomacy Blog* [online], 20 January, Available from: https://uscpublicdiplomacy.org/blog/digital-diplomacy-africa-research-agenda [Accessed 10 March 2020].

Mark, M. (2014), 'Obiageli Ezekwesili: "When they took the girls, our government went under"', *The Guardian* [online], 28 December, Available from: www.theguardian.com/world/2014/dec/28/obiageli-ezekwesili-bring-back-our-girls-boko-haram-school-kidnapping [Accessed 18 July 2022].

Mutiga, M. (2015) 'CNN executive flies to Kenya to apologise for "hotbed of terror" claim', *The Guardian* [online], 14 August, Available from: www.theguardian.com/world/2015/aug/14/cnn-kenya-apologise-obama [Accessed 25 March 2020].

O'Boyle, J. (2019) 'Twitter diplomacy between India and the United States: agenda-building analysis of tweets during presidential state visits', *Global Media and Communication*, 15(1): 121–34.

Portland. (2016) 'How Africa tweets: politics and the Twitter revolution' [online], Available from: https://portland-communications.com/publications/politics-and-the-twitter-revolution/ [25 February 2020].

Rana, K.S. (2011) *21st Century Diplomacy: A Practitioner's Guide*, London: Continuum.

Shumba, E. (2020) 'Twiplomacy in Africa: possibilities and pitfalls for diplomats', *Africa Portal* [online], 9 October, Available from: www.africaportal.org/features/twiplomacy-africa-possibilities-and-pitfalls-diplomats/ [Accessed 20 February 2022].

Statcounter GlobalStats (2022) 'Social media stats Africa' [online], Available from: https://gs.statcounter.com/social-media-stats/all/Africa [Accessed 20 February 2022].

Twiplomacy (2018) *Twiplomacy Study 2018* [online], www.twiplomacy.com/twiplomacy-study-2018/ [Accessed 20 February 2022].

Twiplomacy. (2020) *Twiplomacy Study 2020* [online], 20 July, Available from: www.twiplomacy.com/twiplomacy-study-2020/ [Accessed 20 February 2022].

Uysal, N. and Schroeder, J. (2019) 'Turkey's Twitter public diplomacy: towards a "new" cult of personality', *Public Relations Review*, 45(5) [online], Available from: https://doi.org/10.1016/j.pubrev.2019.101837 [Accessed 20 February 2022].

Zaharna, R.S. (2015) 'From pinstripes to Tweets' [online], Available from: www.thecairoreview.com/issues/winter-2015/ [Accessed 29 April 2024].

8

The Quiet Diplomacy of the Chibok Abductions

Sven Botha

Introduction

Since the end of the Second World War, diplomacy has become a more open and public practice. This development was largely due to the various people-to-people programmes that were administered throughout the war, which found a continued purpose during the cold war (Roberts, 2006). As this volume clearly shows, the professions spanning the diplomatic realm have grown in scope, and non-state actors are not the exception. Quiet diplomacy is a tool that has been well used to reach political solutions when both tensions and expectations have run high. However, as will be shown, quiet diplomacy has been mostly studied from the perspective of the Global North and, when applied to Africa, the focus has been on Kenya's post-independence foreign policy and, more recently, South Africa's diplomatic interactions with the Mugabe administration in Zimbabwe. This reality is problematic, as other states and actors employing quiet diplomacy on the African continent have been ignored. This chapter seeks to help rectify this problem by applying the quiet diplomacy lens to the Chibok abductions which occurred in Nigeria in April 2014. The application and examination of the Chibok abductions brings much-needed diversity to the African discourse on quiet diplomacy as it highlights how non-state actors can influence and participate in the diplomatic process.

Following this introduction, the concept and character of quiet diplomacy will be discussed. Attention will be given to how the characterization of quiet diplomacy occurs when non-state actors are involved in the process. Thereafter, a brief literature review pertaining to quiet diplomacy will be undertake; emphasis is placed on the scarcity of this tool's application within the African context, particularly outside of the South Africa–Zimbabwe paradigm. The review will be followed by a discussion on Boko Haram as a case study. This discussion will focus exclusively on Boko Haram's track record with negotiation as well as the occurrences surrounding the Chibok abductions. Following the discussion of the case study, the characteristics of quiet diplomacy, as determined by the author, will be applied to the Chibok abductions. The final section of this chapter will reflect on the lessons that can be learnt from the negotiation process with Boko Haram and summarize the main arguments.

Quiet diplomacy: concept and character

It has been challenging to find an appropriate definition for quiet diplomacy (Graham, 2008b). The reasoning for this is twofold. First, scholars employ the phrase without assigning specific characteristics to it (see, for example, Thomson, 2008; Jones, 2014; Banim and Pejsova, 2017; Miles, 2021). Some scholars, such as Landsberg (2016), argue that quiet diplomacy is a theory. From this perspective, Landsburg (2016: 128) notes:

> Quiet diplomacy is a theory in its own right. It is an example of African solutions for African problems in practice. This notion conveys the idea that African actors should be afforded the time and space to decide on policy prescripts in seeking to address the continent's vast political and socio-economic problems.

Regardless, all the authors of the sources cited tend to agree that quiet diplomacy is a type of diplomatic practice which is conducted away from the public eye, is facilitated by high-ranking actors, and is peaceful or soft in its approach.

Second, Cooper, Heine and Thakur (2013: 26) note that 'The subject matter of diplomacy has expanded, from the high politics of war and peace to health, environment, development, science and technology, education, law, and the arts'. Consequently, scholarship on diplomacy develops and hosts a vast array of typologies, but severely lacks in theoretical development (Sending et al, 2011). Thus, it is arguable that scholars of diplomacy have been so preoccupied with labelling and categorizing diplomatic practices that little attention is paid to the characterization and theorization of these practices.

Graham (2008b: 124) argues that quiet diplomacy has six characteristics, namely:

- personal or direct diplomacy between heads of state or government or senior officials;
- Little (or no) media involvement;

- the appearance of limited action or even inaction;
- calm and tactful but persistent negotiation or dialogue in a non-threatening atmosphere;
- constructive engagement with the target country to help solve the problems as quietly as possible;
- diplomacy often carried out in the context of bilateral or multilateral efforts.

Graham offers one of the few detailed characterizations of quiet diplomacy, something for which she should be lauded, but within the context of this chapter, the characterization falls short. This is because there is no consideration given to non-state actors and/or third parties in the negotiation process. The non-state actor, as will become clearer, is essential to the application and analysis conducted in this chapter because Boko Haram is technically a non-state actor. Collins and Packer (2006) emphasize that the application of quiet diplomacy differs on a case-by-case basis. Consequentially, context must be considered and must guide the application process. With the need for context in mind, the author adapts Graham's criteria for application to non-state actors as follows:

- personal or direct diplomacy between heads of state or government, senior officials and the head of a non-state organization, a delegation and/or external proxy;
- little (or no) media involvement;
- the appearance of limited action or even inaction;
- calm and tactful but persistent negotiation or dialogue in a non-threatening atmosphere;
- constructive engagement with the target country to help solve the problems as quietly as possible;
- diplomacy often carried out in the context of bilateral or multilateral efforts;
- the optional involvement of a third party (which is either state or non-state in nature) to help make logistical arrangements for an agreement or exchange to be successful.

At this point, some may question the author's preference for the term quiet diplomacy over hostage diplomacy. This preference is justified as hostage diplomacy requires two or more states to employ their legal systems as a coercive tool (Gilbert and Piché, 2021: 14). Unfortunately, the nature and reality of terrorism is more complex than simply deploying a state's legal system. This is largely because few agree on indicators to provide a common definition of terrorism. Furthermore, negotiating with terrorists usually involves large-scale financial transactions which are beyond the purview of a legal system. The lack of purview in such cases usually arises out of the unique character of terrorist groups. As Briggs and Wallace (2022) note:

When large sums of money are potentially at stake, it can be difficult to understand exactly who has committed the crime, as other parties might falsely claim involvement to intercept payments. It can also be unclear if those holding hostages are criminals seeking financial gain, terrorists with political demands or some mix of the two. The lines are not always clear.

Hence, it is clear that an adapted character of quiet diplomacy is a better approach for this chapter.

Quiet diplomacy in the literature

Quiet diplomacy is not a new form of diplomatic practice, nor is it unique to the African context. LaBua (2007) investigates the use of quiet diplomacy by the Carter administration with the aim of promoting human rights in Argentina with limited effect. Despite not yielding the desired result, it is noteworthy that the message and tactic remained the same (LaBua, 2007). Thomson (2008) argues that quiet diplomacy proved ineffectual as a means for implementing US foreign policy against apartheid South Africa, which prompted the Reagan administration to call upon the South African government of the day to abandon apartheid policies. Former President Regan became personally involved, conveying the US's disapproval of the apartheid system when he noted in December 1984:

> [T]here are occasions when quiet diplomacy is not enough – when we must remind the leaders of nations who are friendly to the United States that such friendship also carries responsibilities for them, and for us. ... [We] call upon the government of South Africa to reach out to its black majority by ending the forced removals of blacks from their communities and the detention without trial and lengthy imprisonment of black leaders. (Reagan in Thomson, 2008: 139)

Miles (2021) shed more light on the Reagan administration's use of quiet diplomacy by highting how Reagan elected to employ quiet diplomacy as part of his foreign policy doctrine. This doctrine would rest upon two pillars, namely quiet diplomacy and peace through strength. The first pillar viewed quiet diplomacy as a necessary tool to keep cold war tensions at bay through negotiation and the brokering of agreements, thereby allowing the US to maintain its military dominance (Miles, 2021: 67). The second pillar viewed American strength as a means of upholding the agreements that had been secured by means of quiet diplomacy (Miles, 2021: 67).

Jones (2014) illustrates how the consistent use of quiet diplomacy by Oman allowed the sultanate to host Iran and the US for secret talks which helped to lay the foundations for the Joint Comprehensive Plan of Action in November 2013.

Within the African context, the focus of the literature on quiet diplomacy is twofold. First, Okumu (1973) argues that Kenya opted to use quiet diplomacy to safeguard its geography. Okumu's conceptualization of quiet diplomacy notes that a state chooses to use quiet diplomacy when it is unable to posit or defend a foreign policy position owing to its fragile economic position and thus aims to pursue economic and social advancement (Okumu, 1973: 263). Second, and most recently, the quiet diplomacy discourse has been dominated by Thabo Mbeki's policy towards Zimbabwe (Alden, 2002; Adelmann, 2004; Coetzee, 2004; Kagwanja, 2006; Graham, 2006, 2008a, 2008b; Mkhize, 2008; Hamill and Hoffman, 2009; Malimela, 2010; Mhango, 2012; Chidozie et al, 2013; Landsberg, 2016; Southall, 2019; Cotterill, 2020). While other scholars and commentators such as Dlamini (2002) and Louw-Vaudran (2018) investigate the employment of quiet diplomacy in other states including Burundi, the Democratic Republic of Congo, Côte d'Ivoire, Iraq and Madagascar, such occurrences are rare.

Boko Haram and negotiations: a brief overview

While it is beyond the scope of this chapter to provide a detailed history of Boko Haram,[1] it is worth noting that Boko Haram consists of two leading factions, namely Jamā'a Ahl al-sunnah li-da'wa wa al-jihād (JAS) and Islamic State West Africa Province (ISWAP). JAS is an independent jihadist-inspired terrorist group which was until recently under the leadership of Abubakar Shekau. ISWAP is an offshoot or, as its name suggests, a faction of the Islamic State of Iraq and Syria (ISIS). The term 'Boko Haram' is used within this chapter as a generic point of reference. The fundamental difference between these factions, of relevance to this chapter, is the difference in the way they treat women and girls. From the perspective of Shekau's JAS faction, it was perfectly permissible to mistreat female associates[2] of Boko Haram, including deploying them in combat as suicide bombers (Zenn and Pieri, 2017: 299).

Shortly after Boko Haram declared a jihad against the Nigerian government in 2009, negotiations for a ceasefire began. These talks focused on Boko Haram observing a ceasefire in exchange for better treatment of Boko Haram prisoners (Zenn and Fox, 2021). Unfortunately, these negotiations broke down in 2012 due to a government official leaking the proceedings to the media (Zenn and Fox, 2021). In response, Abu Qaqa, an official spokesperson for Shekau and possibly Boko Haram at large, noted: '"We have closed all possible doors of negotiations with a government of unbelievers; we will never listen to any call to lay down our arms"' (Idris, 2012). Since then, Boko Haram has ruled out negotiations with the Nigerian government on eight different occasions (Zenn and Fox, 2021: 168).

Despite its firm stance on non-negotiation, Boko Haram has shown itself willing to engage in single-issue transition negotiations. Examples include the exchange of wives and children of Boko Haram members for those of Nigerian government officials (Mail and Guardian, 2013); the exchange of some of the Chibok girls for Boko Haram prisoners, and for imprisoned Boko Haram members in 2016 and 2017 (details to follow); the release of the majority of the Dapchi School girls in 2018; the release of two hostages thanks to the efforts of an unnamed Nigerian non-governmental organization in 2019 by ISWAP; failed negotiations with ISAWP to secure the release of two aid workers working for the International Committee of the Red Cross (ICRC) and one working for the United Nations Children's Emergency Fund (UNICEF), all kidnapped in 2018. The former two hostages were executed by ISWAP while the latter was enslaved by the group (Zenn and Fox, 2021: 170). In September 2019 four aid workers from Action Against Hunger were killed and in July 2020 ISWAP killed another four unnamed aid workers after demands for a $500,000 ransom were not met (Zenn and Fox, 2021: 170).

Understanding the Chibok abductions and their aftermath

On 14 April 2014, Boko Haram militants dressed as Nigerian soldiers (Habila, 2016: 106) stormed the government-run Chibok secondary school in Borno State, Nigeria abducting 276 schoolgirls from their dormitories. A week after the Chibok abductions, Obiageli Ezekwesili, a former official of the Nigerian government and then vice president of the African branch of the World Bank, called for the Nigerian government to 'bring back their girls'. This call to action is believed to have set in motion a global outcry against Boko Haram's actions (Berents, 2016: 520). As Sesay (2019: 5) noted: 'their plight [that of the Chibok girls] held the gaze of celebrities worldwide, includ[ing] then first lady Michelle Obama, Angelina Jolie, Beyoncé and Alicia Keys'. This international gaze lit the spark for the conception of the Bring Back Our Girls movement (BBOGM). With its locus in Nigeria, the BBOGM sprouted tentacles that reached countries such as France and the UK in addition to the US (Olutokunbo et al, 2015: 65). By the end of 2014 the phrase had been turned into a social media hashtag that had been tweeted over a million times (Olson, 2016: 773). This ardent and focused attention placed enormous pressure on the Nigerian government to deliver results. In response to the international outcry, Shekau released a video on 21 May 2014 denouncing Christianity and the West as well as all efforts to counter Boko Haram. This was followed by another video release on 1 November 2014 in which Shekau claimed that more than 200 of the Chibok abductees had converted to Islam and those who did not would be treated badly (Kassim, 2018a: 341). Negotiations facilitated by Nigerian civil society actors, the ICRC and the Swiss government helped to secure the release of 21 Chibok girls on 21 October 2016 (Kassim, 2018b: 311). Prior to this, 57 Chibok girls managed to escape. An additional cohort of 28 of the girls were released on 6 May 2017. At the time of writing, 112 Chibok girls are still missing (Kassim, 2018b: 311).

While the emergence of the BBOGM helped to bring attention to an outrageous occurrence, it also helped to turn the Chibok girls into a political brand, which brought Boko Haram considerable local, regional and international attention. This led Boko Haram to develop a keen appreciation for female abductees and participants (Botha, 2019; Pearson and Zenn, 2014). In the months that followed, Zenn (2014: 5) speculated that Boko Haram consisted of various factions and that these factions collaborated on the Chibok abductions. Moreover, given that the treatment of women and girls is a key issue fuelling the factional fire, it has become clear that JAS was responsible for the Chibok abductions. In June 2014, a middle-aged female operative of JAS blew herself up at a security checkpoint in Gombe State, thus becoming the first female suicide bomber in Boko Haram history (Bloom and Matfess, 2016: 105).

While the BBOGM brought with it some positive effects, including drawing the international community's attention to the Boko Haram conflict and its humanitarian consequences, as well as BBOGM founder Oby Ezekwesili attempting to run for the Nigerian presidency in 2019 (Ekott, 2019), it is also worth noting there may have been some negative impacts. For example, the transnational character of the BBOGM has been criticized for lacking impetus due to lack of coordination between the movement's founders in Abuja and international campaigners (Oriola, 2021: 650). It can also be argued that the international hype brought about by the BBOGM gave Boko Haram unintended 'fame', by which it could seek to hold the gaze of the international community. The Dapchi abductions, of an estimated 110 schoolgirls in February 2018, are suggestive of this possibility. Unlike their Chibok counterparts, the Dapchi girls were retuned in March 2021, just over a month after their abduction (Oyweole and Onuoha, 2022: 34, 44). It is worth noting that only 104 of the Dapchi girls were released; some are believed to have died while in captivity (Zenn and Fox, 2021: 170), while one hostage, Leah Sharibu, was not released due to her refusal to convert to Islam (Oyweole and Onuoha, 2022: 44). Factionalism is the causal factor which led to their relatively rapid release. ISWAP facilitated the Dapchi abductions, which caused internal discord as some ISWAP members felt that the actions resembled those of the JAS faction of Boko Haram.

As time has progressed the BBOGM has faded but has not been forgotten. In January 2021 it emerged that an unconfirmed number of Chibok girls had returned from Boko Haram, but these reports were unconfirmed by the Nigerian government (Winsor and Bwala, 2021). In June 2022 it was reported that a further two Chibok girls were released (*Aljazeera*, 2022). With the context provided, the rest of the chapter will now apply the characteristics of quiet diplomacy to the Chibok abductions with the aim of understanding how such diplomacy was used to secure their release. It is imperative to note that these characteristics are not discussed in chronological or systematic order.

Applying the criteria of quiet diplomacy to the Chibok abductions

Personal or direct diplomacy
Prior to the Chibok abductions Swiss diplomat Pascal Holliger was given a mandate by his government to aid the peace-making process vis-á-vis the Boko Haram conflict via the Human Security Division of the Swiss government. As the sole implementer of this mandate, Holliger put together a team of locals to assist him in understanding and navigating the local context. This team consisted of barrister Zannah Mustapha, Tijani Ferobe, Tahir Umar and Fulan.[3] Mustapha was the leading contact and had a vested interest in the conflict resolution process because he ran an orphanage in northern Nigeria for children orphaned by Boko Haram. Ferobe offered extensive information-gathering skills that helped formulate an understanding of Boko Haram's linkages as far afield as Egypt (Parkinson and Hinshaw, 2021: 177). Umar was an ardent follower of Boko Haram's founder, Mohammed Yusuf, but refused to follow the group when Shekau took the helm. Umar was known for getting messages from Boko Haram suspects in the Giwa barracks to their families and vice versa (Parkinson and Hinshaw, 2021: 177). Finally, Fulan operated in multiple settings which gave him an intimate knowledge of militancy. Additionally, he was not afraid to operate behind enemy lines (Parkinson and Hinshaw, 2021: 178). This group became known as the Dialogue Facilitation Team (and with time the Agents of Peace). By 2015 the Agents of Peace realized that the BBOGM had altered the dynamic of the Boko Haram conflict and that any negotiation not featuring the Chibok girls would be futile.

While there is no record of direct contact between Nigeria's top political leaders and the leaders of Boko Haram, it is arguable that consent for the negotiation would need to be given by leaders of both sides for it to happen. For its part, Nigeria, via former president Goodluck Jonathan, stated: '"you have my permission"' and gave the Swiss embassy official clearance to undertake negotiations with Boko Haram to secure the release of the Chibok girls (Parkinson and Hinshaw, 2021: 179). The presidents of Nigeria and Switzerland would meet later during the negotiation process to assess its facilitation (to be returned to under bilateral and multilateral efforts).

Little (or no) media involvement

At the onset of the mapping of negotiation prospects, Holliger wrote in an email to a team member noting that 'everything is being done transparently but quietly away from the fanfare of the other efforts' (Parkinson and Hinshaw, 2021: 177). Given the quiet and confidential nature of these negotiations, the Agents of Peace often held their conversations behind closed doors at the Swiss embassy in Abuja or via encrypted phone apps (Parkinson and Hinshaw, 2021: 179). Despite their best efforts, the names of the Chibok girls were leaked via Twitter shortly after their release; this occurred despite assurances being made to release the names in a controlled and responsible manner (Parkinson and Hinshaw, 2021: 297).

The appearance of limited action or even inaction

The Buhari administration went to great lengths to make it appear as if the government took a one-sided, 'military only' approach to defeating Boko Haram. This became apparent upon his election as president of Nigeria; at this time, Buhari penned an opinion piece for the *New York Times* in which he asserted: 'what I can pledge, with absolute certainly, is that from the first day of my administration, Boko Haram will know the strength of our collective will and commitment to rid the nation of terror' (Buhari, 2015). The use of the word 'strength' demonstrates Buhari's perceived preference for a military response. Furthermore, in January 2016, during a meeting with Chibok parents at the presidential villa, Buhari claimed that the government was yet to choose a credible negotiating proxy (Parkinson and Hinshaw, 2021: 245). However, in September 2016 Nigerian government officials confirmed that three attempts to secure the release of the Chibok girls, in July 2015, November 2016 and December 2016, respectively (Searcey and Stein, 2016), had taken place.

Calm and tactful but persistent negotiation or dialogue

The preceding has illustrated the persistence of the Nigerian government in attempting to secure the release of the Chibok girls. Yet trust between the various parties involved in the negotiation was fragile and required strengthening for any negotiation to succeed. The Agents of Peace spent the greater part of two years building up contacts within Boko Haram aimed at obtaining a better understanding of how the group operated and what the best ports of entry would be. To help build trust with the Nigerian government, the Agents of Peace would not only pass messages from one side to the other, but also refine them before they were seen by the other side. This meant that frank messages from Boko Haram were reworded so as not to offend the government while salutations were often inserted into the messages to Boko Haram from the government to show the appropriate amount of respect to the group's leadership (Parkinson and Hinshaw, 2021: 238). Yet their efforts would almost end up being in vain with the Nigerian airstrikes against Boko Haram in August 2016, as Mustapha received a call from one of his contacts shortly after the airstrikes suggesting that it had killed some of the Chibok girls (Parkinson and Hinshaw, 2021: 259).

Constructive engagement with the target country (or other actors)

While it is essential for a dialogue to be carried out in a non-threatening way, it is also important to illustrate that meaningful change can be achieved (Graham, 2008b: 133). However, the Nigerian context was plagued by intra-governmental rivalry. Nigeria's two intelligence agencies (the Department of the State Services and the Office of the National Security Advisor) had overlapping mandates which led to a constant rivalry, in this case over the release of the Chibok girls. In an attempt to quell the feud, Holliger set up meetings with both the Department of the State Services and the Office of the National Security Advisor encouraging them to put their differences aside and let one department run the Chibok case (Parkinson and Hinshaw, 2021: 238). Unfortunately, Holliger's efforts had minimal impact as many people who met with President Buhari in the wake of this meeting expressed concern that the president was insufficiently briefed on the Boko Haram conflict, which suggested that both agencies were electing to withhold information (Parkinson and Hinshaw, 2021: 238).

To proceed with the negotiation process, the Agents of Peace would either need a direct line to President Buhari or a means to stop the rivalry. The airstrikes (or rather their consequences) would provide a way forward. The airstrikes had reduced Boko Haram's territory, while Shekau was facing internal challenges to his leadership (Parkinson and Hinshaw, 2021: 262, 263).[4] Hence, negotiation and the financial rewards that would follow seemed like a welcome prospect. Shekau reached out to Mustapha via audio message stating: '"if the Zannah I know is the Zannah I am talking to, let him tell me when and where we last met"' (Parkinson and Hinshaw, 2021: 263). Mustapha sent back his reply and Shekau authorized Boko Haram to commence negotiations to facilitate the release of the Chibok girls (Parkinson and Hinshaw, 2021: 263).

Bilateral and multilateral efforts

With both parties now set to strike a deal, the Agents of Peace set to work drafting an agreement that both sides would accept. Unfortunately, the rivalry within the Nigerian state made it difficult for the Agents of Peace to submit a plan to President Buhari for approval (Parkinson and Hinshaw, 2021: 264). Hence, Holliger decided to use his mandate to arrange a one-on-one meeting between President Schneider-Ammann and President Buhari. Both heads of state were due to meet on the sidelines of the 71st United Nations General Assembly Meeting in New York. The primary item on the meeting agenda was to secure the return of Nigerian funds totalling $1 billion which had found their way into Swiss bank accounts during Sani Abacha's rule. The meeting concluded with Switzerland agreeing to return $321 million of the looted funds (Parkinson and Hinshaw, 2021: 267). This success paved the way for Schneider-Ammann to ask for Buhari to approve the deal the Agents of Peace had constructed; Buhari did so.

Third parties to aid logistics

The deal approved by Buhari was to unfold in three phases. Phase 1 would involve the release of a small number of Chibok girls in return for €3 million with no leaks to the press. Provided that the exchange was kept a secret the remaining captives, those not married off to Boko Haram members, would be released along with the exchange of additional ransom funds (Parkinson and Hinshaw, 2021: 268). Phase 2 would involve the ending of airstrikes in exchange for an end to the use of suicide bombers by Boko Haram (Parkinson and Hinshaw, 2021: 268). The final phase of the negotiations would allow for the disarmament, demobilization and reintegration efforts for Boko Haram members and associates wanting to leaving Boko Haram and rejoin society (Parkinson and Hinshaw, 2021: 268). The ICRC, as a neutral international actor, would be responsible for facilitating these exchanges as well as transferring the returned Chibok girls to safety (Tar and Bala, 2022).

Conclusion: lessons learnt and areas of further academic interest

This chapter has sought to apply the typology of quiet diplomacy to the negotiations which led to the release of many of the Chibok girls by using a set of criteria identified by Graham and adapted here. The chapter finds that while the criteria for quiet diplomacy experienced differing degrees of success in their application to the Chibok abductions, all the criteria were met nonetheless. This finding suggests that the negotiations which led to the release of the Chibok girls are a relatively new example of quiet diplomacy on the African continent. In addition, this chapter's case study yields the following lessons, which should be noted for future negotiations and studies pertaining to the terrorism–diplomacy nexus. These lessons are as follows:

- Building trust is a lengthy process which requires extensive knowledge of the local context in which the conflict occurs as well as a neutral actor to liaise between parties.

- Infighting or rivalry between government departments can complicate and, if incorrectly navigated, stall or derail the negotiation process.
- Information pertaining to negotiations was leaked, which could have undermined the trust built between the warring parties. Efforts should be undertaken to tighten the grip on information to ensure that it is not released prematurely. Penalties should also be put in place for those found responsible for the leak, particularly if it originated from within state circles.
- State and non-state actors may need to work in tandem if the terrorism–diplomacy nexus (diplomacy as a means of combatting terrorism) is to succeed.
- Terrorist groups may be more willing to negotiate if, and when, they are most vulnerable. With reference to this chapter's case study, vulnerability occurred when the state actor had a strategic or tactical advantage. Hence, government actors and trust builders should look for such opportunities throughout the negotiation process and should always be open to a negotiated settlement (Nwankpa, 2017).
- States chosen to broker deals on behalf of other state and/or non-state actors must be chosen strategically. With reference to this case study, Switzerland was able to maintain its position as a negotiator due to its holding of funds looted by Sani Abacha, which could be used as a bargaining chip to bolster trust and gain approval for the implementation of a negotiated settlement.
- Negotiators can perform the invaluable task of adapting a negotiator's message to ensure that the receiving party responds favourably to the message.

The Chibok abductions are not the only example of hostages being released by means of negotiation. Hence, future scholarship should seek to study other negotiations involving violent non-state actors on the continent with the aim of identifying points of commonality and discord to determine patterns of behaviour and circumstances which could help inform future theories and practices of negotiation with violent non-state actors.

Notes

[1] Readers wishing to glean a detailed understanding of Boko Haram should refer to Zenn (2020).

[2] The term 'associate(s)' is used as the author acknowledges the fact women do not always join or return to Boko Haram by choice. Their decision may be motivated by grave economic or social circumstances. See Botha (2021) for a more in-depth discussion.

[3] Fulan is the only name provided in the source for this team member. Research suggests that this individual is known by many names due to the various settings they operate in.

[4] In 2015, Shekau pledged allegiance to ISIS, but the pledge was rejected in August 2016 because of Shekau's unilateral and self-centred leadership style.

References

Adelmann, M. (2004) 'Quiet diplomacy: the reasons behind Mbeki's Zimbabwe policy', *Africa Spectrum*, 39(2): 249–76.

Alden, C. (2002) 'South Africa's quiet diplomacy and the crisis in Zimbabwe', *Cadernos de Estudos Africanos*, 2: 1–22.

Aljazeera (2022) 'Two more abducted Chibok girls freed in Nigeria, military says', [online], Available from: www.aljazeera.com/news/2022/6/22/two-kidnapped-chibok-girls-freed-in-nigeria-after-eight-years [Accessed 25 June 2022].

Banim, G. and Pejsova, E. (2017). 'Prevention better than cure: the EU's quiet diplomacy in Asia', *European Union Institute for Security Studies* [onlinc], Available from: www.iss.europa.eu/sites/default/files/EUISSFiles/Report%2033_0.pdf [Accessed 18 December 2022].

Berents, H. (2016) 'Hashtagging girlhood: #IAmMalala, #BringBackOurGirls and gendering representations of global politics', *International Feminist Journal of Politics*, 18(4): 513–27.

Bloom, M. and Matfess, H. (2016) 'Women as symbols and swords in Boko Haram's terror', *Prism*, 6(1): 105–21.

Botha, S. (2019) 'The invisible "gift": the Chibok brand and Boko Haram', *Studia Europaea*, 64(2): 149–69.

Botha, S. (2021) 'The women and girls associated with Boko Haram: how has the Nigerian government responded?', *South African Journal of International Affairs*, 28(2): 263–84.

Briggs, R. and Wallace, J. (2022) '"We do not negotiate with terrorists" – but why?', *Chatham House* [online], 13 January, Available from: www.chathamhouse.org/2022/01/we-do-not-negotiate-terrorists-why [Accessed 7 July 2022].

Buhari, M. (2015) 'Muhammadu Buhari: we will stop Boko Haram', *The New York Times* [online], 14 April, Available from: www.nytimes.com/2015/04/15/opinion/muhammadu-buhari-we-will-stop-boko-haram.html [Accessed 23 June 2022].

Chidozie, F.C., Agbude, G.A. and Oni, S. (2013) 'Nigeria's "megaphone diplomacy" and South Africa's "quiet diplomacy": a tale of two eras', *Covenant University Journal of Politics and International Relations*, 1(2): 235–55.

Coetzee, C. (2004) 'South Africa's foreign policy of quiet diplomacy towards Zimbabwe: constructivism as a framework to highlight the contradictory norms of human rights and African solidarity', Master's thesis, University of Pretoria.

Collins, C. and Packer, J. (2006) *Options and Techniques for Quiet Diplomacy*, Ottawa and Sandöverken: Initiative on Confect Prevention through Quiet Diplomacy and Folke Bernadotte Academy.

Cooper, A.F., Heine, J. and Thakur, R. (2013) 'Introduction: the challenges of 21st-century diplomacy', in A.F. Cooper, J. Heine and R. Thakur (eds) *The Oxford Handbook on Modern Diplomacy*, Oxford: Oxford University Press, pp 1–31.

Cotterill, J. (2020) 'South Africa signals hardening of "quiet diplomacy" with Zimbabwe', *Financial Times*, [online] 23 September, Available from: www.ft.com/content/03528741-c2ab-4734-bf73-de18ae32aa28 [Accessed 23 April 2022].

Dlamini, K. (2002) 'Is quiet diplomacy an effective conflict resolution strategy?' South *African Yearbook of International Affairs*, 3: 171–7.

Ekott, I. (2019) 'Facing down the political establishment', *African in Fact*, 48: 100–105.

Gilbert, D. and Piché, G.R. (2021) 'Caught between giants: hostage diplomacy and negotiation strategy for middle powers', *Texas National Security Review*, 5(1): 12–32.

Graham, V. (2006) 'How firm the handshake? South Africa's use of quiet diplomacy in Zimbabwe from 1999 to 2006', *African Security Review*, 15(4): 113–27.

Graham, V. (2008a) 'A comparison of South Africa's quiet diplomacy towards Nigeria and Zimbabwe's crisis', Master's thesis, University of Johannesburg.

Graham, V. (2008b) 'Deconstructing quiet diplomacy: pinning down the elusive concept', *Journal for Contemporary History*, 33(2): 117–35.

Habila, H. (2016) *The Chibok Girls*, London: Penguin Books.

Hamill, J. and Hoffman, J. (2009) '"Quiet diplomacy" or appeasement? South African policy towards Zimbabwe', *The Round Table*, 98(402): 373–84.

Idris, H. (2012) 'Boko Haram says no more talks with FG', *Daily Trust*, [online], 21 March, Available from: https://allafrica.com/stories/201203210120.html [Accessed 12 February 2022].

Jones, J. (2014) 'Oman's quiet diplomacy', Norwegian Institute of International Affairs [online], Available from: www.nupi.no/en/Publications/CRIStin-Pub/Oman-s-Quiet-Diplomacy [Accessed 12 December 2021].

Kagwanja, P. (2006) 'South Africa: breathing life into "quiet diplomacy"', Electronic briefing paper [online], Available from: https://repository.hsrc.ac.za/handle/20.500.11910/6347 [Accessed 22 February 2022].

Kassim, A. (2018a) 'Shekau speaks on cease-fire and the Chibok girls', in A. Kassim and M. Nwankpa (eds) *The Boko Haram Reader: From Nigerian Preachers to the Islamic State*, Oxford: Oxford University Press, pp 339–42.

Kassim, A. (2018b) 'Message about the Chibok girls' in A. Kassim and M. Nwankpa (eds) *The Boko Haram Reader: From Nigerian Preachers to the Islamic State*, Oxford: Oxford University Press, pp 311–17.

LaBua, J. (2007) 'Outside the public eye: how the Carter administration used "quiet diplomacy" to impact human rights in Argentina', *Iowa Historical Review*, 1(1): 131–39.

Landsberg, C. (2016) 'African solutions for African problems: quiet diplomacy and South Africa's diplomatic strategy towards Zimbabwe', *Journal for Contemporary History*, 41(1): 126–48.

Louw-Vaudran, L. (2018) 'Ramaphosa's quiet diplomacy in Madagascar', *ISS Today* [online], 27 July, Available from: https://issafrica.org/iss-today/ramaphosas-quiet-diplomacy-in-madagascar [Accessed 4 July 2022].

Mail and Guardian (2013) 'New Boko Haram video claims attacks, shows hostages' [online], 13 May, Available from: https://mg.co.za/article/2013-05-13-new-boko-haram-video-claims-attack-shows-hostages/ [Accessed 12 February 2022].

Malimela, L.P. (2010) 'Analyzing Thabo Mbeki's policy of "quiet diplomacy" in the Zimbabwean crisis', Master's thesis, University of Cape Town.

Mhango, G.A. (2012) 'Is quiet diplomacy in consonance with meaningful peacemaking in SADC? Lessons from Zimbabwe', *Southern African Peace and Security Studies*, 1(1): 14–25.

Miles, S. (2021). 'Peace through strength and quiet diplomacy: grand strategy lessons from the Reagan administration', in N.P. Monteiro and F. Bartel (eds) *Before and after the Fall: World Politics and the End of the Cold War*, Cambridge: Cambridge University Press, pp 62–77.

Mkhize, M.C. (2008) 'Assessing South Africa's "quiet diplomacy" towards Zimbabwe: strengths and weaknesses', Master's thesis, University of KwaZulu Natal.

Nwankpa, M. (2017) 'Dialoguing and negotiating with terrorists: any prospect for Boko Haram?', *Behavioural Sciences of Terrorism and Political Aggression*, 9(2): 106–24.

Okumu, J.J. (1973) 'Some thoughts on Kenya's foreign policy', *African Review: A Journal of African Politics, Development, and International Affairs*, 3(2): 263–90.

Olson, C.C. (2016) '#BringBackOurGirls: digital communities supporting real-world change and influencing mainstream media agendas', *Feminist Media Studies*, 16(5): 772–87.

Olutokunbo, A.S., Suandi, T., Cephas, O.R. and Abu-Samah, I. (2015) 'Bring back our girls, social mobilization: implications for cross-cultural research', *Journal of Education and Practice*, 6(6): 1–13.

Oriola, T.B. (2021) 'Framing and movement outcomes: the #BringBackOurGirls movement', *Third World Quarterly*, 42(4): 641–60.

Oyewole, S. and Onuoha, F.C. (2022) 'Boko Haram's abduction of Dapachi schoolgirls and the state response', in T.B. Oriola, F.C. Onuoha and S. Oyewole (eds) *Boko Haram's Terrorist Campaign in Nigeria: Contexts, Dimensions and Emerging Trajectories*, London: Routledge, pp 32–51.

Parkinson, J. and Hinshaw, D. (2021) *Bring Back Our Girls: The Untold Story of the Global Search for Nigeria's Missing Schoolgirls*, New York: Harper Collins.

Pearson, E. and Zenn, J. (2014) 'Women, gender and the evolving tactics of Boko Haram', *Journal of Terrorism Research*, 5(1): 46–57.

Roberts, W.R. (2006) 'The evolution of diplomacy', *Mediterranean Quarterly*, 17(3): 55–64.

Searcey, D. and Stein, C. (2016) 'Nigeran describes 3 failed negotiations with Boko Haram on kidnapped girls', *The New York Times* [online], 17 September 2016, Available from www.nytimes.com/2016/09/17/world/africa/nigeria-boko-haram-chibok.html [Accessed 23 June 2022].

Sending, J., Pouliot, V. and Neumann, I.B. (2011) 'The future of diplomacy: changing practices, evolving relationships', *International Journal*, 66(3): 527–42.

Sesay, I. (2019) *Beneath the Tamarind Tree: A Story of Courage, Family, and the Lost Schoolgirls of Boko Haram*, New York: Harper Collins.

Southall, R. (2019) 'South African diplomacy on Zimbabwe can remain quiet – but it must get tough', *The Conversation* [online], 27 January, Available from: https://theconversation.com/south-african-diplomacy-on-zimbabwe-can-remain-quiet-but-it-must-get-tough-110578 [Accessed 23 April 2022].

Tar, U.A. and Bala, B. (2022) 'Mapping international support for the fight against Boko Haram', in T.B. Oriola, F.C. Onuoha and S. Oyewole (eds) *Boko Haram's Terrorist Campaign in Nigeria: Contexts, Dimensions and Emerging Trajectories*, London: Routledge, pp 215–31.

Thomson, A. (2008) *U.S. Foreign Policy towards Apartheid South Africa, 1948–1994*, New York: Palgrave McMillian.

Winsor, M. and Bwala, J. (2021) 'More Chibok girls have escaped from Boko Haram almost 7 years later, parents say', *ABC News*, [online] 29 January, Available from: https://abcnews.go.com/International/chibok-girls-escaped-boko-haram-years-parents/story?id=75560018 [Accessed 20 January 2022].

Zenn, J. (2014) 'Boko Haram and the kidnapping of the Chibok schoolgirls', *Counter Terrorism Centre Sentential*, 7(5): 1–7.

Zenn, J. (2020) *Unmasking Boko Haram: Exploring Global Jihad in Nigeria*, London: Lynne Rienner.

Zenn, J. and Fox, M.J. (2021) 'Negotiating with Boko Haram? Examining the jihadist exception', *African Conflict and Peacebuilding Review*, 10(2): 158–83.

Zenn, J. and Pieri, C. (2017) 'How much Takfir is too much Takfir? The evolution of Boko Haram's fictionalization', *Journal for Deradicalization*, No. 11.

9

A Diplomatic Conduit: The Role of Science Diplomacy in Africa

Lesley Masters

Introduction

Advancements in science, technology and innovation (STI) saw significant development in countries at the centre of the first industrial revolution of the 18th century. This transformed national social, political and economic environments, but also led to a widening gap between developed and developing countries in the structure of the world system. Those countries on the margins of the industrial revolution continue to find themselves relegated to the periphery in the global structure. Yet in a world where the challenges facing humanity are transnational, all countries, as well as the growing networks of non-state actors, play a role in their resolution. In the 21st century, efforts to address concerns such as climate change, the global COVID-19 pandemic and cyber security need a global partnership. This is a point advanced by the United Nations (UN) Sustainable Development Goal (SDG) 17. The challenge is the gap in access and capacity in STI has driven both cooperation and competition as countries, intergovernmental organizations and non-state actors seek to ensure a voice in decision making.

Communication, negotiation and representation are central to the practice of diplomacy and integral in facilitating global engagement and cooperation (Bjola and Kornprobst, 2013). With the gap between STI 'haves' and 'have nots' growing, the role of 'diplomacy for science', 'science for diplomacy' and 'science in diplomacy' as a means of creating global partnerships is coming to the fore (AAAS/RS, 2010; Rao, 2018; Turekian, 2018; Jacobsen and Olšáková, 2020). Technological advances frequently move faster than politics. For example, progress in artificial intelligence has far outpaced the debates around its governance, accessibility, impact on economies, or international security. On other issues, such as the climate change negotiations, science has provided the foundation for what needs to be achieved in terms of emission reductions, but it is the politics that frequently presents an obstacle to reaching a comprehensive and binding agreement. In the case of the global outbreak of the COVID-19 pandemic in 2019, the delays in coordinated action, vaccine nationalization and the global inequality in access to life-saving medicines patently points to the need for greater engagement in science diplomacy in facilitating cooperation. The value of science diplomacy is that it highlights both the political and scientific pillars of diplomatic engagement.

While the understanding of science diplomacy continues to evolve, its application in statecraft needs further analysis. The political nature of science diplomacy means that it is more than activities of scientific cooperation, where cooperation itself can create 'winners' and 'losers' in the race to address global challenges leading to further structural divisions. In the main, the literature uncritically claims science diplomacy as a panacea for building mutually positive relations between parties; yet, given the global international structure, this is often a one-sided affair dominated by those with a developed capacity in science diplomacy. This exploratory study begins by addressing the concept of science diplomacy, its political purpose and its place as a tool in the diplomatic toolbox. The chapter then considers the role of science diplomacy in the African context and in facilitating communication, negotiation and representation. This aims to move discussions away from addressing the meaning of the concept of science diplomacy to considering questions of capacity, application and its role in practice.

Developments in science diplomacy: where is Africa?

Addressing Africa's peripheral position in the global knowledge structure requires effective science diplomacy (Masters, 2021), yet there is little discussion from Africa, and with Africa, on the concept's meaning and its development. What science diplomacy is, or perhaps more importantly how is it understood, has been the focus of discussion from the late 2000s. This includes a burgeoning literature considering science diplomacy's historical development (Turekian, 2018; Adamson and Lalli, 2021: 1), regional and country application (Rüffin, 2020), and issue-specific analysis – for example on science diplomacy and climate change, the oceans and the role of women in science diplomacy (Doğan et al, 2021).

Discussions on science diplomacy frequently refer to the conceptual understanding espoused in 2010 by the American Association for the Advancement of Science (AAAS)/Royal Society, based in the US and the UK respectively. This includes science diplomacy as 'informing foreign policy objectives with scientific advice (science in diplomacy); facilitating international science cooperation (diplomacy for science); using science cooperation to improve international relations between countries (science for diplomacy)' (AAAS/RS, 2010: v–vi). While this does provide a framework for defining science diplomacy, it has also been critiqued for missing the idea of 'diplomacy in science', as well as failing to account for the multifunctional nature of science diplomacy and the structural nature and impact of knowledge (Adamson and Lalli, 2021). In other words, science diplomacy is frequently understood through a developed-country perspective. This is a point highlighted by Doğan et al (2021) in their discussion of the liberal and realist understanding of science diplomacy, along with the study by Adamson and Lalli (2021: 3), who point to the 'great weight the Anglo-Saxon view has had up to this point in determining how we study science diplomacy'. This certainly calls for the further interrogation of science diplomacy from alternative perspectives.

It is not just the concept of science diplomacy that has an Anglo-Saxon flavour, but its practice. Given the geographical position of the industrial revolution, it is perhaps unsurprising that one of the earliest records of a diplomatic engagement on science is from the 19th century, when the US sent a science attaché to Germany (Linkov et al, 2014). What distinguishes science diplomacy from scientific cooperation is its political considerations, reflecting the interests and priorities of countries (Jacobson and Olšáková, 2020: 471; Doğan et al, 2020: 33). This political consideration was evident in the cold war, when science diplomacy was seen as a means for advancing cooperation in promoting countries' national interests on questions of security and development. One of the significant scientific projects that took place during this period was the 1957–58 International Geophysical Year (IGY), which saw cooperation across 67 states to demonstrate that 'scientific cooperation could transcend political tensions and national boundaries' (Committee for Survey and Analysis of Science Advice on Sustainable Development to International Organizations, 2002: 5). This was hailed as a period of 'highly effective use of science diplomacy to build bridges and connection despite the existence of great political tensions' (Turekian and Neureiter, 2012: 26). While science diplomacy was gaining ground through these interactions, not all nations were able to participate, and not all participated equally given that many of the countries from Africa were newly independent or yet to decolonize. This was a point made evident in the signing of the Antarctic Treaty of 1959, where just 12 countries participated (Van Langenhove, 2019: 18), the only African country present was South Africa, then led by the apartheid National Party.

Science diplomacy as a conduit for communication and cooperation has continued as a means of engagement for developed countries. For instance, the US continues to engage in science diplomacy with countries with which it has strained or significantly reduced relations such as North Korea, Iran, Syria and Cuba (Committee on Global Science Policy and Science

Diplomacy Development, Security and Cooperation, 2012: 30). This has seen the AAAS playing a role in coordinating trips abroad, while funding has been provided by institutions such as the John D. and Catherine T. MacArther Foundation and the Richard Lounsbery Foundation for cooperation in STI (Kramer, 2010b: 28). Within the US State Department there has been the inclusion of a science and technology advisor along with science fellowship programmes which see leading scientists and engineers drawing on their networks in addressing transnational challenges such as climate change and nuclear security (Flink and Schreiterer, 2010: 666; Turekian, 2018: 7). Other examples from developed countries include the UK, which from 2000 set up the Agenda for Global Change, including the creation of science and innovation networks aimed at expanding and replacing the foreign ministry's science counsellor networks. Japan, too, has been at the forefront of using science diplomacy, which it has patently linked to the idea of soft power in its foreign policy. This is evident in the 2008 memorandum issued by the Council for Science and Technology Policy, 'Towards the Reinforcement of Science and Technology Diplomacy', providing a larger role for STI in the country's international relations (Flink and Schreiterer, 2010: 666).

The question of where Africa is in the development of science diplomacy can be answered by looking at developments in the international structure and the impact of colonialism. While the geopolitical North was advancing through STI, Africa has been a target of scientific enquiry since the 1800s. The continent was perceived as primitive, a place in need of civilizing and building a scientific understanding, becoming the focus of scientific expeditions by those in search of resources that would ultimately support the colonial system (Keay, 1976; Gamito-Marques, 2020). As such, STI played a part in shaping the international structure today. This is a point highlighted by Hecht (2012: ix), who points to Africa's marginal position in the global uranium trade, where it is 'clear that colonialism remain[s] central to the nuclear order's technological and geo-political success'.

While research has expanded in countries such as the US and Japan, and across Europe, the increasing presence of emerging states in the field of STI, such as China, South Korea and India, have seen an increase in the proportion of research generated outside of these traditional sites of STI development. With the need for collaboration in addressing truly global challenges, scientists are looking towards engaging developing countries. This has seen a growth in research centres outside the geopolitical North, where knowledge is being developed through collaborative agreements as countries look to address the need for the creation of an 'internationally knowledgeable workforce' (Linkov et al, 2014). Yet work in STI development has also seen tensions arise between countries. Maher and Van Noorden (2021: 317) argued that while the COVID-19 pandemic intensified the focus on science and international collaboration, it also saw heightened tensions between states, particularly the US and China. This signals the need for further discussions on the role of science diplomacy as well as the capacity of African countries to engage in science diplomacy in addressing access and engagement in international STI relations.

Science diplomacy for Africa and by Africa

With STI linked to progress and development, countries are increasingly giving emphasis to research at both a national and global level of decision making (Van Langenhove, 2019). The level of emphasis is not, however, the same across countries and regions and in all global governance forums. This has direct implications for Africa, where capacity for developments in STI has been limited. This includes the ability of countries to invest in research and development, skills shortages including the low number of researchers per capita, lack of infrastructure and the costs associated with STI cooperation (Fellesson and Mählck, 2017; Pathways to Prosperity Commission, 2019; Ndung'u and Signé, 2020, UNGA, 2021). Given the limited ability to engage in research and development it is unsurprising that there has been limited discourse on science diplomacy emerging from Africa. Where there is analysis, this has been focused on the potential of science diplomacy rather than considerations of its role and implementation in practice (Toure, 2018; Ezekiel, 2020; Sharma et al, 2022). It has missed the question of how science diplomacy shapes international engagement and how this is applied in practice by countries for Africa and by Africa.

Science diplomacy: communication and cooperation

Communication and cooperation are central to the definitions of science diplomacy as a means of promoting engagement and collaboration. Hence Fedoroff's (2009: 9) understanding of science diplomacy as 'the use of scientific collaborations among nations to address the common problems facing 21st century humanity and to build constructive international partnerships'. Here, the role of formal diplomatic channels is highlighted, yet science diplomacy also encourages relations through informal networks and across STI communities (Track II diplomacy). The importance of communication and cooperation in science diplomacy is also a point addressed by Flink and Schreiterer (2010: 666), who argue that the purpose of science diplomacy is 'for the enhancement of scientific research and innovation capacities by way of international collaboration with mutual benefits'. Communication and cooperation aim to achieve the goals of science diplomacy, which include access (to researchers, research findings, facilities, natural resources and capital), promotion (of research and development achievements, also to attract best students, researchers and companies) and influence (other countries' public opinion, decision makers and political or economic leaders) (Flink and Schreiterer, 2010: 666).

In the African context, these principles have underpinned the rationale for engagement where relations have been strained. For example, some (but certainly not all) took the decision to continue engaging with apartheid South Africa in scientific collaboration despite the country's growing international isolation. The International Union of Pure and Applied Physics argued that this was a means to enhance understanding between people (Chetty, 2022).

With South Africa's democratic transition in 1994 the country expanded its own focus on science diplomacy as a means of enhancing cooperation and communication, particularly with countries within the Southern African region (Masters, 2016). This includes the Southern African Regional Science Initiative (SAFARI 2000) project, which brought together countries across Southern Africa and the US in exploring the emission, transport and deposition of aerosols and trace gasses within the region (Swap et al, 2002). Initiatives such as the Square Kilometre Array (SKA) radio telescope have also been viewed as a means of facilitating cooperation between countries in the region and internationally. Nevertheless, competition to access the radio telescope resources has been fierce, and by 2014 only 58 out of the 500 radio astronomers who were allocated time were from Africa, with a waiting list of up to five years (DST, 2014).

The literature concerning science diplomacy and Africa provides examples of engagement and the need for cooperation on STI for development, but there is little discussion on the development and conduct of science diplomacy for Africa and by Africa. Moctar Toure (2018: 1–2), former vice president of the World Academy of Sciences and former fellow of the African Academy of Sciences, acknowledges that transnational cooperation constitutes 'the most rational way to develop adequate solutions to the increasing acute and complex challenges facing the continent'. This is a point mirrored by the African Union (AU), and its predecessor the Organization of African Unity (OAU), which urges member states to work together on STI in support of the continent's development. This includes the creation of a Conference of Ministers in charge of science and technology (AMCOST) to support political collaboration and enable a collective voice on STI from the continent (AU, 2014: 14). By 2015 this was replaced by the Specialized Technical Committee Meeting on Education, Science and Technology (STC-EST), which has met at the level of minister in three ordinary sessions, with an extraordinary meeting called on 30 April 2020 (Addis Abba) to address the spread of the COVID-19 pandemic and to reiterate the role of science, technology and innovation in addressing the pandemic and continental development needs (AU, 2020). The STC-EST has also been part of an AU–European Union (EU) high-level policy dialogue for

STI, concluding the seventh plenary meeting in January 2022. The focus of the meeting was on addressing potential cooperation on a joint EU–AU innovation agenda (EU, 2022).

Yet the value of science diplomacy in supporting communication and cooperation between member states, and between an organization and its external milieu, is an area in need of further discussion. Initiatives like SAFARI, SKA and STC-EST are designed to promote cooperation, but do not always address the politics (priorities and interests), which undermines the sustainability of these projects. For instance, in the case of cyber security, while there was initial movement on creating a continental agreement (negotiated in 2015), as of April 2023 only 14 states had ratified the convention, leaving it one short of being adopted (AU, 2023). Egypt, Kenya, South Africa and Nigeria have failed to sign or ratify the agreement, leaving out some of Africa's leading states in cyber development (Fidler, 2016; AU, 2023).

In the case of COVID-19, which became the focus of the STC-EST and cooperation between Centres for Disease Control (CDC) across Africa, the division between the politics and the scientists limited cooperation where borders, and increasing national priorities, undermined engagement. As a researcher from Ghana pointed out, the continent had a shortfall in accessing reagent components, which meant reliance on resources from Europe, calling for 'African governments … to build scientific capacity sustainably rather than resorting to firefighting only when a pandemic hits. We should be preparing for the next pandemic as soon as this one ends' (Awandare, 2020: 586). In the case of COVID-19, the lack of communication and cooperation was extended to other regions of the world, where scientists in Europe too pointed to their ill-preparedness as well as lack of protective equipment, scarcity of doctors, nurses and technicians, and a political system that was not able to effectively manage the crisis (André, 2020: 586–7). These failings have demonstrated a necessary role for science diplomacy between countries in navigating the challenges of national priorities and interests. Addressing these shortfalls has seen, for example, the creation of a consortium of national academies of science from across Sub-Saharan Africa in addressing the impact of COVID-19, working with funding institutions from Canada, Sweden, the UK and the US (Kalele and Maphosa, 2021).[1] Nevertheless, these activities require the capacity to engage with research organizations across the region as well as ensuring that African interests are served in partnership and collaborative initiative with institutions from the Global North.

Science diplomacy: negotiation and representation

Science diplomacy aims to build channels of communication and facilitate cooperation, but as a political activity it is also about navigating priorities and interests of competing stakeholders when it comes to the governance of, and access to, STIs (Committee on Global Science Policy and Science Diplomacy Development, Security and Cooperation, 2012). Developing countries are confronted by inequality in addressing access to resources, research capacity and representation within STI negotiation forums. As has become evident, STI itself can act as a barrier to cooperation. For example, Hornsby and Parshotam (2018) point out that the science of developed countries has shaped the food trade standards, which in turn impede developing country agricultural exports to these countries. In other words, in addition to supporting cooperation and collaboration, science diplomacy plays a part in negotiating international structural inequalities while addressing country interests and priorities across bilateral and multilateral platforms (Doğan et al, 2021). This highlights the point that science diplomacy is for a political purpose, giving effect to foreign policy, creating advantage through expanding knowledge bases, presenting a means to manage conflict, as well as supporting capacity building and development commitments (Jacobson and Olšáková, 2020: 465–6). Science diplomacy is, at its core, diplomacy. Indeed, while the science may be perceived as rational, value neutral and universal (Adamson and Lalli, 2021), international politics has meant those engaged in science diplomacy face an environment where countries with a relative comparative advantage in STI may not want to engage in discussions on regulatory or governance system that may disrupt the current status quo (Seth, 2019: 4–5).

The politicization of science and the use of science diplomacy is evident within international forums. Developed countries such as the US have looked to take advantage of science diplomacy, with budgets allocated and priority given to STI research and development. As Alex Dehgan (in Kramer, 2010a: 30), science and technology advisor at the United States Agency for International Development, notes:

> many of the challenges for our foreign service officers around the world are going to be found in science and technology. There are going to be issues, like depletion of fisheries, global climate change, and how we manage energy, that are going to require a diplomatic corps that is much savvier about science and technology.

During the Obama administration (2009–17), science diplomacy played an active role in US foreign policy. The administration committed the US to 'open centres of scientific excellence in Africa, the Middle East and Southeast Asia, and appoint new science envoys to collaborate on programs that develop new sources of energy, create green jobs, digitize records, clean water, and grow new crops' (Turekian and Neureiter, 2012: 28). The EU too is, since February 2022, negotiating expanding scientific cooperation, including a focus on Africa through EU–Africa cooperation on research and innovation. Here there is evidence of an emerging role for science diplomacy by representatives from the African continent. This was apparent in the input from Africa's participants, who were openly critical of past engagement, noting that Europe should be supporting the levelling up of Africa's STI, with researchers offered the same opportunities in both Africa and Europe. It was also proposed that a database of African research be created to enhance visibility of contributions coming from the continent (Collins, 2022).

The preponderance of science on the international agenda for developed countries was also evident in the 2021 G7 summit hosted in Cornwall (UK). Here agreement was reached on a research compact with a focus on science and research collaboration in addressing global challenges (G7, 2021). Within the research compact, G7 countries committed to using their positions as 'leading science nations', ensuring transparency, integrity and the free flow of data in advancing innovation and knowledge, but with the proviso that the intellectual property and the security of the 'research ecosystem' is protected (G7, 2021). These discussions, however, serve to showcase the challenges of inequality and access for developing countries in negotiating STI, with only India and South Africa present as observers to the meeting.

While Africa may be looking to include science diplomacy within the diplomatic toolbox, the ability to adopt this approach in their statecraft is often lacking. As the AU (2014: 18) points out, this then only serves to increase inequality within relations:

> Bilateral and multilateral partnerships have shaped STI development in Africa (e.g. the European Union–Africa Joint Strategy, the India–Africa Science and Technology Initiatives and the China–Africa Science and Technology Partnership). However, most of these interventions and cooperation mechanisms are not adequately designed to promote African ownership, accountability and sustainability.

Negotiations, starting from the 1960s, presented STI as a solution to Africa's development; here Africa was the subject of science diplomacy. As African countries achieved their independence, the scope to address this position remained limited as the existing framework of negotiations discounted the local applicability of technology resources, social impact and economic costs, with many of Africa's countries unable to meet what was agreed on paper. The resulting disillusionment meant that later conferences saw a growing suspicion of Western approaches to technological development (Gaillard, 1992: 212–33).

With capacity limited in science and in the development of science diplomacy, when it comes to negotiation and representation Africa is playing catch-up. Representation is not always guaranteed in the world of science, where those without resources are often not included, and where access to STI knowledge can be 'wielded as an economic and cultural instrument as countries and institutions assert epistemic hegemony' (Adamson and Lalli, 2021: 7). The impact of colonization and underdevelopment have left Africa on the periphery of international negotiations when it comes to STI, where post-colonial countries continue to face low levels of STI productivity and deteriorating conditions in which research is carried out (Gaillard, 1992: 213). The challenge is that African countries are confronted by the realities of poverty, inadequate infrastructure, limited finance and lack of government support. This limits a county's options to engage in science diplomacy as most have only weak capacity for research and policy activities. There is also evidence that the foreign services of many African countries are not well prepared, or aware of the challenging tasks encompassing science diplomacy (Flink and Schreiterer, 2010).

Building capacity in science diplomacy in Africa is further hampered by an environment where there are increased restrictions on the mobility of researchers, weak public–private partnerships, shortfalls in communication between research agencies (in South–South as well as North–South cooperation), no incentives, lack of human capital and resources, divisions within research communities and failure of governments to follow up on their negotiated commitments (Committee on Global Science Policy and Science Diplomacy Development, Security and Cooperation, 2012). As scientists have pointed out when it comes to engagement, 'The drivers and the rewards for team science just really aren't there, yet' (Trudie Lang in Maher and Van Noorden, 2021: 317).

Science may provide answers, but politics can undermine solutions. This is evident in the case of the continued disagreement between the riparian states of the river Nile. While scientific evidence has been used to support an agreement in the dispute between Sudan and Egypt against Ethiopia, political interests have prevailed as Ethiopia continues to fill its Grand Renaissance Dam, citing its importance for water conservation and hydroelectricity to the country and region (UNSC, 2021). Science on its own does not drive agreement without the inclusion of diplomacy. In the context of the dispute on the waters of the Nile, there is an opportunity for the riparian states to employ science diplomacy, yet despite the potential this has not been pursued as an approach to negotiation. This points to a division between rhetoric and practice when it comes to the role of STI and science diplomacy. Science diplomacy is promoted as a means of furthering relations, yet it has not been considered in practice as an avenue for building cooperation.

There are long-standing policy developments within the AU aimed at addressing the role of STI in shaping inter- and intra-continental relations. This includes policy development on digital strategies, the creation of technology hubs, ICT strategies, a convention on cyber security and the protection of personal data (Masters, 2021). The Science, Technology and Innovation Strategy for Africa 2024 acknowledges the need for increased attention to STI, built on networks across the continent's research communities and those within the diaspora (AU, 2014: 9). In practice the African Academic of Sciences (AAS) has played a central role in supporting networks across the continent, particularly in the context of the COVID-19 pandemic. For instance, in February 2020, the AAS participated in the global World Health Organization (WHO)/Global Research Collaboration for Infectious Disease Preparedness and Response Forum (Kalele and Maphosa, 2021). In March 2020, the AAS went on to host a continent-wide webinar, including 250 scientists from Africa, on developing the continent's response to the pandemic, although it became evident that those engaged in STI research were not prepared or supported in managing the international politics in responding to the global pandemic.

There is a gap between policy and capacity in driving an African approach to science diplomacy. This is evident in the limited support African science academies receive from governments. Only half of the countries across Africa have national academies of science, and for those that do, rather than acting as a platform in promoting science diplomacy the science academies are mostly not functional or are even non-existent, undertaking ad hoc work (through lack of funding) rather than building sustained relations (Kalele and Maphosa, 2021). In fact, capacity constraints mean that Africa has few possibilities to participate in STI talks, unless developed countries focus on supplying technology to Africa, leaving Africans as consumers of knowledge (Masters, 2016). For example, while the continent is a major source of uranium for use in nuclear technology, there is a void in the conversation about Africa's role in shaping international nuclear governance. As Hecht (2012) points out, Africa is on the periphery of transnational technological systems, and those involved in mining have few options for challenging huge international mining companies' bad safety policies. While African countries may host the SKA radio telescope, it is primarily used by industrialized countries. On the question of STI and space, Asiyanbola and colleagues (2021: 55) argue for the importance of developments in space technology for managing water, infrastructure development, climate change, creating effective land policies and managing disasters but highlight Africa's lack of innovation, which 'translates to [Africa] buying satellites, lack of continuous funding, under-representation in international space forums and absence from the space sector'.

Conclusion

Science diplomacy as an emerging field of study and research has seen growth in its role and application in international relations. This is led by the developed countries, whose capacity and interests have seen states such as the US, Japan and those from across Europe building expertise within foreign ministries as well as providing financial and governmental support to institutions engaged in building collaborative international networks. Africa has been on the periphery of these developments given the context of colonial and continued underdevelopment. As such, discussions on science diplomacy have seen Africa as a theatre of discussion rather than as an active participant.

On paper and in the political rhetoric, the AU, a regional organization, and member countries give considered attention to the value of STI in promoting development, yet in practice there is little investment in the practice of science diplomacy. Given the impact of STI on society and its role in addressing global challenges, this is a discussion that the continent can ill afford to miss. Yet the biggest drawback to an emerging science diplomacy for and by Africa is that many of the AU's member countries lack the scientific communities and capacity within foreign ministries to bring together STI and diplomacy in practice. There is evidence of its embryonic role in projects among Africa's more developed countries, including examples such as the SKA, and cooperation between academies in support of efforts to address the COVID-19 pandemic, but this strategy must evolve beyond cooperation to include the development of science diplomacy to effectively navigate international relations.

Note

[1] According to Kalele and Maphosa (2021) this included the Botswana Academy of Sciences, Kingdom of Eswatini Academy of Sciences, Mauritius Academy of Science and Technology, Zambia Academy of Sciences, Zimbabwe Academy of Sciences, South Africa Young Academy of Science, Zimbabwe Young Academy of Science, Mauritius Young Academy of Science, and the Democratic Republic of Congo Young Academy of Science.

References

AAAS/RS (American Association for the Advancement of Science/Royal Society) (2010) *New Frontiers in Science Diplomacy: Navigating the Changing Balance of Power*, Royal Society Policy document 01/10 [online], 12 January, Available from: https://royalsociety.org/topics-policy/publications/2010/new-frontiers-science-diplomacy/ [Accessed 7 July 2022].

Adamson, M. and Lalli, R. (2021) 'Global perspectives on science diplomacy: exploring the diplomacy–knowledge nexus in contemporary histories of science', *Centaurus*, 63(1): 1–16.

André, E. (2020) 'Science advisers from around the world on 2020', *Nature*, 588: 24–31 [online], December, Available from: https://media.nature.com/original/magazine-assets/d41586-020-03557-x/d41586-020-03557-x.pdf [Accessed 15 October 2021].

Asiyanbola, O.A., Ogunsina, M.A., Akinwale, A.T. and Odey, J.B. (2021) 'Towards African space autonomy: developmental framework and incorporated synergies', *New Space*, 9(1): 49–62.

AU (African Union) (2014) *Science, Technology and Innovation Strategy for Africa 2024*, African Union Commission [online], Available from: https://au.int/documents/20200625/science-technology-and-innovation-strategy-africa-2024 [Accessed 28 November 2023].

AU (African Union) (2020) *Communique of the Bureau of the Specialised Technical Committee Meeting on Education, Science and Technology of the African Union* [online], 9 April, Available from: https://au.int/en/pressreleases/20200409/communique-bureau-specialized-technical-committee-education-science-and [Accessed 28 November 2023].

AU (African Union) (2023) *List of Countries Which Have Signed, Ratified/Acceded to the African Union Convention on Cyber Security and Personal Data Protection* [online], 11 April, Available from: https://au.int/sites/default/files/treaties/29560-sl-AFRICAN_UNION_CONVENTION_ON_CYBER_SECURITY_AND_PERSONAL_DATA_PROTECTION.pdf [Accessed 28 November 2023].

Awandare, G. (2020) 'Science advisers from around the world on 2020', *Nature*, 588: 24–31 [online], December, Available from: https://media.nature.com/original/magazine-assets/d41586-020-03557-x/d41586-020-03557-x.pdf [Accessed 15 October 2021].

Bjola, C. and Kornprobst, M. (2013) *Understanding International Diplomacy: Theory, Practice and Ethics*, London: Routledge.

Chetty, N. (2022) 'Scientific diplomacy and cooperation in this time of war', *University World News* [online], 10 March, Available from: www.universityworldnews.com/post.php?story=20220309104524206 [Accessed 29 June 2022].

Collins, C. (2022) 'Conference report: Africa's research system must be strengthened and driven by opportunity, not aid', *ScienceBusiness* [online], 28 April, Available from: https://sciencebusiness.net/news/conference-report-africas-research-system-must-be-strengthened-and-driven-opportunity-not-aid [Accessed 6 July 2022].

Committee on Global Science Policy and Science Diplomacy Development, Security, and Cooperation (2012) *U.S. and International Perspectives on Global Science Policy and Science Diplomacy: Report of a Workshop*, Washington, DC: National Academies Press.

Committee for Survey and Analysis of Science Advice on Sustainable Development to International Organizations (2002) *Knowledge and Diplomacy: Science Advice in the United Nations System*, Washington, DC: National Academies Press.

Doğan, E.Ö., Uygun, Z. and Akçomak, I.S. (2021) 'Can science diplomacy address the global climate change challenge?', *Environmental Policy and Governance*, 31(1): 31–45.

DST (Department of Science and Technology) (2014) *Annual Report 2013–2014* [online], Available from: www.dst.gov.za/images/pdfs/DSTAnnual Report_1314.pdf [Accessed 10 July 2015].

EU (European Union) (2022) '7th plenary meeting of the AU–EU High Level Policy Dialogue for Science, Technology and Innovation, *European Commission News* [online], 27 January, Available from: https://ec.europa.eu/info/news/7th-plenary-meeting-au-eu-high-level-policy-dialogue-science-technology-and-innovation-2022-jan-27_en [Accessed 1 July 2022].

Ezekiel, P. (2020) 'Engaging science diplomacy for nanotechnology development in Africa', *IOP Conference Series: Materials Science and Engineering*, 805 012039 [online], Available from: https://iopscience.iop.org/article/10.1088/1757-899X/805/1/012039 [Accessed 1 July 2022].

Fedoroff, N.V. (2009) 'Science diplomacy in the 21st century', *Cell*, 136(9): 9–11.

Fellesson, M. and Mählck, P. (2017) 'Untapped research capacities? Mobility and collaboration at the intersection of international development aid and global science regimes', *International Journal of African Higher Education*, 4(1): 1–24.

Fidler, M. (2016) *Cyber Diplomacy with Africa: Lessons from the African Cybersecurity Convention*, Net Politics, Council on Foreign Relations [online], Available from: www.cfr.org/blog/cyber-diplomacy-africa-lessons-african-cybersecurity-convention [Accessed 1 July 2022].

Flink, T. and Schreiterer, U. (2010) 'Science diplomacy at the intersection of S&T policies and foreign affairs: towards a typology of national approaches', *Science and Public Policy*, 37(9): 665–77.

G7 (2021) *G7 Research Compact* [online], Available from: www.consilium.europa.eu/media/50365/g7-2021-research-compact-pdf-356kb-2-pages-1.pdf [Accessed 24 July 2022].

Gaillard, J. (1992) 'Science policies and cooperation in Africa: trends in the production and utilization of knowledge', *Knowledge: Creation, Diffusion, Utilization*, 14(2): 212–33.

Gamito-Marques, D. (2020) 'Science for competition among powers: geographical knowledge, colonial–diplomatic networks, and the Scramble for Africa', *Berichte zur Wissenschaftsgeschichte*, 43(4): 473–92.

Hecht, G. (2012) *Being Nuclear: Africans and the Global Uranium Trade*, Cambridge, MA: MIT Press.

Hornsby, D.J. and Parshotam, A. (2018) 'Science diplomacy, epistemic communities, and practice in sub-Saharan Africa', *Global Policy*, 9(3): 29–34.

Jacobsen, L.L. and Olšáková, D. (2020) 'Diplomats in science diplomacy: promoting scientific and technological collaboration in international relations', *Berichte zur Wissenschaftsgeschichte*, 43(4): 465–72.

Kalele, P. and Maphosa, S. (2021) 'Connecting the dots: the role of African National Academies of Science in informing the COVID-19 response', *Science and Diplomacy* [online], 22 January, Available from: www.sciencediplomacy.org/article/2021/connecting-dots-role-african-national-academies-science-in-informing-covid-19-response [Accessed 1 November 2021].

Keay, R. (1976). 'Scientific cooperation in Africa', *African Affairs*, 75(298): 86–97.

Kramer, D. (2010a) 'At work in the trenches of science diplomacy', *Physics Today*, December: 30–31.

Kramer, D. (2010b) 'Science diplomacy enlisted to span US divide with developing world', *Physics Today*, December: 28–30.

Linkov, I., Trump, B., Tatham, E., Basu, S. and Roco, M. (2014) 'Diplomacy for science two generations later', *Science and Diplomacy* [online], 13 March: 1–8, Available from: www.sciencediplomacy.org/perspective/2014/diplomacy-for-science-two-generations-later [Accessed 7 July 2022].

Maher, B. and Van Noorden, R. (2021) 'The challenges facing research collaborations', *Nature*, 594 [online], 17 June, Available from: https://media.nature.com/original/magazine-assets/d41586-021-01570-2/d41586-021-01570-2.pdf [Accessed 15 October 2021].

Masters, L. (2016) 'South Africa's two-track approach to science diplomacy', *Journal for Contemporary History*, 41(1): 169–86. 10.18820/24150509/jch.v41i1.9.

Masters, L. (2021) 'Africa, the Fourth Industrial Revolution, and digital diplomacy: (re)negotiating the international knowledge structure', *South African Journal of International Affairs*, 28(3): 361–77.

Ndung'u, N. and Signé, L. (2020) 'Capturing the Fourth Industrial Revolution: a regional and national agenda', *Foresight Africa*, Brookings Institute [online], Available from: www.brookings.edu/wp-content/uploads/2020/01/ForesightAfrica2020_Chapter5_20200110.pdf [Accessed 17 January 2020].

Pathways for Prosperity Commission (2019) *Digital Diplomacy: Technology Governance for Developing Countries*. Oxford, UK: Pathways for Prosperity Commission, Available from https://pathwayscommission.bsg.ox.ac.uk/sites/default/files/2019-10/Digital-Diplomacy.pdf [Accessed 28 February 2024].

Rao, J.E. (2018) 'A career in science policy and diplomacy: from Banana Slug to diplomat', *Molecular Biology of the Cell*, 29(21): 2516–18.

Rüffin, N. (2020) 'EU science diplomacy in a contested space of multi-level governance: ambitions, constraints and options for action', *Research Policy*, 49(1): 103842, ISSN 0048-7333, Available from: https://doi.org/10.1016/j.respol.2019.103842.

Seth, N. (2019) 'The changing face of diplomacy and the enhanced role of science diplomacy in the post-2015 world', *Science & Diplomacy* [online], 19 June, Available from: www.sciencediplomacy.org/perspective/2019/changing-face-diplomacy-and-enhanced-role-science-diplomacy-in-post-2015-world [Accessed 28 November 2023].

Sharma, J., Valerino, D.R., Widmaier, C.N., Lima, R., Gupta, N. and Varshney, S.K. (2022) 'Science diplomacy and COVID-19: future perspectives for South–South cooperation', *Global Policy*, 13: 294–99.

Swap, R.J., Annegarn, H.J. and Otter, L. (2002) 'Southern African regional Science Initiative (SAFARI 2000): summary of science plan', *South African Journal of Science*, 98(March/April): 119–24].

Toure, M. (2018) 'Integrating Africa: prospects and promise for science diplomacy', *Science & Diplomacy*, 7(3) [online], September, Available from: www.sciencediplomacy.org/perspective/2018/integrating-africa-prospects-and-promise-for-science-diplomacy [Accessed 24 August 2022].

Turekian, V. (2018) 'The evolution of science diplomacy', *Global Policy*, 9(3): 5–7.

Turekian, V. and Neureiter, N. (2012) 'Science and diplomacy: the past as prologue', *Science & Diplomacy*, 1(1) [online], March, Available from: www.sciencediplomacy.org/editorial/2012/science-and-diplomacy [Accessed 11 July 2022].

UNGA (United Nations General Assembly) (2021) *Globalization and Interdependence: Science, Technology and Innovation for Sustainable Development*, Seventy-Sixth session, Second Committee. Agenda item 22(a) [online], 11 October, Available at: https://digitallibrary.un.org/record/3950839?ln=en [Accessed 24 July 2022].

UNSC (United Nations Security Council) (2021) *Egypt, Ethiopia, Sudan Should Negotiate Mutually Beneficial Agreement over Management of Nile Waters, Top Official Tells Security Council*, Security Council 8816th Meeting, SC/14576 [online], 8 July, Available from: www.un.org/press/en/2021/sc14576.doc.htm [Accessed 28 November 2023].

Van Langenhove, L. (2019) 'Who cares? Science diplomacy and the global commons', *Australian Quarterly*, 90(4): 18–27.

10

Africa's Health Diplomacy

Jo-Ansie van Wyk

Introduction

Africa's response to health challenges entered a new phase with the establishment of the African Union (AU) in 2002. Building upon the foundation laid by its predecessor, the Organization of African Unity (OAU), the AU added health to its founding document, the Constitutive Act of the AU. In Article 4, one of the AU's objectives is to cooperate with its international partners to eradicate preventable diseases and improve African health (AU, 2002). Despite this, the health of Africans has not significantly improved due to a plethora of national and international reasons. The poor state of the continent's health was further diminished with the outbreak of the novel corona virus in Wuhan, China in 2019.

On 11 March 2020, the World Health Organization (WHO) declared the coronavirus (COVID-19) a global pandemic. The COVID-19 pandemic was and remains a turning point in global health requiring rapid responses and the massive mobilization of medical and financial resources. The declaration has had global ramifications, adding to Africa's existing health and developmental challenges.

It is impossible to address all 55 African states' bi- and multilateral health diplomacy, as well as that of the AU, in a limited-word chapter such as this. However, the purpose of the chapter is fourfold. First, it sets out to explore the concept of health diplomacy. Second, it sketches the state of health in Africa and the AU's health architecture. Third, the chapter analyses Africa's health diplomacy. Finally, it outlines Africa's health diplomacy in the context of the global COVID-19 pandemic.

Health diplomacy

There is conceptual disagreement regarding the concept and practice of health diplomacy. Definitions and practices have tended to describe health diplomacy as a component of routine and established diplomatic practices. This has shifted towards a more universal acceptance of health diplomacy as a unique and distinct diplomatic practice requiring technical expertise and diplomatic specialization. Global differences in population health have added an additional normative and social justice layer to the health and wealth of states, often attracting global non-governmental actors' attention followed by increased pressure on governments and multilateral institutions.

The World Health Organization (WHO) and the Rockefeller Foundation have developed a definition of health diplomacy:

> The policy-shaping processes through which States, inter-governmental organisations, and non-State actors negotiate responses to health challenges or utilize health concepts or mechanisms in policy-shaping and negotiation strategies to achieve other political, economic, or social objectives. (Fidler, 2013: 693)

Here, health diplomacy is regarded as a process involving a multiplicity of actors shaping policy through negotiation to achieve 'other' objectives, implying the cross-cutting nature of health. Other definitions focus on health diplomacy as a political process aiming to achieve improved global health while simultaneously advancing the interests of individual states through their representation at these organizations and global events (Novotny and Kevany, 2013: 302). Cooperation and competition are thus recognized as an integral part of heath diplomacy; elements it shares with other niche diplomatic areas. An example of these 'other' objectives is contained in the continent's developmental blueprint, *Agenda 2063: The Africa We Want*, adopted in 2015 (AU, 2015a). There, the continent reiterated its intention to reduce its global marginalization and enhance internal unity and its influence in global affairs (AU, 2015a). Besides this, Agenda 2063, read with the Constitutive Act, expresses Africa's collective aspirations to terminate global inequality and achieve equity. Aspiration 7 of Agenda 2063 (Africa as a strong, united, resilient and influential global player and partner) formulates this as:

> improving Africa's place in the global governance system (UNSC [United Nations Security Council], financial institutions, global commons such as outer space); improving Africa's partnerships and refocusing them more strategically to respond to African priorities for growth and transformation; and ensuring that the continent has

the right strategies to finance its own development and reducing aid dependency. (AU, 2015a)

Another determinant of an actor's health diplomacy is the state of its population's health and its health architecture, the focus of the next section.

Health in Africa: state and architecture

Historically, the continent and individual African states during colonization and afterwards, have not achieved universal health (Giles-Vernick and Webb, 2013), an aspect that informs its contemporary actions and responses to the population's health. The state of the health of Africa's population remains unsatisfactory as the continent's disease burden compares unfavourably to other continents. In Africa, tuberculosis (TB), malaria, HIV/AIDS and other communicable and non-communicable diseases are exacerbated by, for example, low life expectancy, poverty, malnutrition, gender inequality, human displacement, humanitarian crises, conflict- and climate-induced food insecurity, and unavailable and underperforming health services (WHO, 2018: xi–xii). Besides this, Africa seems to be the epicentre of zoonotic diseases, as the WHO (2022) has reported a 63 per cent increase during the past decade (2012–22) compared to its previous reporting period (2001–11).

The AU's health architecture has expanded parallel to global and African health issues and agreements, and Africa's efforts to achieve continental integration. Within the AU bureaucracy, its health architecture includes the role of the AU Assembly in deciding upon and coordinating African efforts regarding health as well as a dedicated Specialized Technical Committee on Health responsible to the AU Executive Council (AU, 2002). This is complemented by the Division on Health, Nutrition and Population and the Division on AIDS, TB, Malaria and Other Infectious Diseases.

The health aspirations of the continent were included in its development blueprint, Agenda 2063, adopted in 2015 (AU, 2015a) and coinciding with the UN's adoption of the Sustainable Development Goals (SDGs) (UN, 2015a). Following Agenda 2063, the AU adopted its second health strategy, the Africa Health Strategy 2016–30 in 2016 (AU, 2016). The strategy emphasizes, among other matters, international cooperation at bi- and multilateral level, and with humanitarian organizations, civil society and the private sector to achieve universal health in Africa (AU, 2016: 32). Additional institutionalization to strengthen the AU's health architecture included the establishment of the Africa Centres for Disease Control (CDC) in 2016 to support AU members' health initiatives. Besides the Africa CDC, the continent established its second health agency, the African Medicines Agency, in 2019. The latter's functions include, inter alia, the harmonization of health regulations between members and regional economic communities (RECs), and to improve the continent's access to medical products.

In response to the outbreak of COVID-19 on the continent and the WHO's declaration of the global COVID-19 pandemic, the continent's health diplomacy shifted into a higher gear. Access to personal protective equipment (PPE), detection technology and equipment, treatment facilities and medical products, including vaccines, became just a few challenges to the continent's health diplomacy.

The poor state of the health of Africa's population remains a grave concern. In terms of Africa's health diplomacy and its results, the establishment of the AU in 2002 and its adoption of Agenda 2063 can be recorded as milestones. However, the continent's efforts to establish and operationalize its health architecture have produced mixed results due to, for example, variables negatively affecting the population's health, the high cost of these efforts and, possibly, bureaucratic inertia at national, regional and continental level. These matters are expected to be addressed once the AU's current institutional reform process in terms of the Kagame Report concludes and becomes fully operational (Kagame, 2017). It may also be that the continent's health architecture is not fit for purpose, or that it requires a decolonized approach to health and a decolonized health architecture. Be as it may, as indicated, Africa's health diplomacy has produced intended and unintended results, as discussed in the next section.

African health diplomacy: agony or agency?

Despite the diplomatic efforts of individual African states and the AU to respond to and improve health crises, the continent has not achieved its intended objectives. Despite this, a few examples of African agency regarding health diplomacy exist where either individual African states or the continental collective have contributed to shaping global health governance. One example of this is South Africa and Senegal's cooperation with Brazil, France, Indonesia, Norway and Thailand in 2007 to establish the Global Health and Foreign Policy Initiative that resulted in the Oslo Ministerial Declaration. The latter has been a significant turning point for global health diplomacy as it declared that 'health is one of the most important, yet still broadly neglected, long-term foreign policy issues of our time' and that 'health as a foreign policy issue needs a stronger strategic focus on the international agenda' (Brazil, France, Indonesia, Norway, Senegal, South Africa and Thailand, 2007). Although only two African states were involved in this process, the global impact of the declaration has not been denied. In 2008, the UN General Assembly Resolution 63/33 (UNGA, 2008) on global health and foreign policy was adopted recognizing the 'close relationship between foreign policy and global health and their interdependence' (UNGA, 2008).

The cross-cutting nature of health issues and health diplomacy has been included in the WHO and the Rockefeller Foundation's definition of health diplomacy. It therefore makes sense to include African health issues on the agenda of the continent's engagements with its international partners. Besides African states' membership of the WHO and other UN agencies, it is also engaged in efforts driven by regional organizations such as the European Union (EU), and individual states of the Global North and South. The EU–AU partnership has been one of the continent's oldest such relations. Health matters also feature in the continent's diplomatic engagements with China (Forum on China–Africa Cooperation, FOCAC), France (new Africa–France summits) and Russia (Russia–Africa summits), and solidarity engagements such as the joint Africa–Arab heads of state and government summit.

Compared to long-term health challenges, the continent has been more successful in dealing with short-term communicable health emergencies such as the Ebola outbreak in West Africa (2014–16). One explanation lies in the pathology of these diseases. Their highly communicable nature often results in high incidences of death.

Other explanations point to the power of bi- and/or multilateral health diplomacy. First, the rapid response of national governments to call on international assistance in terms of its existing bi- and/or multilateral relations. A second explanation relates to the rapid response by non-governmental humanitarian organizations such as the International Committee of the Red Cross and Médecins Sans Frontières. In the third instance, the establishment of a dedicated UN mission, the UN Mission for Ebola Emergency Response (UNMEER), the UN's first-ever health emergency mission, in September 2014 could add to these explanations. UNMEER's allocation of financial, logistical and human resources, and training and assistance regarding communication of the outbreak to Guinea, Liberia and Sierra Leone, the epicentre of the Ebola outbreak, contributed to ending the health disaster (UN, 2022). A final, but not exhaustive, explanation relates to the diplomatic efforts to assist the affected states during the outbreak and in their post-Ebola recovery. The World Bank, for example, convened a High-Level Meeting, 'Ebola, the Road to Recovery', in April 2015 with the governments of Guinea, Liberia and Sierra Leone. These governments presented their recovery plans, prepared with the cooperation of their international partners, to the World Bank. This meeting was followed in July 2015 by the International Ebola Recovery Conference hosted by the UN secretary general but held in cooperation with the governments of Guinea, Liberia and Sierra Leone, and in partnership with the AU, the African Development Bank (ADB), the EU and the World Bank. One of the outcomes of this conference was the allocation of US$5.2 billion to these three states to assist with their post-Ebola recovery (UN, 2015b).

After these two events and later in July 2015, the AU also convened an event, the International Conference on Africa's Fight against Ebola. The AU conference on Ebola was deliberately themed 'Africans helping Africans in the Ebola Recovery and Reconstruction', echoing an earlier declared mantra of the AU: 'African solutions for African problems'. The conference theme reiterated Africa's commitment to continental unity, solidarity and Pan-Africanism. Besides focusing on what is required for recovery, the conference's reference to health diplomacy became evident in the call to accelerate the establishment of the Africa CDC to assist African states during future pandemics. The conference also committed to the implementation of the African Medicines Regulatory Harmonization to, inter alia, implement the continent's Pharmaceutical Manufacturing Plan for Africa (AU, 2015b). Further evidence of African health diplomacy in the context of the Ebola outbreak includes South Africa's provision of humanitarian assistance amounting to R32.5 million to Ebola-affected states (DIRCO, 2015). Another instance of South Africa's health diplomacy with fellow African states is its involvement in the multilateral MOSASWA (Mozambique, South Africa and Swaziland – now Eswatini) project on the elimination of malaria (Health Reporter, 2017).

African health diplomacy has not distinguished itself from the health diplomacy of other actors in terms of its substance and practice. Instances of African agency have been recorded alongside the continent's efforts to reform global governance structures, and achieving African unity, Pan-Africanism and solidarity with like-minded actors. However, the continent remains significantly dependent on external actors, such as its diplomatic partners and non-governmental organizations, to provide health services. This compromises the continent's agential opportunities, and achieving Aspiration 7 of Agenda 2063 (Africa as a strong, united, resilient and influential global player and partner) (AU, 2015a). The next section focuses on Africa's health diplomacy in the context of the global COVID-19 pandemic.

COVID-19 and Africa's health diplomacy

The COVID-19 pandemic has reiterated, for example, global inequality, the spread of communicable diseases due to increased global human mobility, and the challenges posed by the recurrence of zoonotic diseases. Besides this, the pandemic has manifested the urgency to address longstanding issues around, for example, technology transfer and sharing between developed and developing states, indigenous knowledge systems, ethno-botany, traditional medicine and intellectual property rights. It has also highlighted the political and economic influence of private sector pharmaceutical companies and global responses against vaccines developed by state-owned pharmaceutical companies of non-Western countries and African allies such as China, Cuba and Russia. The concepts of vaccine apartheid and vaccine nationalism have entered the diplomatic lexicon as actors compete to benefit economically as well as to speed their recovery from the economic effects of the pandemic. Moreover, racial undertones also resurfaced as the world responded to the pandemic. Reference to the coronavirus as the China Virus by then US President Donald Trump illustrated tensions between the US and China. Similarly, reference to the Omicron variant as 'the South African variant' added to the othering of non-Western countries. In addition to this, COVID-19 agnosticism (a disbelief in the existence of the virus and suspicion of vaccines) also affected diplomatic relations. Former Brazilian president and African ally, Bolsonaro, for example, can be included in this category.

Another aspect highlighted by the pandemic was the politics of global health governance. By the time the COVID-19 pandemic was declared, the US under the leadership of President Donald Trump had committed acts of unilateralism that negatively affected multilateral efforts to address global efforts. Africa became caught up in these developments when the US announced its withdrawal from the WHO and that it would cancel financial support for the organization, ostensibly due to the WHO's failure to respond to the COVID-19 outbreak in China towards the end of 2019 and the beginning of 2020, followed by an attack against the WHO and its African director general, Ethiopian Dr Tedros Adhanom Ghebreyesus (Rogers and Mandavilli, 2021). In response, the incumbent AU chairperson and South African president, Cyril Ramaphosa, unequivocally expressed the continent's support for and gratitude to the WHO and Dr Ghebreyesus for their leadership 'from the very earliest stages of this unprecedented global health crisis' (AU, 2020c).

South Africa led the AU and African Peer Review Mechanism[1] when the global pandemic was declared in March 2020. As chairperson of the AU at the time, South Africa's President Cyril Ramaphosa convened a virtual meeting of the bureau of the AU Assembly of the Heads of State and Government on 26 March 2020. The bureau, consisting of the presidents of Mali, Kenya, the Democratic Republic of the Congo (DRC) and Egypt, agreed on a coordinated continental response. This included the establishment of a continental anti-COVID-19 fund to which bureau members immediately contributed US$12.5 million as seed-funding and a further contribution of US$4.5 million to the Africa CDC to fight the pandemic. The bureau also called on the G20, the World Bank, the International Monetary Fund (IMF), the ADB and other regional institutions to assist African through, for example, debt relief initiatives to counter the economic impact of the pandemic (AU, 2020a).

A follow-up meeting of the bureau on 3 April 2020 revealed several aspects of African diplomacy in general, and health diplomacy specifically. Besides the bureau, the presidents of Rwanda, Senegal, Ethiopia and Zimbabwe attended. French President Emmanuel Macron, WHO Director General Tedros Ghebreyesus and the head of the Africa CDC addressed the meeting, which agreed on the establishment of 'humanitarian and trade corridors in a spirit of African solidarity and integration', and a continental ministerial coordination committee on health, finance and transport to coordinate the comprehensive continental strategy (AU, 2020b). As an illustration of African solidarity and Pan-Africanism, the meeting called for the 'immediate lifting of all' economic sanctions against Zimbabwe and Sudan to fight the pandemic, which the bureau considered 'intolerable and inhumane in the present context' (AU, 2020b). The bureau also discussed developments in the Sahel (where France is involved in peace efforts) that needed 'special attention in the light of terrorist activity' and expressed 'solidarity' with countries in the region (AU, 2020b). Finally, the meeting expressed its gratitude to Africa's international partners, and China was commended for its commitment and 'solidarity with Africa' (AU, 2020b).

In June 2021, South Africa, upon the invitation of the G7, attended the group's summit in the UK. By now the pandemic had killed a substantial number of Africans and decimated African economies, and calls to end vaccine apartheid became louder. Ramaphosa reiterated the growing gap regarding access to vaccines between developed and developing states. By broadening the access gap, Ramaphosa as AU chairperson thus also expressed African solidarity with other regions in a similar position. A few months later, Ramaphosa rejoined G7 leaders for an emergency meeting to discuss South Africa's identification of the Omicron variant of COVID-19. He reiterated the increasing economic implications for developing countries as developed countries sought to reimpose earlier pandemic-induced travel restrictions (Harrison, 2021). Realizing these calls might not have produced sufficient results, in his capacity as AU chairperson Ramaphosa appointed a team of AU special envoys from each of the AU's regions, including Ngozi Okonjo-Iweala (Nigeria), Donald Kaberuka (Rwanda), Tidjane Thiam (Côte d'Ivoire), Trevor Manuel (South Africa), Benkhalfa Abderrahmane (Algeria) and Mbaya Kankwenda (DRC), to mobilize international support from the EU, the G20 and international financial institutions for Africa's efforts to address the economic fall-out of the pandemic (The Presidency, 2020). President Ramaphosa also appointed a seventh special envoy, Zimbabwean businessman Strive Masiyiwa, who coordinated private sector support for the procurement of PPE and other supplies for Africa in terms of the Africa Medical Supplies Platform, another AU initiative introduced by Ramaphosa during his AU tenure (Ramaphosa, 2021). These envoys had 'extensive engagements' with the G20, the World Bank and the IMF that resulted in these entities' deployment of 'significant financial resources' for Africa's COVID-19 response (Ramaphosa, 2021).

As AU chairperson, in November 2020 Ramaphosa had been instrumental in the negotiations, AU endorsement and establishment of the African Vaccine Acquisition Task Team to secure African access to vaccines for which the continent required approximately US$13 billion (AU, 2020d).

As chair of the AU during 2020, Ramaphosa had been central in negotiating the African Vaccine Acquisition Task Team, endorsed by the AU (AU, 2020c). Lack of access to COVID-19 vaccines reinforced the urgency for the full implementation of the AU's 2007 Pharmaceutical Manufacturing Plan for Africa and the development of an African Medicines Agency. South Africa's emphasis on multilateralism enabled it to join the COVID-19 Vaccines Global Access (COVAX)facility, contributing $19.2 million to the Vaccine Alliance (South Africa, 2020). Besides this, South Africa's cooperation with the WHO and COVAX partners enabled the South African consortium (Biovac, Afrigen Biologics and Vaccines, a network of universities and the Africa CDC) to establish the first hub for COVID-19 vaccine technology transfer (WHO, 2021).

In its capacity as AU chair, South Africa coordinated the African response to the pandemic, and worked to achieve equitable access to appropriate health equipment and equipment. The country continued with its efforts to achieve this for the continent after its tenure ended. President Ramaphosa's health diplomacy as AU chairperson was recognized when the DRC, South Africa's successor as AU chair in 2021, appointed Ramaphosa as Africa's 'Champion for the COVID-19 vaccine strategy and acquisition by AU Member States' to continue to coordinate the AU's response to the pandemic and to acquire and distribute vaccines (AU, 2021)

A clear sign of African agency in terms of its health diplomacy, especially regarding the pandemic, emerged during deliberations of the World Trade Organization (WTO). Developing states' increased concern about a lack of access to vaccines developed and manufactured elsewhere on the globe sparked concerns about 'vaccine apartheid'. Developing states, among others, called on the WTO to waive trade-related intellectual property rights (TRIPS) relating to the production of vaccines to enable other countries to produce vaccines as global demand outstripped production. From October 2020, South Africa and India took the lead in this initiative (WTO, 2021) and, through diplomatic engagements, were able to obtain support from African states, the Global North and the Global South, including the African Group, Bolivia, Egypt, Eswatini, Fiji, Indonesia, Kenya, the Least Developed Country (LDC) Group, Maldives, Mozambique, Mongolia, Namibia, Pakistan, Vanuatu, Venezuela, the US and Zimbabwe (WTO, 2021).

Compared to before the pandemic, the continent's health diplomacy has achieved some successes, most notably global awareness of the commonality of the pandemic and a shift towards social justice. Other diplomatic success has been the elevation of continent through its role in the WTO TRIPS waiver, a major normative development favouring Africa and its solidarity partners in the Global South. Moreover, the continent's diplomacy has also been in the spotlight due to the scope of the pandemic. Novel diplomatic initiatives were undertaken, especially during South Africa's tenure as chair of the AU, but were largely initiated in terms of either existing partnerships or guidelines issued by the WHO. These aspects do not diminish Africa's efforts to respond to the pandemic, but it remains to be seen how sustainable these efforts will be and whether Africans' health can improve quantitatively.

Conclusion

The cross-cutting nature of health makes it a major political issue at the national and international level. Africa remains an unhealthy continent, a condition exacerbated by a plethora of other continental crises such as conflict, war, environmental change and food insecurity. Besides these material conditions, Africa has elevated its role in international affairs, but achieving African unity, promoting Pan-Africanism and expressing solidarity with its allies are continuously tested.

Africa is unlikely to achieve the goals set out in Agenda 2063 and the SDGs. Of this, the COVID-19 pandemic has made sure. The continent can, at least, aim to work towards an operational African, regional and national health sector and facilities, improved health governance at national level, and continental political stability.

Note

1. The African Peer Review Mechanism (APRM) is a mutually-agreed mechanism of the African Union whereby states evaluate their governance to promote political stability, regional and continental integration, economic growth and development.

References

AU (African Union) (2002) *Constitutive Act of the African Union* [online], Available from: https://au.int/sites/default/files/pages/34873-file-constitutiveact_en.pdf [Accessed 14 July 2022].

AU (African Union) (2015a) *Agenda 2063. The Africa We Want. Framework Document* [online], Available from: https://au.int/sites/default/files/documents/33126-doc-framework_document_book.pdf [Accessed 12 July 2022].

AU (African Union) (2015b) 'International conference on Africa's fight against Ebola', Press release 170/2015 [online], Available from: https://au.int/fr/node/27027 [Accessed 12 July 2022].

AU (African Union) (2016) *Africa Health Strategy 2016–2030* [online], Available from: https://au.int/sites/default/files/pages/32895-file-africa_health_strategy.pdf [Accessed 14 July 2022].

AU (African Union) (2020a) *Communique of the Bureau of the Assembly of the African Union (AU) Heads of State and Government Teleconference on COVID-19* [online], 26 March, Available from: www.dirco.gov.za/docs/2020/au0326.pdf [Accessed 6 May 2020].

AU (African Union) (2020b) *Communique of the Bureau of the Assembly of the African Union (AU) Heads of State and Government Teleconference Meeting on COVID-19* [online], 3 April, Available from: www.dirco.gov.za/docs/2020/au0404.pdf [Accessed 6 May 2020].

AU (African Union) (2020c) *African Union Reaffirms Its Unwavering Support to the WHO* [online], 8 April, Available from: www.dirco.gov.za/docs/2020/au0408.pdf [Accessed 6 May 2020].

AU (African Union) (2020d) *Statement on AU Vaccines Financing Strategy* [online], 8 November, Available from: https://au.int/en/pressreleases/20201108/statement-au-vaccines-financing-strategy [Accessed 24 May 2021].

AU (African Union) (2021) '34th AU summit strives to ensure that, as a continental body, no country is left behind in the COVID-19 responses "as we enhance integration"', Press release [online], 6 February, Available from: https://au.int/en/pressreleases/20210206/34th-au-summit-strives-ensure-continental-body-no-country-left-behind-covid [Accessed 11 June 2021].

Brazil, France, Indonesia, Norway, Senegal, South Africa and Thailand (Ministers of Foreign Affairs of) (2007) 'Oslo Ministerial Declaration. Global health: a pressing foreign policy issue of our time', *The Lancet*, 369(95): 1373–8.

DIRCO (Department of International Relations and Cooperation) (2015) *DIRCO and ARF Performance and Financial Report. Quarter 2 & 3*, Presentation to the Portfolio Committee on International Relations and Cooperation [online], 4 March, Available from: https://pmg.org.za/committee-meeting/20107/ [Accessed 14 April 2020].

Fidler, D. (2013) 'Health diplomacy', in A.F. Cooper, J. Heine and R. Thakur (eds) *The Oxford Handbook of Modern Diplomacy*, Oxford: Oxford University Press, pp 691–707.

Giles-Vernick, T. and Webb, J. (eds) (2013) *Global Health in Africa: Historical Perspectives in Disease Control*, Athens: Ohio University Press.

Harrison, V. (2021) 'Omicron variant: G7 to hold emergency COVID meeting as Japan closes its borders', *The Guardian* [online], 29 November, Available from: www.theguardian.com/world/2021/nov/29/omicron-variant-g7-to-hold-emergency-covid-meeting-as-japan-closes-its-borders [Accessed 26 January 2021].

Health Reporter (2017) 'Malaria day: strong cross border collaboration is key to elimination', *Independent Online* [online], 10 November, Available from: www.iol.co.za/lifestyle/health/malaria-day-strong-cross-border-collaboration-is-key-to-elimination-11946510 [Accessed 12 May 2020].

Kagame, P. (2017) *The Imperative to Strengthen our Union. Report of the Proposed Recommendations for the Institutional Reform of the African Union* [online], Available from: https://au.int/sites/default/files/pages/34915-file-report-20institutional20reform20of20the20au-2.pdf [Accessed 11 July 2022].

Novotny, E. and Kevany, S. (2013) 'The way forward in global health diplomacy: definition, research and training', in E. Novotny, I. Kickbusch and M. Todd (eds) 21st *Century Global Health Diplomacy*, Singapore: World Scientific Publishing Co, pp 299–324.

Ramaphosa, C. (2021) *Handover Statement by President Cyril Ramaphosa on the Occasion of the 34th Ordinary Session of the Heads of State and Government of the African Union* [online], 6 February, Available from: https://au.int/sites/default/files/speeches/39954-sp-handover_remarks-_au_chair-assembly.pdf [Accessed 11 June 2021].

Rogers, K. and Mandavilli, A. (2021) 'Trump administration signals formal withdrawal from W.H.O.', *The New York Times* [online], 22 September, Available from: www.nytimes.com/2020/07/07/us/politics/coronavirus-trump-who.html [Accessed 28 November 2023].

South Africa (Government of) (2020) 'Health on securing South Africa's COVAX participation as solidarity fund concludes down payment', Statement [online], 22 December, Available from: www.gov.za/speeches/health-securing-south-africa%E2%80%99s-covax-participation-solidarity-fund-concludes-down-payment [Accessed 26 January 2022].

The Presidency (of the Republic of South Africa) (2020) 'African Union chair, President Cyril Ramaphosa, appoints special envoys to mobilise international economic support for continental fight against COVID-19', Media statement [online], 12 April, Available from: www.dirco.gov.za/docs/2020/au0412.htm [Accessed 6 May 2020].

UN (United Nations) (2015a) *Transforming Our World: The 2030 Agenda for Sustainable Development*, A/RES/70/1 [online], Available from: https://sdgs.un.org/publications/transforming-our-world-2030-agenda-sustainable-development-17981 [Accessed 14 July 2022].

UN (United Nations) (2015b) *International Ebola Recovery Conference. Summary* [online], 10 July, Available from: https://ebolaresponse.un.org/sites/default/files/summary_report.pdf [Accessed 14 July 2022].

UN (United Nations) (2022) *United Nations Mission for Ebola Emergency Response (UNMEER)* [online], Available from: https://ebolaresponse.un.org/un-mission-ebola-emergency-response-unmeer [Accessed 14 July 2022].

UNGA (United Nations General Assembly) (2008) *Resolution 63/33 (2008). Global Health and Foreign Policy*, A/RES/63/33 [online], Available from: https://digitallibrary.un.org/record/642456?ln=en&v=pdf [Accessed 30 April 2024].

WHO (World Health Organization) (2018) *The State of Health in the WHO African Region: An Analysis of the Status of Health, Health Services and Health Systems in the Context of the Sustainable Development Goals*, Brazzaville: WHO Regional Office for Africa.

WHO (World Health Organization) (2021) 'WHO supporting South African consortium to establish first mRNA vaccine technology transfer hub', Press release [online], 21 June, Available from: www.who.int/news/item/21-06-2021-who-supporting-south-african-consortium-to-establish-first-covid-mrna-vaccine-technology-transfer-hub [Accessed 26 January 2022].

WHO (World Health Organization) (2022) 'In Africa, 63% jump in diseases from animals to people seen in last decade', Press release [online], 14 July. Available from: www.afro.who.int/news/africa-63-jump-diseases-spread-animals-people-seen-last-decade [Accessed 14 July 2022].

WTO (World Trade Organization) (2021) *Waiver from Certain Provisions of the TRIPS Agreement for the Prevention, Containment and Treatment of Covid-19*. Revised Decision Text. IP/C/W/669/Rev.1 [online], 25 May, Available from: https://docs.wto.org/dol2fe/Pages/SS/directdoc.aspx?filename=q:/IP/C/W669R1.pdf&Open=True [Accessed 11 June 2021].

11

Ghana's Cultural Diplomacy

Sandra Asafo-Adjei

Introduction

Rapid globalization continues to shrink distances between states and has enabled a global sentiment of human interconnectedness manifesting in, for example, the increasingly borderless nature of fashion, music, film, culture, trade and religion (James and Steger, 2018: 21–39). Globalization as a process whereby governments, people and institutions interconnect and integrate through trade, investment and information technology (James and Steger, 2018: 21–39), albeit sometimes complex, has been shown to strengthen global social interaction beyond territorial borders and has fostered exchanges which, either directly or indirectly, promote relations between states.

Besides material exchanges and mobilities, non-material social goods and capital such as ideas and knowledge have also become highly mobile through the processes associated with globalization. The invention of the internet and a variety of social media platforms such as Facebook, YouTube, Instagram and Twitter have generated and enabled the sharing of knowledge and the exchange of ideas peculiar to specific communities and regions (James, 2002). This process continues to influence national economies, political systems and culture within and across the globe. Access to news, fashion trends, popular music or films has significantly improved as the internet provides opportunities for states, people and institutions to share and learn from their respective cultures. This has had and continues to have an impact on diplomacy as the maintenance of relations and exchange of ideas between states. Another objective of diplomacy is to influence the choices, responses and attitudes of foreign governments and their citizens. This process involves dialogue and peaceful negotiations rather than coercion and violence (Berridge, 2002). Besides these objectives, diplomacy is also an official mode of communication between states, often in the form of dialogue, negotiation and discussion of pertinent issues within the international system to arrive at agreements and aligned positions. Whereas these objectives tend to focus on the cooperative nature and objectives of diplomacy, some scholars, for example Morgenthau (2006), are of a strong conviction that diplomacy is a technique employed by states to project and promote their national, rather than communal, interests by peaceful means.

The essence of diplomacy can thus be regarded as the process to establish and maintain goodwill between states while simultaneously advancing national interests and resolving issues of international concern in a peaceful way. To achieve this, there are various diplomatic strategies available to states. These diplomatic strategies have been categorized under two broad fields, namely traditional diplomacy and public diplomacy (Javaid, 2019). Traditional diplomacy, also known as government-to-government diplomacy, is centred on efforts of officials of a state to influence officials of another state to make certain choices through dialogues and negotiations (Javaid, 2019). Public diplomacy, on the other hand, as a soft power tool is a process whereby a state seeks to build trust and understanding by engaging a broader foreign public through organizing educational and culture-related programmes in a target country. Usually, the sending country's prime concern is to capture the attention of the large audience in the target country and establish awareness there. Typically, these programmes help the advocate country to institute a positive opinion and image in a target country that will persuade the political leaders and publics of the target country to make conclusive decisions which will be advantageous and in line with the foreign policy goals of the advocate country (Melissen, 2005).

Through media relations and cultural events such as art exhibitions and other cultural events, the sending country is capable of building understanding in the target country. As a result, many members of the foreign audience are likely to develop an interest in the unique culture of the advocate country. The exchange of ideas, information, art, language, fashion styles and other features of culture between states to maintain mutual understanding and trust is done through a process called cultural diplomacy (Cull, 2009). A unique type and aspect of traditional and public diplomacy, cultural diplomacy can be defined as a state's goal to ensure that its cultural assets and accomplishments are recognized abroad and embedded in its foreign policy to advance the interests of the state as well as communicate aspects of its culture, adding to its diplomatic attractiveness (Cull, 2009). Practically, cultural diplomacy is often regarded as a subdivision of public diplomacy, where the culture (which includes fashion, language, film, dance, art, music, cuisine and religion) of a state is projected abroad in such a way that it meets the foreign policy objectives of the state. The idea is to first tackle stereotyping against the advocate state in the target state by developing mutual understanding and pursuing national reputation and relationships abroad (Lovrinić, 2018: 138–41).

Organizations such as the British Council of the United Kingdom, the Confucius Institute of China, the Goethe Institute (Germany) and the *Alliance Française* (France), among others, have been created by states to project unique examples of their culture and foreign policy objectives, thereby aligning with the purpose and practice of diplomacy. Cultural diplomacy plays a significant role in the global competitiveness of states for political influence, status, prestige, dominance, trade, tourism and investment. Cultural diplomacy also has some linkage with global competition through soft power (political) and the creative economy (economic). These constitute the socio-economic and political elements and objectives of states' cultural diplomacy that allows countries to present their national and cultural identity abroad (Lovrinić, 2018: 138–41).

African states are not novices regarding the purpose and practice of cultural diplomacy. In fact, it has become a unique feature of a state such as Ghana's foreign policy and diplomacy. This has historical roots. Upon attaining independence in 1957 as the first Sub-Saharan African country to do so, Ghana became a pioneer in the promotion of cultural diplomacy when its first prime minister and later president, Kwame Nkrumah, issued a cultural policy document which endured until 2004, when it was revised (Arku, 2013).

Ghana's use of cultural diplomacy and its intended outcomes hold great potential in projecting a sense of national identity, international status and prestige, and a source of revenue through tourism and tourism-related foreign direct investment (FDI), that could advance the developmental and economic agenda of Ghana.

Against that background, this chapter focuses on Ghana's utilization of cultural diplomacy as an instrument of its foreign policy, and to promote tourism and attract FDI. The chapter highlights the cultural identity and architecture of the people, the government and the diaspora of Ghana to position the Ghanaian state as a pacesetter in cultural engagements by reconnecting them to their roots and culture and, ultimately, contribute to the development of Africa, particularly Ghana, through FDI. Furthermore, the chapter discusses the challenges that hinder Ghana from fully benefitting from its cultural engagements alongside what the country stands to achieve in strengthening its cultural diplomatic relations with other states.

Ghana's cultural identity

The Republic of Ghana, formerly known as the Gold Coast, is a West African country which is a former colony of the British Empire. The country attained its independence on 6 March 1957. Ghana's neighbours include Burkina Faso (north), Togo (east), Côte d'Ivoire (west) and the Gulf of Guinea (south). The country is culturally rich, with, for example, over 100 ethnic groups, of which the largest are Akan, Moshi-Dagbani, Ewe and Ga (Briggs and Connolly, 2017).

Ghana is divided into 16 regions (as of February 2019) with each having a distinct cultural identity but intertwined to represent the national identity of Ghana. Cultural elements such as festivals, music, dance, food, traditions, customs and traditional symbols, as well as ways of dressing, present an opportunity to decipher the cultural identity of these different regions (Salm and Falola, 2022). These cultural elements significantly add to Ghana's unique identity. Besides external recognition in this regard, Ghana internally also recognizes the strength of its culture and continues to pivot towards the diplomatic opportunities it presents to ultimately reap the benefits and thus advance the development of the country. This internal reawakening has contributed to the country's renewed engagement in cultural diplomacy, as this chapter outlines. Ghana, through its cultural elements such as *kente* (a colourful hand-woven piece of fabric with symbolic patterns), is garnering international recognition and this has proven to be a promising source of revenue for the country. Aside from the fact that *kente* is favoured by tourists and foreigners worldwide, it has become very popular among students during their graduation ceremonies (who, with their graduation gowns, wear stoles with the beautiful colours and unique patterns of *kente* hanging around their necks), particularly in some parts of Europe, America and Asia (Touring Ghana, 2016).

Cultural diplomacy is a recent phenomenon in Africa due to the conditions of slavery, colonialism and apartheid. Ghana has had various governments, and its economic heritage is intricately tied to its culture and traditions. Before colonial times, the leadership structure was established on a strong foundation of traditions, customs and values. At the time, the culture and identity of indigenes were inseparable and activities in trade and politics were conducted based on mutual respect (Papaioannou, 2018: 448–51).

Culture in Ghana: policy and practice

Cultural diplomacy has emerged as a preferred form of diplomacy that best projects the values of a state as it aims at enhancing relations among countries within the international system (US Department of State, 2005). It is, therefore, crucial for states to seize the opportunity to utilize cultural diplomacy as an instrument of soft power in building and fostering friendly relations that will pave the way for potential benefits in line with their national interests, and that will play a role in influencing public opinion through increasing the cultural appeal of states.

In Ghana, democracy and politics have evolved to enable the establishment of a partisan state that recognizes diverse traditions, culture and customs in national development. In boosting national development, successive Ghanaian governments have engaged in diplomatic activities as a method of advancing their national interests. A key effort in this regard has been Ghana's efforts to maximize its cultural identity and relations since the release of a national cultural policy document in 1957, soon after it gained independence. In this early period of decolonization, under Nkrumah, Ghana was keen to ensure the promotion of its culture and traditions to forge a united national identity. However, successive administrations failed to implement the policy. This may have been due to, for example, Nkrumah's exit from Ghanaian politics and subsequent political instability which forced administrations to focus on national, rather than international, politics. It was only in 2004 that the Kufuor administration reconsidered this aspect of the country's diplomatic relations, revised the Nkrumah era's national cultural policy and released the Cultural Policy of Ghana that has served as a blueprint for subsequent administrations to preserve and promote Ghana's culture (National Commission on Culture, 2004).

The Cultural Policy of Ghana, among other aspects, outlines and prescribes traditional and cultural practices that have been agreed officially by a group of experts with a background in Ghana's cultural heritage and related fields (National Commission on Culture, 2004: 2). It prescribes the preservation and promotion of Ghana's cultural heritage between generations without trivializing its substance and benefits to the nation. Importantly, the Cultural Policy of Ghana outlines the main objectives it seeks to achieve, namely to:

- document and promote Ghana's traditional cultural values;
- ensure the growth and development of cultural institutions and make them relevant to human development, democratic governance and national integration;
- enhance Ghanaian cultural life and develop cultural programmes to contribute to the nation's human development and material progress through heritage, preservation, conservation, promotion and the use of traditional and modern arts and crafts to create wealth and alleviate poverty (National Commission on Culture, 2004: 10).

Achieving these objectives has become a primary mandate of the country's National Commission on Culture. Established by Provisional National Defence Council (PNDC) Law 238 in 1990, the National Commission on Culture is one of the cornerstones of the country's cultural architecture. Its mandate includes the administration, implementation and management of the Cultural Policy of Ghana. The Commission operates through several cultural institutions and agencies, but is the main institution mandated to liaise with all district assemblies, the Ghana Education Service, non-governmental organizations (NGOs) such as media agencies, the traditional council, individuals, various club associations and other stakeholders towards implementing the cultural policy.

Nonetheless, the implementation plan of the National Commission on Culture ought to observe important practical guidelines to attain the successful implementation of the policy. These guidelines are:

- Ghana's cultural policy targets the entire population and gives scope for all individuals and segments of society to access and participate in cultural events.
- Although the Cultural Policy of Ghana is guided by a holistic approach to culture, it recognizes that not all aspects of culture and cultural processes can be regulated by policy. It affirms the basic freedoms and fundamental human rights guaranteed by the constitution and which are essential to creativity and artistic self-expression.
- Cultural goods and services are an integral part of the national economy. However, for creativity and cultural entrepreneurship to thrive and contribute to wealth and employment generation, it is necessary to protect cultural goods and services from forces and logic of the free market economy through tax relief and other measures (National Commission on Culture, 2004: 13–15).

Ghana's cultural diplomacy

Article 40 of the 1992 Constitution of Ghana underpins the fundamental principles that guide the nation's foreign policy objectives by developing and maintaining diplomatic relations with other countries. These principles include the promotion of Ghana's interests, the promotion of respect for international law, commitment to multilateralism, achieving development and upholding international peace. Institutions such as the Ministry of Foreign Affairs and Regional Integration, the Ministry of Tourism, Culture and Creative Arts, the National Commission on Culture, the Ministry of Trade and the Ministry of Information have been mandated by the executive arm of government to carry out its mission and vision from the grassroots, decentralizing its operations to the various regional and district levels of culture locally and internationally.

The bulk of Ghana's revenue is derived from the export of traditional cash crops, followed closely by the tourism sector (Ministry of Foreign Affairs and Regional Integration, 2019). To generate revenue and simultaneously enhance the international image of Ghana, the Ministry of Tourism, Culture and Creative Arts in conjunction with Ministry of Foreign Affairs and Regional Integration has arranged activities and programmes for the Ghanaian diaspora through various Ghanaian diplomatic missions abroad (Ministry of Foreign Affairs and Regional Integration, 2019). For instance, during National Day celebrations, Ghana's diplomatic missions usually organize art exhibitions of Ghana's traditional attire and adinkra symbols, and offer a variety of traditional cuisines to commemorate the day. Furthermore, Ghanaian ambassadors and high commissioners who present their letters of credence to the head of state of the country they have been assigned to are usually clad in *kente*, *batakari* or African wax print designs and ornaments made with beads and/or from gold, portraying Ghana's unique culture. This serves as a way of expressing Ghana's national identity and attracts the interest of foreigners.

Ghana also practises cultural diplomacy through various initiatives such as recognizing and supporting Ghana's unique national culture and heritage, promoting cultural Made in Ghana products and commemorating the transatlantic slave trade.

Recognizing and promoting Ghana's unique national culture and heritage

The Ministry of Tourism, Arts and Culture (2022a), in conjunction with the National Commission on Culture, has over the years organized the National Festival of Arts and Culture to bring together stakeholders in Ghana's arts and culture industry where they showcase the talents of fashion designers, sculptors, weavers and film makers through art exhibitions while projecting the values of Ghana's cultural heritage.

Similarly, the Ghana Tourism Authority under the auspices of the Ministry of Tourism, Arts and Culture and its agencies have launched the 'See Ghana, Eat Ghana, Wear Ghana, Feel Ghana' campaign to evoke the spirit of nationalism through traditional food, clothes, music and significant sites (Ghana Tourism Authority, 2017). This campaign is an attempt at rebranding Ghana's historic sites and marketing Ghana to promote tourism and attract FDI. Former Minister of Tourism, Culture and Creative Arts Catherine Afeku, in her speech during the campaign launch in 2017, stated that Ghana's tourism has a lot to offer through its exciting cultural products (Ghana Tourism Authority, 2017). Furthermore, she maintained that Ghanaians are mindful of the fact that the creative and cultural industries have made a positive impact on economies all over the world. For this reason, the Ghanaian creative and cultural industries should be revitalized (Ghana Tourism Authority, 2017). Hence the creation of the 'See Ghana, Eat Ghana, Wear Ghana, Feel Ghana' campaign.

Furthermore, occasions like festivals help to portray Ghana's diverse culture through, among others, clothes, music and food. Usually, dignitaries from other countries are invited and sometimes during the celebrations are clothed in *kente* or *batakari* by their hosts which are later given to them as gifts. Guests at these festivals are also introduced to Ghanaian cuisine, traditional music and customs, creating a memorable experience; foreigners end up purchasing these before leaving the country as a reminder of the rich culture and traditions they encountered on their visit to Ghana. During important occasions such as wedding ceremonies, naming ceremonies, church services, graduations and so on, Ghanaians make a point of projecting their culture through their garments, food, music and cuisine. Most Ghanaians use traditional artefacts and symbols such as the *adinkra* for interior decorations for their homes and offices.

Promotion of cultural Made in Ghana products

In 2004, the government launched the 'National Friday Wear Programme', an initiative that sought to portray Ghana's identity using locally manufactured fabric and designs that are to be worn to work every Friday. This encouraged private companies, the public sector and schools to opt for Friday wear for their workers and students, respectively. The promotion of Ghana-made textiles was an attempt to promote the unique patterns and revive the textile and clothing industry but also to influence expatriates, the diaspora community and other foreigners to embrace Ghana's culture (Axelsson, 2021: 20–36).

Commemorating the transatlantic slave trade

In 2019 the Akufo Addo government launched the Year of Return campaign that has a become a major instrument to summon the global African family, home and abroad, to mark 400 years of the arrival of the first enslaved Africans in Jamestown, Virginia. Although August 2019 marked 400 years since enslaved Africans arrived in the US, the Year of Return initiative celebrated the resilience of all the victims of the transatlantic slave trade who were displaced and scattered all over the world.

The Year of Return campaign aimed to encourage the African diaspora to visit Ghana and reconnect with their culture and roots. The campaign involved a series of events such as festivals and music, focusing on Ghana's culinary culture and Ghanaian traditional wear (Year of Return, 2019). As an expression of cultural diplomacy, the Year of Return campaign also intersected with celebrity diplomacy. Aside from the fact that states and non-state actors (including NGOs and multinational companies) often facilitate diplomatic relations, there is an increasing trend of public figures engaging in the field of diplomacy. These public icons are now regarded as influential actors within the international system due to their ability to reach popular and elite audiences while building authority, legitimacy and influence, impacting on local and global processes of governance (Richey and Budabin, 2016). These icons also serve as ambassadors and activists in various ways with regard to promoting the cultural diplomacy of their states.

Through them, a state's cultural elements such as clothing, music, sports and cuisine, to mention a few, are often projected to foreign audiences in target countries. An example of such icons is Ghana's first prime minister (and later president), Kwame Nkrumah, who in 1957, together with his colleagues, 'stood at the Old Polo Grounds in Accra on the eve of Ghana's political independence to declare the country's freedom from British Colonial rule' (Arku, 2013). While addressing the nation, Nkrumah and his colleagues were adorned in traditional garments, the *batakari* as well as wristbeads. This signified the starting point of Ghana's quest to portray the African and, for that matter, the Ghanaian personality as proof that Ghana has something to offer which is uniquely African (Arku, 2013).

Celebrated global personalities who attended some events of the Year of Return initiative included, among others, Steve Harvey, Idris Elba, Boris Cudjoe, Anthony Anderson, Naomi Campbell, Kofi Kingston and Tina Knowles. Steve Harvey, for instance, visited the Cape Coast Castle built in 1555 as a transit point for slaves during the transatlantic slave trade era. Harvey was given a tour around the castle. Moved by its history, he called on the African diaspora to visit Ghana and reconnect with their ancestry and culture (Ghana Tourism Authority, 2019). Award-winning Jamaican dancehall artiste Popcaan, after visiting Cape Coast Castle during the Year of Return campaign, felt a strong connection to the history of the slaves housed at the castle and decided to purchase a house in Ghana (Adeola, 2020)

Ultimately, these experiences not only served the purpose of reconnecting the global African community at home and abroad with their roots and culture but also attained the goal of leveraging Ghana's culture and cultural diplomacy to boost its tourism industry, positioning Ghana as an ideal destination of choice for the African diaspora and promoting FDI into Ghana. The Year of Return campaign welcomed a total of about 700,000 visitors into the country (BBC News, 2020). Through activities of the initiative, $1.9 billion (£1.5 billion) was added to Ghana's economy (BBC News, 2020). It is evident that cultural diplomacy holds a lot of potential to bring significant amounts of money into a country's economy and to advance development.

To sustain the conversation around reconnecting the African diaspora to their roots and culture as well as encouraging them to make investments in Africa, and particularly Ghana, in 2020 the government of Ghana established the Beyond the Return Secretariat, following on from the Year of Return campaign of 2019. Beyond the Return essentially aims at highlighting Ghana as a global tourism brand, showcasing the investment potential of the country's tourism and creative sectors to the African diaspora and beyond. Although there was a lineup of events as a follow-up to the success of the Year of Return initiative, the outbreak of the COVID-19 pandemic made it impossible to hold the events. However, post-COVID-19, the Beyond the Return Secretariat is actively seeking to fulfil its purpose (Ministry of Tourism, Arts and Culture, 2022b).

All these instances of Ghana's state institutions, public figures and citizenry promoting cultural elements while engaging with foreigners not only to changes perceptions of Africa but also shows that Ghana has a lot to offer as a nation.

What Ghana stands to achieve in promoting cultural diplomacy

Countries all over the world seek to win the hearts and minds of global audiences through their cultural diplomatic engagements with other states within the international arena. Ghana's international cultural programmes focus on the country's music, cuisine, festivals and fashion. Ghana's pursuit of cultural diplomacy has been beneficial as it has boosted employment opportunities, tourism and FDI, and has promoted international recognition, especially as Ghana's *kente* is well-represented abroad.

Ghana is not as technologically advantaged as other states, such as those that manufacture car brands like Toyota, BMW and Honda, or phone brands like Samsung, iPhone, and Motorola. However, it has rich cultural elements that attract many tourists into the state to experience what Ghana has to offer. People's experiences when they travel from one country to another make a significant impact on their perceptions of the countries they have visited (Mabvuto, 2016). Ghana's tourism industry has proven to contribute to the country's economic development. The cultural elements of any country can attract foreigners to the country, anticipating an unforgettable experience. And this normally opens the country to more investors.

States that can project a positive image through their cultural offerings gain status and recognition by other countries and can be considered 'champions of global cultural diversity' (Ahearne, 2018). Ghana's pursuit of cultural diplomacy continues to serve as a channel to achieve its national interests, and the welfare of its citizens is a priority. The promotion of cultural diplomacy through cultural products offers various opportunities that add to its economic growth.

Over the years, Ghana's engagement in cultural diplomacy has encountered some major setbacks that have prevented the government and other stakeholders from fully achieving desired results. Issues of financial shortcomings, patent rights, inadequate support from the private sector and inconsistent policies of governments challenge Ghana's cultural diplomacy and the gains therefrom. Government can overcome these hurdles by encouraging private entities to sponsor more cultural-related programmes and creating some incentives for investors interested in its tourism sector. In addition, governments ought to be consistent in implementing cultural policies regardless of which administration is in power. Again, government needs to pursue legal protection for Ghana's *kente* patterns and *adinkra* symbols, which are being imitated by East Asian countries on a large scale without any compensation to the originators of the design (Boateng, 2011).

Conclusion

Ghana can leverage its rich traditional and cultural values to project a sense of national identity and gain a source of alternative revenue through the promotion of tourism and increased FDI to advance its national interest while promoting the image of Ghana.

Cultural diplomacy promotes Ghana's national interest, economic development and prestige. Despite Ghana's rich cultural diversity, more can be done to get to the point where Ghana is considered a master of cultural diplomacy within the international sphere and, ultimately, enjoy fully the gains of its cultural relations with the rest of the world. Therefore, Ghana must create awareness of and promote its cultural heritage. In instilling the 'I am Ghanaian' spirit, the government can increase the capacity of all country actors (celebrities, politicians, ambassadors, key business leaders and students) by organizing periodic programmes or workshops to teach Ghana's workforce and citizenry how to promote Ghana's culture as ambassadors of its cultural diplomatic engagements. Ghana must also adopt a well-structured framework for dissemination of information and implementation of the policies of the cultural policy document. There should be an end-to-end process detailing what state institutions and organs must practise in diplomacy based on traditional values, customs and cultural beliefs. This will ensure that cultural diplomacy is absorbed into the day-to-day activities of all stakeholders for the promotion of arts and culture. To ensure its effectiveness, there is the need for a monitoring and evaluation process as well as the provision of sufficient budgetary support for such a programme.

Finally, to achieve synergy and collaboration between relevant institutions, the Ministry of Foreign Affairs and Regional Integration, the National Commission on Culture, the Ministry of Tourism and the Ghana Tourism Authority should work hand in hand and not in isolation to champion the course of Ghana's cultural diplomacy.

References

Adeola, N. (2020) 'Jamaican star Popcaan buys $5.5m mansion in Ghana after "Year of Return"', *Face2Face Africa* [online], 23 January, Available at: https://face2faceafrica.com/article/jamaican-star-popcaan-buys-5-5m-mansion-in-ghana-after-year-of-return [Accessed 18 July 2022].

Ahearne, J. (2018) 'International recognition regimes and the projection of France', *International Journal of Cultural Policy*, 24(6): 696–709.

Arku, J. (2013) 'Re-living old Polo Grounds – now Nkrumah Mausoleum', *Graphic Online* [online], 11 July, Available from: www.graphic.com.gh/features/features/re-living-accra-old-polo-grounds-now-nkrumah-mausoleum.html [Accessed 23 June 2022].

Axelsson, L. (2021) 'Wearing the Ghanaian border: performing borders through the National Friday Wear programme', Space and Polity, 25(1): 20–36.

BBC News (2020) 'African diaspora: did Ghana's Year of Return attract foreign visitors?' [online], 20 June, Available from: www.bbc.com/news/world-africa-51191409 [Accessed 19 July 2022].

Berridge, G. (2002) *Diplomacy: Theory and Practice* (2nd edn), London: Palgrave.

Boateng, B. (2011) *The Copyright Thing Doesn't Work Here. Adinkra and Kente Cloth and Intellectual Property in Ghana*, Minneapolis: University of Minnesota Press.

Briggs, P. and Connolly, S. (2017) *Ghana* (7th edn), Buckinghamshire: Bradt Travel Guides.

Cull, N.J. (2009) *Public Diplomacy: Lessons from the Past*, Los Angeles, CA: Figueroa Press.

Ghana Tourism Authority (2017) 'Visit Ghana – "See, Eat, Wear, Feel Ghana" campaign launched' [online], July, Available from: https://visitghana.com/see-eat-wear-feel-ghana-campaign-launched/ [Accessed 23 June 2022].

Ghana Tourism Authority (2019) 'Visit Ghana – Year of Return: Steve Harvey reiterates call on black people in diaspora to "come home" as he tours Cape Coast Castle' [online], August, Available from: https://visitghana.com/year-of-return-steve-harvey-reiterates-call-on-black-people-in-diaspora-to-come-home-as-he-tours-cape-coast-castle/ [Accessed 23 June 2022].

James, J. (2002) 'Information technology, transactions costs and patterns of globalization in developing countries', *Review of Social Economy*, 60(4): 507–19.

James, P. and Steger, M.B. (2018) 'Globalization and global consciousness: levels of connectivity', in R. Robertson and D. Buhari-Gulmez (eds) *Global Culture: Consciousness and Connectivity*, London: Routledge, pp 21–39.

Javaid, N. (2019) 'Public diplomacy in comparison to traditional diplomacy', unpublished paper [online], Available from: www.academia.edu/11292698/Public_Diplomacy_in_Comparison_to_Traditional_Diplomacy#:~:text=Traditional%20diplomacy%20has%20more%20focus,%2Dto%2Dpeople%20positive%20relations [Accessed 23 June 2022].

Lovrinić, B. (2018) 'Book review: Cultural diplomacy: arts, festivals and geopolitics', *Croatian International Relations Review*, 24(82): 138–41.

Mabvuto, N. (2016) 'The role of tourism in a country's public diplomacy', *Linkedin Pulse* [online], 25 October, Available from: www.linkedin.com/pulse/role-tourism-countrys-public-diplomacy-percy-mabvuto-ngwira [Accessed 23 June 2022].

Melissen, J. (2005) 'The new public diplomacy: between theory and practice', in J. Melissen (ed) *The New Public Diplomacy. Soft Power in International Relations*, New York: Palgrave, p 3.

Ministry of Foreign Affairs and Regional Integration (2019) *Diaspora Engagement Initiative Concept Paper* [online], Available from: https://ghanaemberlin.de/wp-content/uploads/2019/12/DAB_CONCEPT_PAPER.pdf [Accessed 23 June 2022].

Ministry of Tourism, Arts and Culture (2022a) 'National Festival of Art and Culture (NAFAC)' [online], Available from: http://motac.gov.gh/index.php?option=com_content&view=article&id=106&catid=13&Itemid163 [Accessed 23 June 2022].

Ministry of Tourism, Arts and Culture (2022b) 'Beyond the return' [online], Available from: https://beyondthereturngh.com/ [Accessed 23 June 2022].

Morgenthau, H.J. (2006) *Politics among Nations: The Struggle for Power and Peace* (7th edn), New York: McGraw-Hill Higher Education.

National Commission on Culture (2004) *The Cultural Policy of Ghana* [online], Available from: www.academia.edu/31748891/THE_CULTURAL_POLICY_OF_GHANA_NATIONAL_COMMISSION_ON_CULTURE [Accessed 18 July 2022].

Papaioannou, K. (2018) 'Cultural policy, cultural diplomacy, culture: pillars of soft power', *Proceedings of SOCIOINT 2018 – 5th International Conference on Education, Social Sciences and Humanities*, Dubai, United Arab Emirates [online], 2–4 July, Available from: www.academia.edu/69145598/Cultural_Policy_Cultural_Diplomacy_Culture_Pillars_of_Soft_Power [Accessed 23 June 2022].

Richey, L. and Budabin, A. (2016) 'Celebrities in international affairs', *Oxford Handbooks Online*, Oxford: Oxford University Press [online], Available from: www.oxfordhandbooks.com/view/10.1093/oxfordhb/9780199935307.001.0001/oxfordhb-9780199935307-e-3 [Accessed 19 July 2022].

Salm, S.J. and Falola, T. (2002) *Culture and Customs of Ghana*, Westport, CT: Greenwood Publishing Group.

Touring Ghana (2016) *Bonwire Kente Weaving Village* [online], Available from: https://touringghana.com/bonwire-kente-weaving-village/ [Accessed 28 June 2022].

US Department of State (2005) *Cultural Diplomacy: The Linchpin of Public Diplomacy*. A Report of the Advisory Committee on Cultural Diplomacy [online], 1 September, Available from: www.state.gov/cultural-diplomacy-the-linchpin-of-public-diplomacy/ [Accessed 19 July 2022].

Year of Return (2019) 'Celebrating 400 years of African resilience' [online], Available at: www.yearofreturn.com/ [Accessed 23 June 2022].

12

Morocco's Cultural Diplomacy with Africa

Faiza Koubi

Introduction

A state's foreign policy is, among other factors, shaped by historical, geopolitical, geo-economic and geo-cultural determinants, which affect and determine its international and regional behaviour. Typically, a state adopts either a defensive or offensive posture depending on its reading of the environment and the definition of its national interests. The Kingdom of Morocco (hereafter Morocco or the Kingdom) is no exception in this regard. However, Morocco has been in an exceptional position regarding its relations with the rest of the African continent. Whereas Morocco had been a founding member of the Organization of African Unity (OAU), it withdrew its membership in 1984. Morocco also did not join the African Union (AU) along with its fellow African states when it was established in 2002 as the successor to the OAU. Morocco based these decisions on its opposition to other African states' support for Western Sahara and the Polissario Front, which had been campaigning for secession from Morocco. Moreover, the AU has recognized Western Sahara's independence as the Sahrawi Arabic Democratic Republic (SADR), which was accepted as an AU member. Despite this apparent diplomatic isolation from the rest of the continent, Morocco, before it joined the AU in 2016, had maintained significant relations with other African states and non-state actors. The Kingdom emphasized its cultural capital such as religion, history and tradition in its diplomatic interactions with the rest of Africa (Wüst and Nicolai, 2023: 554).

In Morocco, religious diplomacy is a common aspect of cultural diplomacy because it integrates Islamic culture into Moroccan identity. While some states, most notably France after the French Revolution, have separated the state, politics and religion from foreign policy, Morocco considers moderate Islam to be an essential asset in exercising soft power in regional, continental and international affairs. In 2021, the Commission Spéciale sur le Modèle de Développement expressed the need to renew Morocco's soft power strategy, which requires the country to draw on history, heritage and culture as tools of cultural diplomacy and nation branding (Commission Spéciale sur le Modèle de Développement, 2021). In this context, public decision making reaffirms the idea that promoting cultural diplomacy is not soft power on its own but that this diplomacy is a source of soft power deployed to achieve foreign policy objectives under a pragmatic national strategy. In this view, one can regard cultural diplomacy as a soft power tool that can serve a country's hard power and complement it, so this diplomacy could be seen as smart power. Therefore, Morocco is encouraging civil initiatives to intervene in cultural diplomacy and contribute to the nation's branding. This concerted approach requires the support and application of the country's diplomatic corps at home and abroad.

This chapter explains and analyses Morocco's diplomatic relations with the rest of the continent despite its ostensible isolation and exclusion between 1984 and 2016. Religion is a major aspect of Morocco's identity and culture, and therefore a significant driver of its cultural diplomacy. The chapter outlines Morocco's practice of cultural diplomacy as an instrument of its foreign policy with special emphasis on its relations with African states. Cultural diplomacy, as a distinct diplomatic practice, can be defined as the 'purposeful cultural cooperation' (Ang et al, 2015: 366) between states and the 'orchestrated government intervention to channel the flow of culture to advance national interests' (Arndt in Ang et al, 2015: 371). Drawing upon these definitions, the chapter outlines the evolution, tenets and practice of Morocco's cultural diplomacy with other African states and significant African non-state actors.

The chapter proceeds to outline the evolution of Morocco's cultural diplomacy. Thereafter, it turns to the role of religion in Morocco's cultural diplomacy with Africa. Finally, it concludes with an assessment of Morocco's cultural diplomacy.

Morocco's evolving cultural diplomacy

Cultural diplomacy is an evolving diplomatic practice that, like any other type of diplomacy, must adapt to domestic and international developments (Boutabssil, 2021: 209). Despite the dynamics of cultural diplomacy, a state's culture remains relatively stable, which allows it to practise cultural diplomacy to channel 'the flow of culture to advance national interests' (Arndt in Ang et al, 2015: 371).

Several distinct periods of Morocco's cultural diplomacy, which, inter alia, reveals its evolution and adaptive capacity, can be identified. These periods are presented here, followed by a discussion on the country's practice of cultural diplomacy.

Institutionalization and early manifestations of culture in diplomacy

During the first period, 1956–74, Morocco created a foreign affairs ministry and developed its diplomatic and consular network worldwide. In the early years after its independence, Morocco's cultural diplomacy was directed towards the classical circles of its belonging and identity, namely the country's African, Arab-Islamic and Mediterranean neighbourhoods. Despite the lack of resources and personnel, culture did feature, albeit less prominently, in Moroccan diplomacy. In early independence, Morocco was caught in the grip of revolutionary regimes that increased their hegemony via a wave of pan-Arabism. King Hassan II stabilized these regimes by focusing on religion. As a result, he achieved national cohesion through the population's shared Muslim religion. The King's status as Commander of the Faithful places his religious legitimacy above political forces (Bouasria, 2012). This silenced his opponents. Hassan II also made religion a significant dimension of Morocco's foreign policy and thus its cultural diplomacy. This increased Morocco's multilateral presence and influence. Notable examples of a focus on culture during this period include Morocco joining the United Nations Educational, Scientific and Cultural Organization (UNESCO), a multilateral organization promoting, for example, culture, and the Arab League, an organization that aims to promote relations between Arab states. Another example of culture in the country's diplomacy included Morocco's call for the creation of the Organization of Islamic Cooperation. King Hassan II's earlier proposal to establish a pan-Islamic organization resulted in the establishment of the Organization of the Islamic Conference on 25 September 1969. By 2023, the Organization of Islamic Cooperation (as it was subsequently renamed) is, after the United Nations, with 57 member states, the largest international organization spread across all continents (OIC, 2023).

Moreover, culture has also been mentioned in Morocco's cooperation agreements such as the Association Agreement with the European Economic Community (Aydoun and Kenbib, 2016: 25).

Thus, this period saw the establishment of the country's foreign ministry and its diplomatic missions. A second notable aspect of this period is the manifestation of Morocco's identity that informs its culture, namely its alignment with fellow Arab and Islamic states.

Ambition and cultural cooperation

The second distinguishable period of Morocco's cultural diplomacy covers 1975 to 1986 (Aydoun and Kenbib, 2016: 25). During this era, Morocco's international relations should be considered in the context of the Green March. On 6 November 1975, King Hassan II led Moroccans in a peaceful protest against Spain's occupation of the southern parts of the Kingdom (Entelis, 1996: 59). Spain eventually withdrew from the territory and Morocco restored its territorial integrity. The Green March bolstered Morocco's international confidence, national cohesion and the Kingdom's relations with its immediate African neighbourhood (Entelis, 1996: 59). In the aftermath of the Green March, the Kingdom pursued the promotion of its history and heritage, emphasizing its historical links with other countries. In this period, Moroccan diplomacy proliferated through cultural cooperation agreements, the creation of the Academy of the Kingdom of Morocco in 1977, research in the social sciences and fine arts, and attracting scholars from across the globe.

Culture on the diplomatic agenda

Between 1986 and 1999, the third phase of Moroccan cultural diplomacy, the Kingdom began to organize cultural events with an international audience in mind (Aydoun and Kenbib, 2016: 25). For example, it launched the year-long 'Time of Morocco in France' initiative in June 1999 to portray Morocco as a modern state rooted in history and with a rich heritage. The initiative was organized under the aegis of the two heads of state at the time, King Hassan II and French President Jacques Chirac, and introduced the Kingdom to French citizens, the Moroccan diaspora and the tourism market (Kapchan, 2007: 151).

Reformulation of foreign policy and consolidation of cultural diplomacy as a diplomatic practice

After King Hassan II's death in 1999, his son Mohammed VI succeeded him. Like his father, Mohammed VI expressed an interest in international affairs and commenced a reformulation of the country's foreign policy. One of the key features of this reformulated foreign policy was a renewed interest in Africa. In the 2000s, the Institute of African Studies, originally established by Mohammed VI's father to serve as a scientific bridge between Morocco and Africa, was actively involved in the development of the African policy of the new King (Koubi, 2021). Several royal speeches have reiterated the preponderance of culture in Morocco's diplomacy (Mohammed VI, 2013). Besides the reformulation of Morocco's foreign policy under the new King, further institutionalization of Morocco's culture occurred. In 2011, Morocco adopted a new constitution that enshrines the diversity of Moroccan identity and culture. The Preamble of the constitution refers to the origins of these diversities, which include Arab-Islamic, Amazigh and Saharan-Hassani components enriched by its African, Andalusian, Hebrew and Mediterranean elements (Morocco, 2011). The domestic institutionalization and thus acknowledgement of these cultural diversities soon found expression in Morocco's diplomatic relations, as will be outlined later.

In 2021, the Moroccan Higher Education Authority merged the Institute of African Studies with the Institute of Euro-Mediterranean Studies and Ibero-American Studies to integrate Africa into other spheres of Moroccan influence and cooperation.

Morocco's cultural diplomacy evolved over several distinct periods in response to domestic changes and international developments. These periods saw the institutionalization of the country's foreign policy, the introduction of its cultural capital in its foreign policy and diplomacy, and the acceleration of this as the country withdrew from the OAU in 1984. More importantly, Morocco's adaptive capabilities regarding its cultural diplomacy enabled it to use its unique culture to maintain historical relations and establish new horizons.

Practising cultural diplomacy with Africa

A state's culture, and therefore what it wants to channel internationally to advance its national interests, stem from numerous sources, including its national identity. In the case of Morocco, its national identity and culture stem from several sources, including geography (Africa, the Maghreb and its coastal locations), religion (Islam), 'Moroccanness' (translated in the local language as '*tamaghrabit*' denoting the state's exceptional and diversified identity, and Arabness (Mouline, 2022).

The practice of Morocco's cultural diplomacy with Africa is, among other aspects, determined by the substance and features of Moroccan culture to be channelled to foreign audiences. Morocco's practice of cultural diplomacy entails at least two elements, namely a focus on openness and diversity, and on religion and culture.

Openness

The constitutional changes of 2011 had several objectives, including to reflect Morocco as an open, diverse and tolerant society. The country has, for example, established a programme to renovate religious buildings such as synagogues, cathedrals and mosques. The renovation of these spaces symbolizes, for example, the cultural diversity of Morocco. This openness is also evident in the country's cultural cooperation, scientific cooperation, international cultural and student exchanges, and intercultural and interreligious dialogues and events. In addition to this, Morocco established cultural centres abroad to promote the country's heritage and history.

Morocco has a well-defined foreign policy decision-making process. The traditional and constitutionally prescribed actors involved in this process are the King and the foreign affairs ministry. However, foreign policy decision making is highly dependent on the King as royal speeches and statements guide foreign policy, which, in turn, guides Moroccan diplomats in implementing royal instructions.

The practice of cultural diplomacy in Morocco was initially restricted to the royal household and the diplomatic corps, but over time opened to other actors. The country's cultural diplomacy has become accessible to traditionally non-diplomatic actors and the government of Morocco is also increasingly sharing its cultural diplomacy strategy with domestic stakeholders such as think tanks, the clerical corps and educational institutions. The symbolic value of these initiatives is significant as it presents Morocco as a tolerant, open, multi-ethnic and diversified society; this gives credence to the country's cultural diplomacy (Boutabssil, 2021: 203–13).

Religion and culture

Cultural diplomacy is based on the persuasion of the masses by cultural values, which are not necessarily naturally acquired or objectively perceived (Molénat, 2016: 152). The constructivist approach also shows that culture and norms are constructed through a process of socialization which creates a particular reality. In Morocco, public corporations and civil society focus on African culture through arts festivals, international forums and the country's film industry. Moroccans maintain that Africanity is an intrinsic characteristic of Moroccan identity and reality; an aspect that is reflected in Morocco's cultural diplomacy. The country's African identity is pervasive. The glories of yesteryear, for example, the Charifian empire, began in its southern part, which is intimately linked with and anchored in Africa. Cultural practices in Morocco also reflect this reality, as does the country's constitution, royal and ministerial speeches, art exhibitions, rituals and spiritual practices. Admittedly, all these cultural manifestations of Morocco's African essence are social constructions, but they are internalized by all Moroccans. The country's relations with the rest of Africa have been socially constructed over time, and Morocco's cultural diplomacy with the continent reflects this social reality and the country's African identity. Moroccan culture, of which Africanity is one component, has been grafted over time via a process of spontaneous socialization within Morocco and between Morocco and the rest of the continent. Marrakech, the Moroccan imperial city, and the city of Essaouira illustrate this. Here, local traditions denote centuries of interactions between Morocco and the rest of the continent. In Essaouira, the annual Gnawa/Gnaoua Music Festival expresses the country's African heritage through a mixture of Sub-Saharan African, Arabic and Berber music and rituals (Kapchan, 2014: 7–14).

On a theoretical level, cultural diplomacy is a prime example of the antithesis of the realist theory of international relations. The English School of international relations, with Hobbes and his extreme realism at its origin, brought the great liberal ideas of state relations through exchanges, dialogues and international cooperation. Regarding cultural diplomacy, Hedley Bull's remarks on international society better reflect the power of transnational flux of values under a liberal approach (Bull, 1995). The liberalism paradigm explains that the anarchy of global society allows states to confront and know each other and therefore to opt for cooperation (rather than conflict) by taking advantage of shared values and/or interests. This is evident in some parts of Africa, which has long been subject to struggles for survival. The African past teaches us that the conflict that has punctuated the history of inter-African relations has pushed states to get to know each other better and forge links. Thus, one moves from an inevitable conflict towards a mutual understanding built around shared interests.

The third millennium had been called the African millennium (Klay Kieh, 2008). This re-evaluation of Africa's role and status in the international community is a recurring theme in the speeches of African leaders. There is also a greater awareness of the power of cultural diplomacy in Africa to affirm the continent's role and status in international affairs. A mutual understanding of culture can advance continental stability, solidarity and integration.

The predominance of the liberal approach over the practice of cultural diplomacy represents an emergence of multilateral forms of cultural action in Africa. The proliferation of cultural initiatives by community, national and regional intergovernmental and non-governmental organizations in Africa demonstrates the relevance of ideas to liberalism. It also suggests an awareness of the need for branding to bolster African states' agency. It could be said that 'making Africa great' is remaking Africa. The French political scientists Badie and Devin (2007) affirm that if it is possible to think of cooperation, states must not despair of international institutions. For Nye (1990: 32), states are interested in cooperation if there is evidence of some benefit to derive from cooperation. By avoiding war, one saves money and maximizes one's interests. Nye (1990: 32) observed that power also derives from intangible sources such culture, ideology and institutions.

The objectives of Moroccan foreign policy are to preserve its territorial integrity, strengthen the idea of the Moroccan nation state and position itself within its regional context. Cultural diplomacy buffers the Kingdom against its complex regional context and persistent instability in its neighbours. Historically, Africa was a hinterland for imperial influences. Through its cultural diplomacy and, more particularly, its religious dimension, Morocco has been able to confront historical and contemporary risks and threats, and the impact of regional instability. Violent extremism and terrorism remain contributing factors to insecurity and religious freedom of Moroccans and other Africans who confess the same faith.

To defend its territorial integrity, Morocco endeavours to maintain its ties with its African neighbourhood and extends its diplomacy beyond the traditional areas of influence. Therefore, it emphasizes its cultural assets and a common historical heritage with its African neighbourhood. Morocco's discourses maintain that its cultural heritage has been enriched by different civilizations in flux: Phoenician, Roman, Amazigh, Arab, Mediterranean and African. Moreover, Morocco stresses its cultural heritage expressed in, for example, its architectural historical heritage, intergenerational craftsmanship, literature and art. In the last decade, Morocco has adapted this approach and expanded it to project its cultural diplomacy towards other geographical areas, specifically North America, Latin America and Asia. This redirection signifies Moroccan confidence and ambition to expand its alliances and defend its national interests. Thus, Moroccan diplomacy became more pragmatic in its choices of allies during this era.

Effectively, culture as a component of Moroccan diplomacy can facilitate the national projection by a triple modality. Culture can be used as a shared component to consolidate pre-existing links and relations in some spheres of the Mediterranean, African or Arabic regions. Second, culture is a national branding tool to initiate new relations or promote a good image of the country. Finally, Moroccan culture can be used as an instrument of reconciliation to resolve or appease conflicts in its African and Islamic neighbourhood.

The country's cultural diplomacy focuses on shared religious doctrinal foundations in, for example, Sub-Saharan Africa, where it maintains its status and influence through cultural cooperation in academia and scientific areas. Morocco has realized that academic cooperation and exchanges have the potential to build goodwill and maintain a shared cultural and political understanding (Powell, 2001). The soft power of educational cooperation promotes Morocco's influence and national interests. Moroccan universities and higher education establishments focus on cooperation with African academic institutions and are increasingly hosting a significant number of foreign students. In 2021, Morocco announced a 15-year higher education and research development model and strategy to establish the country as a regional higher education, science and innovation hub (Commission Spéciale sur le Modèle de Développement, 2021).

Academic exchanges between Morocco and the rest of Africa aim to improve the country's standing in and relations with the rest of the continent and to accelerate the internationalization of the higher education sector (El Kirat El Allame and Kaaouachi, 2023). Since the 2000s, student mobility from African countries to Morocco has increased significantly. The country is becoming a desirable educational destination for African and non-African students. In 2020, for example, Morocco hosted 24,226 foreign students compared to 14,220 in 2014 (El Kirat El Allame and Kaaouachi, 2023). One of the reasons for the increase is the large number of bursaries offered to Sub-Saharan African students by the Moroccan Agency for International Development (Sawahel, 2021).

Religion in Morocco's cultural diplomacy and geo-cultural struggles in Africa

In the aftermath of the attacks on the United States of 11 September 2001, Moroccan expatriates, most notably Mounir al-Motassadek and Amir Azizi, were implicated in terrorism abroad (Celso, 2014: 89–92; BBC News, 2018). King Mohamed VI, who was enthroned in 1999, realized that international perceptions might question Morocco's identity as a bulwark against radicalization. To counter this, Morocco embarked on an intensification of its cultural diplomacy, particularly its religious dimension (Wüst and Nicolai, 2023: 554–79).

Since the pro-democracy protests in North Africa that started in 2010 (the Arab Spring), the African continent has again become an area of geo-cultural struggles. The Sahel from the Gulf of Guinea to the Red Sea faces several hybrid security threats. In response, Morocco identified three threats likely to affect its national security and regional stability, namely a proliferation of terrorist attacks, increased violent extremism and the spread of Shiitism. Morocco considers these elements a clear danger to the security and stability of the entire region. To counter these threats, Morocco again employed religion and religious diplomacy to prevent a possible shift towards violent religious radicalization and challenges to the 'Moroccan official Islam', a key element of the country's cultural identity (Nejjar, 2018: 1). Sunni Islam is the constitutionally enshrined religion in Morocco and the Moroccan monarchy its designated religious authority. In the wake of the Arab Spring, Maliki jurisprudence and rites were reaffirmed. The Sunni Malikite dogma is widespread in Africa and is practised by almost all Muslims in the Maghreb. Therefore, Morocco countered support for Shia Islam, which had been gaining a foothold in its African neighbourhood. Speaking at the 2013 Franco-African Summit on Peace and Security, the King reiterated the Sunni identity of his country and the bonds that link the country with the remainder of the continent: 'Building on its time-honoured spiritual bonds with the countries of the Sahel, on the Commandership of the Faithful and on its successful reform of the religious domain, Morocco has sought to protect and promote the moderate, open, tolerant Sunni Islam which has long existed in the region' (Mohammed VI, 2013).

Morocco's consistent adherence to Sunni Islam has brought stability to the country and sees the growth of Shia Islam in several African states, due to what it considers Iranian support, as an imminent national and regional security threat (Jacobs, 2018). Morocco is, therefore, opposing the spread of the sectarian wars between Shiites and Sunnis in the Middle East to Africa, and is particularly critical of Iran, a Shia Islam state; it has broken diplomatic ties with Iran at least twice (2009 and 2018) (Jacobs, 2018; Hami, 2023). Besides this, Morocco has been actively restoring the image and influence of the Sufi Brotherhoods (*Zawya*). Historically, these Brotherhoods included the Tidjaniya Tariqa, the Qadiria Tariqa, the Shadilia-Jazulia Tariqa, the Taibia Tariqa and the Sanusia Tariqa and were described as the 'main engines for strengthening relations' between Morocco, its African neighbours and other Sufi Brotherhoods in these countries (Hami, 2023). The second significance of these Brotherhoods lies in their support of Morocco in its struggle against Portugal, Spain, France and the Ottoman Empire. In the third instance, these Sufi Brotherhoods are pacifist, culturally tolerant and follow a unifying spiritual dogma that rejects all violence in religious practices (Bouyahya, 2016: 42–3). The Sufi Tijaniyya Brotherhood, for example, was established in 1781 by Sidi Ahmed Tijani in the Moroccan city of Fez, the spiritual capital of Morocco. It soon spread to other parts of Africa such as Mali and Senegal, where it remains active today, and their attachment to Morocco remains a source of their legitimacy (Hami, 2023). For Morocco, these Sufi Brotherhoods are an instrument of its cultural diplomacy as the country uses them to secure and maintain support in its African neighbourhood, prevent destabilization and maintain spiritual leadership in an African area renowned for ancestral ties with Morocco (Hami, 2023). Moreover, Moroccan kings and sultans have supported these Brotherhoods financially, lavishing them with gifts, and brings them together annually for a gathering (Hami, 2023). The attachment to these historical relationships and these shared religious values maintain Morocco's symbolic presence, leadership and status among cross-border communities of worshippers and practitioners of the rites developed by these Brotherhoods across Africa.

Despite historical ties and a common religion, the Brotherhoods exist and operate in a complicated political context crossing national borders. This has, for example, manifested in tensions between Morocco and its neighbour Algeria, which claims its share in the Sufi landscape and influence. Algeria has been claiming the origin of Zawya Tijaniyya (the Tijaniyya Brotherhood) as its founder, Sidi Ahmed Tijani, was born in Ain Madi in present-day Algeria (Hami, 2023). Although these Brotherhoods are deeply anchored in the history of worship in the Maghreb, Morocco was one of the few countries that institutionalized and integrated these practices. Despite these Moroccan–Algerian tensions, Morocco maintains its symbolic and real influence, as is evident in, for example, its mobilization of public actors in maintaining relations between the Moroccan Brotherhoods and their loyal adherents (called the Mouridis) across Africa, particularly in Senegal and Mali. Second, Morocco continues to allocate resources for scientific and religious cooperation between Morocco and countries where these Brotherhoods exist. The third reason why Morocco maintains its influence in its neighbourhood is the established links between the Zawyas of Morocco and their affiliates in African countries which recognize the Moroccan sovereign as Commander of the Faithful. Finally, Morocco has institutionalized relations between the Moroccan Muslim clerical sector and those of other African states through, for example, the Moroccan Foundation of African Ulemas (Muslim theologians) and the annual gathering of African Sufi Brotherhoods.

Conclusion

The chapter set out to outline Morocco's cultural diplomacy as an instrument of the country's foreign policy. Cultural diplomacy uses a state's culture as diplomatic capital to transmit and exchange ideas about a country to a foreign audience such as another government or organization.

Contemporary Morocco is the product of its unique location and history that continues to inform and determine the country's present-day foreign policy and diplomacy. In fact, the hand of history and its location have produced a highly diverse society that through social construction has produced a unified and coherent national identity and thus a unique culture. For post-independence Morocco, culture became the country's diplomatic currency. Since independence, the country's cultural diplomacy has evolved over four distinct periods, showing an increased awareness of and use of culture in Morocco's interactions with its immediate African neighbourhood and further afield. Cultural diplomacy has also been a significant driver of the country's foreign policy and ambitions.

Religion underlies Morocco's cultural diplomacy. Historical experiences and events have contributed to its establishment and that of its immediate African neighbourhood as Sunni Islam. Besides the shared religious doctrine, Morocco has also enshrined the role of its monarch as the Commander of the Faithful in its constitution. Thus, Morocco maintains its status as an influential African state. It also maintains this position due to its self-reference as a diverse and open society. Moreover, and especially during the time of Hassan II and Mohamed VI, the country has actively focused on religion as an essential element of its cultural identity and cultural diplomacy. Moroccan public authorities have opened cultural diplomacy to non-institutional actors to reinforce the effect of Morocco's nation branding as open and diverse. This fluidity of the decision-making process in favour of expanding the stakeholders in cultural diplomacy promises to stimulate more initiatives, provided that these new actors have the financial means to act and to coordinate their actions. Furthermore, the use of religious diplomacy, in terms of impact, has a comparative advantage over other areas of cultural diplomacy. The rationales are the strong organization of the national religious field and the standardization of religious actors' intervention. As explained earlier, one can also add the abundance of funds dedicated to religious diplomacy regarding the security issue in the national and regional landscape.

On a practical level, Morocco's cultural diplomacy is rooted in the logic of South–South cooperation. In the fields of education, academia and capacity building, Morocco seeks to export know-how to African countries not only for purposes of nation branding but also to lay the foundations for cooperation with the African regions that share the same challenges in terms of development. Morocco is developing its conception of cultural diplomacy to provide collective responses to national and transnational problems, such as the training and qualification of young people, their employability and the opening of other alternatives for African youth. Educational and university diplomacy remains one of the oldest dimensions of Moroccan African relations that allow Morocco to shape its image with an audience in the making. This cultural action is often presented under the nexus of diplomacy, culture/development and stability. However, the francophone factor is potent in this type of diplomacy. Although this allows Morocco to maintain its position among the French-speaking club, it is not enough to develop an African cluster of the knowledge economy on a global scale.

Morocco encourages the African dimension by highlighting its heritage in the field of artistic creation. Thus, it has been working since 2020 to increase cooperation agreements in the cultural industry with African countries. Aware of the difficulty for this sector on the continent, the country aims to set up platforms to support African creators, publishers and artists to produce and transmit their work and to provide the necessary regulatory facilities throughout the artistic value chain. The conclusion drawn from this chapter holds that through cultural diplomacy in Africa or elsewhere, Morocco highlights a characteristic intrinsic to its identity, that of its African roots. By boosting these aspects of its cultural diplomacy, Morocco is branding for Africa. It presents itself as the hub between Africa and Europe and as the gateway to Africa (King Mohammed VI, 2017). An illustration of this representation appears clearly in the speech by King Mohammed VI (2017) on the reintegration of the AU: 'Some argue that Morocco would aim to acquire leadership in Africa. I tell them that it is to Africa that the Kingdom seeks to give leadership.' Indeed, Morocco's soft power is recognized in, for example, the Global Soft Power Index 2022, which ranked the country 46th of 120 states surveyed, and leading the Maghreb Region (Zouiten, 2022).

References

Ang, I., Raj Isar, Y. and Mar, P. (2015) 'Cultural diplomacy: beyond the national interest?', *International Journal of Cultural Policy*, 21(4): 365–81.

Aydoun, A. and Kenbib, M. (2016), *La Diplomatie culturelle marocaine. Proposition d'un modèle rénové*, Institut Royal d'Etudes Stratégiques, Rabat [online], December, Available from: www.ires.ma/images/Publications/RAPPORT-DIPLOMATIE-CULTURELLE.pdf [Accessed 19 July 2022].

Badie, B. and Devin, G. (2007) *Le multilatéralisme: Nouvelles formes de l'action internationale*, Paris: La Découverte.

Bouasria, A. (2012) 'The second coming of Morocco's "Commander of the Faithful". Mohammed VI and Morocco's religious policy', in B. Maddy-Weitzman and D. Zisenwine (eds) *Contemporary Morocco: State, Politics and Society under Mohammed VI*, London: Routledge, pp 35–58.

Bouyahya, D. (2016) 'Religious tourism and Sufism in Morocco', *European Journal of Multidisciplinary Studies*, 1(5): 40–50.

Boutabssil, F.Z. (2021) 'Evaluation of the impact of Moroccan cultural diplomacy: tools, challenges and insights – the Ministry of Foreign Affairs, African cooperation and Moroccan expatriates as a case-study', *International Journal of Linguistics, Literature and Translation*, 4(2): 203–13.

BBC News(2018) 'Mounir al-Motassadek: Germany releases 9/11 accomplice' [online], 15 October, Available from: www.bbc.com/news/world-europe-45862560 [Accessed 3 December 2023].

Bull, H. (1995) *The Anarchical Society – A Study of Order in World Politics*, 2nd ed., London: Macmillan.

Celso, A. (2014) *Al-Qaeda's Post-9/11 Devolution: The Failed Jihadist Struggle against the Near and Far Enemy*, New York: Bloomsbury Academic.

Commission Spéciale du Modèle de Développement (2021) *Le Nouveau modèle de développement. Libérer les énergies et restaurer la confiance pour accélérer la marche vers le progrès et la prospérité pour tous* [online], Available from: https://csmd.ma/documents/Rapport_General.pdf [Accessed 29 November 2023].

El Kirat El Allame, Y. and Kaaouachi, A. (2023) 'The internationalization of Moroccan higher education. Achievements, intended and unintended outcomes, and future prospects', in S. Kamyab and R. Latiner Raby (eds) *Unintended Consequences of Internationalization in Higher Education: Comparative International Perspectives on the Impacts of Policy and Practice*, New York: Routledge, pp 182–90.

Entelis, J.P. (1996) *Culture and Counterculture in Moroccan Politics*, Lanham, MD: University Press of America.

Hami, H. (2023) 'Islamic Brotherhoods' enduring relevance in North Africa–Sub-Saharan Africa relations', *Morocco World News* [online], 22 May, Available from: www.moroccoworldnews.com/2023/05/355578/islamic-brotherhoods-enduring-relevance-in-north-africa-sub-saharan-africa-relations [Accessed 3 December 2023].

Jacobs, A. (2018) *Why Did Morocco Cut Its Diplomatic Ties with Iran?*, Moroccan Institute for Policy Studies [online], Available from: https://mipa.institute/en/6813 [Accessed 3 December 2023].

Kapchan, D. (2007) *Travelling Spirit Masters: Moroccan Gnawa Trance and Music in the Global Marketplace*, Middletown, CT: Wesleyan University Press.

Kapchan, D. (2014) 'Introduction. Intangible rights: cultural heritage in transit', in D. Kapchan (ed) *Cultural Heritage in Transit. Intangible Rights as Human Rights*, Philadelphia: University of Pennsylvania Press, pp 177–93.

Klay Kieh, G. (ed) (2008) *Africa and the Third Millennium*, Trenton, NJ: Africa World Press.

Koubi, F. (2021) 'The Moroccan cultural action in Sub-Saharan Africa', International Institute for Middle East and Balkan Studies (Ifimes) [online], 20 March, Available from: www.ifimes.org/en/researches/the-moroccan-cultural-action-in-sub-saharan-africa-for-a-peaceful-space/4753# [Accessed 19 July 2022].

Mohammed VI (2013) 'Message to participants in Elysée Summit on Peace and Security in Africa', *Moroccan World News* [online], 6 December, Available from: www.moroccoworldnews.com/2013/12/114975/king-mohammed-sends-message-to-participants-in-elysee-summit-on-peace-and-security-in-africa [Accessed 3 December 2023].

Mohammed VI (2017) *Speech delivered to the 28th African Union Summit in Addis Ababa* [online], 31 January, Available from: www.maroc.ma/en/royal-activities/full-speech-hm-king-28th-african-union-summit [Accessed 19 July 2022].

Molénat, X. (2016) 'Peter Berger et Thomas Luckmann: l'homme est une production sociale', in N. Journet (ed) *Les grands penseurs des Sciences Humaines*, Auxerre: Éditions Sciences Humaines, pp 151–54.

Morocco (Kingdom of) (2011) *Constitution* [online], Available from: www.constituteproject.org/constitution/Morocco_2011.pdf [Accessed 19 July 2022].

Mouline, M. (2022), 'Le capital culturel, historique et des loisirs', Institut Royal d'études Stratégique*s* Presentation [online], 11 April, Available from: www.youtube.com/watch?v=fWcpv9QZMoY [Accessed 19 July 2022].

Nejjar, S. (2018). *Morocco's Political Use of Islam and Its Religious Diplomacy*, EuroMeSCo Policy Brief, No 86 [online], 7 November, Available from: www.euromesco.net/wp-content/uploads/2018/11/Brief86_Morocco-Political-Use-of-Islam-1.pdf [Accessed 3 December 2023].

Nye, J. (1990) *Bound to Lead: The Changing Nature of American Power*, New York: Basic Books.

OIC (Organization of Islamic Cooperation) (2023) *History* [online], Available from: www.oic-oci.org/page/?p_id=52&p_ref=26&lan=en [Accessed 3 December 2023].

Powell, C. (2001) *Statement on International Education Week 2001*, US Department of State Archive [online], 7 August, Available from: https://2001-2009.state.gov/secretary/former/powell/remarks/2001/4462.htm [Accessed 19 July 2022].

Sawahel, W. (2021) 'A roadmap for making Morocco a regional hub', *University World News Africa Edition* [online], 10 June, Available from: www.universityworldnews.com/post.php?story=20210608120107741#:~:text=Morocco%20has%20unveiled%20a%2015,Mohammed%20VI%20on%2025%20May [Accessed 29 November 2023].

Wüst, A. and Nicolai, K. (2023) 'Cultural diplomacy and the reconfiguration of soft power: evidence from Morocco', *Mediterranean Politics*, 28(4), 554–79.

Zouiten, S. (2022) 'Morocco leads the Maghreb region in Soft Power Index', *Morocco World News* [online], 17 March, Available from: www.moroccoworldnews.com/2022/03/347715/morocco-leads-the-maghreb-region-in-soft-power-index [Accessed 19 July 2022].

13

Understanding Knowledge Diplomacy in Africa[1]

Jane Knight

Introduction

Diplomacy is used and defined in a multitude of ways. At the macro level, diplomacy is described as a lens to understanding international relations (Pouliot and Cornut, 2015). The definitions vary according to whether diplomacy is being articulated in terms of functions, forms or actors and whether the theory or practice of diplomacy is being examined. Kerr and Wiseman (2013) identify two fundamental aspects regarding the ongoing debates about contemporary diplomacy. The first relates to the epistemological underpinnings as they believe that 'what we mean by diplomacy' is breaking down. The second is identifying the key differences between contemporary diplomacy and diplomacy in the past (Kerr and Wiseman, 2013). The purpose of this chapter is to examine the changing roles of international higher education, research and innovation (IHERI) in the complex and evolving world of contemporary diplomacy through the concept of knowledge diplomacy. An interdisciplinary approach is required to understand how scholars and experts from both diplomacy and international higher education fields of study understand the forms, functions and contributions that IHERI makes to international relations.

Among the multitude of terms traditionally used to conceptualize and label the role of IHERI in international relations, the most common are cultural, public and science diplomacy and soft power. Having multiple and even contradictory terms causes confusion and so-called terminology chaos. Each term has its pros and cons and has been chosen by the scholar, diplomat or policy maker for specific reasons. It is evident that 'one size does not fit all', and the local context of each actor, country and sector must be respected. However, the plethora of terms is not helping to advance a robust analysis of the contemporary role of IHERI and international relations. This chapter addresses that challenge and presents a definition and conceptual framework for the concept of knowledge diplomacy, differentiates knowledge diplomacy from the more commonly used terms previously mentioned such as cultural, science, education and public diplomacy, and illustrates how the key elements of knowledge diplomacy can be applied to the Pan-African University (PAU).

Defining knowledge diplomacy

The definition proposed for knowledge diplomacy is 'the process of building and strengthening relations between and among countries through international higher education, research and innovation' (Knight, 2021: 161 and 162). In this definition, diplomacy is intentionally framed as a process – a series of actions to receive a result – not a policy per se. This approach to defining knowledge diplomacy is consistent with the understanding that diplomacy is generally understood as the process of developing relations between and among countries to operationalize foreign policies (Griffiths et al, 2014).

It is important that a generic definition of knowledge diplomacy be used to increase its relevance and use in a diversity of settings, cultures or countries. Many of the proposed definitions of diplomacy by scholars and policy experts emanate from and relate to a specific set of circumstances, making it difficult to use the definitions more broadly. To illustrate the difference between a definition and a description, an example of a description of knowledge diplomacy is proposed as follows:

> Knowledge diplomacy involves diverse state and non-state actors such as universities and research organizations involved in collaborative education, research and innovation initiatives which are based on mutual benefits and reciprocity and designed to build and strengthen relations between and among countries to increase mutual understanding and address global issues. (Knight, 2021: 149)

This description includes actors, strategies, values and intended outcomes and is different to a concise definition.

It is worth noting that the proposed definition of knowledge diplomacy does not actually include the term knowledge. Instead, higher education, research and innovation are used as the fundamental concepts to represent the transfer (teaching and learning/education) of knowledge, production of knowledge (research) and application of new knowledge (innovation). These three concepts form the backbone of the definition.

Not including knowledge in the definition was deliberate and can be both a strength and a weakness. While knowledge is inclusive of higher education, research and innovation, it can also be used in many different and contradictory ways. Different disciplines and sectors have their own lens to understand and define knowledge and there are countless ways to modify the concept of knowledge, such as implicit knowledge, tacit knowledge, technical knowledge and scientific knowledge (Lehrer, 2000). Furthermore, by including knowledge in the definition, the term knowledge diplomacy could be misunderstood as a form of issue diplomacy and become one more hyphenated type of diplomacy such as climate, health or refugee diplomacy, where advocacy plays a key role. It is important to avoid knowledge diplomacy being seen as being about knowledge itself rather than the use of knowledge in building and strengthening international relationships. In this way, the meaning of knowledge diplomacy is like the concept of cultural diplomacy and different from climate diplomacy (Light, 2017). Cultural diplomacy is not about advocating for or solving issues about culture, it is about using culture to promote relations and mutual understanding among countries (Gienow-Hecht and Donfried, 2010; Goff, 2013). This differs from climate diplomacy or food security, for example, which is about addressing the issues of climate change, not using climate to strengthen relations between countries.

Knowledge diplomacy can also be understood as a two-way process. IHERI can strengthen relations between and among countries. However, the converse direction is also true, meaning that international relations can strengthen the capacity and impact of IHERI. An example of the latter is when governments or international organizations develop policies, sign agreements or establish new initiatives that are intended to increase capacity or forge new partnerships to further education, research and innovation, build trust, find common ground and strengthen cooperation between participating countries and actors.

It is recognized that the working definition of knowledge diplomacy is not neutral, as it infers a positive outcome. While the intention is to strengthen relations between and among countries, as in states and society, as well as to enhance IHERI, there can also be unexpected negative outcomes. Unstable and conflicted relations between states can have negative repercussions on IHERI and vice versa. There are examples where bilateral higher education cooperation schemes have been cancelled and borders closed to academics and students due to strained relations between countries, as evidenced by the US ban on issuing visas for students/scholars from Arab countries in 2017 and by United Arab Emirates requiring all students and academics to leave Qatar during the 2017 blockade. Another example involves the closing of China's Confucius Institutes in several countries because of deteriorating relationships.

It is important to note that while knowledge diplomacy is oriented to positive outcomes, it is not intended to be a normative concept in the sense that it suggests what a state ought to do or that it is always the preferred approach. Different needs, priorities, rationales and expected outcomes in the use of IHERI in international relations can necessitate different approaches. The use of IHERI in knowledge diplomacy is one of these approaches that has an intended positive response which is strengthening relations between states and societies based on collaboration, reciprocity and trust. There are instances where using IHERI in a more competitive way would serve national interests (Wojciuk, 2018).

Towards a conceptual framework for knowledge diplomacy

Conceptual frameworks can be used as analytical tools to explore the meaning and deepen the understanding of a phenomenon and concept such as knowledge diplomacy (Ravitch and Riggan, 2016). Table 13.1 presents the foundational elements of the knowledge diplomacy framework including intentions, actors, principles, modes and activities. An elaboration of each of the major categories follows. The examples noted in the framework are meant to be illustrative, not comprehensive. However, the principles and values remain steadfast and are key to understanding the process of knowledge diplomacy.

The following sub-sections discuss each constituent element of the structure of the conceptual framework in Table 13.1.

Intentions, purpose, rationales

Because knowledge diplomacy brings together a network of different partners from various sectors to address common issues, there will different intentions, self-interests and implications for the individual countries and actors involved. This means that despite common concerns, actors will bring different needs, priorities and resources to the partnership. These differences will need to be respected and negotiated to ensure that the strengths and opportunities for each partner are optimized. This is done through a horizontal collaborative type of relationship that acknowledges the different but collective rationales, needs and resources of the group of partners to reach a common understanding.

Actors and partners

Several international relations scholars suggest that distinctions should be made between cultural diplomacy and cultural relations (Pajtinka, 2014),

Table 13.1: Conceptual framework for IHERI in a knowledge diplomacy relationship

Intentions, purpose 1	Actors, partners 2	Principles, values 3	Modes, approaches 4	Activities, instruments 5
To build/strengthen relations between and among countries through IHERI	Government departments and agencies related to education, science, technology, innovation at all levels	Reciprocity	Negotiation	*Generic:*
		Mutuality	Communication	Networks
		Cooperation	Representation	Joint projects
		Common ground	Conflict Resolution	Conferences
To use IHERI to help address global challenges and promote peace and prosperity	Intergovernmental agencies related to IHERI	Partnership	Compromise	Summits
		Common good	Collaboration	Coalitions
	NGOs related to IHERI	Interdisciplinary	Exchange	Track II
		Multi-sector	Mediation	Agreements
	HEIs	Transparency	Conciliation	Working groups
To strengthen IHERI through enhanced relations between and among countries	Research centres		Partnerships	Institution building
	Think-tanks		Building trust	*IHERI specific:*
	Centres of excellence		Dialogue	Int'l joint universities
	Research Networks			Student/scholar exchanges
	Foundations			Joint research networks
	Innovation centres			Regional universities
	Experts			Education/ knowledge hubs
	Private sector – multinational corporations			Scholarships
				ODA projects
				Twinning and joint degree programmes

Source: Knight (2021).

education diplomacy and education relations (Piros and Koops, 2020), and science diplomacy and science cooperation (Copeland, 2015). This is predicated on the belief that 'diplomacy' involves state actors only while 'relations' involves state and non-state actors. On one hand, this helps to avoid diplomacy being used as a catch-all phrase for any international activity by diverse actors. On the other hand, it seems to contradict the reality that in contemporary diplomacy it is not only state actors that are involved in addressing many of the major national, regional and global issues (Cooper et al, 2013). Ruffini (2020: 11) asserts that 'science diplomacy draws its appeal from being properly attuned to its time, and it does this in two ways. First, global issues are put at its centre. Second, non-state actors find their place in it'. A multi-actor and multi-stakeholder approach to diplomacy is needed in today's interconnected world, where countries face common challenges (Pigman, 2010).

While universities and colleges are key players in knowledge diplomacy, a broad range of other state and non-state IHERI actors is involved. These include national, regional and international centres of excellence, research institutions, foundations, think-tanks, professional associations, private sector companies, non-governmental organizations, education and knowledge hubs and cities, and different sector governmental departments/agencies. In many cases the IHERI actors are working with other sectors and/or disciplines depending on the nature of the initiative. Common partners include industry, civil society groups, foundations and governmental agencies. Working with a diversity of IHERI and other partners is a key feature of knowledge diplomacy and often differentiates knowledge diplomacy from higher education internationalization. Knowledge diplomacy includes actors and partners working together in bilateral/multilateral relationships and at national, regional and international levels with the aim of building stronger relationships between countries as well as sharing education, research and innovation to address national, regional or global issues.

Principles and values

As noted, principles and values are an integral part of diplomacy (Rathbun, 2014) and foreign policy (Srinivasan et al, 2019) and are thus core to understanding knowledge diplomacy and differentiating it from other terms. As identified in Table 13.1, the values of cooperation, reciprocity and mutuality are fundamental building blocks of knowledge diplomacy. Different needs and resources of actors will result in different benefits (and potential risks) for partners. Mutuality of benefits does not mean that all actors/countries will receive the same benefits in a symmetrical fashion. It does mean, however, that the principle of mutuality and reciprocity of benefits will guide the process and there will be collective and different benefits for different actors and countries. The conceptual framework makes the fundamental principles/values of knowledge diplomacy explicit. Whether these values are interpreted to be inherently good or desirable is in the eye of the beholder – in other words, actors and states – and depend on desired outcomes. Making values explicit does not necessarily imply that they are normative in nature and indicate a preferred approach. For instance, cooperation and reciprocity can be seen as desirable in some cases where in other circumstances competition can be seen as more attractive and advantageous.

Modes and approaches

Knowledge diplomacy is based on horizontal relationships between and among major actors and countries and focuses on collaboration, negotiation and compromise to ensure that the goals are met and there are benefits for all. There is no doubt that despite common concerns, there will be potential conflict given inevitable differences in self-interest and expectations among actors. It is naïve to deny this reality. However, a diplomatic approach in general, and knowledge diplomacy more specifically, rely on negotiation, mediation and conflict resolution to address these differences and find common ground. In general, knowledge diplomacy is based on a collaborative win–win approach to addressing common issues as well as meeting individual countries' self-interests.

Activities and instruments

The activities/instruments generally associated with international relations and diplomacy include joint meetings, conferences, Track II negotiations, summits and coalitions (Cooper et al, 2013). These are central to diplomacy in general and apply to knowledge diplomacy. However, because knowledge diplomacy has IHERI at its core, there are additional salient activities which differentiate it from other types of related diplomacies. These activities include international joint universities, student/scholar exchanges, thematic research networks, education/knowledge hubs, regional centres of excellence, scholarships, development cooperation projects, international branch campuses, alumni networks, centres of excellence and twinning programmes, to name a few.

Knowledge diplomacy in relation to cultural, science and education diplomacy

Knowledge diplomacy is framed as a more comprehensive process than individual traditional higher education internationalization activities, and different from soft power and other forms of diplomacy such as cultural, public, science and education diplomacy. Understanding these differences involves understanding the inherent intentions, values and activities attached to the different approaches. The following sub-sections discuss points of differentiation between knowledge diplomacy and other types of diplomacy used by scholars and experts to discuss the role of IHERI in international relations.

Knowledge diplomacy is broader than cultural diplomacy

Cultural diplomacy has been a popular term for decades. While the meaning and activities have evolved, it is primarily oriented to international exchanges, exhibitions and events in all fields of the arts, music, theatre, literature, film, media and architecture as well as sports and other cultural expressions (Goff, 2013). The goal of cultural diplomacy is primarily to enhance cross-cultural awareness, trust and relations between and among countries (Gienow-Hecht and Donfried, 2010). When higher education is referred to as part of cultural diplomacy, the most common activities cited are student/scholar exchanges, language learning, international sport competitions and cultural events (Pajtinka, 2014). While cultural diplomacy can include a wide range of people-to-people education and cultural exchanges, it is not broad enough to include the central elements of IHERI, such as research and innovation. Furthermore, the focus is primarily related to people mobility, as in student/scholar exchanges. The recent increase in the scope and scale of universities and other private higher education providers moving across borders to offer foreign education programmes and qualifications in the students' home country is not usually accommodated in the notion of cultural diplomacy. Thus, while cultural diplomacy includes some IHERI activities, and is an appropriate term to discuss student and scholar mobility and exchange, the concept is not broad enough to encompass the wide range of contemporary higher education, research and innovation activities.

Knowledge diplomacy is inclusive of science diplomacy but is more comprehensive

More attention is being given to science diplomacy, as evidenced by an increase in national government science policies, international meetings on the topic, and the rising number of academic references and projects (Knight, 2021). A frequently asked question is whether science diplomacy and knowledge diplomacy are not one and the same. This is a question worthy of consideration and depends on how broadly science is being defined and used. If science is broadly interpreted to mean knowledge, as in the Latin word *scientia*, then there is a close relationship. But traditionally science diplomacy has been seen in terms of natural sciences and more recently it has been placed within the broader framework of science and technology (Miremadi, 2016; Rungius, 2018). There is no doubt that this reflects the centrality of science and technology in today's knowledge economy. However, the focus on science and technology largely excludes other sectors, issues and disciplines related to the social sciences and humanities. For instance, it is unlikely that science diplomacy initiatives or negotiations would include humanitarian or societal issues such as migration, ageing, refugees, gender, poverty or human rights initiatives. Thus, while full acknowledgement is given to the importance and role of science diplomacy, it does not exclude the necessity of knowledge diplomacy, which is a more inclusive concept in terms of higher education and the production and application of knowledge and is consistent with the holistic concept of a knowledge society (Cerroni, 2020). It is inevitable that countries and actors will continue to use both 'science diplomacy' and 'science and technology diplomacy' according to their own policy priorities and contexts. However, the difference between these terms and the more comprehensive perspective of knowledge diplomacy also needs to be recognized.

Education diplomacy

The term education diplomacy is usually applied to basic education. The Association for Childhood Education International (ACEI) believes that 'education diplomacy uses the skills of diplomacy grounded in human rights principles to advance education as a driver for human development' (Höne, 2016). This raises the question whether the term education diplomacy or knowledge diplomacy is more appropriate for higher education as a more advanced education and knowledge space. In addition to education and training, knowledge diplomacy includes the use of research and new knowledge for innovation which are not usually associated with basic education. Furthermore, the drivers and outcomes differ. Education diplomacy, as interpreted by ACEI, is oriented to human development while knowledge diplomacy has a broader mandate and focuses on strengthening relations between and among countries. It also addresses a diversity of global challenges facing countries in all regions of the world which are not usually part of early childhood education.

An important question to ask after reviewing the use of the terms cultural, science and education diplomacy is whether constructing conceptual frameworks for these terms would bring more clarity to their use and help distinguish them from knowledge diplomacy. This is a challenge for scholars exploring the contemporary role of IHERI in international relations.

Soft power and knowledge diplomacy are guided by different intentions, values and modes

Developed by Nye (2004), the concept of soft power is popularly understood as the ability to influence others and achieve national self-interest through attraction and persuasion, rather than through military force or economic sanctions – commonly known as hard power. According to Nye (2010), co-option and compliance, not coercion, is the predominant idea in soft power. Lively debate focuses on the rhetoric, potential and limitations of soft power (Hayden, 2012), but in general Nye's concept of soft power has been influential in the study of international relations even though there are multiple interpretations and understandings of the concept. Thus, a soft power approach to the use of IHERI in international relations is primarily based on attraction and persuasion rather than collaboration and exchange to achieve self-interests and dominance. For example, scholars such as Lo (2011) argue that soft power is an alternative way to understand the dominance of the Western paradigm in higher education and its role in international relations. Jones (2010) cites the renowned European Union (EU) programmes such as Erasmus Mundus, Asia-Link and Asia-Europe Meeting as examples of cultural diplomacy used as 'soft power instruments to influence future relations via co-option and internalized agent cooperation' (Jones, 2010: 43). Wojciuk (2018) emphasizes the geopolitical power and competitive advantage gained from the soft power of knowledge and technology. This type of relationship can occur between and among countries where soft power can also be perceived as a means of neo-colonization (Woldegiorgis, 2018). Thus, the core values of soft power (dominance, co-option and competitive advantage) are not the same for knowledge diplomacy (mutuality, common ground and cooperation), and more attention needs to be given to this critical difference (Knight, 2021).

This section has discussed the differences and similarities between the proposed concept of knowledge diplomacy and the traditionally used terms of cultural, science and education diplomacy and soft power. The discussion has not suggested that knowledge diplomacy 'ought' to be used, thereby taking a normative position. Instead, it has noted when the related terms are most used and how the concept of knowledge diplomacy differs or is more comprehensive. This involves key features of contemporary diplomacy such as the engagement of state and non-state actors and expanding the types of IHERI activities beyond scholarships and academic exchanges to include joint universities, multilateral research networks, education hubs and regional centres of excellence, among others.

Illustrating the key elements of the knowledge diplomacy framework: the Pan-African University

The purpose of this section is to demonstrate and clarify how the key and often abstract concepts of the knowledge diplomacy framework can be applied to real-life IHERI initiatives using the Pan-African University as a case study.

The PAU is an example of a contemporary IHERI initiative involving a university with multiple campuses located across the African continent. It was initiated in 2013 to establish a regional university system to serve the entire continent by addressing key development priorities and to strengthen the regional integration goal of the Africa Union's (AU) *Agenda 2063: First Ten Year Implementation Plan 2014–2023* (AU, 2015). The initiative was started by the member states of the AU and is funded jointly by the African Development Bank (AfDB), African host countries, the World Bank and international partners. The PAU is made up of five postgraduate, training and research institutes, hosted at leading universities in the West, North, East, Central and South regions of the African continent. Each institute focuses on one of the strategic areas for African advancement, as determined by the Conference of Ministers of Education of the AU. The research institutes are:

- Kenya: Basic Sciences, Technology and Innovation located at Jomo Kenyatta University of Agriculture and Technology.
- Nigeria: Life and Earth Sciences, including Health and Agriculture, located at University of Ibadan.
- Cameroon: Governance, Humanities and Social Sciences located at University of Yaoundé II.
- Algeria: Water and Energy Sciences located at the Abou Bakr University of Tlemcen.
- South Africa: Space Sciences Institute located at the Cape Peninsula University of Technology (AU, 2016).

Intentions, purpose and rationales

The PAU is a key player and contributor to the operationalization of the first ten-year phase of the AU's Agenda 2063, which outlines a vision for pan-African unity for the creation of an 'integrated, prosperous and peaceful Africa, driven by its own citizens, representing a dynamic force in the international arena' (AU, 2015). Agenda 2063, adopted in 2015, charts a path for inclusive and sustainable development, a politically integrated continent, peace and security, fused together by a strong 'cultural identity, common heritage, shared values and ethics' (AU, 2015).

The five regional networks of universities and research partners are connected and strengthened by a continental framework. A review of the stated objectives reveals how PAU strives to enhance collaboration and integration between and among African countries through IHERI activities. The two primary academic objectives are to:

- stimulate collaborative, internationally competitive, cutting-edge fundamental and development-oriented research, in areas having a direct

bearing on the technical, economic and social development of Africa while recruiting, training and retaining African talent;
- enhance the mobility of students, lecturers, researchers and administrative staff between African universities to improve teaching, leadership and collaborative research and create regional/continental integrating networks (AU, 2016).

Actors

The AU, the AfBD and five national African governments are the key state drivers behind the PAU. State and non-state actors include universities, centres of excellence, foundations and research centres that are members of the five regional networks. International universities and governments are additional partners, and share expertise, participate in joint research projects and provide some funding opportunities. For instance, Germany cooperates with the research institute in Algeria; Sweden works with the institute in Cameroon; India and Japan are involved in supporting the institute in Nigeria; and China collaborates with the institute in Kenya. The EU has also been involved by providing initial funding for student scholarships. The AfBD was the main funder of the project and the World Bank provided additional start-up funds.

Key principles/values

Partnership and collaboration are key principles driving the development and operation of regional networks which are coordinated by a continent-wide strategy. Cooperation with African-based public and private organizations for internships, joint research and knowledge exchange is a priority and illustrates the importance of mutual benefits. The theme of each network illustrates the multi-sector and interdisciplinary nature of the entire PAU initiative. In terms of mutual benefits, African researchers and graduate students benefit from the increased collaboration in their region as well as the international support and exchange with their international thematic partners. National governments in the host African countries have benefitted from increased research capacity at their institutions and their leadership role in their region to collaborate with industry and non-governmental organizations while addressing major societal issues facing the continent. International partners have benefitted from finding common ground, building trust and deepening relationships with African research institutes and industry. In turn, these activities and benefits contribute to operationalizing the Agenda 2063 goal of inclusive and sustainable development, a politically-integrated continent, peace and security, fused together by a strong 'cultural identity, common heritage, shared values and ethics' (AU, 2015).

Modes

A project as large and ambitious as the PAU is not without conflicts and differing priorities among the major players and funders. Negotiation, conflict resolution, mediation and compromise are necessary to reach common ground and a way forward in knowledge diplomacy. The creation of five regional networks consisting of multiple state and non-state actors also requires a consultative and collaborative approach to negotiating priorities, budgets and strategies. These are fundamental modes used in diplomatic relationships.

Activities

Based on the primary goals and operating principles of PAU, the main IHERI activities focus on graduate-level programmes including internships, knowledge production and innovation; academic exchange of students and scholars across Africa; and joint research within the networks and with international partners. Scholarships are available to students from African countries as well as those from the African diaspora. Enrolment quotas are in place to ensure regional representation and gender parity. No more than 20 per cent of new students can be from the host country and an equal number of men and women must be accepted (AU, 2016). An interesting and important feature of PAU is that graduate programmes are intentionally designed to build a unified African identity beyond national differences. Students are required to take two general education courses to further this aim: General History of Africa and Gender and Human Rights. All students are required to collaborate with industrial or governmental partners throughout their programme, with internships being mandatory. Finally, students must sign a contract committing to work in Africa after the completion of their programme, to ensure that the new talent continues to work towards African development priorities (AU, 2016).

Two flagship research projects illustrate the emphasis on collaboration, partnerships and mutuality of benefits as well as the types of global/regional issues being addressed. The West African Science Centre on Climate Change and Adapted Land Use project was developed jointly by researchers from the universities of Cotonou (Benin), Bonn (Germany) and Miami (US) and their industry and governmental partners. The aim of this project was to create sustainable institutional relationships to develop a community of experts in areas of natural resource management aiming to conduct joint research and offer practical applications. The Institute for Water and Energy Sciences in Algeria offers another example of the PAU's collaborative research projects, with its researchers working with German universities to host international

Table 13.2: The Pan-African University's application of key elements of knowledge diplomacy conceptual framework

Element of conceptual framework	As illustrated in the Pan-African University initiative
Intentions/purpose	PAU is seen as a key player to realize Agenda 2063 which charts a path for 'inclusive and sustainable development, a politically-integrated continent, peace and security, fused together by a strong cultural identity, common heritage, shared values and ethics' (AU, 2015)
State and non-state actors and partners	African national governments, universities, research centres and industry AU, AfDB, World Bank International partner governments, universities, foundations and industry
Guiding principles and values	Partnership Cooperation Mutual benefits Commonality of issues Multidisciplinary/multi-sector
Modes/approaches of relationship	Negotiation Conflict resolution Mediation Compromise Collaboration Dialogue
IHERI activities	Joint research projects among African universities, research centres, industry, governmental agencies Collaborative academic and research initiatives between African and international universities, foundations, research centres, industry Scholarships for African graduate students, industry internships Student and scholar mobility within Africa Regional, continental, international workshops and seminars hosted in Africa

Source: Knight (2021).

research symposia bringing together specialists in water and energy sciences from around the world (Koli et al, 2019).

When fully realized, the PAU will be the sum of five thematic regional institutions/networks with 50 related centres of excellence across the African continent working towards and using IHERI to achieve the long-term goal and core aspiration of Agenda 2063, which is to make Africa a 'strong, united, resilient and influential global player and partner' (Table 13.2).

The analysis of the PAU initiative illustrates how the key elements of the conceptual framework can be operationalized. The diversity of partners involved in collaborative IHERI activities illustrates how the knowledge diplomacy approach includes both state and non-state actors. The establishment of bilateral and multilateral IHERI networks across countries, disciplines and sectors based on collaboration, exchange and partnerships were commonly used to build and expand stronger relationships between and among countries and yielded mutual but different benefits for partners. Traditional IHERI activities such as scholarships and student/scholar exchange, as well as contemporary IHERI projects such as regional multi-campus universities and multi-stakeholder thematic research networks, illustrate several of the key activities used in a knowledge diplomacy approach.

In conclusion, this chapter has argued that knowledge diplomacy is a valuable idea for exploring, understanding and capturing IHERI's current and expanding importance in enhancing ties between and across countries. It is important to note that the analysis of the concept of knowledge diplomacy is not suggesting it is the best approach for IHERI's role in international relations. To avoid the current confusion and terminology chaos resulting from the multiple terms used to describe the role of IHERI in international relations, a definition and a conceptual framework for knowledge diplomacy were introduced to explain and justify the use of the term. The conceptual framework for knowledge diplomacy clearly articulated the intentions, actors, principles, modes and activities, acknowledging that they were illustrative and not necessarily comprehensive. To clarify the understanding and use of IHERI in a knowledge diplomacy approach, the differences between knowledge diplomacy and other terms such as cultural, education and science diplomacy as well as soft power, which are traditionally used to frame IHERI in international relations, were examined. Finally, an analysis of the Pan-African University was undertaken to demonstrate and clarify how the key and often abstract concepts of the knowledge diplomacy framework can be applied to real-life IHERI initiatives.

Facing the future

Knowledge diplomacy is not without challenges. It can easily become a buzzword to camouflage national and regional ambitions to promote self-interest at the expense of mutual interests and benefits. As the concept of knowledge diplomacy becomes more commonplace in Africa, there can be unrealistic expectations about its role and contributions. Knowledge diplomacy is not a silver bullet. Expectations of its contribution to international relations need to be managed to avoid early misunderstandings or dismissal of its value and potential. Finally, developing a framework, policies, strategies and commitment to knowledge diplomacy cannot be done without facing the harsh realities of international politics both internal and external to Africa and the challenges of the more competitive, nationalistic and turbulent world in which we live. However, it must be asked whether we can afford to ignore the potential of knowledge diplomacy to address and contribute to the resolution of national, regional and global challenges.

Note

[1] This chapter draws on J. Knight (2022) *Knowledge Diplomacy in International Relations and Higher Education.* Springer Cham. https://doi.org/10.1007/978-3-031-14977-1.

References

AU (African Union) (2015) *Agenda 2063: First Ten Year Implementation Plan 2014–2023* [online], Available from: https://au.int/en/agenda2063/ftyip [Accessed 19 July 2022].

AU (African Union) (2016) *Revised Statute of the Pan African University* [online], Available from: https://au.int/sites/default/files/treaties/33127-treaty-0059_-_ revised_statute_pan_african_university_e.pdf [Accessed 19 July 2022].

Cerroni, A. (2020) *Understanding the Knowledge Society: A New Paradigm in the Sociology of Knowledge*, Cheltenham: Edward Elgar.

Cooper, A., Heine, J. and Thakur, R. (2013) *The Oxford Handbook of Modern Diplomacy*, Oxford: Oxford University Press.

Copeland, D. (2015) *Science and Diplomacy after Canada's Lost Decade: Counting the Costs, Looking Beyond*, Canadian Global Affairs Institute [online], Available from: https://d3n8a8pro7vhmx.cloudfront.net/cdfai/pages/690/attachments/original/1446661660/Science_and_diplomacy.pdf?1446661660 [Accessed 19 July 2022].

Gienow-Hecht, J. and Donfried, M. (2010) *Searching for a Cultural Diplomacy*, Oxford: Berghahn Books.

Goff, P. (2013) 'Cultural diplomacy', in A. Cooper, J. Heine and R. Thakur (eds) *The Oxford Handbook of Modern Diplomacy*, Oxford: Oxford University Press, pp 419–35.

Griffiths, M., O'Callaghan, T. and Roach, S. (2014) *International Relations: The Key Concepts* (3rd edn), London: Routledge.

Hayden, C. (2012) *The Rhetoric of Soft Power. Public Diplomacy in Global Contexts*, Lanham, MD: Lexington Books.

Höne, K. (2016) *Education Diplomacy: Negotiating and Implementing the Sustainable Development Goals – Looking Back and Looking Ahead*. Centre for Education Diplomacy and Leadership, Childhood Education International [online]. Available from: www.academia.edu/33207197/Education_Diplomacy_Negotiating_and_Implementing_the_Sustainable_Development_Goals_Looking_Back_and_Looking_Ahead_April_2016_?auto=download [Accessed 15 April 2024].

Jones, W. (2010) 'European Union soft power: cultural diplomacy & higher education in Southeast Asia', *Silpakorn University International Journal*, 9–10: 41–70.

Kerr, P. and Wiseman, G. (2013) *Diplomacy in a Globalizing World: Theories and Practices*, Oxford: Oxford University Press.

Knight, J. (2021) *Towards a Knowledge Diplomacy Framework: The Role of International Higher Education, Research and Innovation in International Relations*, PhD dissertation, University of Antwerp, Belgium [online], Available from: https://repository.uantwerpen.be/desktop/irua [Accessed 19 July 2022].

Koli, M., Tambo, E., Cheo, E., Oduor, B.O. and Nguedia-Nguedoung, A. (2019) 'Pan-African University and German government higher education cooperation in Algeria', in *Universities, Entrepreneurship and Enterprise Development in Africa – Conference Proceedings 2018*, Sankt Augustin, Germany [online], 13–14 September 2018, Available from: https://pub.h-brs.de/frontdoor/deliver/index/docId/4422/file/GAUP_Conference_Proceedings_2018_136.pdf [Accessed 19 July 2022].

Lehrer, K. (2000) *Theory of Knowledge* (2nd edn), Boulder, CO: Westview Press.

Light, A. (2017) 'Climate diplomacy', in R. Gardiner and A. Thompson (eds) *The Oxford Handbook of Environmental Ethics*, Oxford: Oxford University Press, pp 487–500.

Lo, W.Y. (2011) 'Soft power, university rankings and knowledge production: distinctions between hegemony and self-determination in higher education', *Comparative Education*, 47(2): 209–22.

Miremadi, T. (2016) *A Model for Science and Technology Diplomacy: How to Align the Rationales of Foreign Policy and Science* [online], Available from: https://ssrn.com/abstract=2737347 or http://dx.doi.org/10.2139/ssrn.2737347 [Accessed 15 April 2024].

Nye, J.S. (2004) *Soft Power: The Means to Success in World Politics*, New York: Public Affairs.

Nye, J.S. (2010) *The Powers to Lead*, Oxford: Oxford University Press.

Pajtinka, E. (2014) 'Cultural diplomacy in the theory and practice of contemporary international relations', *Politické vedy*, 17(4): 95–108.

Pigman, G. (2010) *Contemporary Diplomacy: Representation and Communication in a Globalized World*, London: Polity Press.

Piros, S. and Koops, J. (2020) 'Towards a sustainable approach to EU education diplomacy? The case of capacity-building in the Eastern Neighbourhood', in C. Carta and R. Higgot (eds) *Cultural Diplomacy in Europe*, Cham: Springer International, pp 113–38.

Pouliot, V. and Cornut, J. (2015) 'Practice theory and the study of diplomacy: a research agenda', *Cooperation and Conflict*, 50(3): 297–315.

Rathbun, B.C. (2014) *Diplomacy's Value: Creating Security in 1920s Europe and the Contemporary Middle East* [online], Cornell Scholarship Online, Available from: https://doi.org/10.7591/cornell/9780801453182.001.0001 [Accessed 19 July 2011].

Ravitch, S.M. and Riggan, M. (2016) *Reason & Rigor: How Conceptual Frameworks Guide Research* (2nd edn), London: Sage.

Ruffini, P.B. (2020) 'Introduction to the Forum on Science Diplomacy', *The Hague Journal of Diplomacy*, 15(3): 355–58.

Rungius, C. (2018) *S4D4C Using Science for/in Diplomacy for Addressing Global Challenges: State of the Art Report*, EU Horizon [online], Available from: www.s4d4c.eu/wp-content/uploads/2018/08/S4D4C_State-of-the-Art_Report_DZHW.pdf [Accessed 19 July 2022].

Srinivasan, K., Mayall, J. and Pulipaka, S. (eds) (2019) *Values in Foreign Policy: Investigating Ideals and Interests*, London: Rowman & Littlefield.

Wojciuk, A. (2018) *Empires of Knowledge in International Relations: Education and Science as Sources of Power for the State*, New York: Routledge.

Woldegiorgis, E. (2018) 'Policy travel in regionalization of higher education: the case of the Bologna Process in Africa', in A. Curaj, L. Deca and R. Procopie (eds) *European Higher Education Area: The Impact of Past and Future Policies*, Cham: Springer Nature, pp 43–59.

14

African Agency: The Case of Russian Nuclear Programmes in Egypt, Ghana, South Africa and Zambia

Dzvinka Kachur and Robyn Foley

Introduction

Access to affordable, reliable, sustainable and modern energy is one of the United Nations (UN) Sustainable Development Goals (SDGs). Currently, the majority of Africa's energy is predominantly generated from fossil fuels, perpetuating climate change risks (Statista, 2020). Africa has the fastest growing population and economy and thus requires just energy transitions that will simultaneously tackle poverty, industrialization and decarbonization (Mohlakoana and Wolpe, 2021). The developmental agenda dominates the local discourse around energy in African countries, and nuclear energy, with lower greenhouse gas emissions, albeit heavily loaded with geopolitics, is often presented as the best response to the challenges of the developmental agenda. For example, nuclear energy is one of the decarbonized options that the African Union (AU) is actively working on with the International Atomic Energy Agency (IAEA) for sustainable development in Africa (IAEA, 2018, 2022a).

On the other hand, analysis of the motivation of Middle Eastern countries for a nuclear energy push when alternative decarbonized energy resources are available suggests geopolitical considerations, 'political posturing' and geopolitical rivalry (Al-Saidi and Haghirian, 2020). But to what extent do geopolitical influences shape African countries' energy choices?

The colonial past has to a large extent driven the nuclear developments on the continent. For example, the South African nuclear energy industry was driven by the UK and US's interest in nuclear weapons during the Second World War (Fig, 2010). The French nuclear testing and British imperialism were behind nuclear aspirations in Algeria, Nigeria and Ghana (Hill, 2018). The interconnectedness between nuclear weapons and nuclear energy has been used as an instrument of influence for the colonial and post-colonial states, creating the notion of power behind those linked to the nuclear industry. Nuclear energy's intangible power might be the factor that still affects the choices of energy in African countries today.

Nuclear energy on the African continent

The South African 1.9 MW nuclear power plant (NPP), at Koeberg outside of Cape Town, is the only one on the continent. However, this could change in the next decade. Egypt is closest to joining the nuclear club with a 1.2 GW NPP under construction in El Dabaa (TASS, 2022; Egypt State Information Service, 2023). In addition, some African countries have been using nuclear research reactors for over five decades. These are often seen as a first step towards the NPP and are operating in Algeria, DRC, Egypt, Ghana, Libya, Morocco, Nigeria and South Africa (IAEA, 2022b) (see Table 14.1).

At least 17 countries, despite the different levels of their current capacity, are looking into developing nuclear technology for their needs: Algeria, Angola, Burundi, Democratic Republic of the Congo (DRC), Egypt, Ethiopia, Ghana, Kenya, Malawi, Morocco, Rwanda, Sudan, Tunisia, Tanzania, Uganda, Zambia and Zimbabwe. Some African countries have already signed international agreements with potential partners and taken practical steps to set up necessary regulations, and while only a decade ago the technical potential for new nuclear programmes on the continent was seen as implausible, the situation is changing.

Jewel (2010) analysed the potential nuclear advances by different countries and concluded that the development of nuclear technology is unlikely in African countries.[1] A similar analysis done in 2018 judged Nigeria and South Africa to be countries where the development of nuclear energy for peaceful purposes is very likely, Ghana and Kenya to be countries with strong motivation but the need for more substantial financing, and Sudan, Tanzania and Zimbabwe to be in the category with stronger financing and over a longer time horizon (Sah et al, 2018).

China, France, Russia, South Korea and the US are offering their nuclear technologies to African countries (van der Merwe, 2021). However, the Russian state-owned enterprise Rosatom has the largest number of contracts signed and is seen as a leader in promoting nuclear energy on the continent (see Table 14.2). Thus, this chapter investigates the geopolitical influences that shape the development of nuclear aspirations on the continent from

Table 14.1: Research reactors in Africa

Country	Facility name	Type	Thermal power	Status
Algeria	Nur	Pool	1,000	Temporary shutdown
	Es-Salam	Heavy water	15,000	Operational
DRC	Trico I	Triga Mark I	50	Permanent shutdown
	Trico II	Triga Mark II	1,000	Extended shutdown
Egypt	ETRR–1	Tank WWR	2,000	Extended shutdown
	ETRR–2	Pool	22,000	Operational
Ghana	GHARR–1	MNSR	30	Operational
Libya	IRT-1	Pool, IRT	10,000	Temporary shutdown
	TNRC critical facility	Crit assembly	0.1	Operational
Morocco	MA–R1	Triga Mark II	2,000	Operational
Nigeria	NIRR–1	MNSR	30	Operational
	Multipurpose research reactor	Pool	10,000	Planned
South Africa	Safari-1	Tank in pool	20,000	Operational
	Pelinduna-0	Crit fast	0	Decommissioned

Source: IAEA (2022b).

Table 14.2: Africa nuclear power programme status

Country	Agreement	Type	INIR Mission, FU	Operator	Regulator	Capacity/1 GW
Algeria	Russia, China, France, SA, US, Argentina,	Cooperation agreement, NPP, uranium ore, Fuel, rad waste, SMR			Yes	19.2
Egypt	Russia	NPP, EPC, fuel, spent fuel, tech support and maintenance	Phase2	Yes	Yes	4.5
Ghana	Russia	Financing, skills dev, NPP	Phase1, FU	Yes	Yes	4.4
Kenya	Russia, China South Korea	Financing, skills dev, NPP technical support, research, application	Phase1	Yes	Yes	2.4
Morocco	Russia, France	NPP, uranium ore	Phase1			8.3
Namibia	Russia	Mining, and proposal for small NPP				0.54
Niger			Phase1		yes	0.28
Nigeria	Russia	Financing, skills dev, NPP*, financial options, SMR	Phase2	Yes	yes	12.5
South Africa	France, China, US, Russia	R&D, trg for NPP* project invite	Phase2, FU	Yes	Yes	51
Sudan	China, Russia	Research, sc and tech, NPP	Phase1		Yes	3.4
Tunisia	Russia, France	Desalination, research, applications, NPP			yes	5.8
Uganda	Russia, China	Financing, skills dev, application			Yes	0.95
Zambia	Russia	Peaceful application, training, research			Yes	2.8

Source: Klutse (2020).

the other end, focusing on the agency of South Africa, Egypt, Ghana and Zambia in their bilateral relations with Russia.

Context and framing

Before embarking on any deliberation of nuclear diplomacy in Africa, it is important to first reflect on the broader context in which this discussion unfolds and outline the epistemological and theoretical foundations that inform the analysis. Most discourse around Russia–Africa nuclear relations focuses primarily on Russia's foreign policy objectives and the implications for 'other competing powers' (read: the West), with little interest or consideration regarding the African partner. This power imbalance is partially created because there are only nine countries that possess nuclear weapons: the United States, Russia, France, China, the United Kingdom, Pakistan, India, Israel and North Korea. From the perspective of the Global South, this tendency to consider 'Africans as peripheral agents of the international system' (Coffie and Tiky, 2021: 244) needs to be disrupted.

The view of Africans as peripheral agents and of the empirical limitations of African agency (when considering the real constraints of weak economic power and military capabilities) are deeply rooted in its colonial past and reinforced by continuation of Eurocentric coloniality in international relations theory (Zondi, 2016; Coffie and Tiky, 2021). The reality that Africa's underdevelopment was deliberately enacted to build and maintain control over the continent's wealth and its people, which one may argue was the basis for the industrial development of Europe and North America, is hardly ever reflected in international relations discourse. The traumatic memory of this not-so-distant violent past still shapes and informs the way in which Africa engages the rest of the world. It embeds a deep level of mistrust in relations with former colonizers and this mistrust is in turn leveraged by other great powers to foster a sense of allyship (neglecting to acknowledge their own acts of colonialism). This mistrust is justified, particularly while most nations' primary foreign policy objectives continue to reflect the predatory colonial logics of domination, exploitation and extraction.

Africa's development potential is immense, with significant untapped mineral and natural resources and a dynamic young population. It presents a significant opportunity for economic growth and a target for extraction by more powerful states. While the global challenges of climate and the large-scale underdevelopment in certain parts of the world call for decolonized forms of international cooperation (focused on finding just and generative solutions), the realities are that the international dialogue continues to depict 'Africa as a passive or supplicant actor in international politics' (Coffie and Tiky, 2021: 245).

It is important to emphasize that while acknowledging the broader power dynamics at play in international relations and the commonality of colonialism whose legacy has shaped the current state of underdevelopment, the authors do not mean to fall foul of their own criticism. The prevailing perception is that 'African agents (states, organizations and diplomats) are consumers of international norms and practices designed in the affluent countries of the Global North' (Coffie and Tiky, 2021: 243). This perception must be abandoned and if we are to decolonize the Eurocentric narratives of international relations, we must recognize African agency in global politics.

Africa is not a country but a continent of 54 countries, each with its own complex history, diverse cultures and religions, with different approaches to development, resulting in a distinctive set of societal norms, different political systems and unique economic interests/offerings, all of which inform how they manifest agency within international relations. Understanding these complexities requires expanding our scope of agency to non-state actors.

Agency can be understood as 'the ability of states, intergovernmental organisations, civil society and individual actors to exert influence in their interactions with foreign entities to maximise their utilities and achieve a set of goals' (Coffie and Tiky, 2021: 245). The type of governance regime, the capacity of the state, the influence of business elites, the legal and regulatory frameworks and the extent of public participation (civil society agency) all contribute to shaping how an African country engages with the rest of the world. How agency manifests also depends on the complexities that reside in the type of diplomacy that is being enacted between international actors. The analysis is concerned with nuclear diplomacy, which is discussed in greater detail in the next section.

Appreciating that Africa is not a monolith and that there is complexity embedded in each form of engagement or exchange that takes place between an African state and other international actors, the analysis does not attempt to draw direct comparisons between countries or derive a generalizable theory for African agency. Rather, the sections that follow focus on specific cases where the different African countries engage with a specific international power (in this case, Russia) and its strategy in nuclear diplomacy.

Nuclear power, agency and geopolitics

African countries are often regarded as those with little agency due to their low economic development. However, African countries played a key role in brokering the network of like-minded countries in the Global South and North, which shaped the institutions and agenda of, for example, the Treaty on the Non-Proliferation of Nuclear Weapons (NPT) to include a three-fold objective: non-proliferation, disarmament and technological transfers for peaceful use (Kornprobst, 2020).

There are few areas that define potential geopolitical influence as much as the construction of nuclear power stations (Česnakas and Juozaitis, 2017; Schepers, 2019). In addition, there are some barriers that limit the agency of African countries. The reason for this is twofold: African countries lack the economic capacity to embrace nuclear energy as well as them being relative newcomers to the industry.

First, the large capital investment and long-term political commitment increase the risk of geopolitical influence, interference and manipulation. The financial investment in nuclear energy globally was close to 5 per cent, concentrated in China, India and Russia (IEA, 2021). The cost of a nuclear project is tightly connected to the national regulation and safety requirements. If available, domestic funding would reduce the project risk, but the magnitude of the required costs means that African countries must rely on international partnerships. The pure project financing schemes (that are available for other energy sources such as renewable energy) currently do not work, limiting the option to large corporations or government-to-government financing schemes (Lucet, 2018). The NPP in Egypt is financed via an intergovernmental loan from the Russian Federation.

The costs of construction by different international partners vary significantly. For example, a US or French nuclear power plant comes to almost double those constructed by China or South Korea, which is not exclusively, but largely, linked to the differences in regulation and safety requirements (ANBP, 2020). The risk distribution between the owner and the vendor also affects the financing model. It requires long-term political commitments and state guarantees to reduce the costs of interest rates (IAEA, 2021). Thus, by choosing an international partner, the country is often caught in a compromise between the best pricing and the long-term geopolitical affiliation and governance principles.

Second, nuclear energy also requires upfront *human capital building*. Most of the technology providers, such as Russia, China and France, also provide scholarships for African student's studies. For example, in 2017 Rosatom introduced 60 scholarships for African students (Study in Russia, 2018). In 2021, 20 fully funded scholarships in nuclear sciences were provided only for Zambian students (Zambia Daily Mail, 2021). Such investment in human capital in African countries also provides an opportunity for soft diplomacy – influencing decision making about the choice of technology, the future corporate culture of the industry, and understanding and communicating the risks and benefits to the public.

The capacity of the African countries to train their own specialists is growing but remains quite limited. For example, the School of Nuclear and Allied Sciences under the Ghana Atomic Energy Commission annually produces Master's and PhD students in various areas of the nuclear field, including nuclear engineering. South Africa remains the only Southern

African Development Community (SADC) country that renders assistance in nuclear safety and security to other African countries (Velichkov, 2021). Therefore, the increased capacity to train nuclear experts on the continent would also contribute to the growth of decision-making agency.

Third, there is a need for a developed grid and technical infrastructure that can enable the NPP connection and would allow the NPP to be under 10 per cent of the overall generation capacity (Lucet, 2018). Jewell (2010) found that indicators for the potential of nuclear power include the size of the national grid, the presence of international grid connections and the security of fuel supply for electricity production. The development of the grid and infrastructure is often funded independently from the nuclear programme and provides additional financial pressures for a country's budget.

International regulation is also driven by the early adopters of nuclear technology. Nuclear is a low-probability high-risk industry. When developed, the nuclear industry did not account for many risks, but as large nuclear accidents have occurred in Three Mile Island (1979), Chornobyl (1986) and Fukushima (2011), the safety standards of the industry have increased. The IAEA provides support and guidelines for new nuclear countries, but the regulations for safe waste management, NPP decommissioning and other safety requirements come with additional costs. At the same time, the cost of alternative types of energy has dropped, making nuclear energy less financially attractive (IEA et al, 2020).

Regional cooperation as an expression of agency

Several regional initiatives aim to facilitate cooperation between African countries regionally, to increase knowledge exchange and capacity development. As an example of leadership in nuclear non-proliferation, the African continent is the only nuclear weapons-free zone (UNODA, 2022) based on the Treaty of Pelindaba (enforced in 2009). The African Commission on Nuclear Energy (AFCONE) was established in response to the Pelindaba Treaty and aims to promote non-proliferation and support nuclear technology development for sustainable development (AFCONE, 2022). It is seen as an organization that can 'champion the nuclear energy research and development agenda through the African Union and other platforms' (Mbambo, 2020).

Regional initiatives include the African Regional Cooperative Agreement for Research, Development and Training Related to Nuclear Science and Technology (AFRA), which enables regional cooperation and is funded by local members. AFRA's 30 members (AFRA, 2023: 1) aim 'to maximise the utilisation of available infrastructure and expertise in Africa' and move towards 'regional self-sufficiency' in peaceful applications of nuclear energy (Mbambo, 2020). In 2020, AFCONE and AFRA joined forces and signed a Memorandum of Understanding that would allow for the strengthening of the African voice pertaining to nuclear energy.

Another initiative is the Forum of Nuclear Regulatory Bodies in Africa as well as strong regional cooperation based in the AU. The African Union's Agenda 2063 reiterates the importance of building competitive productive capacity in manufacturing and the industrialization of African economies (AU, 2022).

Russian nuclear diplomacy: the use of energy resources for geopolitical influence

For the Russian Federation, nuclear energy is not only the official geopolitical strategy, but also a source of personal pride for President Putin: 'We really have overtaken everybody' (Russian View, 2020). In 2007, the Russian Federation launched a long-term programme to promote its nuclear reactors worldwide (Government of the Russian Federation, 2006) through Rosatom, a 100 per cent state-owned company, which is a hybrid between a state organization and a privately owned company. Rosatom is under the control of President Putin, who sets the strategic objectives and appoints directors and board members. Rosatom is a powerful institution responsible for the country's nuclear power industry, nuclear weapons division, nuclear research institutions, and nuclear and radiation safety. This allows Rosatom to enjoy the full support of the Russian government and to use diplomatic routes for the company's promotion. Regular corruption scandals involving top management support the notion that Rosatom is a key player in Putin's elaborate neo-patrimonial network (Slivyak, 2019).

Rosatom entered the African nuclear market in 2012, opening a marketing office for Sub-Saharan Africa in Johannesburg and actively engaging with African governments (Rossiyskaya Gazeta, 2012). Currently, Rosatom is the leader in promoting nuclear energy on the continent and has signed agreements on nuclear cooperation with at least 18 African countries.

There are a few advantages for prospective buyers of Russian nuclear technology. First, unlike many other nuclear technology providers, Russia does not seek further assurances from partners concerning uranium enrichment and plutonium reprocessing technologies. Second, Russia is one of the few suppliers that takes back spent nuclear fuel from foreign reactors, which is an additional benefit for countries that do not have their own waste-management capacities (Schepers, 2018). And third, Russia (and China) provides state funding for its nuclear projects.

For Russia, energy resources for geopolitical influence are part of the national energy strategy (Gonchar et al, 2017). For example, the Russian Federation's 'Energy Strategy of Russia for the period up to 2020' mentions that Russian energy resources are 'the basis for economic development, an instrument for conducting domestic and foreign policy' (Government of the Russian Federation, 2003).

There are multiple examples of how such geopolitical influence with the use of the energy resources is exercised. In 2000, Russia threatened the gas supply during the presidential elections in Georgia in order to exert pressure; in 2006 the supply of electricity and gas was blocked during the winter months when the government of Georgia started to implement pro-Western policies (Orttung and Overland, 2011). In July 2008, the Czech Republic signed an agreement with Washington to place a missile defence system on its territory, and the day after that Transneft cut the oil supply by 40 per cent (Gonchar et al, 2017). In 2010 in Ukraine, the Russian Federation traded a 30 per cent gas discount for a 25-year extension of the lease for Russia's naval base in Ukraine. Russia has used energy leverage for political gains in Belarus (winter 2004 and 2006), Latvia (2003) and Lithuania (2006). All these energy crises were regulated politically and accompanied by an information campaign to show the benefits of the contracts offered by the Russian Federation, including accusing the governments concerned of being unreliable (Gonchar et al, 2017). These examples show how Russia can use energy resources in combination with information campaigns for geopolitical gains.

In the case of nuclear energy, beneficiary countries are expected to make a long-term commitment to use Russian technology, specialists and training. For Victor Polikarpov, the head of the 'Rosatom-International Network', a long-term commitment to Russian-built nuclear power plants influences the country's economy and politics for the next 50–100 years (Salakhetdinov and Sidorov, 2018).

There are several events and developments which suggest that Russia is already using its nuclear programme to achieve geopolitical influence. For instance, after Hungary and Slovakia signed a nuclear agreement with Russia, they adopted 'a rather favourable attitude towards Russia regarding the Ukrainian–Russian conflict during the EU's internal negotiations on sanctions against Russia' (Česnakas and Juozaitis, 2017). Similarly, in 2010 Rosatom signed the agreement with Turkey to implement the Akkuyu project with a price well below other NPPs. It was suggested that Russia expected to gain geopolitical influence and recover the costs via high tariffs (Česnakas and Juozaitis, 2017). After a Turkish jet was shot down by a Russian aircraft in 2015, the project stalled (IISS, 2017). In 2018, after Turkey, against warnings from the US and the North Atlantic Treaty Organization (NATO), purchased S-400 batteries from Russia, Rosatom announced it alone would continue with the Akkuyu construction, as no private investors had joined it (WNA, 2021). In 2020, as the Russia–Turkey clash over conflicts in Syria, Libya and Nagorno-Karabakh grew, information was shared by a Turkish journalist that the Russian company RAO (1 per cent of Akkuyu project, controlled by Putin-proxy Igor Sechin) would withdraw its support for the project (Ülker, 2020). Thus, despite the high electricity tariff agreed, the project is permanently in the stop/go mode due to geopolitical battles.

African nuclear aspirations: a tale of four countries
Egypt
In the case of Egypt, the El Dabaa NPP that is currently under construction has been planned for approximately 40 years. The political leadership is driving the nuclear programme, while civil society organizations are sidelined and do not have enough information for meaningful and public participation.

Since the mid-1900s, Egypt has desired to develop its nuclear capabilities to include power generation; however, over the years its development has been interrupted by, among other factors, high costs and political will. In the 1950s, Egypt established a nuclear regulatory framework and by 1964 it launched its first light-water research reactor, procured from the Soviet Union. Since then, it has maintained capacities in terms of training nuclear scientists and the research reactor is still operational to date.

Under the Jamal Abd al-Nasser administration, after attempts at procuring nuclear weapons (during the 1960s) from the Soviet Union and China, Egypt moved towards adopting a non-proliferation approach to developing nuclear capabilities.

In the 1970s, following Nasser's death, the administration of President Anwar al-Sadat restarted the nuclear power plant project. This time Egypt would look to the US as a potential partner in the construction of a nuclear power plant, but due to instability in the region the US backed out and the project faltered.

In 1981, El Dabaa was identified as a potential site for the nuclear power plant, however the project was effectively put on hold as there were no active attempts to pursue further development of the country's nuclear capabilities. It was only towards the end of Hosni Mubarak's nearly 30-year rule, in the mid-2000s, that the NPP project resurfaced. This was reported as being primarily due to the influence of Mubarak's son Gamal and the increase in the country's energy needs at the time (Turianskyi and van Wyk, 2021). From 2006 to 2011 Egypt signed several cooperation agreements related to its development of nuclear power, with Russia and China (and later South Korea). In 2009, WorleyParsons was contracted to oversee the initiation phase of the project, including site investigations, project planning and managing the procurement process. The project was again put on hold though, following the uprising in January 2011 (part of the Arab Spring), when Mubarak was ousted and ultimately Mohamed Morsi, from the Muslim Brotherhood, came to power.

Under the Morsi administration, between 2011 and 2013, there was very little progress on the NPP project. Following the coup d'état in July 2013 and General Abd al-Fattah al-Sisi's subsequent ascendence to the presidency in June 2014, it would appear that the plans for developing nuclear energy were renewed, with the NPP at El Dabaa seen as a key project in Al-Sisi's agenda of 'restoring security and stabilising the economy' (Turianskyi and van Wyk, 2021). However, it is important to note that several important steps were taken during this period of political instability: in April 2013 Egypt approached Russia to renew its nuclear cooperation agreements, focusing on construction of a NPP at El Dabaa, and in October 2013 the minister for electricity and energy officially reactivated plans for El Dabaa (WNA, 2022). In January 2014, the ministry announced that there would be a tender process undertaken for the development, using WorleyParsons as consultants. It is unclear if WorleyParsons' involvement was undertaken under a new agreement or if this was merely a continuation of their original 2009 agreement, but the continuity of the consulting services they have provided on the project over the years, under various administrations, is worth noting.

By December 2014 Egypt made clear that any proposal for developing the nuclear power station would need to come with substantial financing. Ultimately, in July 2015 Russia was selected as the preferred bidder for the El Dabaa project, with several other countries such as Japan, France, China and South Korea having also reportedly submitted proposals (Turianskyi and van Wyk, 2021). Worth noting is that in February 2015 there was a meeting in which the Ministry of Electricity and Renewable Energy Egypt and Rosatom (the Russian nuclear power parastatal) 'agreed to launch detailed discussions on the prospective project involving construction of two 1,200 MWe nuclear power units, with the prospect of two more' (in WNA, 2022). Whether there were similar meetings with other potential service providers is unknown. Similarly, very little is publicly available about the tender adjudication process, with Russia the successful bidder.

As per Egypt's requirements, the nuclear build programme in El Dabaa is accompanied by a financing agreement whereby Rosatom has committed to providing a long-term loan of an estimated $25 billion (at 3 per cent interest) that would cover approximately 85 per cent of the capital investment requirements for the project (Turianskyi and van Wyk, 2021). The nuclear programme is also accompanied by a third agreement with Russia, for the supply and removal of nuclear fuel for the power plant. The build project itself, however, is not limited to Rosatom, with various parts of the development and construction of the project being contracted to a variety of suppliers from Egypt and across the world.

Ghana

Ghana is among the few West African countries that constantly rate as a democracy and has had two decades of peaceful transfer of leadership between the major political parties with an actively involved civil society allowing for multifaceted leadership and broad political debate on critical strategic issues (Gopaldas, 2021; Democracy in Action, 2022).

The Ghanaian government roadmap to nuclear power is to have 700 MW of capacity ready for commissioning by 2025 and later expand it to 1,000 MW. In 2015, Ghana signed a nuclear cooperation agreement with Rosatom that allows partners to develop mutual contractual and legal frameworks for cooperation and promote Russian nuclear technology in the West African sub-region (Sah et al, 2018).

The energy crisis in 2007 spurred then President John Kufuor to set up an eight-member committee to advise the government on the potential use of nuclear energy for electricity generation and to develop a roadmap, to culminate in a pre-feasibility study. There are clear drivers for the inclusion of nuclear energy in the Ghana energy mix: the long-term vision outlined in Ghana's development plan and the drive towards industrialization, increasing electricity demand, limited hydro and gas resources, and pressures for decarbonization (Debrah et al, 2020). And a few reporters suggested that Ghana's preferred bidder is Russian Rosatom (Debrah et al, 2020).

Ghana is experiencing regular energy shortages – 1983–84, 1997–98, 2003, 2006–7 and 2011–17 – but it was a combination of energy needs and political leadership that have been driving the nuclear programme in Ghana. Ghana is among the early adopters of nuclear energy as its Nuclear Power Programme was launched by the first president, Kwame Nkrumah (1957–66), at the beginning of 1960 to promote Pan-Africanism. The ambition was to position Ghana on the global map as a developed, prosperous, industrialized country, and nuclear energy was a symbol of a developed country. In only a few years the Kwabenya Nuclear Reactor Project was set, and Ghana Atomic Energy was established (Foy and Bosman, 2021). However, as soon as the political leadership changed, the nuclear programme stagnated. A revival of the nuclear programme in Ghana is linked to the stable political leadership of Jerry J. Rawlings (1982–2000). Rawlings was seen as a leader who gave 'back Ghanaians their national pride' (Foy and Bosman, 2021). Under Rawlings' leadership, Ghana acquired the Ghana Research Reactor-1 (GHARR-1) from China and approved new legislation that targeted the commercialization of nuclear energy research and development in 2000[2] (GAEC, 2022).

Ghana is party to many international agreements that regulate nuclear energy and safety issues and hosted two IAEA Integrated Nuclear Infrastructure Review (INIR) missions. As early as 2007, it signed the first intergovernmental framework for nuclear cooperation with the US; in 2011 with Rosatom; and in 2018 with China.

The initial nuclear expertise in Ghana comes from the Ghana–Soviet Union agreement for training of specialists in Moscow, 1962–64; however, later, the specialists would go on, with IAEA support, to study in the UK and other European countries (Adu-Gyamfi et al, 2017). This initial training allowed the Ghana Atomic Energy Commission to establish a graduate school that provides a variety of specialities on nuclear energy technology and safety. More recently, Ghana signed two bilateral agreements with South Korea (2018) and Rosatom (2019) that focus on the training and expertise development of nuclear scientists (Foy and Bosman, 2021). As a result of managing multiple geopolitical influences, Ghana managed to establish one of the most substantial nuclear expert centres on the continent, capable of developing the feasibility study and assessing the risks and opportunities for Ghana's nuclear programme.

While Ghana managed to establish multiple institutions involved in regulating the industry, there is still a need for a wider involvement of stakeholders. Ghana's civil society organizations are actively participating in the energy policy debate (Turianskyi and van Wyk, 2021). The transparency of the procurement process and the ability of the regulatory institutions to conduct public participation would be critical in shaping the perception of nuclear energy in the country.

Ghana has issued a 'Request for Interest' and five vendors – the US, Russia, Canada and South Korea – have submitted their proposals (GNA, 2021). The estimated cost for the programme is US$8–10 billion; Ghana has been discussing financial assistance with Russia, China and the Republic of Korea and has established the Ghana Infrastructure Investment Fund, an institution that would support the funding process for 'flagship infrastructural projects' (Foy and Bosman, 2021).

While Ghana might choose Russia as a preferred bidder, the development of local capacity, legislation and setting up nuclear institutions have been playing a key role in the industry's development.

South Africa

As already mentioned, South Africa could be considered the most advanced nuclear-developed country in Africa. It is home to the only commercial energy-producing nuclear power plant in Africa; it developed nuclear weapons under the apartheid regime and since disarmament has continued to develop various nuclear programmes that are governed by a well-established legal framework (Kachur, 2021a).

The strong legislative and regulatory requirements in place dictate the various processes that need to be followed in the development of larger-scale energy infrastructure. For instance, the pursuit of any large-scale energy infrastructure needs to align with the country's Integrated Resource Plan (DMRE, 2019) – a living document that outlines the preferred energy mix for the country based on technical and financial considerations, such as cost of production, demand and supply capabilities. The Public Finance Management Act additionally requires that all large-scale investments should be signed off by the National Treasury before conclusion of any international agreements that would commit South Africa to financial obligations to another state, ensuring project feasibility and protecting financial sovereignty (South Africa, 1999). Public participation is built into the legislative frame for various processes that need to be followed when government is looking to procure nuclear energy.

Early in the democratic dispensation the country looked at maintaining and possibly expanding on its nuclear capabilities, particularly to energy production and innovation. The pebble bed modular reactor programme was established in 1993 and in 2008, during the first occurrence of nationwide rolling blackouts, the first bidding process for a new nuclear power plant was initiated. This programme was, however, halted shortly after Mbeki was removed from ANC presidency (Kachur, 2021a). Under the new leadership of President Zuma, South Africa would once again pursue nuclear power, with renewed vigour. The nuclear deal with Russia pursued with the Zuma administration proposed the development of a 9.6 GW NPP, which it is estimated would have cost over R1 trillion (Kachur, 2021a).

The relationship between Zuma and Putin appears to have played a significant role in how the deal was conceived and formal processes circumvented. It is understood that the deal was developed over several visits that took place between Zuma and Putin, starting in March 2013. The backroom dealing would come to an end when in December 2015 Zuma fired the finance minister, which shook markets and caused a backlash from society (resulting in greater scrutiny of the nuclear deal). Alive to the potential dangers that the deal presented, in relation to implementing a nuclear development with little regard to public participation or the financial risks to the country, two local non-profit environmental advocacy organizations took the government to court and halted the nuclear deal (Kachur, 2021a).

Following the removal of Zuma from the presidency in 2018, President Ramaphosa indicated that the nation will only consider developing its nuclear programme at 'at a pace and scale that the country can afford' (DMRE, 2019: 48). But while South Africa is no longer vigorously pursuing the development of a nuclear power station, the preparation for the programme continues and it remains a matter of public debate.

This case demonstrates several dimensions to African agency. The first is the agency of personalized relationships between state leaders and competing logics that prevail under patrimonial/authoritarian styles of leadership. This is perhaps most readily visible in the case of then President Zuma trying to pressurize the finance minister into signing an unlawful agreement on the sidelines of a diplomatic visit to Russia or the various cabinet reshuffles that were made in pursuit of fast-tracking the nuclear deal with Russia. The second is the agency displayed by the finance minister in not signing off on the agreement. However, the finance minister was later removed from office. Nevertheless, in the case of the nuclear deal with Russia, South Africa's constitutional framework safeguarded the country against making a decision that would have been detrimental. The third is the agency that resides within civil society. Had it not been for the interventions of civil society halting the nuclear deal, South Africa would be indebted to Russia for a nuclear energy plant it could not afford.

Zambia

Zambia has been a member of the IAEA since 1969, but the ambition to develop the national nuclear programme was only fully embraced when President Edgar Lungu (January 2015 to August 2021) was elected. He announced an interest in nuclear power only a few weeks after taking office, in order to diversify into a sustainable energy mix by adding nuclear energy (Republic of Zambia, 2019). Zambia's potential to mine uranium was another strong argument to support a nuclear programme, even though the low global uranium prices at the time made it unprofitable.

In 2016, Zambia signed its first agreement on peaceful uses of nuclear energy with Rosatom. Zambia planned to construct the research centre within five years and to build two units of the nuclear power plant by 2040. The excess power generated from this plant could be made available for export to neighbouring countries under the SADC Power Pool framework arrangement, which would significantly benefit Zambia economically.

Lungu saw nuclear energy as an opportunity to solve the Zambian electricity crisis. His vision was to increase the external debt but to develop the country's infrastructure, which would improve employment, the investment climate and boost the economy. The challenge for the partially democratic Zambia is that the external debts, especially those with China and Russia, became very opaque, leading to increased corruption. During the five years of Lungu's presidency the external debt grew from 20 per cent of gross domestic product (GDP) to over 70 per cent, with China being the key debtor (Reuters, 2021; IMF, 2022).

Funding became the major stumbling block for the nuclear programme's implementation. Russia refused to provide loans to Lungu's government, fearing that it would not be capable of repaying them, and therefore asking for access to Zambian's natural resources (TASS, 2020). The nuclear negotiations intensified diplomatic connections between Russia and Zambia, including trade and interparliamentary relations, resulting in Zambian nuclear legislation largely replicating the Russian experience (Kachur, 2021b). As Table 14.3 shows, the nuclear cooperation between Russia and

Table 14.3: Agreements between Russia (or Rosatom) and Zambia

Date concluded	Description of agreement
May 2016	Intergovernmental Agreement on Peaceful Uses of Nuclear Energy between Russia and Zambia
December 2016	Memorandum of Understanding (MoU) with Rosatom signed in Lusaka – a non-binding agreement that sets out a 15-year nuclear cooperation plan with the eventual goal of constructing a nuclear power plant
February 2017	Intergovernmental Agreement on Cooperation in Building a Nuclear Science and Technology Centre on Zambian Territory – provides for a 10MW multipurpose nuclear research water-cooled reactor
April 2017	Agreement (came into force in 2018) on military and technical cooperation Provisions for the supply of weapons and delivery of spare parts
May 2017	Ministers of foreign affairs, Harry Kalaba and Sergei Lavrov, meet in Moscow They discuss military and nuclear collaboration, investments in IT and banking systems, and international cooperation in anti-terrorism and extremism
October 2017	A Zambian delegation headed by the speaker of the National Assembly, Patrick Matibini, takes part in the 137th Assembly of the Inter-Parliamentary Union in St Petersburg
Autumn 2017	A Memorandum of Cooperation in the creation of an educational cluster is signed between the Peoples' Friendship University of Russia and the Ministry of Higher Education of Zambia
April 2018	Visit to Moscow by Zambian parliamentary delegation The delegation includes Mr Matibini and foreign affairs and agriculture representatives, and visits the Novovoronezh nuclear power plant
May 2018	General engineering, procurement and construction (EPC) contract with the Ministry of Higher Education of Zambia – the key agreement signed during AtomExpo-2018, it expands on details of the construction of the CNST 10km outside Lusaka
July 2018	Vladimir Putin and Edgar Lungu meet at the 10th BRICS summit in Johannesburg Russian and Zambian diplomats identify this meeting as a turning point in the relationship
February 2019	Meeting of the ministers of foreign affairs: Sergei Lavrov meets with a Zambian delegation headed by Joseph Malanji
April 2019	A Memorandum of Understanding and Cooperation is signed between the Moscow and Zambian chambers of commerce and industry
May 2019	A delegation of Zambia's Ministry of Finance visits Russia The minister meets with the management of Gazprombank JSC
February 2019	Mr Malanji pays a working visit to Moscow

Table 14.3: Agreements between Russia (or Rosatom) and Zambia (continued)

Date concluded	Description of agreement
October 2019	Mr Malanji, as head of the Zambian delegation, takes part in the first Russia–Africa summit in Sochi Russia and Zambia sign an agreement on visa-free travel for holders of diplomatic passports (enters into force 1 July 2020)
January 2020	Zambian delegation headed by Minister of Finance Bwalya Ng'andu visits Moscow Discussion on funding for a nuclear power plant and the supply of mineral fertilizers with Uralkali PJSC
February 2020	A Russian delegation headed by chairwoman of the Federation Council Valentina Matviyenko meets with the Zambian president and speaker
September 2020	First Joint Coordination Committee meeting under an intergovernmental agreement to explore peaceful uses of nuclear energy
March 2021	A Zambian delegation, headed by Ng'andu, visits Rostov region

Source: Kachur (2021b).

Zambia intensified links between different institutions including parliaments, municipalities, research centres and presidencies.

In August 2021, Zambia held presidential elections, and the leadership was transferred to the opposition leader Hakainde Hichilema, who declared the goal to significantly cut down on public expenditures and focus on Zambia's macroeconomic stability. As the leadership in Zambia changed, interest in nuclear energy also declined, and the major focus shifted towards renewable energy (Rosatom, 2021). The Russian embassy initiated a dialogue (Russian Embassy in Zambia, 2022), but it is unclear at this stage that the nuclear programme will regain momentum.

Conclusion

Political stability and the perception of nuclear technology as a symbol of African development are common factors in pursuing a nuclear programme on the continent. However, each African country shows different responses to the Russian nuclear programme, depending on the country's institutional and political composition. The nuclear programme contributes to bilateral contacts between different institutions, including government ministries, parliamentarians, municipalities and scientists.

The context of nuclear cooperation is continuously changing, and the future of the various programmes is once again uncertain. On 24 February 2022, Russia invaded Ukraine in violation of the UN Charter principles and international law. In the first week of the war Russia seized the Chornobyl NPP, and on 4 March 2022 troops shelled and then captured the largest nuclear plant in Europe, Zaporizhzhia NPP. 'Rosatom specialists' were brought in to take over the control of Zaporizhzhia NPP; however, the IAEA has expressed 'great concerns' and warned that the fundamental principles of safely operating such facilities had been violated (IAEA, 2022c). Russia has already violated six major nuclear safety principles.

Russia has put to the test its geopolitical strategy. On 2 March 2022, Egypt, Ghana and Zambia all supported the UN resolution condemning the Russian invasion of Ukraine, but South Africa, despite its long-standing tradition on preventing and mitigating violence, abstained. The weakening of Russia and its geopolitical power might shift the perception of energy dependency and carbon dependency, undermining the appeal of nuclear energy programmes. Recent events could also see a return of cold war-era geopolitics, reinforcing 'great power' narratives and an increase towards more authoritarian tendencies on the continent – all of which undermines African agency. The future of nuclear programmes on the continent will be once again tested.

Notes

[1] The criteria for determining capacity included current and projected grid capacity, GDP and GDP/capita, Government Effectiveness Indicator and Political Stability Indicator by the World Bank and Political Instability Task Force, and the motivation was determined by the magnitude and average demand growth rate of electricity consumption and import dependency and diversity of the primary electricity sources (Jewell, 2010).

[2] Parliament enacted the new Ghana Atomic Energy Commission Act No. 588, which came to replace Act 204. Act 588 enabled the GAEC to 'undertake commercialisation of its research and development results'.

References

Adu-Gyamfi, S., Amakye-Boateng, K., Yartey, H.T., Dramani, A. and Adoteye, V.N. (2017) 'Nuclear energy in Ghana? History, science and policy', *Journal of Social and Development Sciences*, 8(3): 11–34.

AFCONE (African Commission on Nuclear Energy) (2024) *Who we are* [online], Available from: www.afcone.org/who-we-are/ [Accessed 15 April 2024].

AFRA (African Regional Cooperative Agreement for Research, Development and Training related to Nuclear Science and Technology) (2023) *Status List* [online], 3 October, Available from: www.iaea.org/sites/default/files/22/06/afra_status.pdf [Accessed 24 November 2023].

Al-Saidi, M. and Haghirian, M. (2020) 'A quest for the Arabian atom? Geopolitics, security, and national identity in the nuclear energy programs in the Middle East', *Energy Research & Social Science*, 69 [online], Available from: https://doi.org/10.1016/j.erss.2020.101582 [Accessed 6 February 2022].

ANBP (2020) *Are Safety Requirements the Only Driver of Nuclear Construction Cost?* [online], Available from: https://www.linkedin.com/pulse/safety-requirements-only-driver-nuclear-construction-cost–ababou/ [Accessed 6 February 2022].

Česnakas, G. and Juozaitis, J. (2017) *Nuclear Geopolitics in the Baltic Sea Region: Exposing Russian Strategic Interests behind Ostrovets NPP*, Atlantic Council Global Energy Center [online], Available from: www.atlanticcouncil.org/in-depth-research-reports/issue-brief/nuclear-geopolitics-in-the-baltic-sea-region/ [Accessed 30 November 2023].

Coffie, A. and Tiky, L. (2021) 'Exploring Africa's agency in international politics', *Africa Spectrum*, 56(3): 243–53.

Debrah, S.K., Nyasapoh, M.A., Ameyaw, F., Yamoah, S., Allotey, N.K. and Agyeman, F. (2020) 'Review article: Drivers for nuclear energy inclusion in Ghana's energy mix', *Journal of Energy*, 11: 1–12.

Democracy in Action (2022) *Democracy in Ghana* [online], Available from: https://democracyinafrica.org/democracy-monitor/ghana/ [Accessed 15 February 2022].

DMRE (Department of Mineral Resources and Energy) (2019) *Integrated Resource Plan 2019*, Pretoria: DMRE.

Egypt State Information Service (2023) *El Dabaa Nuclear Energy Plant Project* [online], 4 February, Available from: www.sis.gov.eg/Story/176389/El-Dabaa-Nuclear-Energy-Plant-Project?lang=en-us [Accessed 29 November 2023].

Fig, D. (2010) *Nuclear Energy Rethink? The Rise and Demise of South Africa's Pebble Bed Modular Reactor*, Institute for Security Studies (ISS) Paper 210 [online], Available from: https://issafrica.s3.amazonaws.com/site/uploads/210.pdf [Accessed 30 October 2020].

Foy, H. and Bosman, I. (2021) *Nuclear Energy in Ghana. Special Report* , South African Institute for International Affairs (SAIIA) [online], March, Available from: https://saiia.org.za/research/nuclear-energy-in-ghana/ [Accessed 19 July 2022].

GAEC (Ghana Atomic Energy Commission) (2022) *About Us – Ghana Atomic Energy Commission* [online], Available from: https://gaecgh.org/about-us/ [Accessed 24 March 2022].

GNA (Ghana Nuclear Authority) (2021) *Five Vendors Express Interest in Ghana's Nuclear Power Programme* [online], Available from: https://gna.org.gh/2021/09/five-vendors-express-interest-in-ghanas-nuclear-power-programme/ [Accessed 12 December 2023].

Gonchar, M., Chubyk, A., Dyachenko, S., Ishchuk, O., Lakiichuk, P., Hychka, O. and Mukhrynsky, S. (2017) *Wars – XXI: Russia's Polyhybression*, Kyiv: Avega Publishing House.

Gopaldas, R. (2021) 'Democracy in decline in Africa? Not so fast', *Institute for Security Studies (ISS) Today* [online], 4 November, Available from: https://issafrica.org/iss-today/democracy-in-decline-in-africa-not-so-fast [Accessed 29 March 2022].

Government of the Russian Federation (2003) *On the Approval of the Energy Strategy of Russia for the Period up to 2020 # 1234-r (Ob Utverzhdenii Energeticheskoi strategii Rossii na period do 2020 goda)*, Pravitelstvo Rossiiskoi Federacii [online], Available from: https://docs.cntd.ru/document/901872984 [Accessed 29 March 2022].

Government of the Russian Federation (2006) *О федеральной целевой программе 'Развитие атомного энергопромышленного комплекса России на 2007–2010 годы и на перспективу до 2015 года'*, Moscow: Government of the RF.

Hill, C.R. (2018) 'Britain, West Africa and "The new nuclear imperialism": decolonisation and development during French tests', *Contemporary British History*, 33(2): 274–89.

IAEA (International Atomic Energy Agency) (2018) *IAEA and the African Union Commission Sign First-Ever Practical Arrangements for Sustainable Development in Africa* [online], Available from: www.iaea.org/newscenter/news/iaea-and-the-african-union-commission-sign-first-ever-practical-arrangements-for-sustainable-development-in-africa [Accessed 12 December 2023].

IAEA (International Atomic Energy Agency) (2021) *Financing Nuclear Power Plants*, IAEA-TECDOC-1964 [online], Available from: www-pub.iaea.org/MTCD/Publications/PDF/TE-1964web.pdf [Accessed 19 July 2022].

IAEA (International Atomic Energy Agency) (2022a) *IAEA and AU Strengthen Cooperation on Nuclear Applications for Development in Africa* [online], Available from: www.iaea.org/newscenter/pressreleases/iaea-and-au-strengthen-cooperation-on-nuclear-applications-for-development-in-africa [Accessed 16 February 2022].

IAEA (International Atomic Energy Agency) (2022b) *Research Reactor Database (RRDB)* [online], Available from: https://nucleus.iaea.org/rrdb/#/home [Accessed 17 February 202].

IAEA (International Atomic Energy Agency) (2022c) *Update 13 – IAEA Director General Statement on Situation in Ukraine* [online], 6 March, Available from: www.iaea.org/newscenter/pressreleases/update-13-iaea-director-general-statement-on-situation-in-ukraine [Accessed 31 March 2022].

IEA (International Energy Agency), NEA (Nuclear Energy Agency) and OECD (Organisation for Economic Co-operation and Development) (2020) *Projected Costs of Generating Electricity* [online], Available from: https://iea.blob.core.windows.net/assets/ae17da3d-e8a5-4163-a3ec-2e6fb0b5677d/Projected-Costs-of-Generating-Electricity-2020.pdf [Accessed 7 April 2022].

IISS (Institute for International Security Studies) (2017) *Geopolitics of Nuclear Energy in the Middle East*, Istanbul [online], Available from: www.iiss.org/blogs/analysis/2018/02/Nuclear-Middle-East [Accessed 28 February 2022].

IMF (International Monetary Fund) (2022) *IMF Data – Zambia* [online], Available from: https://data.imf.org/?sk=85b51b5a-b74f-473a-be16-49f17 86949b3 [Accessed 29 March 2022].

Jewell, J. (2010) 'Ready for nuclear energy? An assessment of capacities and motivations for launching new national nuclear power programs', *Energy Policy*, 39(2011): 1041–55.

Kachur, D. (2021a) 'How state capture went nuclear', in N. Callaghan, R. Foley and M. Swilling (eds) *Anatomy of State Capture*, Cape Town: African Sun Media, pp 329–58.

Kachur, D. (2021b) *Russia's Resurgent Interest in Africa: The Cases of Zambia and Tanzania. Special Report*, South African Institute for International Affairs (SAIIA) [online] December, Available from: www0.sun.ac.za/cst/wp-content/uploads/2022/01/Special-Report-kachur-1.pdf [Accessed 20 February 2022].

Klutse, C.K. (2020) *Nuclear Power Programme in Africa: Current Status and Challenges*, Presentation to African Commission on Nuclear Energy (AFCONE) webinar [online], 10 December, Available from: www.afcone.org/wp-content/uploads/2020/12/07-Dr-Charles-KLUTSE-Ghana-Nuclear-Power-Programme-in-Africa-Final-15-12-20201.pdf [Accessed 28 March 2022].

Kornprobst, M. (2020) 'African agency and global orders: the demanding case of nuclear arms control', *Third World Quarterly*, 41(5): 898–915.

Lucet, F.P. (2018) 'Conditions and possibilities for financing new nuclear power plants', *Journal of World Energy Law & Business*, 12(1): 21–35.

Mbambo, Z. (2020) *Statement by the Republic of South Africa* [online], 7 September, Available from: www.energy.gov.za/files/media/pr/2020/AFRA-Chair-Statement-at-the-signing-ceremony-of-the-MOU.pdf [Accessed 16 February 2022].

Mohlakoana, N. and Wolpe, P. (2021) *A Just Energy Transition to Facilitate Household Energy Access and Alleviate Energy Poverty*, Trade and Industrial Policy Strategy Policy Brief: 5/2021 [online], Available from: www.tips.org.za/policy-briefs/item/4199-a-just-energy-transition-to-facilitate-household-energy-access-and-alleviate-energy-poverty [Accessed 19 July 2022].

Orttung, R.W. and Overland, I. (2011) 'A limited toolbox: explaining the constraints on Russia's foreign energy policy', *Journal of Eurasian Studies*, 2: 74–85.

Republic of Zambia (2019) *Zambia National Energy Policy 2019* [online], Available from: https://www.reuters.com/article/zambia-debt-idUSKBN2HA2L5/ [Accessed 19 July 2022].

Reuters (2021) 'Zambia owes nearly $27 billion in foreign and local public debt' [online], 20 October, Available from: www.reuters.com/article/zambia-debt-idUSKBN2HA2L5 [Accessed 29 March 2022].

Rosatom (2021) 'Nuclear can help Africa jumpstart its 4th industrial revolution' [online], Available from: https://rosatomnewsletter.com/centralafrica/nuclear-can-help-africa-jumpstart-its-4th-industrial-revolution/ [Accessed 29 March 2022].

Rossiyskaya Gazeta (2012) 'Rosatom's foreign orders portfolio reaches $ 50 billion' [online], 23 April, Available from: www.zato26.org/korporaczii-i-biznes/984 [Accessed 19 July 2022].

Russian Embassy in Zambia (2022) 'A.A.Yarakhmedov held a meeting with Minister of Foreign Affairs of Zambia S.Kakubo' [online], Available from: https://zambia.mid.ru/en/press-centre/news/a_a_yarakhmedov_held_a_meeting_with_minister_of_foreign_affairs_of_zambia_s_kakubo/ [Accessed 20 February 2022].

Russian View (2020) '20 Questions with Vladimir Putin – Interview to TASS News Agency' [online], Available from: www.youtube.com/watch?v=-LlBoCrUmD8&list=PLtH7t4KO6uGiIuA8Tdy2k4JWPxmN-pdkB [Accessed 24 March 2022].

Sah, A., Lovering, J., Maseli, O. and Saxena, A. (2018) *Atoms for Africa: Is There a Future for Civil Nuclear Energy in Sub-Saharan Africa?*, Centre for Global Development Policy Paper, Washington, DC [online], Available from: www.cgdev.org/publication/atoms-africa-there-future-civilnuclear-energy-sub-saharan-africa [Accessed 19 July 2022].

Salakhetdinov, E.R. and Sidorov, V. (2018) 'Russian projects and energy cooperation in South Africa', *Studies on Russian Economic Development*, 29(3): 336–42.

Schepers, N. (2018) *Russian Incentives for Nuclear Hopefuls in Africa*, Institute for International Security Studies (IISS) [online], 30 April, Available from: www.iiss.org/blogs/analysis/2018/04/russia-nuclear-africa [Accessed 24 March 2022].

Schepers, N. (2019) *Russia's Nuclear Energy Exports: Status, Prospects and Implications*, Stockholm International Peace Research Institute (SIPRI) Non-Proliferation and Disarmament Paper No 61 [online], February, Available from: www.sipri.org/publications/2019/eu-non-proliferation-and-disarmament-papers/russias-nuclear-energy-exports-status-prospects-and-implications [Accessed 19 July 2022].

Slivyak, V. (2019) *Dreams and Reality of the Russian Reactor Export* [online], Available from: https://ecdru.files.wordpress.com/2019/03/rosatom-report2019.pdf [Accessed 19 July 2022].

South Africa, Republic of (1999) *Public Finance Management Act [No 1 of 1999] (PFMA)*, Pretoria, South Africa: Government Gazette 33059 [online], Available from: www.treasury.gov.za/legislation/PFMA/act.pdf [Accessed 24 November 2023].

Statista (2020) *Distribution of Energy Production in Africa as of 2020* [online], Available from: www.statista.com/statistics/1277860/distribution-of-energy-production-in-africa-by-source/ [Accessed 20 March 2022].

Study in Russia (2018) *Stipends for Foreign Students to Study in Russia 2014–2018* (*Стипендии на обучение в России для иностранцев, квота на образование иностранных граждан*) [online], Available from: https://studyinrussia.ru/en/actual/scholarships/ [Accessed 1 December 2018].

TASS (2020) 'Matvienko says Russia is ready to help Zambia in mineral exploration' (Matvienko zaiavila, chto Rossia gotova pomoch' Zambii v razvedke poleznyh iskopaemyh) [online], Available from: https://tass.ru/ekonomika/7785635 [Accessed 24 March 2022].

TASS (2022) 'Construction of El Dabaa NPP in Egypt to begin in July – Rosatom' [online], Available from: https://tass.com/economy/1389379 [Accessed 16 February 2022].

Turianskyi, Y. and van Wyk, J. (eds) (2021) *Nuclear Power and Governance Frameworks: Egypt, Ghana and South Africa*, South African Institute for International Affairs (SAIIA) Special Report [online], March, Available from: https://saiia.org.za/research/nuclear-power-and-governance-frameworks-egypt-ghana-and-south-africa/ [Accessed 15 February 2022].

Ülker, K. (2020) 'Key Russian company withdraws from Turkish nuclear project', *Ahwal News* [online], 31 October, Available from: https://ahvalnews.com/russia-turkey/key-russian-company-withdraws-turkish-nuclear-project-columnist [Accessed 24 February 2022].

UNODA (United Nations Office for Disarmament Affairs) (2022) *Nuclear-Weapon-Free Zones* [online], Available from: www.un.org/disarmament/wmd/nuclear/nwfz/ [Accessed 29 March 2022].

Van der Merwe, L. (2021) *International Involvement in the African Nuclear Market*, South African Institute of International Affairs (SAIIA) Occasional Paper 329 [online], September, Available from: https://saiia.org.za/research/international-involvement-in-the-african-nuclear-market/#:~:text=There%20are%20no%20nuclear%20vendors,operates%20a%20nuclear%20power%20plant [Accessed 19 July 2022].

Velichkov, K. (2021) *Synchronising Nuclear Governance in SADC Member States Through Regional Cooperation*, South African Institute of International Affairs (SAIIA) Occasional Paper [online], October, Available from: https://saiia.org.za/research/synchronising-nuclear-governance-in-sadc-member-states-through-regional-cooperation/ [Accessed 19 July 2022].

WNA (World Nuclear Association) (2021) *Nuclear Energy in Finland* [online], Available from: https://world-nuclear.org/information-library/country-profiles/countries-a-f/finland.aspx [Accessed 24 March 2022].

WNA (World Nuclear Association) (2022) *Nuclear Energy in Egypt* [online], Available from: https://world-nuclear.org/information-library/country-profiles/countries-a-f/egypt.aspx [Accessed 24 March 2022].

Zambia Daily Mail (2021) 'Nuclear technologies key for Africa's renascence and prosperity' [online], 26 January, Available from: https://web.archive.org/web/20221203221659/http://www.daily-mail.co.zm/nuclear-technologies-key-for-africas-renascence-and-prosperity/ [10 April 2024].

Zondi, S. 2016) 'A decolonial turn in diplomatic theory: unmasking epistemic injustice', *Journal for Contemporary History*, 41(1): 18–37.

15

Challenges and Triumphs for Women Leaders in African Diplomacy

Jennifer Chiriga, Rudo Chitiga and Hesphina Rukato

Introduction

Diplomacy is one of the most critical instruments of foreign policy and governance globally. Holsti (1995) defines diplomacy as ideas or actions created by policy makers to address challenges or encourage changes in policies, attitudes or actions of other states and non-state actors in the international economy or in the physical environment of the world. As a result of the world's interdependencies and connectedness, diplomacy has been refined and institutionalized to guide formal relations established between countries and regions as well as continents. Diplomacy has gained popularity from the growing number of cross-border issues ranging from conflicts and disagreements to trade negotiations, spurred by globalization. As a result, many professions have been created around diplomacy including ambassadors, consuls and negotiators (Akokpari, 2016: 3).

Although in recent years the world has witnessed an upsurge of women's participation in the political and diplomatic space, there continues to be a huge gap between men's and women's participation in leadership positions both globally and in Africa, particularly in politics. The huge participation deficit in women's participation in political leadership positions continues to be central to contemporary political discourses. According to Rahman-Figueroa (2012), diplomacy is not symbolic of men's status and views of world affairs, but rather it is reflective of a whole society. In respect to this, diplomacy of the 21st century must be represented equally by men and women of equivalent merit and standing. Women's equal participation in diplomacy plays a crucial role in the general process of the advancement of women in any field.

In the context of Africa, many African Union (AU) member states have put in place progressive legal frameworks that are supposed to guarantee gender equality in social, economic and political affairs. While this is a mark of normative progress, the continent still must practically demonstrate its commitment to equal gender representation across all spheres.

Although women make up more than 50 per cent of Africa's population, they remain under-represented in leadership roles across political, financial, economic, investment and entrepreneurial markets. This is even though African women have been and continue to be the *invisible and undercounted* backbone of the continent (World Bank, 2019).

Yet, according to Pardon (1971), diplomacy is a feminine art. This is because 'women have been skilled in diplomacy for thousands of years … to learn how to get what they want for the interests of their families' (Pardon, 1971). The low representation of women in the diplomatic sector starts from the low numbers of women in the international relations field, which is dominated by men (Bimha, 2021). The role of women in international relations remains unjustifiably under-studied in the social sciences (Bimha, 2021). The historical domination of men in diplomacy, the military and government still inform international relations studies.

African women have always been at the forefront of diplomacy, even though their actions were not categorized or termed as such. That is the case with Annie Jiagge. She was the first Ghanaian woman to become a High Court judge and the first woman judge of the Commonwealth; she was a leading women's rights activist of her time, and author of the basic draft and introduction to the United Nations (UN) Declaration on the Elimination of Discrimination against Women.

Another leading illustration of women's diplomacy is the Pan African Women's Organization (PAWO). Before the formation of the Organization of African Unity (OAU) in 1963, PAWO was already in existence, emphasizing the early and active role of African women in the continent's diplomatic affairs. Established in Dar es Salaam, Tanzania, in 1962, PAWO played a significant role in building unity and solidarity among African women during crucial periods in the struggle for political emancipation. Over the last six decades PAWO has been steered by strong women leaders who have been at the helm as secretary generals:

- Jeanne Martin Cissé (Guinea), 1962–74;
- Fathia Bethabar (Algeria), 1974–86;
- Maria Ruth Neto (Angola), 1986–97;
- Assetou Koite (Senegal), 1997–20;
- Grace Kabayo (Uganda), 2020 to present.

This chapter provides personal reflections of three women – Jennifer Chiriga, Hesphina Rukato and Rudo Chitiga – who have served in diplomatic fields in their careers. This is within the context of the AU's normative frameworks, and the overall milieu of the challenges and successes of African women's foray into the diplomatic sphere. The chapter focuses on specific issues of interest in women's participation in diplomacy, both global and continental.

The authors reflect on their experiences in the context of their lived participation in leadership and diplomacy globally and in Africa. In doing so, they draw on relevant normative frameworks, especially of the UN at the global level, and of the African Union at the continental level. The chapter also utilizes theoretical frameworks in gender and leadership studies. It ends by highlighting emerging lessons and recommendations.

The role and dominance of women in Track II diplomacy

The groundswell for the advancement of women manifested in the UN global women's conferences (1975–85), which began when the UN hosted the First World Conference on Women in Mexico in 1975 and was christened the Decade for Women. This was followed five years later in 1980 by the Second World Conference in Copenhagen. This recognition of the need to promote the advancement of women produced a blueprint for UN member states to work towards achieving women's equality globally, which was adopted as the Nairobi Forward-Looking Strategies for the Advancement of Women in 1985 in Nairobi, Kenya. The Fourth World Conference on Women was held in Beijing in September 1995, setting the stage for a review of previous initiatives and design of new approaches for the implementation of action plans in areas of concern. African women were highly mobilized and participated in these processes, and their input helped inform the various action plans, protocols and frameworks.

UN Secretary General Kofi Annan (2002), during a UN Security Council meeting on women, peace and security, noted that 'women, who know the price of conflict so well, are also better equipped than men to prevent or resolve it'. This relates to the participation of women in formal diplomacy, which is also known as Track I diplomacy. Since the UN meetings on the Decade for Women culminating in the Beijing Conference, a parallel Track II process has emerged where women in civil society and non-government organizations (NGOs) have become major negotiators and participants in international meetings. The introduction of consultative status and observer status in the UN and AU have enabled the women's movement to sit in official meetings, to advise their governments on positions and to find sponsors to promote policies which advance gender equality.

The pinnacle of this process was the Women Peace and Security Movement, which advocated for the UN Security Council to adopt Resolution 1325 of 2000 (S/RES/1325) on Women, Peace and Security. The resolution calls for the protection of women and the prevention of violence against women in conflict situations. It also calls for the inclusion of women in peace negotiations and in peacekeeping missions. This was a major milestone on women, peace and security at the UN. UNSC Resolution 1325 (2000) has since given rise to additional UNSC Resolutions to sharpen it. For instance, the AU and the regional economic communities (RECs) such as the Southern African Development Community (SADC) have also adopted the Resolution in their gender protocols. Additionally, NGOs like the Working Group for Women, Peace and Security maintain a permanent presence at the UN, make speeches and interventions in UN debates, represent a feminist political viewpoint and constituency, and attempt to influence the behaviour of member states through informal negotiations and public communications strategies. These are all diplomatic practices.

Africa has demonstrated great leadership in Track II diplomatic negotiations for peace. For example, the Mano River Women's Peace Network (MARWOPNET) in Freetown, Sierra Leone, is a network of women's organizations from Sierra Leone, Liberia and Guinea established in May 2000 to promote their participation in the process of restoring peace in Africa, and specifically in the Mano River region (Liberia, Sierra Leone and Guinea). The network participated formally in peace talks in the three countries and were signatories to the 2003 peace agreement in Liberia. Despite the challenges and setbacks, initiatives like the MARWOPNET are testimony that recognition and acceptance of women's inclusion in Africa's diplomatic arena has been steadily increasing.

Another progressive development in this area was the 2014 appointment of a special envoy on women, peace and security – Bineta Diop – by then chairperson of the AU Commission. The position is meant to advocate for the importance of women's diplomacy in the prevention and resolution of conflicts and peace building. The special envoy's mandate (as per Commitment 8 of the AU gender policy) is to 'enhance the role of women in creating an enabling, stable and peaceful environment for the pursuit of Africa's development agenda' (AU, 2009). The special envoy has provided high-level advocacy support and solidarity missions to Central Africa Republic, South Sudan, Nigeria and Somalia.

The African Union's normative framework for gender equality

The AU is Africa's apex intergovernmental body, made up of 55 member states. In this respect, it is Africa's representative in matters of diplomacy with the rest of the world. Through the African Union, Africa has created normative frameworks for gender equality.

The Constitutive Act, which is the foundational instrument for the AU, clearly articulates Africa's progressive stance on gender equality (AU, 2002). This stance is indicative of the diplomatic prowess of a women's movement that already knew of its aspiration for women's role in diplomacy in the 21st century. At the start of the crafting of the Constitutive Act, women deftly worked to ensure that it reflected women's aspirations. Former AU Commission chairperson, Nkosazana Dlamini Zuma (2016), buttressed this point:

> through the lobbies of civil society women, meeting on the sidelines of Summits, coordinating with the few women Foreign Ministers inside Summits, we lobbied our Presidents and won the Gender Parity principle. So, from zero women in the leadership of our Union, we leapfrogged to the 50:50 representation in the AU Commission that we still have today.

To their credit, African governments responded positively to the call for a Constitutive Act that reflected African women's aspirations. Specifically, Article 4(l) of the Constitutive Act speaks to the 'promotion of gender equality' and provides the guiding principle for gender parity (AU, 2002). Normatively, this was a huge diplomatic success for African women. The next battle was, and continues to be, in the implementation field.

In 2002, the AU adopted the principle of gender parity. The ground-breaking clause in the Constitutive Act stipulated that half of the eight commissioners elected had to be female. This broke the tradition of an AU Commission/OAU Secretariat which had been led by men in the positions of secretary general and assistant secretary general since the formation of the OAU in 1963. This example is demonstrative of the political will to advance women's participation in diplomacy and political leadership. However, even though the AU gender policy and the parity principle 'represents the most advanced global commitment to equal representation between men and women in decision-making' (AU, 2009), the Assembly of the AU (heads of state level) remains exclusionary to women (Makinda and Okumu, 2007: 40). To date, only three African countries out of 55 have had female heads of state (Liberia, Malawi and Tanzania).

At the global level, 54 African countries are UN members. As such, the 30 per cent affirmative action quota agreed upon at the 1995 Beijing Conference has been a target for most countries, some of which have registered progress in women's representation and participation in decision-making structures. According to the Inter-Parliamentary Union, the overall representation of women in national parliaments in Sub-Saharan Africa is estimated at 26.1 per cent (IPU, 2022). This represents an encouraging improvement of 7 per cent since the 1990s. Africa has also witnessed the appointment and election of women in strategic and executive positions in governments, NGOs and in the private sector, including as deputy presidents and strategic ministries such as foreign affairs, defence and finance ministers. The AU envisions a 50 per cent representation of women in decision making as a yardstick for member states (AU, 2009).

These examples speak to the gap between having the normative frameworks and the challenging environments of practically effecting these aspirations. The fact that two out of the three female heads of state and government that Africa has had since independence got their positions by succeeding deceased heads of their political parties, and not through elections, speaks to national psyches, cultures, traditions and environments that are not conducive to women's equal participation in high offices, even though technically the normative space exists.

To give an impetus to the implementation of the Beijing Platform for Action as well as the AU Assembly Decision on the 2018–28 Gender Equality and Women's Empowerment strategic programmes, the AU Assembly declared the period 2010–20 the African Women's Decade. However, as with many other declarations, implementation remained a challenge, and not much progress was recorded on women's advancement in political leadership and diplomacy as *purposefully* stemming from this declaration.

The Solemn Declaration on Gender Equality in Africa is an important policy instrument adopted for attaining gender equality on the continent (AU, 2004). The declaration is also a reporting tool to keep gender equality issues alive at the highest political level in Africa. It aims to ensure the full and effective participation and representation of women in peace processes as stipulated in UNSC Resolution 1325 of 2000, and also to appoint women as special envoys and special representatives (AU, 2004). Although only a limited number of member states have submitted their reports, it remains a relevant tool that needs leadership to drive its effectiveness. This again points to the lack of advancement of women's participation at the national level.

As part of the African Women's Decade, AU heads of state and government launched the Fund for African Women. This is meant to devote at least 0.5 per cent of the AU's operational budget to women's empowerment. Much needs to be done (including the political will of member states) to activate this instrument. It should also be noted that money alone is not enough to remove the barriers that hamper women's advancement in the political and diplomatic realm. There are fundamental patriarchal, cultural and societal challenges that need to be confronted.

Defining national/organizational interests through a gender lens

Having addressed the continental context for women's participation in leadership and diplomacy, it is important to share some reflections on national imperatives and the challenges they present for women's participation

The strong interest among policy makers to increase the representation of women in diplomacy has not been matched by efforts in the foreign policy of the countries (Bimha, 2021). In peace negotiations men are still largely seen as the most credible negotiators and special envoys. According to a UN Women (2012) study, women only constitute 9 per cent of all negotiators, 2.5 per cent of all chief mediators and 4 per cent of signatories of peace agreements. The reasons given include that peace, or any negotiations, are hard and last long, which may be inconvenient to women. Women in the negotiating teams often provide only the administrative, secretarial and logistical support, while the negotiators are predominately male. The content of agreements therefore often misses out on the gender issues and dimensions that women could bring if they were present at the negotiating table.

Foreign policy statements in most African countries hardly mention gender. Gender issues only come about during the annual Commission on the Status of Women, the Convention on the Elimination of all Forms of Discrimination Against Women (CEDAW) Committee hearings and sometimes at the Human Rights Commission. This is even though some of the biggest development partners for Africa, such as Canada and the Nordic countries, describe their foreign policy as feminist (Thompson, 2020). By shying away from gender equality as a foreign policy objective, countries miss support for gender equality programmes, which could be a critical component in their cooperation agreements with these countries.

Determinants and prospects for women's participation in diplomacy

The previous section articulated some of the efforts being made by governments at the continental level to advance the participation of women in politics and diplomacy. However, before a woman can look forward to overcoming the continental and global barriers, there are other local and personal challenges she must face.

The first stepping stone to entering the diplomatic field is a solid foundation of quality education that provides an individual with knowledge, problem-solving skills and aptitude to execute novel ideas, all of which are key to a successful diplomatic career.

In addition, entry to the field of diplomacy is also determined by the politics of the day, and this applies equally to national, regional and continental diplomacy. For instance, in the context of the AU, high-level positions require an 'endorsement' from one's government. This is to ensure candidates presented and occupying strategic positions are model citizens and can represent the country or institution at an international level. Given that African governments' leadership is predominantly male, it follows that in such cases a woman's foray into the diplomatic field happens at the behest of a male-dominated leadership.

In a nutshell, the key determinants and prospects for women's participation in diplomacy lie in a good education as a foundation, followed by post-education mentorship, especially in the early years of a career. Relevant experience and a nurturing work environment are also key, as some work environments can stunt women's prospects for entering the diplomatic field. Another key ingredient is building and sustaining support networks, as this is critical to staying afloat in a world that is not conducive to women's participation, especially for young women rising in the diplomatic world.

In addition to the technical and often discussed challenges facing women in diplomacy, Bimha (2021) quotes a key informant in her study who noted that in order to survive, women had to learn to live 'with the pebble in the shoe' to forge ahead with their career path and to be on the list for diplomatic postings. Those who stopped to shake out the pebble did not go far. These pebbles include policies which go against one's principles and staying silent about sexual harassment and other unpalatable dynamics. To be appointed an ambassador one must be seen as completely loyal to the leadership and the 'system'. This loyalty often means living with a few inconvenient 'pebbles'. This is common not only to Africa but to all countries around the world. These are 'soft and unspoken' issues which women are commonly confronted with.

Personal reflections

Diplomacy in intergovernmental processes: the African Union
One of the most significant developments in the 50-year history of the AU Commission was the election of the first ever woman chairperson in 2012. In this position, Africa had its first female top diplomat. All eyes were on her, in Africa and globally. She had the challenge of demonstrating to the world what African female leadership and diplomacy looks like. Chiriga reflects that Dlamini Zuma's legacy at the AU Commission could be categorized into two areas: recruitment and acknowledging women's role. In the area of recruitment, she had an unshakable principle of no tolerance for shortlists without female candidates. She also appointed the first female peace and security envoy, and selected women as head of field missions in Chad, deputy head of mission in Somalia, special representative of AU office in Madagascar and AU permanent representatives to Washington and New York.

Dr Dlamini Zuma also had the knack of seeing and acknowledging the role of other women in Africa's political and diplomatic field. PAWO was formed in 1962, a year before the establishment of the OAU. It took a female leader at the AU Commission to have PAWO honoured and celebrated. A portrait of the founding members of PAWO and a plate inscribed with all their names have now taken their rightful place alongside the founding fathers of the continent in the AU Commission building as a reminder and acknowledgement of the contribution of women to the establishment of the OAU (AU, 2017). The key message here is that female diplomats see other females and acknowledge them. The recruitment of women in senior positions also sends a clear message that they deserve equal chances, especially if they are educated, ready for the positions and can deliver. She demonstrated that if someone is dedicated to women's advancement, then Africa is not short of candidates for diplomacy. Women are ready to take the roles of leadership and diplomacy.

Chiriga further reflects that Dr Dlamini Zuma created a series of firsts: She had a female chief of staff, Jennifer Chiriga, two female deputy chiefs of staff (in succession) and a female secretary general. In addition, the recruitment process was unequivocally in support of gender balance, and the shortlists and interview reports presented for approval or appointment were processed only if there were female candidates on them:

> Beyond the gender parity at the level of elected officials, there was a relentless commitment to ensure that every recruitment brought to her for approval took gender balance into consideration. She fought resistance and arguments that insistence on gender balance might compromise meritorious recruitment. Whenever she was presented with three male candidates for any position, she would not consider any of them until and unless they included women. (Du Plessis, 2017: 85)

Chiriga reflects further that there were advantages and challenges to being a cog in the wheel of the command centre of Africa's premier diplomatic institution. Being chief of staff was a leadership role where management and coordination were key to facilitating interdepartmental and inter-agency processes, and managing relationships with representatives of member states and multilateral bodies, as well as strategic and international development partners. This was a role of institutional leadership and making politically sensitive decisions under the authority of the chairperson whose mandate was to deliver on the development agenda of the Commission.

Her experience in advancement of the AU's development and integration agenda made her realize the need for Africa to create synergy with other parts of the world through strategic partnerships. That is why Africa continues to engage the international community and to seek cooperation with various international bodies and groups, countries and continents. One of Chiriga's highlights of engagement with Africa's partners was her involvement in diplomatic negotiations of the AU Commission partnerships unit with the strategic counterparts, including representatives of Japan, China and India. What remains a fact (and a recurring challenge) for her is the continued male dominance of the diplomatic processes. She cites the Tokyo International Conference on African Development, which she says had only two women in the collective delegations of both sides – with the women at senior level being the World Bank representative and AU Commission chief of staff.

One of her insights from her experience is that the fragility of African states offers a compelling case for the continent to embrace a collective, a multilateral approach to diplomacy, rather than bilateral diplomacy. Being on the sidelines and, at times, amid multilateral engagements was thus a strategic position. Some of the significant engagements were actively representing, participating in and articulating the AU Commission position in multilateral forums such as consultation meetings hosted by the Secretariat of the Chinese Follow-up Committee of the Forum on China–Africa Cooperation (FOCAC). These were high-level discussions to review the framework of the FOCAC summit, share notes and expedite its preparatory work through collaboration between the Chinese side, the African diplomatic corps in Beijing and representatives of the AU Commission. As usual, the delegates in the conference room, particularly those with speaking slots, were always overwhelmingly male.

Agenda setting and consensus building

The running theme emerging in this chapter is that spaces for diplomatic consultations and negotiations tend to be very male oriented, which sometimes creates barriers for married women or women with young children. For Chitiga, as deputy director at the Commonwealth Foundation, it was a major advantage to be able to keep all hours, negotiating key points with colleagues in the Secretariat during smoking breaks outside the building. Quitting smoking brought an abrupt end to the networking, and the trail of information dried up.

Chitiga says that during her tour of duty in Paris, as Zimbabwe's ambassador accredited to France:

> 'I realized very quickly that agreements and strategies were formed at spaces created by the diplomats such as over lunch, dinner, other spaces including in the private boxes at the Paris Saint Germain stadium where one could find senior diplomats from the Arab states. On the occasions where I found myself at the stadium, most of the time was spent in the hospitality lounge, and often we would ask the waiters what the score was as we were busy discussing some business matter. In Addis and in Paris I discovered that there were spaces for women which were very feminine. These were mostly the nail bar, the spa or hairdressers where a group of female colleagues met after the treatments

over coffee to discuss and agree on matters. These experiences were mostly in relation to multilateral affairs.'

She further reflects that although there is guidance in terms of the bilateral relations one's government has with others and the need to work closely with one's regional bloc, it was also important to explore relations with other representatives who may not be on the top list of friendly countries. Having represented Zimbabwe during the time it was under Western sanctions, she realized that re-engagement efforts included building relations with representatives of countries that were seen as influencers and could open doors and help to thaw hostilities against her country. These led to long-lasting and productive relationships and opened opportunities for cooperation. This helped in setting the agenda and achieving cross-regional consensus. Being present president of the G77 and China, and being part of the Africa group at UNESCO, gave access to other regional chairpersons and created opportunities to influence the agenda at UNESCO, which would have been difficult had she not been in those positions. She also managed to develop cooperation programmes between Africa and China, as well as with Germany, from which Zimbabwe benefitted. There was a lot of quid pro quo to influence key members and gain support on certain issues in exchange for mutual support on an issue important to the group. Much can be achieved when there is an opportunity to exercise leadership in important processes.

Challenges of leadership: building networks and alliances and influencing agendas

In this section focusing on leadership, Rukato reflects that in her experience, one of the challenges of female leadership is the mistaken belief that a good female leader is one who exhibits male leadership qualities. This is sometimes expected of female leaders to make the men they lead feel at ease, and can have the effect of constraining women leaders from being natural and innovative leaders, trying too hard to be like their male counterparts. There must be ways of building alliances and networks without a female diplomat losing her unique feminine attributes, which have an indispensable value in the world of diplomacy. It is key for women to be able to identify these attributes, and then use them strategically.

Another important challenge is that of symbolism and visuals. Global female leaders are often seen wearing severely tailored suits (Angela Merkel, Christine Lagarde, Kamala Harris and Hillary Clinton are good examples, to name a few). In Africa, the leader who ran for elections and won, Ellen Sirleaf Johnson, presented a female brand. Ngozi Okonjo Iweala is also setting a trend that you can wear your *doek* (headscarf) when leading a global institution, the World Trade Organization (WTO). Nkosazana Dlamini Zuma presents a distinctly African brand too. This conveys to young women seeking to enter the world of diplomacy that they can be an effective African female diplomat by looking African and not downplaying their feminine attributes.

The world needs to become accustomed to the image of an African female diplomat clad in ethnic clothing, and associate this image with as much credibility as the image of a Western male or female diplomat in a dark suit. The world of diplomacy also needs to become accustomed to seeing this same image with a younger face. Therefore, experienced women diplomats providing training and mentoring of the younger generation is essential to equip future leaders who, in collaboration with national instruments, can compel governments to bring capable women into the diplomatic service.

Currently, the world does not necessarily equate older African female diplomats with competence. Upon Ngozi Okonjo Iweala's appointment as head of the WTO, a Swiss newspaper announced: 'This grandmother will become the boss of the WTO', with no reference to her impressive credentials (Ishiekwene, 2021). After several women heads of UN agencies and more than 120 ambassadors in Geneva signed a petition calling out the headline as racist and sexist, the paper apologized (Ishiekwene, 2021). When women leaders form strong lobby groups, the impact can be powerful. Strong networks of women can breach the frontiers of discrimination and inequity.

Networking with both women and men is key to remaining abreast of issues. In a world dominated by social media, choosing the issues to engage on wisely can shift the narrative about women's capabilities. The contest should be one of ideas and this logically means that one must be on top of issues at hand and be well-informed and well-read. Diplomacy needs a clear understanding of international relations, as well as a broad range of general knowledge and expertise as a prerequisite for effective representation. These attributes can help break down stereotypes. For example, there is a balance to be struck between being authentically loud voiced and effective (without being judged aggressive or too assertive) and being soft voiced and effective (without this being seen as weak). Women diplomats should not be expected to be either/or.

Lessons learnt

- Africa has many capable women deserving of being given a chance to participate in diplomacy and leadership.
- As a woman diplomat, one fights for the image and credibility of women and sisterhood and carries the burden of the whole of womanhood.
- Delivery and preparedness are key. Even though men fail in diplomacy every day, one woman's failure can be projected to be a failure by all women.

- Issues of women's participation in political and diplomatic spaces need to be practically addressed at the national level. As has been demonstrated, the normative frameworks exist, including through national constitutions, but the patriarchal, institutional, cultural and traditional practices bar women's advancement. These need to be structurally removed to pave the way for more women to advance. There is a need to go beyond slogans.
- It is not enough to have a vision; leaders must take the normative frameworks beyond theory, and take decisive action for implementation of gender equity.

Conclusion

At international level it is now imperative to include women and ensure that they participate fully in the entire range of actions diplomats usually perform. Much emphasis has been placed on building of a critical mass that can become a strong lobby (strength in numbers) to build a legacy of women's leadership and leverage male allies to advocate for women's advancement. A case in point is how this was done by looking at all the UN agencies in Vienna, and lobbying male colleagues to join the Gender Champions Initiative, a leadership network of permanent representatives and heads of organizations that brings together female and male decision makers to break down gender barriers. Leaders are asked to make commitments on an individual level to lead by example in promoting gender equality within the organizations they lead. Working with progressive men is very important, Rwanda would not be what it is today if not for the progressive leadership of President Kagame and his commitment to mainstreaming gender and promoting women's empowerment, and therefore contributing to the prosperity of Rwanda.

A policy framework for mainstreaming gender can only succeed where those who must carry out the mainstreaming activities are sensitized on gender dynamics – such as gender analysis training targeted at bureaucrats and diplomats in addition to national instruments which will force governments to commit to an action plan to train and support women. There is already a framework provided by UN Resolution 1325 (2000), which deals with the inclusion, support and protection of women in peace and security activities. Training in mediation, negotiation and diplomacy can pave the way and broaden women's inclusion in negotiating teams, whether it be in economic, political, or peace and security fields.

The AU is a key international relations institution due to its role as interlocutor between Africa and the rest of the world. Therefore, the AU should spearhead the campaign for inclusion of more female leaders, such as special envoys, within the AU system and its RECs. Supporting recruitment data and indication of the types of posts women hold in African states is important information that should be incorporated into the AU's strategy on Gender Equality and Women's Empowerment 2018–28. The plan already calls for participation of women in political affairs to amplify their voices and integrate gendered perspectives (Bimha, 2021).

References

Annan, K. (2002) *Remarks by Secretary-General Kofi Annan to the Security Council Meeting on Women and Peace and Security*, SG/SM/7598 [online], 24 October, Available from: https://reliefweb.int/report/burundi/secretary-general-calls-council-action-ensure-women-are-involved-peace-and-security [Accessed 19 July 2022].

AU (African Union) (2002) *Constitutive Act of the African Union* [online], Available from: https://au.int/sites/default/files/pages/34873-file-au_constitutive_act_ar.pdf [Accessed 19 July 2022].

AU (African Union) (2004) *Solemn Declaration on Gender Equality in Africa*, Assembly/AU/Decl.12 (III) Rev.1 [online], Available from: https://au.int/sites/default/files/documents/38956-doc-assembly_au_decl_12_iii_e.pdf [Accessed 19 July 2022].

AU (African Union) (2009) *Gender Policy* [online], Available from: www.usip.org/sites/default/files/Gender/African_Union_Gender_Policy_2009.pdf [Accessed 19 July 2022].

AU (African Union) (2017) 'African Union commemorates Pan-African Women's Day', Press release [online], 31 July, Available from: https://au.int/pt/node/32734 [Accessed 19 July 2022].

Akokpari, J. (2016) 'The challenges of diplomatic practice in Africa', *Journal for Contemporary History*, 41(1): 1–17.

Bimha, P.Z.J. (2021) 'The status of African women in foreign policy', *e-International Relations* [online], 6 May, Available from: www.e-ir.info/2021/05/06/the-status-of-african-women-in-foreign-policy/ [Accessed on 20 July 2022].

Dlamini Zuma, N. (2016) *Remarks by AUC Chairperson during Celebration of International Women's Day* [online], 8 March, Available from: https://au.int/ar/node/21056 [Accessed 29 November 2023].

Du Plessis, C. (2017) *Woman in the Wings: Nkosazana Dlamini Zuma and the Race for the Presidency*, Johannesburg: Penguin Books.

Holsti, K.J. (1995) *International Politics: A Framework of Analysis* (7th edn), Englewood Cliffs, NJ: Prentice Hall.

IPU (Inter-Parliamentary Union) (2022) *Global and Regional Averages of Women in National Parliaments* [online], 1 July, Available from: https://data.ipu.org/women-averages?month=7&year=2022&op=Show+averages&form_build_id=form-FVhIv9Ab4QeqHKsZGXIgkn84b4gSryc3s4s49-L7YEU&form_id=ipu__women_averages_filter_form [Accessed 19 July 2022].

Ishiekwene, A. (2021) 'World Trade Organisation: the Black African "grandmother" who could just save the world from itself', *Daily Maverick* [online], 21 February, Available from: www.dailymaverick.co.za/opinionista/2021-02-21-world-trade-organisation-the-black-african-grandmother-who-could-just-save-the-world-from-itself/ [Accessed 19 July 2022].

Makinda, S.M. and Okumu, F.W. (2007) *The African Union: Challenges of Globalisation, Security and Governance*, New York: Routledge.

Pardon, C. (1971) 'The foreign service wife and diplomacy in the '70s', *Foreign Service Journal* [online], September, Available from: https://afsa.org/foreign-service-journal-september-1971 [Accessed 29 November 2023].

Rahman-Figueroa, T. (2012) 'Celebrating the rise of women in diplomacy', *Grassroots Diplomat* [online], Available from: www.grassrootdiplomat.org/news/celebrating-the-rise-of-women-in-diplomacy [Accessed 20 July 2022].

Thomson, J. (2020) 'The growth of feminist (?) foreign policy', *e-International Relations* [online], 10 February, Available from: www.e-ir.info/2020/02/10/the-growth-of-feminist-foreign-policy/ [Accessed 20 July 2022].

UN Women (2012) *Women's Participation in Peace Negotiations: Connections between Presence and Influence* [online], Available from: https://asiapacific.unwomen.org/en/digital-library/publications/2016/01/women-s-participation-in-peace-negotiations [Accessed 29 November 2023].

World Bank (2019) *Population, Female (% of Population) – Sub-Saharan Africa* [online], Available from: https://data.worldbank.org/indicator/SP.POP.TOTL.FE.ZS?locations=ZG [Accessed 20 July 2022].

16

African Diplomacy: An Agenda for Practice and Research

Jo-Ansie van Wyk and Sven Botha

Introduction

African diplomacy, as a unique diplomatic practice and area of study, stands at the centre of this volume. Whether a unique African diplomatic practice exists, or not, the continent's diverse diplomatic actors are subject to international law and customs regulating diplomacy. However, within these legal confines, African states and non-state actors have in recent years crafted a diplomatic niche for themselves in response to a changing international landscape and, in some instances, adding to its significant diplomatic achievements. This is not only limited to individual African states but also seems to be emerging within the context of the African Union (AU) and its building blocks, the regional economic communities (RECs).

The editors of and contributors to this volume set out with several caveats. First, this volume does not aim to make contributions to diplomatic theory despite an intellectual gap that remains in this area. Theory building is a unique intellectual undertaking that requires scientific rigour and time. This volume is, however, the first in a series by Bristol University Press (BUP) dedicated to the study of Africa's international relations and diplomacy. In this regard, the publication has laid some of the empirical and analytical groundwork for future scholarship in this area, a key objective of this BUP series. The volume has presented several diplomatic typologies to determine unique and shared elements of African diplomacy. Its focus and findings on African diplomacy present a unique contribution voicing African diplomatic typologies, relations and practices. Another unique aspect is the wide-ranging nature of illustrative instances of African diplomacy presented by African and Afro-centric scholars and practitioners. Here, the volume contributes to non-Western knowledge production and sharing (aspects highlighted in Chapter 13 by Jane Knight) and unveiling unique practices from and about the continent. In this sense, the volume is a contribution to African epistemology and ontology. It is also mindful of and recognizes previous scientific efforts and contributions in this regard. It is hoped that this volume will become a key milestone in the study, discovery and contribution to African diplomacy.

This chapter proceeds by returning to the conceptual and analytical framework of the volume. It commences with an outline of the functions of African diplomacy based on contributors' findings. Thereafter the chapter focuses on the practice of African diplomacy deduced from the volume. The penultimate section provides recommendations for the future agenda of African diplomacy before proceeding to the volume's concluding remarks.

The functions of African diplomacy

The editors offered an expanded list of the functions of African diplomacy, namely communication and information gathering, gaining and maintaining influence, regulation, conflict resolution, common purpose and socialization, and diversity and innovation (see Chapter 1).

Diplomacy as communication and information gathering

Communication and information gathering are two of the traditional functions of diplomacy. In this regard African diplomacy is no exception. African diplomatic actors ranging from heads of state and government, governments, diplomats and foreign policy decision makers communicate, for example, via Twitter (Chapter 7), maritime diplomacy (Chapter 6) and cultural diplomacy (see Chapters 11 and 12), with each other and with a broader continental and international audience. Chapter 6 has shown that diplomatic signalling such as the adoption of an African maritime strategy, a SADC naval operation such as Operation Copper, or a joint naval exercise such as IBSAMAR are also examples of diplomatic communication. In this chapter, the intended audience for maritime diplomacy as communication and information gathering includes non-state actors like illegal fishing companies, pirates and states perceived to be involved in illegal fishing. Chapter 7 unveiled the power and perceptions involved in the practice of Twitter diplomacy. The number of Twitter followers of African heads of state and government varies across the continent. As Twitter followers can be from across the globe, the number of followers of a diplomatic actor reveals its national and international appeal, influence and standing. Similarly, criticism via Twitter has resulted in diplomatic actors' suspension of their accounts, ostensibly to counter negative perceptions. Chapter 7 also confirms the practice of Twitter diplomacy as part of African diplomacy to communicate diplomatic positions, events and achievements. Besides this, social media platforms such as Twitter provide unique information-gathering services to its clients upon request. This is useful for diplomats and diplomatic interactions to gain a competitive advantage and manage perceptions. Perception management, nation branding and self-promotion via Twitter has thus become an important diplomatic function and practice. However, for this practice to function optimally and improve nation branding and regime legitimation, the authors caution that digital inequality in Africa remains prevalent and will continue to challenge 'Twitter diplomats' on the continent, particularly if it functions as an official communication tool in the context of public diplomacy to sell their foreign policy to the African people. Moreover, the authors warn that given the penetration of other social media platforms on the continent compared to Twitter, African diplomatic actors should diversify their digital presence and practice.

Diplomacy as influence

Influence has been described as one of the types of agency (Munyi et al, 2020: 3). Hence, diplomacy and appropriate diplomatic practices can improve the influence of an African state and the continent, and thus enhance its agency. More importantly, influence enables access, agenda setting and material and/or non-material rewards. Influence means that a diplomatic actor can coerce, compel or persuade another actor to serve the influencer's interests. Influence can be formal or informal, ascribed or constructed. This latter aspect is clear in Chapter 12, which deals with Morocco's cultural diplomacy with Africa. Despite Morocco's decades-long unwillingness to join the AU, it has been able to maintain diplomatic relations with several African states, most notably through the construction of influence by practising religio-cultural diplomacy that locks into the country's triple identity as an African, Muslim and traditional monarchical state.

Another example of diplomacy as influence is evident in Chapter 3 on common African positions (CAPs). Building on the continent's historical mission to achieve unity, Pan-Africanism and solidarity, the AU's Constitutive Act states that one of the objectives of the AU is to craft and promote common African positions to achieve its historical mission (AU, 2002). The effect of the plethora of CAPs adopted by the AU is that the continent's international marginalization has been reduced and some degree of Pan-African unity on common interests achieved. Moreover, CAPs have improved Africa's collective bargaining power in multilateral fora. A CAP is endorsed by 55 African states, a significant voting bloc in any multilateral organization. In the context of the UN, for example, Africa represents almost a quarter of UN members. More importantly, CAPs are expressions of the normative commitment of the continent, aspects that have influenced, for example, the UN's adoption of the Sustainable Development Goals (SDGs).

Chapter 6 presents an example of diplomacy as influence by focusing on maritime diplomacy. The AU and African regional organizations have adopted maritime strategies to combat piracy and ensure maritime security. Typically, states participating in, for example, joint naval operations and exercises project their influence in this domain.

The continent is not isolated from international developments, as clearly illustrated by the outbreak of the COVID-19 pandemic. Although the pandemic reiterated the limitations of the territorial state to prevent the spread of disease, global interconnectedness could continue through technology and social media, for example, which also opened new technological platforms for diplomatic practices. Chapter 7 focuses on the practice of Twitter diplomacy as an increasingly institutionalized practice of African diplomacy. Technological platforms were one of the enablers of the international response to the COVID-19 outbreak. As outlined in Chapter 10, Africa's response to the pandemic included online diplomatic interactions between the chairperson of the AU at the time, the South African president Cyril Ramaphosa, and other heads of state and government.

Diplomacy as influence can, however, lead to the opposite effect. In their contribution, Dzvinka Kachur and Robyn Foley turn the focus to the great power politics in and about Africa, and the geopolitical influences that shape some African countries' energy ambitions and choices (see Chapter 14). Here, the focus is specifically on the agency of South Africa, Egypt, Ghana and Zambia in their bilateral relationships with Russia. Kachur and Foley posit that the hegemonic discourse about Russo-African nuclear relations focuses on Russia's foreign policy objectives and its implications for the West and other powers present in Africa. Africa is thus marginalized. Kachur and Foley do not deny Russia's competitive advantage in Africa compared to other states. They are mindful that Russian nuclear diplomacy in the context of their selected African cases has highlighted Russia's use of energy resources for its increased geopolitical influence in Africa. However, Russia has put its African partners to the test. On 2 March 2022, Egypt, Ghana and Zambia all supported the UN resolution condemning the Russian invasion of Ukraine, while South Africa, despite its long-standing tradition of preventing and mitigating violence, abstained (see Chapter 14).

Diplomacy as regulation

Perceptions regarding Africa and African diplomacy often oscillate between positive and negative views. Opinions of the continent have shifted to the positive end of the scale due to some of the achievements of African diplomacy. However, this has not diminished the prevalence of and concerns about major unresolved conflicts and challenges on the continent. These realities inform African diplomacy and reflect Africans' lived experience, presenting a challenge to hegemonic discourses about development and diplomacy. The importance of these lived experiences, for example in a diplomatic context, is voiced in this volume with a contribution by African women diplomats (see Chapter 15).

Diplomacy as common purpose and socialization

Diplomacy is a social institution and a social practice between states. Besides the regulatory function of international law vis-à-vis diplomacy, there are socialization agents such as customs, culture and multilateralism. A more intimate socialization setting exists at bilateral level. Routinized bilateral relations embed this intersubjectivity, which can be disrupted if bilateral relations are ruptured or enter a new phase by mutual consent.

Diplomacy as common purpose in Africa was energized by the transition from the Organization of African Unity (OAU) to the AU. Since its establishment in 2002, the AU has renewed the notion of common purpose in Africa and enshrined it in its Constitutive Act (AU, 2002). For the AU, the continent's common purpose is to achieve unity, Pan-Africanism and solidarity. Its common purpose has been operationalized through diplomatic practices such as the adoption of an integrated continental maritime strategy (see Chapter 6) and CAPs (see Chapter 10) that typically follow diplomatic negotiations along various paths. The continent's shared purpose enables diplomatic discussions to create and accept a CAP based on intersubjective understandings of common difficulties and questions on the continent, though this is not always easy. A CAP thus serves as a socialization agent for African states in constituting and operationalizing a CAP. A similar mutually constitutive process is currently under way as the continent implements the African Continental Free Trade Area (AfCFTA) Agreement to establish a continental free trade area (see Chapter 4). Besides the establishment of the AU, the AfCFTA will be African diplomacy's greatest achievement.

Diplomacy as common purpose often diminishes the possibility of coercive diplomatic practices, but to achieve common and shared objectives requires diplomatic competence. Following Bélanger (2021: 39), competence is understood here as 'possessing the relevant knowledge, skills and expertise embedded within a specific setting to perform a particular activity in a capable and proficient way'. One can thus deduce that diplomatic competence requires not only competent decision makers but also institutions, norms and appropriate practical and technical expertise and experience. Once competence becomes embedded in diplomatic practices then common purpose is easier to achieve. An area where competence is always the gold standard is innovation, science and technology (IST). Chapter 10 outlines the role of science diplomacy for and in Africa, whereas Jane Knight shows the limitations of the concept and practice of science diplomacy and posits that knowledge diplomacy is inclusive but more comprehensive compared to science diplomacy (see Chapter 13).

Diplomacy as conflict regulation

Communication is considered a key function of diplomacy to build trust among actors, facilitate cooperation and defuse misunderstandings. It is thus also an instrument to regulate competing interests through diplomatic practices such as negotiation, cultural exchanges and trade. Essentially, and ideally, diplomacy as conflict regulation reduces actors' vulnerability and exposure to risk while also securing their national interests. This is of particular importance to small and weaker states such as Africa's small island developing states (SIDS) that, as Chapter 5 outlines, have resorted to smart diplomacy as a diplomatic practice to reduce their vulnerabilities. Diplomacy as conflict resolution is also referred to in Chapter 6 on Africa's maritime diplomacy and Chapter 12 on Morocco's cultural diplomacy.

Diplomacy as diversity and innovation

Diversity is the spice of diplomatic life, more so in Africa where besides 55 sovereign states, thousands of unique ethnic identities and cultures prevail. The unification project of Africa's post-colonial independent states attempted to supersede ethnic diversity to forge a new post-colonial identity. As the cultural turn in international relations has shown, the politico-economic mobilization of, for example, cultural diversity can achieve national objectives such as development and attracting foreign direct investment (FDI). As the example of Ghana (see Chapter 11) shows, cultural diversity can manifest in an innovative diplomatic practice – cultural diplomacy – that, among other outcomes, can attract FDI. Similarly, in the case of Morocco (see Chapter 12), cultural diplomacy has achieved significant outcomes for the country. By mobilizing its cultural diversity through the practice of cultural diplomacy, Morocco has been able to maintain a strong diplomatic presence in Africa despite its withdrawal from the OAU in 1984 until it joined the AU in 2016.

Besides cultural diversity, gender diversity can also advance or undermine diplomacy. Jennifer Chiriga, Rudo Chitiga and Hesphina Rukato, experienced African women diplomats, focus on the participation, role and agency of women in African diplomacy and the AU's normative framework on this aspect (see Chapter 15). They conclude that a 'huge participation deficit' prevails in women's participation in politics and leadership in Africa (see Chapter 15). Despite some successes by African women diplomats, Chiriga, Chitiga and Rukato refer to the imperative to include more women in the diplomatic processes on the continent. Drawing on their lived personal experiences as diplomats and from academic literature, they identify the challenges faced by women that need to be overcome to enhance women's access to, participation in and agency in respect of African diplomacy. Chiriga, Chitiga and Rukato mention the challenges women diplomats face. These, according to them, include patriarchy and political systems that advance men rather than women. They also refer to the gap between the AU's normative framework on gender and women, and the reality in African states and institutions. However, where women have been involved, this has not always been acknowledged. Chiriga, Chitiga and Rukato make several recommendations pertaining to the advancement of women in African diplomacy (see Chapter 15).

The practice of African diplomacy

Diplomatic practices are often complex, requiring states and their representatives to balance interests, needs and values within the context of what Frost (2021: 21) refers to as a 'mega-practice' between a multitude of states. African diplomacy is no exception in this regard. Despite overlaps with traditional and more recently developed diplomatic practices, African diplomacy at national, regional and continental level contains some unique aspects, as contributions to this volume show. These include the presence and undoing of history, mega-diplomacy through institution building and collective decision making, diplomatic syncretism, commonality of purpose and collective bargaining and culture.

The presence and undoing of history

As François Theron posits in Chapter 2, 'African diplomacy and its objectives are deeply rooted in the history of African nationalism, which, in turn, is intimately connected to the founding figures of African independence and nationalism'. Theron thus focuses on the significance of history in African diplomacy and, as he terms it, 'a yearning for unity' (see Chapter 2). The shared experience of colonialism is fundamental to defining and understanding contemporary African diplomacy and practice. 'Undoing history' refers to the continent's repeated commitment and efforts to end the its historical marginalization, reform the international system, and achieve the triple goals of the continent: unity, Pan-Africanism and solidarity.

Mega-diplomacy through institution building and collective decision making

As Theron and other contributors indicate, the establishment of the institution of the AU has and continues to have a major impact on African diplomacy.

Besides its evolving architecture, the AU is instrumental in providing bureaucratic support, resources and legitimacy to African diplomatic decisions. The latter has benefitted significantly from the institutionalization of CAPs as a diplomatic practice (see Chapter 3). Besides the institution of the AU, the implementation of the AfCFTA is another mega-diplomatic development and practice on the continent (see Chapter 4).

Diplomatic syncretism

Despite claims that Africa practises a distinct style or form of diplomacy, the continent has maintained colonial borders and guards territorial sovereignty jealously (see Chapter 2). This state-centrism in the Westphalian tradition remains prevalent on the continent, but, as some contributors show, has evolved in Africa (see Chapter 5). Evidence presented here points to African diplomacy as diplomatic syncretism, that is, a diplomatic practice resulting from an amalgamation of traditional and post-traditional agendas, styles and forms of diplomacy. In this regard, the continent is not unique. However, what is unique is that through the AU and individual states it has indigenized diplomacy by adopting a position stressing the urgency of reforming an unequal and unjust international system.

Commonality of purpose and collective bargaining

The establishment of the AU has re-energized the continent's commonality of purpose to achieve the stated historical mission. Capitalizing on its numerical advantage in a multilateral organization such as the UN, African-led initiatives have revealed and added to the agential and normative power of the continent (see Chapter 3).

Culture

Ghana and Morocco are presented as two examples of African states' use of cultural diplomacy (see Chapters 11 and 12 respectively). Sandra Asafo-Adje concludes that Ghana's pursuance of cultural diplomacy continues to serve the country in achieving its national interests and the welfare of its population (see Chapter 11). Whereas Asafo-Adjei shows that Ghana has predominantly focused on an external diplomatic audience, including the African diaspora and descendants of the transatlantic slave trade, Faiza Koubi demonstrates that Morocco's cultural diplomacy has increasingly been directed towards African actors. Both authors attest to the economic potential and benefits of cultural diplomacy.

Koubi posits that cultural diplomacy among African actors enables solidarity between African states. Koubi indicates that regional organizations, or intergovernmental or non-governmental structures, are proof of this awareness and the need for African branding to undo negative perceptions about the continent and even to resolve conflicts. Koubi shows that Morocco's cultural diplomacy, which includes a significant religious base, has been one of the instrumental enablers of Morocco's African relations before and since it joined the AU.

These are not an exhaustive list of unique aspects of African diplomacy. As the contributors to this volume show, the continent's agency, status and participation have significantly changed since the establishment of the AU, which is illustrative of successful African diplomacy. However, the future agenda of African diplomacy should be mindful of some of the findings, conclusions and recommendations offered by the volume's authors.

A future agenda of African diplomacy

Diplomatic practices are often complex, requiring states and their representatives to balance interests, needs and values within the context of what Frost (2021: 21) refers to as a 'mega-practice' between a multitude of states.

African diplomacy has produced mixed results, but what is its future and how can it be improved to the continent's advantage? Contributors to the volume highlight issues, developments and practices that must be addressed to advance the African diplomatic agenda and achieve its intended functions and objectives. These are peace and security, an alignment of norms and practices, an appropriate diplomatic architecture, streamlined decision making, the alignment and harmonization between national, regional and continental agendas, policies and institutions, brand management, refining cultural, health, science, technology, energy and knowledge diplomacy, as well as advancing the role of women in African diplomacy.

A second proposal for the future agenda of African diplomacy is to streamline the process of collective action through, for example, crafting and adopting CAPs (see Chapter 3). Although consultative processes have improved, the absence of a clearly defined process has resulted in the ad hoc nature and process leading to the adoption of a CAP.

A third proposal for a future agenda of African diplomacy emanated from the establishment of the AfCFTA as one of Africa's mega-diplomatic initiatives. Sanusha Naidu, Faith Mabera and Arina Muresan highlight the need for future alignment and harmonization between national, regional and continental agendas, policies and institutions, especially in the context of the AfCFTA (see Chapter 4). Although their chapter focuses on South Africa's diplomacy, they make an instructive comment that applies to the rest of the continent, and thereby add a fourth item to the future agenda of African diplomacy in the context of economic diplomacy and the AfCFTA by calling for a 'dynamic brand management strategy and adeptness in navigating the intricacies of global economic governance and participation in institutions such as the World Trade Organization (WTO) and the G20' (see Chapter 4).

Although the AfCFTA is a mega-diplomatic initiative, it is a land-based initiative. Francois Vreÿ reminds us in Chapter 6 that the continent's maritime domain is of similar importance, especially in the context of illegal maritime activities, rising global maritime competition, the developmental promise of the blue economy and the security concerns linked to climate change.

Given technological advances in the context of the evolving Fifth Industrial Revolution, it is imperative for Africa to keep up and step up. Suzanne Graham, Victoria Graham and Lesley Masters allude to the state of digital and science technology and innovation on the continent, as well as its potential and current inequalities (see Chapters 5, 7 and 9). A future agenda of African diplomacy should capitalize on the continent's evolving science diplomacy.

Asafo-Adje reiterates the economic contribution and potential of cultural diplomacy (see Chapter 11). Ghana's *kente* fabrics and patterns are, like *adinkra* symbols, globally known. Despite this, she identifies challenges regarding Ghana's cultural diplomacy, such as financial constraints, intellectual property rights pertaining to designs and cultural elements and symbols, inadequate support from the private sector and inconsistent government policies. She reiterates that Ghana's cultural diplomacy should also focus on and involve the domestic and international private sector to invest in the cultural and tourism sectors, which, in turn, will benefit economic growth in Ghana. Moreover, Asafo-Adje recommends legal backing for Ghana's cultural products and symbols, which, according to her, are imitated by East Asian countries without any compensation to Ghana.

In reference to Morocco, Koubi observes the evolution of Morocco's conception of cultural diplomacy, with a continued emphasis on 'educational and university diplomacy … one of the oldest dimensions of Morocco–Africa relations that allows Morocco to shape its image with an audience in the making' (see Chapter 12). Whereas Asafo-Adje warns of challenges to Ghana's cultural diplomacy posed by, for example, Asian countries, Koubi observes that 'the francophone factor is potent in this type of diplomacy. Although this factor allows Morocco to maintain its position among the French-speaking club, it is not enough to develop an African cluster of the knowledge economy on a global scale' (see Chapter 12).

Janet Knight introduces the concept and practice of knowledge diplomacy, utilizing the Pan-African University (PAU) as an illustrative case (see Chapter 13). Knight warns that knowledge diplomacy 'is not a silver bullet' and concludes that it 'does not come without challenges' and can be easily used to promote national rather than mutual benefits (see Chapter 13).

Knight proposes that expectations need to be managed to avoid early discord and dismissal of the value and potential of knowledge diplomacy. She also proposes that the development of a framework, policies, strategies and commitment to knowledge diplomacy must be mindful of 'the harsh realities of international politics' indigenous and exogenous to Africa (see Chapter 13).

As foreign policy statements of African governments barely mention gender, Chiriga, Chitiga and Rukato recommend a definition and/or redefinition of national, regional and continental interests through a gender lens. Moreover, given the objectives and status of the AU, it 'should spearhead the campaign for inclusion of more female leaders such as special envoys within the AU system and its RECs' (see Chapter 15). This will require national investment in women's education and refined recruitment strategies regarding the appointment of women to relevant government, regional, or AU departments. These aspects, according to Chiriga, Chitiga and Rukato, should be incorporated into the AU's strategy on Gender Equality and Women's Empowerment 2018–28 (see Chapter 15).

Conclusion

Africa is a diverse continent consisting of 55 sovereign states. The editors and contributors have attempted to illustrate this diversity in the context of the diplomacy of African state and non-state actors, here collectively referred to as African diplomacy. The volume set out to present the functions and practices of African diplomacy at various levels – bilateral, regional, continental, international and polylateral – in an increasingly complex international arena. The continent cannot ignore these levels and complexities.

Including contributions from a wide variety of practitioners, diplomats and academics varying in geography, gender and race, the volume provides new perspectives on African diplomacy. It shows that the functions of African diplomacy coincide with the conventional functions of diplomacy but with an expansion to include communication and information gathering, gaining and maintaining influence, regulation, conflict resolution, common purpose and socialization, and diversity and innovation. In the third instance, the volume positions African diplomatic actors and developments within the broader African and international context. Africa at the AU level and at national level have historically been active diplomatic participants. It has maintained this status, albeit oscillating between national and continental interests.

In the fourth instance, the continent has achieved major diplomatic successes at three levels. The establishment of the AU and the AfCFTA are two of the continent's internal diplomatic successes and show continental agency asserted through internal coherence and cooperation. Diplomatic efforts to align individual AU member states, RECs, the AU and the AfCFTA have yielded some results.

Advances in IST have empowered many African states. It has also emerged as an instrument of national security and risk reduction. However, inequalities pertaining to IST persist. The volume reflects on some of the advances accrued due to IST diplomacy and an emerging form of African diplomacy, namely knowledge diplomacy through the establishment of the PAU.

The diplomatic scope of the AU and African states is comprehensive and includes, as shown here, IST, health, culture, education, maritime matters, women, knowledge and nuclear energy. The continent is, however, subject and sometimes vulnerable to the larger international political arena. Besides this, insecurity, war and conflict on the continent continue, compounded by the human and economic legacy of, for example, the COVID-19 pandemic.

Africa's colonial experience has left an indelible mark on the continent and will surely affect future diplomatic relations. The task to analyse and explore all facets of African diplomacy remains incomplete.

References

AU (African Union) (2002) *Constitutive Act of the African Union* [online], Available from: https://au.int/sites/default/files/pages/34873-file-constitutiveact_en.pdf [Accessed 12 December 2023].

Bélanger, J. (2021) 'Coercive diplomacy and continued relevance of hard power: the role of competence and context', in J. Spence, C. Yorke and A. Masser (eds) *New Perspectives on Diplomacy: A New Theory and Practice of Diplomacy*, London: I.B. Tauris, pp 37–53.

Frost, M. (2021) 'The global diplomatic practice: constituting an ethical world order', in J. Spence, C. Yorke and A. Masser (eds) *New Perspectives on Diplomacy: A New Theory and Practice of Diplomacy*, London: I.B. Tauris, pp 15–35.

Munyi, E.N., Mwambari, D. and Ylönen, A. (2020) 'Conceptualising agency and influence in African international relations', in E.N. Munyi, D. Mwambari and A. Ylönen (eds) *Beyond History: African Agency in Development, Diplomacy, and Conflict Resolution*, London: Rowman and Littlefield, pp 3–11.

Index

References to figures appear in *italic* type; those in **bold** type refer to tables.
References to endnotes show both the page number and the note number (116n2).

A

Abacha, Sani 115, 116
Abiy Ahmed Ali 91, 92, 98
Academy of the Kingdom of Morocco 166
Acemoglu, D. 16
Adamson, M. 123
Adegbulu, F. 18, 19
Ad'ha Aljunied, S.M. 58
adinkra 157, 160, 245
Afeku, Catherine 156
Africa Centres for Disease Control (CDC) 127, 139, 142, 143, 144
Africa Health Strategy 2016–30 139
African Academic of Sciences (AAS) 131
African Commission on Nuclear Energy (AFCONE) 203–4
African Continental Free Trade Area (AfCFTA) 6–7, 43, 47, 53, 240, 243, 244–5, 246, 247
  mobility of people and goods 52
  reciprocity 51
  rules of origin 51
  trade facilitation 51–2
African Development Bank (AfDB) 141, 143, 188, 189
African diaspora 8, 131
  Cabo Verdean 63
  Ghanaian 155, 157–8
  Moroccan 166
  and Twitter/X diplomacy 93–4, 99
African diplomacy 1–2, 6, 236–7, 246–7
  after independence 21–4
  collective bargaining 243
  and colonialism 16–18
  common African positions (CAPs) 6, 29–39, 238–9, 240, 243, 244
  common purpose 5, 240–1, 243
  communication and information gathering 237–8
  conflict regulation 241
  cultural diplomacy 8, 150–60, 163–74, 238, 241, 243–4, 245
  culture 243–4
  diplomatic syncretism 243
  diversity and innovation 241–2
  economic diplomacy 7, 42–53
  energy diplomacy 8, 196–214
  and Eurocentric international order 24
  functions of 4, 237–42
  future agenda of 244–6
  health diplomacy 8, 137–46
  and Islam 19
  knowledge diplomacy 8, 178–93, 241, 245–6
  maintaining influence 238–9
  maritime diplomacy 7, 71–83, 237, 239, 245
  mega-diplomacy through institution building and collective decision making 242–3
  perceptions of 2–5
  practice of 242–4
  pre-colonial 18–21, 23
  presence and undoing of history 242
  quiet diplomacy 7, 105–16
  regulation 239–40
  science diplomacy 8, 121–32, 241, 245
  smart diplomacy 7, 59–66, 241
  socialization 240–1
  Twitter/X diplomacy 5, 7, 88–101, 237–8, 239
  West Africa 19–21, 25
  women in 4, 8–9, 59, 221–34, 239, 241–2, 245
African Medicines Agency 139–40, 145
African Medicines Regulatory Harmonization 142
African nationalism 21–2, 242
African Peace and Security Architecture (APSA) 23, 24

248

INDEX

African Peer Review Mechanism 143
African Regional Cooperative Agreement for Research, Development and Training Related to Nuclear Science and Technology (AFRA) 203–4
African Standby Force 23
African Union (AU) 1, 3, 6, 9, 22, 25, 94, 126, 129, 132, 137, 163, 174, 196, 203, 233–4, 236, 240, 242–3, 246–7
  Agenda 2063: The Africa We Want 8, 33, 53, 76, 82, 138, 139, 140, 142, 188, 189, 191, 204
  Constitutive Act of the African Union 6, 23, 24, 29, 38, 39, 137, 138, 225, 238, 240
  and Ebola outbreak in West Africa (2014–16) 141, 142
  normative framework for gender equality 224–6
  STI-related policy developments 130–1
  women in diplomacy 228–30
  see also common African positions (CAPs)
African Union Mission in Somalia 79
African Vaccine Acquisition Task Team 145
Africa's Integrated Maritime Strategy (AIMS-2050) 75–6, 78, 79, 82, 240
agency, African 3, 4, 8, 65, 169, 201, 243
  and CAPs 33, 36, 37, 38, 39
  and colonialism 200
  and health diplomacy 140, 142, 145
  maintaining influence 238–9
  and nuclear energy 202, 203–4, 210–11
  and smart diplomacy 60
Agenda 2063: The Africa We Want 8, 33, 53, 76, 82, 138, 139, 140, 142, 188, 189, 191, 204
Agents of Peace 112, 113, 114
Ahmed, Tijani 172
Akkuyu nuclear power plant project 205–6
Akufo-Addo, Nana 91, 92, 157
Algeria 188, 189, 197
  and Sufi Brotherhoods (*Zawya*) 172
  Twitter/X diplomacy of 97
Algiers Declaration on Climate Change (2009) 35
American Association for the Advancement of Science (AAAS) 122, 124
ancient Greeks 12
Anderson, Anthony 158
Anglo-Spanish Treaty (1713) 13
Annan, Kofi 31, 223
Antarctic Treaty (1959) 123
Anyaoku, Emeka 21, 22
Arab League 165
Arab Spring 171, 206
Argentina 108
Arsenault, A. 89, 100
artificial intelligence 121–2
Asafo-Adje, Sandra 243, 245
Asante state 20
Asiyanbola, O.A. 131

Assembly of the African Union *see* AU Assembly
Association for Childhood Education International (ACEI) 186
Assyria 11
AU Assembly 35, 139, 143, 225, 226
AU Commission 22, 34, 35, 36, 224, 225, 228–9, 230
AU Executive Council 36, 139
AU Special Fund for Climate Change (AUPSC) 36
Austria 14
Azizi, Amir 171

B

Badie, B. 169
balance of power 13–14
Baltag, D. 5
batakari 156, 158
Beijing Platform for Action 226
Bélanger, J. 240
Belarus 205
Berenger, Joanna 64
Berlin Conference of 1884–85 17–18, 21, 25
Berridge, G.R. 11, 72
Bethabar, Fathia 222
Beyond the Return Secretariat, Ghana 158–9
Bimha, P.Z.J. 228
Bismarck, Otto von 17, 18
blue diplomacy *see* ocean diplomacy
blue economy 60, 65, 76, 82
Boko Haram 97, 116n2
  Chibok schoolgirls abductions 110–15
  factions of 109
  negotiations with Nigerian government 109–10
Bolsonaro, Jair 143
Botswana 91
Bouteflika, Abdelaziz 23
Boutros-Ghali, Boutros 12
Brand South Africa (Brand SA) 50
Brazil 81, 143
Brazil, Russia, India, China and South Africa (BRICS) 24
Brexit 2
Briggs, R. 107–8
Bring Back Our Girls movement (BBOGM) 110, 111, 112
#BringBackOurGirls movement 97–8
Britain *see* United Kingdom
Brook, Joshua 94
Bueger, C. 60, 78
Buhari, Muhammadu 92, 100, 113, 114, 115
Bull, Hedley 72, 169
Burundi 23

C

Cabo Verde 56, 60
  digital capabilities of 61, 62

249

representation of women in government in 64
stakeholder diplomacy of 63
Twitter/X diplomacy of 99
Callières, François de 13
Cameroon 188, 189
Campbell, Naomi 158
Cardinal Richelieu of France 13
Carter, Jimmy 108
Casablanca Group 21, 22
Castlereagh, Lord 17
celebrity diplomacy 157–8
Central African Republic (CAR) 98, 224
Chad 98
Charles VIII 13
Cheeseman, N. 56
Chibok schoolgirls abductions 7, 97–8, 105, 110–12
and BBOGM 110, 111, 112
negotiations 111, 112–13, 114, 115
and quiet diplomacy 112–15
China 3, 24, 53, 141, 189, 206, 208, 211
Confucius Institutes 180
and COVID-19 pandemic 125, 143, 144
Forum on China–Africa Cooperation (FOCAC) 230
Maritime Silk Road initiative 82
relations with South Africa 44
String of Pearls strategy 64–5
Chirac, Jacques 166
Chiriga, Jennifer 8, 228, 229–30, 241–2, 246
Chitiga, Rudo 8, 230–1, 241–2, 246
Ciolek, Melanie 91
climate change 35–6, 122
climate diplomacy 180
Clinton, Hillary 57
Cold War 22, 72, 105, 108, 123
collective bargaining power 6, 39, 238, 243
Collins, C. 107
colonialism 6, 15, 17, 63, 201, 242
and African agency 200
Berlin Conference of 1884–85 17–18, 21, 25
destruction of Africa's diplomatic traditions 18
and nuclear developments 196–7
and STI development in Africa 124, 130
commercial diplomacy 44–5, 49
see also economic diplomacy of South Africa
Commission on the Status of Women 34, 227
Commission Spéciale sur le Modèle de Développement, Morocco 164
Committee of Permanent Representatives (COREPER) 33
Committee of Ten (C-10) 32
common African positions (CAPs) 5, 6, 29–30, 238–9, 240, 243, 244
applying and upholding 37–8
appointment of ad hoc high-level committee 35, 37
commonality and compromise 36–7
consolidation of a historical position on an issue 34
consultative process 35, 37
diplomatic path to 33–6, 38
elements, nature and objectives of 31–3
initiative of AU Commission and/or AU commissioner 35
common positions 30–1
common purpose 5, 240–1, 243
communication 4, 25, 150–1, 237–8, 241
digital diplomacy 89
public diplomacy 89–91, 98
and science diplomacy 125–7
Twitter/X diplomacy 7, 88–101, 237–8
Comoros 56, 65
digital capabilities of 61
representation of women in government in 64
stakeholder diplomacy of 62–3
Concert of Europe 14, 15
conflict regulation/resolution 31, 112, 170, 241
Confucius Institutes 180
Congress of Vienna (1814–15) 14–15, 16–17, 25
Congress System 14, 17
Constitution of Ghana (1992) 155
Constitution of Morocco (2011) 166–7
Constitutive Act of the African Union 6, 23, 24, 29, 38, 39, 137, 138, 225, 238, 240
Contact Group on Piracy off the Coast of Somalia 60
Convention on the Elimination of all Forms of Discrimination Against Women (CEDAW) 227
Coolsaet, R. 12–13
Cooper, A.F. 106
Corbett, J. 56
Council for Science and Technology Policy, Japan 124
COVID-19 pandemic 5, 8, 122, 124–5, 131, 137, 239
agnosticism 143
and digital diplomacy 89
and health diplomacy 140, 142–6
and science diplomacy 126, 127
and Twitter/X diplomacy 91, 94
vaccines 142–3
COVID-19 Vaccines Global Access (COVAX) 145
Cowan, G. 89, 100
Crimean War (1853–56) 14, 15
Cudjoe, Boris 158
cultural diplomacy 5, 47, 62, 151–2, 153, 169, 180, 245
definition of 164

Ghana 8, 152–60, 241, 243, 245
  and knowledge diplomacy 185
  Morocco 8, 163–74, 238, 241, 243–4, 245
  and religion 163–4, 165, 171–3, 174
Cultural Policy of Ghana 154, 155
cuneiform diplomacy 11–12
customary law 19
Customs and Excise Duty Act, South Africa 51
cyber security 127
Czech Republic 205

D

Dapchi schoolgirls abductions 111
decolonization 16, 21, 25, 154, 201
Dee, M. 95
defence diplomacy 71, 73
Dehgan, Alex 128
democracy 24, 153, 207–8
Democratic Republic of the Congo (DRC) 145
Department of International Relations and Cooperation (DIRCO), South Africa 46, 48–9, 98
Department of Trade, Investment and Competition (DTIC), South Africa 49
developmental diplomacy 22–3, 47
Devin, G. 169
diaspora diplomacy 93–4
digital capabilities 5, 9n2, 58–9, 61–2
digital diplomacy 89, 90, 101
  see also Twitter/X diplomacy
digital inequality 92, 238
Digital Mauritius 2030 Strategic Plan 61
Diop, Bineta 224
diplomacy 5–6, 24–5, 71, 88, 150–1
  bilateral 16
  celebrity 157–8
  common positions 30–1
  cuneiform 11–12
  defence 71, 73
  definition(s) of 11, 57, 72, 178, 221
  developmental 22–3, 47
  diaspora 93–4
  and dynamic state of international relations 72
  evolution of 12–13
  functions of 3–4
  global state system 15–16
  gunboat 75
  hostage 107
  and modern state system 12–15
  multilateralism 16
  networked 94
  new 72, 73, 75
  origins of 11–12
  regulatory function of 4
  and representation/governance 72, 75
  Track II 223–4
  traditional 101, 151
  see also African diplomacy

diplomatic competence 240
diplomatic marriages 19
diversity, and diplomacy 5, 241–2
Dlamini, K. 109
Dlamini-Zuma, Nkosazana 22, 225, 228–9, 232
Dlomo, Maud 98
Doğan, E.Ö. 123
Donaldson, A. 100
Du Plessis, A. 73
Dvali, Beka 98

E

Ebla 11
Ebola outbreak in West Africa (2014–16) 141–2
Economic Community of Central African States (ECCAS) 63
Economic Community of West African States (ECOWAS) 3
Economic Community of West African States Monitoring Group 79
economic diplomacy of South Africa 6–7, 42–3, 52–3
  and AfCFTA 51–2
  and commercial/trade dynamics 44–5
  engaging businesses 50–1
  inner workings of bureaucratic machinery 48–9
  positioning of Africa in South Africa's foreign policy orientation 45–8
  post-apartheid foreign policy 43–5
  state-owned enterprises 49–50
Economic Diplomacy Strategic Framework (EDSF), South Africa 46
Economic Reconstruction and Recovery Plan (ERRP), South Africa 46
Edmunds, T. 78
education diplomacy 186
  see also knowledge diplomacy
e-government 61
E-Government Development Index (EGDI) 61
Egypt 4, 20, 36, 130, 214
  maritime diplomacy of 79
  nuclear energy expansion in 8, 197, 202, 206–7, 239
Eighty Years' War (1568–1648) 13
El Dabaa nuclear power plant (Egypt) 197, 206–7
Elba, Idris 158
energy diplomacy *see* nuclear energy
Essaouira 168–9
Ethiopia 36, 143
  Grand Renaissance Dam 130
  Twitter/X diplomacy of 94
EU Council 33, 34
EU Council of Ministers 33
European diplomacy 13–15, 20

European Parliament 33, 34
European Union (EU) 5, 24, 53, 126–7, 141, 187, 189
  and African Union, partnership between 141
  common positions 30, 31, 33–4
  science diplomacy of 128–9
Ezekwesili, Obiageli 97, 110, 111
Ezulwini Consensus 31–2

F

Faki Mahamat, Moussa 98
Faleye, O.A. 24
Faure, Barry 99
Fayot, Frantz 99
Fedoroff, N.V. 125
feminist foreign policy 59, 63–4
Ferobe, Tijani 112
festivals 156–7, 168–9
Final Act of the Congress of Vienna 16–17
First World War (1914–18) 15, 18, 25
Fletcher, Tom 15
Flink, T. 125
Fofana, Kassory 91
Foley, Robyn 8, 239
food systems, CAP on 35
foreign direct investment (FDI) 47, 50, 241
  and cultural diplomacy 152, 156, 158, 160
  of small island developing states 56
foreign policy 2, 13, 21, 72, 163
  Asante 20
  definition of 57
  feminist 59, 63–4
  and health 140
  of SIDS 56, 60
  smart power 57–8
  of South Africa 7, 43–8, 49, 53
  statements, gender issues in 227
  see also African diplomacy
Foreign Service Act, South Africa 48–9
Forum of Nuclear Regulatory Bodies in Africa 204
Forum on China–Africa Cooperation (FOCAC) 230
France 13, 14, 166
French Revolution (1789–99) 14, 25
Frost, M. 242, 244
Fulan 112
Fund for African Women 226

G

G7 summit (2021) 129, 144
Geingob, Hage 90
Gender Champions Initiative 233
gender equality *see* women in diplomacy
gender parity 225
geopolitics 47
  and nuclear energy 196, 202, 204–6, 209, 214, 239
  and soft power 187

Georgia 205
Germany 17, 18, 123, 189
Ghana 4, 5, 152–3, 197, 214
  cultural identity of 153
  independence of 21
  nuclear energy expansion in 8, 207–9, 239
  Twitter/X diplomacy of 91
Ghana, cultural diplomacy of 8, 152, 155–6, 159–60, 241, 243, 245
  challenges 159
  commemoration of transatlantic slave trade 157–9
  National Day celebrations 156
  policy and practice 153–5
  promotion of cultural Made in Ghana products 157
  recognition and promotion of national culture and heritage 156–7
Ghana Atomic Energy Commission (GAEC) 202, 208, 209, 214n2
Ghana Infrastructure Investment Fund 209
Ghana Research Reactor-1 (GHARR-1) 208
Ghana Tourism Authority 156
Ghana–Guinea Union 22
Ghazi, Y.E. 58, 65
Ghebreyesus, Tedros Adhanom 143, 144
Global Compact on Safe, Orderly and Regular Migration, CAP on 34
Global Competitiveness Report 48
Global Diplomatic Forum 58
Global Health and Foreign Policy Initiative 140
global state system 15–16
globalization 16, 72, 150, 221
Gnawa/Gnaoua Music Festival 168–9
Gobin-Rahimbux, B. 60
good governance of small island developing states 60–1
government-to-government diplomacy *see* traditional diplomacy
Graham, Suzanne 7, 56, 245
Graham, Victoria 7, 56, 106–7, 115, 245
Grand Renaissance Dam, Ethiopia 130
Green March (1975) 166
Group of 20 (G20) 47, 143, 144
Guinea 141, 224
Guinea-Bissau 56, 63
  digital capabilities of 61–2
  narco-state label of 65
  representation of women in government in 64
Gulf of Aden 77
Gulf of Guinea 76–7, 80
gunboat diplomacy 75
Gurib-Fakim, Bibi Ameenah Firdaus 63
Gwaambuka, T. 22

H

Haile Selassie I 22
Hamilton, K. 11

INDEX

Harvey, Steve 158
hashtag diplomacy *see* Twitter/X diplomacy
hashtags 88, 91, 92, 97
Hassan II, King 165, 166, 173
health architecture 139–40
health diplomacy 8, 138–9
 of Africa 140–6
 and COVID-19 pandemic 140, 142–6
 Ebola outbreak in West Africa (2014–16) 141
 population health and health architecture of Africa 139–40
Hecht, G. 124, 131
Heine, J. 106
Heng, Y.-K. 58
Hichilema, Hakainde 90, 213
Holliger, Pascal 112, 113, 114
Holsti, K.J. 221
Hong Kong 44
Hornsby, David 128
hostage diplomacy 107
Houphouët-Boigny, Félix 22
humanitarian effectiveness, CAP on 32–3, 37–8
Hungary 205

I

IBSAMAR 81, 237
India 3, 81, 189
 health diplomacy of 145
 relations with Mauritius 64
India–Brazil–South Africa Dialogue Forum 81
Indian Ocean Rim Association (IORA) 65, 81
information and communications technology (ICT) 91
information gathering, diplomacy as 237–8
innovation, and diplomacy 5, 241–2
Institute for Water and Energy Sciences, Algeria 190–1
Institute of African Studies, Morocco 166
Institute of Euro-Mediterranean Studies and Ibero-American Studies, Morocco 167
Integrated Nuclear Infrastructure Review (INIR) missions 208
Integrated Resource Plan, South Africa 209–10
International Atomic Energy Agency (IAEA) 196, 203, 208, 209, 214
International Committee of the Red Cross (ICRC) 5, 111, 115, 141
International Conference on Africa's Fight against Ebola 142
International Criminal Court (ICC) 23
International Ebola Recovery Conference 141
International Geophysical Year (IGY) 123
international higher education, research and innovation (IHERI) 178, 179, 180–1, **182**, 183, 185, 192
 see also knowledge diplomacy; Pan-African University (PAU)

international law 4, 12, 19, 75, 236
International Monetary Fund (IMF) 143, 144
international society 24, 169
International Union of Pure and Applied Physics 126
internet
 and exchange of ideas 150
 penetration in Africa 92, **93**, 99, 100
Invest SA One-Stop-Shop, South Africa 49
Investment Promotion (Smart City Scheme) Regulations 2015, Mauritius 61
Iran 108–9, 172
Irwin, G.H. 18, 19, 20
Islam 19, 163–4, 165, 171–3
Islamic State West Africa Province (ISWAP) 109, 110, 111
Italy 13, 82
ius gentium (law of nations) 12

J

Jamā'a Ahl al-sunnah li-da'wa wa al-jihād (JAS) 109, 111
James, A. 72
Japan 124, 189
Jewell, J. 197, 203
Jhummun, D.S. 60
Jiagge, Annie 222
John D. and Catherine T. MacArther Foundation 124
Johnson, T. 56
Joint Comprehensive Plan of Action 109
Jonathan, Goodluck 112
Jones, J. 108–9
Jones, W. 187
Jugnauth, Pravind 99

K

Kabayo, Grace 222
Kachur, Dzvinka 8, 239
Kagame, Paul 90, 91, 92, 100, 233
Kalele, P. 132n1
Kamoto, Maria Margaret 90
Karabo, T. 2, 3
kente 153, 156, 159, 160, 245
Kenya 36, 105, 188, 189
 maritime diplomacy of 79
 quiet diplomacy of 109
 Twitter/X diplomacy of 92, 94–5
Kenyatta, Uhuru 92, 95
Kerr, P. 178
Kingdom of Mali 20
Kingston, Kofi 158
Kissinger, Henry A. 2
Knight, Jane 8, 241, 245–6
knowledge diplomacy 8, 178, 192–3, 241, 245–6
 activities and instruments 184
 actors and partners 181, 183
 conceptual framework 181, **182**, 183–4

253

and cultural diplomacy 185
defining 179–81
and education diplomacy 186
intentions, purposes and rationales 181
modes and approaches 184
Pan-African University (PAU) 187–92
principles and values 183–4
and science diplomacy 185–6
and soft power 186–7
Knowles, Tina 158
Koite, Assetou 222
Kony, Joseph 97
#Kony2012 movement 97
Koubi, Faiza 8, 243–4, 245
Kufuor, John 154, 208
Kwabenya Nuclear Reactor Project, Ghana 208

L

LaBua, J. 108
Laidi, Z. 24
Lalli, R. 123
Landsberg, C. 106
Langhorne, R. 11
Lascurettes, K. 15
Latvia 205
Laxton, Rowan 98
Le Mière, C. 74, 75
League of Nations 16
liberalism 14, 169
Liberia 141, 224
Libya 77
Lithuania 205
Lloyd, L. 11
Lo, W.Y. 187
Louw-Vaudran, L. 109
Luh, S. 5
Lungu, Edgar 211
Luxembourg 99

M

Mabera, Faith 6, 244
Macron, Emmanuel 144
Maher, B. 124
Mali 172, 173
Mancham, James 57
Mandela, Nelson 43, 44
Mano River Women's Peace Network (MARWOPNET) 224
Manor, I. 91, 93, 101
Mansa Kankan Musa 20
Maphosa, S. 132n1
maritime agenda 7, 71, 75–6, 78, 83
maritime diplomacy 7, 71–4, 83, 237, 239, 245
  coercive 74, 75, 76, 77, 78–9, 82
  cooperative 74, 75, 76, 77, 78, 80–1, 82
  hard power 82
  interagency and transnational cooperation 78
  international collaboration 80–1
  and international oceans agenda 78
  multilevel partnerships 77–8
  national, regional and continental positions 77
  naval acquisitions 81–2
  naval capabilities 78–9, 82
  non-traditional threats 77, 80
  persuasive 74, 75, 76, 77, 78, 79, 82
  presence of African/international navies 77
  regional cooperation 80
  towards Africa 81–3
  utility of 74–5
  visits by naval and other agencies to African ports 82
maritime security 60, 63, 65, 73, 75, 76–7, 78–80, 239
Marrakech 168
Martin Cissé, Jeanne 222
Mashego-Dlamini, Candith 98
Masisi, Mokgweetsi 91
Masiyiwa, Strive 144
Masser, A. 2
Masters, Lesley 8, 245
Mauritius 5, 56, 60, 65
  cultural diplomacy of 62
  digital capabilities of 61
  relations with India 64
  representation of women in government in 63–4
  stakeholder diplomacy of 62
  Twitter/X diplomacy of 99
Mbeki, Thabo 23, 44, 45, 109, 210
Médecins Sans Frontières 141
mega-diplomacy 242–3, 244–5
middle power 9n1, 45
migration and development, CAP on 36
Miles, S. 108
Millennium Development Goals (MDGs) 23
Ministry of Electricity and Renewable Energy (Egypt) 207
Ministry of Foreign Affairs and Regional Integration (Ghana) 155
Ministry of Tourism, Arts and Culture (Ghana) 155, 156
modern state system 12–15
Mohamed, Amina 94
Mohamed bin Zayed 90
Mohammed, S.A. 18
Mohammed VI, King 166, 171, 173, 174
Monrovia Group 21–2
Morgenthau, H.J. 151
Moroccan Agency for International Development 171
Moroccan crises (1905–6, 1911) 18
Moroccan Foundation of African Ulemas 173
Morocco 5, 173
  and African Union 163
  foreign policy decision-making process in 168
  Green March 166

national identity of 167
threats to national/regional security 171, 172
Twitter/X diplomacy of 97
Morocco, cultural diplomacy of 8, 163–5, 238, 241, 243–4, 245
  academic cooperation and exchanges 170–1
  Africanity 168
  ambition and cultural cooperation 165–6
  artistic creation 174
  culture on the diplomatic agenda 166
  institutionalization of culture 165, 166–7
  Moroccan culture 168–9, 170
  openness 167–8
  reformulation of foreign policy 166
  and religion 163–4, 165, 169–70, 171–3, 174
  South–South cooperation 174
Morsi, Mohamed 206
Al-Motassadek, Mounir 171
Mozambique 77, 78, 79
Mthembu, Jackson 50
Mubarak, Gamal 206
Mubarak, Hosni 206
Mugabe, Robert 96, 105
Munyi, E.N. 3
Muresan, Arina 6, 244
Murithi, T. 2, 3
Museveni, Yoweri 22, 92
Mustapha, Zannah 112, 114
Mwambari, D. 3

N

Naidu, Sanusha 6, 244
Nairobi Forward-Looking Strategies for the Advancement of Women (1985) 223
Napoleon 25
Napoleonic Wars (1799–1815) 14
Al-Nasir Muhammad 20
Al-Nasser, Jamal Abd 206
nation branding 50, 94–5, 101, 164, 170, 173, 238
nation states 13, 16, 18
National Commission on Culture, Ghana 154–5, 156
National Economic Development and Labour Council (NEDLAC), South Africa 50–1
National Festival of Arts and Culture, Ghana 156
National Friday Wear Programme, Ghana 157
nationalism 75
  African 21–2, 242
  and Ghanaian cultural diplomacy 156
  vaccine nationalism 134
naval diplomacy 73, 74
naval exercises 79, 81, 237
Neto, Maria Ruth 222
Network of Women Parliamentarians in Cabo Verde 64

networked diplomacy 94
new diplomacy 72, 73, 75
New Partnership for Africa's Development (NEPAD) 23
Nicolson, Harold 11, 17
Nigeria 23, 79, 100, 188, 189, 197, 224
  Chibok schoolgirls abductions 7, 97–8, 105, 110–15
  Dapchi schoolgirls abductions 111
  intra-governmental rivalry 114
  negotiations with Boko Haram 109–10
Nigro, L.J. 12
Nkrumah, Kwame 21, 23, 152, 154, 158, 208
non-state actors 72, 163, 236
  and knowledge diplomacy 179, 183, 189, 192
  and maritime diplomacy 77–8, 237
  and quiet diplomacy 4–5, 7, 105, 107, 116
  see also Morocco, cultural diplomacy of
Ntshinga, Ndumiso 24
nuclear energy 4, 8, 196–7, 239
  on African continent 197, 200
  capital investment for 202
  Egypt 206–7
  Ghana 207–9
  grid and technical infrastructure development 203
  human capital building 202–3
  international regulation 203
  nuclear power programme status **199**
  regional cooperation as an expression of agency 203–4
  research reactors 197, **198**
  Russian nuclear diplomacy 204–6
  South Africa 209–11
  Zambia 211, **212–13**, 213
nuclear weapons 197, 200, 201, 209
Nye, Joseph 57, 169, 186–7
Nyerere, Julius 21

O

Obama, Barack 57, 94–5, 128
Obama, Michelle 97
Obangame Express 81
Obasanjo, Olusegun 23
ocean diplomacy 60
  see also maritime diplomacy
Ohsan Bellepeau, Agnes Monique 63
Okonjo Iweala, Ngozi 231
Okumu, J.J. 109
Olonisakin, F. 3
Oman 108–9
One China Policy 44
Operation Copper 79–80, 237
Organization of African Unity (OAU) 22, 23, 25, 29, 126, 163, 167, 225, 229, 240
Organization of the Islamic Conference/Organization of Islamic Cooperation 165

Oslo Ministerial Declaration 140
Oumouri, Hadjira 64

P

Packer, J. 107
Pan African Women's Organization (PAWO) 222, 228–9
Pan-African Parliament (PAP) 24
Pan-African University (PAU) 8, 179, 187–8, **191**, 245, 246
  activities 190–2
  actors and partners 189
  intentions, purposes and rationales 188–9
  modes 190
  principles and values 189
Pan-Africanism 2, 6, 21–2, 23, 33, 144, 208
pan-Arabism 165
Pandor, Naledi 98
Pardon, C. 222
Paris Peace Conference (1919) 15
Parshotam, Asmita 128
Patel, Ebrahim 53
Pax Romana 12
Peace and Security Council (PSC) 23, 35–6
Peace of Westphalia (1648) 13, 25
Pebble Bed Modular Reactor (PBMR), South Africa 210
Pharmaceutical Manufacturing Plan for Africa 142, 145
Polikarpov, Victor 205
Popcaan 158
population health 138, 139, 140
  see also health diplomacy
post-2015 Development Agenda, CAP on 35
principle of effectivity 17
Protestant Reformation 13
Protocol to the African Charter on Human and People's Rights on the Rights of Women in Africa (2003) 59
Prussia 13, 14
public diplomacy 89–91, 98, 100, 101, 151
  see also Twitter/X diplomacy
Public Finance Management Act, South Africa 210
Pudaruth, S.K. 62
Putin, Vladimir 204, 210

Q

Qaqa, Abu 109
Quadruple Alliance 14
quiet diplomacy 7, 105
  appearance of limited action or even inaction 113
  bilateral and multilateral efforts 114–15
  calm and tactful but persistent negotiation/dialogue 113–14
  and Chibok schoolgirls abductions 112–15
  concept and character of 106–8

constructive engagement with target country/actors 114
literature review 108–9
media involvement 113
personal/direct diplomacy 112
third parties to aid logistics 115
Quintuple Alliance 14

R

Rahman-Figueroa, T. 221
Ramaphosa, Cyril 46, 48, 52, 92, 94, 143, 144–5, 210, 239
Rana, K.S. 47, 90
Rawlings, Jerry J. 208
Reagan, Ronald 108
Red Sea 77, 79
regional economic communities (RECs) 36, 38, 140, 224, 233, 236, 246
regional integration 52, 188
  and CAPs 38
  economic integration 22, 43, 46–7
Règlement de Vienne 15
religious diplomacy 163–4, 165, 169–70, 171–3, 174
resident ambassadors 13
Responsibility to Protect (R2P) 3
Richard Lounsbery Foundation 124
Robinson, J.A. 16
Rockefeller Foundation 138, 141
Roman Catholic Church 12
Roman law 12
Romans 12
Rosatom 8, 197, 202, 204, 207, 208, 211
Rouhani, Hassan 97
Royal Society 122
Ruffini, P.B. 183
Rukato, Hesphina 8, 231–2, 241–2, 246
rules of origin 51
Russia 3, 8, 14, 141
  energy strategy 204–5
  invasion of Ukraine 4, 213–14, 239
  nuclear diplomacy of 197, 200, 204–6, 207, 208, 209, 210–11, **212–13**, 213, 239
Ruto, William 92
Rwanda 143, 233
  genocide 23
  Twitter/X diplomacy of 90, 92

S

Al-Sadat, Anwar 206
Sahib-Kaudeer, N.G. 60
Sahrawi Arabic Democratic Republic (SADR) 163
Sall, Macky 91
Sanches, E.R. 56
Santos, Jorge 99
São Tomé and Príncipe 56, 60
  digital capabilities of 61, 62
  stakeholder diplomacy of 63

INDEX

Satow, Ernest 11, 18
Schneider-Ammann, Johann 115
School of Nuclear and Allied Sciences, Ghana 202
Schreiterer, U. 125
science, technology and innovation (STI) 8, 121, 124, 128, 130–1, 132, 240, 247
Science, Technology and Innovation Strategy for Africa 2024 131
science diplomacy 5, 9, 121–2, 131–2, 183, 241, 245
  for Africa and by Africa 125–31
  AU policy developments 130–1
  capacity 125, 128, 129–30, 131
  collaborations 124, 125
  communication and cooperation 125–7
  conceptual understanding of 122–3
  of developed countries 123–4, 128–9
  developments in 122–5
  and knowledge diplomacy 185–6
  negotiation and representation 127–31
  political considerations of 123
Scramble for Africa 17
sea blindness 74, 76
Second World War (1939–45) 16, 25, 105, 197
'See Ghana, Eat Ghana, Wear Ghana, Feel Ghana' campaign 156
Senegal 23, 143
  health diplomacy of 140
  Sufi Brotherhoods (*Zawya*) in 172, 173
Senghor, Léopold 22
Serumaga, Amanda 99
Seychelles 5, 56, 57, 65
  digital capabilities of 61
  ocean diplomacy of 60
  Twitter/X diplomacy of 99
Shekau, Abubakar 109, 110, 114, 116n4
Shia Islam 171, 172
Sierra Leone 141, 224
Sirleaf, Ellen Johnson 59, 231
Al-Sisi, Abd al-Fattah 92, 207
slave trade 16–17, 157–9
Slovakia 205
small island developing states (SIDS) 5, 7, 56, 58, 65–6, 241
  digital capabilities of 58–9, 61–2
  feminist foreign policy of 59, 63–4
  foreign policy of 56, 60
  good governance of 60–1
  niche diplomacy of 64–5
  political strategy of 60
  stakeholder diplomacy of 59, 62–3
  Twitter/X diplomacy of 99
Smart City Scheme, Mauritius 61
smart diplomacy 5, 7, 9n2, 73, 241
  definition of 58
  maritime diplomacy 78
  of small island developing states 58, 59–65

smart power 7, 57–8, 75, 164
Smith, R. 19, 20
social media 5, 7, 89, 92–3, *93*, 97, 100, 110, 150
  see also Twitter/X diplomacy
socialization 5, 31, 39, 168, 240–1
Sofer, S. 72
soft diplomacy 73, 75, 82, 202
soft power 57, 60–1, 62, 73, 94, 96, 101, 124, 151, 152, 153, 164, 174, 186–7
Solemn Declaration on Gender Equality in Africa (2004) 226
Somalia 79, 224
South Africa 7, 22, 23, 36, 105, 108, 123, 188, 202–3, 214
  BRICS 24
  economic diplomacy of 7, 42–53
  economic reforms 46, 48
  economic stagnation of 45
  foreign policy orientation, positioning of Africa in 45–8
  health diplomacy of 140, 142, 143, 144–5
  inequality in 45–6
  maritime diplomacy of 78–9, 81
  middle power label of 45
  National Development Plan 48
  naval exercises 81
  nuclear energy expansion in 8, 209–11, 239
  nuclear energy industry of 196–7
  Operation Copper 79–80, 237
  post-apartheid foreign policy 43–5
  quiet diplomacy of 109
  science diplomacy of 126
  Twitter/X diplomacy of 91, 92, 98
South Korea 209
South Sudan 224
Southern African Customs Union 51
Southern African Development Community (SADC) 47, 79–80, 211, 224
Southern African Development Community Mission in Mozambique (SAMIM) 78–9
Southern African Regional Science Initiative (SAFARI 2000) project 126
South–South cooperation 174
Soviet Union 206, 208
  see also Russia
space technology, developments in 131
Spain 166
Sparta 12
Specialized Technical Committee Meeting on Education, Science and Technology (STC-EST) 126–7
Speller, I. 78
Spencer, J. 2
Spies, Yolanda K. 1, 23
Square Kilometre Array (SKA) radio telescope 126, 131
stakeholder diplomacy 59, 62–3
state-owned enterprises (SOEs) 49–50

Sudan 19, 130, 144
Sufi Brotherhoods (*Zawya*) 172–3
Suluhu Hassan, Samia 92
Sunni Islam 171–2, 173
Sustainable Development Goals (SDGs) 8, 23, 76, 121, 139, 196, 239
sustainable tourism 62–3
Sweden 189
Switzerland 112, 115, 116

T

Taiwan 44
Tanzania 79
Tavares, Luís Filipe 99
technology 121–2
  digital capabilities 5, 9n2, 58–9, 61–2
  science diplomacy 121–32, 241
  Twitter/X diplomacy 7, 88–101, 237–8, 239
  see also science diplomacy
terrorists, negotiation with 107–8, 111, 112–13, 114, 115, 116
Thakur, R. 106
Theron, François 5–6, 242
Thirty Years' War (1618–48) 13
Thomson, A. 108
Tijaniyya Brotherhood 172
Till, G. 74, 78
'Time of Morocco in France' initiative 166
Tofa, M. 3
Tokyo International Conference on African Development 230
Touadera, Faustin-Archange 98
Toure, Moctar 126
tourism 62–3, 152, 156, 158–9, 160
Track II diplomacy, role of women in 223–4
trade
  and economic diplomacy of South Africa 44–5, 49, 51–2
  maritime 82
  slave trade 16–17, 157–9
traditional diplomacy 101, 151
transatlantic slave trade 16, 157–9
Transneft 205
trans-Saharan slave trade 16
Treaty of Aix-la-Chapelle 14
Treaty of Pelindaba 203
Treaty on the Non-Proliferation of Nuclear Weapons (NPT) 201
Trump, Donald 91, 143
trust 95–6, 115, 116, 151, 241
Turianskyi, Y. 5
Turkey 79, 82, 205–6
Twiplomacy *see* Twitter/X diplomacy
Twitter/X diplomacy 5, 7, 88, 89, 90–2, 237–8, 239
  in Africa 92–5
  African regional bodies using Twitter/X **95**
  Chibok schoolgirls abductions 97–8
  during COVID-19 pandemic 91, 94, 239

diaspora diplomacy 93–4
disastrous consequences of 96
of international organizations 99
nation branding 94–5
networked diplomacy 94
politicization of Twitter/X 96, 97
and trust between diplomats 95–6

U

Uganda 22
Ukraine 4, 99, 205, 213–14, 239
Umar, Tahir 112
UN Charter 4
UN Human Rights Commission 227
UN Mission for Ebola Emergency Response (UNMEER) 141
Union of African States (UAS) 22
United Arab Emirates 90, 180
United Kingdom 14, 16–17, 94
  Brexit 2
  science diplomacy of 124, 126
United Nations (UN) 3, 16, 21, 22, 39, 233, 238
  E-Government Survey 2022 61
  Ezulwini Consensus 31–2
  Millennium Development Goals (MDGs) 23
  Sustainable Development Goals (SDGs) 8, 23, 76, 121, 139, 196, 239
  United Nations Decade for Women 223
  United Nations Development Programme (UNDP) 61–2, 99
  United Nations Educational, Scientific and Cultural Organization (UNESCO) 62, 165, 231
  United Nations General Assembly (UNGA) 4, 23, 115
    Resolution 63/33 140
    Session on the World Drug Problem (2016) 34
  United Nations Security Council (UNSC) 31
United States 206
  and COVID-19 pandemic 125, 143
  quiet diplomacy of 108
  science diplomacy of 123–4, 128
  visa ban on students/scholars from Arab countries 180
UNSC Resolution 1325 224, 226, 233
uranium 124, 131, 204, 211
US State Department 124

V

vaccines, COVID-19 142–3
  African Vaccine Acquisition Task Team 145
  TRIPS waiver 145–6
  vaccine apartheid 143, 144, 145
  vaccine nationalism 134
  vaccine passport 35

Van Noorden, R. 124
van Wyk, Jo-Ansie 6, 8, 59
Veenendaal, W.P. 56
Verwijk, Margaret 90
Vienna Convention on Diplomatic Relations 15
Vreÿ, Francois 7, 245

W

Wade, Abdoulaye 23
Wallace, J. 107–8
Wallström, Margot 59
Wekesa, B. 5
Weltpolitik 18
West Africa 25, 81
  Ebola outbreak (2014–16) 141–2
  pre-colonial diplomacy 19–21
West African Science Centre on Climate Change and Adapted Land Use project 190
Western Sahara 163
Westphalian state system 6, 13–14, 23, 25, 243
Wilhelm II, Kaiser 18
Wiseman, G. 178
Wivel, A. 60
Wojciuk, A. 187
women in diplomacy 4, 8–9, 59, 63–4, 221–3, 239, 241–2, 245
  African Union's normative framework for gender equality 224–6
  agenda setting and consensus building 230–1
  building networks and alliances and influencing agendas 231–2
  determinants and prospects for participation 227–8
  intergovernmental processes (African Union) 228–30
  national/organizational interests 226–7
  Track II diplomacy 223–4
Women Peace and Security Movement 224
Working Group for Women, Peace and Security 224
World Bank 141, 143, 144, 188, 189, 230
World Conference on Women 223, 225
World Economic Forum (WEF) 48
World Health Organization (WHO) 137, 138, 139, 141, 143, 145, 146
World Trade Organization (WTO) 47, 232, 245
WorleyParsons 206, 207

Y

Yaoundé Architecture for Maritime Security 80
Yaoundé Code of Conduct (YCC) 80
Year of Return campaign, Ghana 157–8
Ylonen, A. 3
Yorke, C. 2
Yusuf, Mohammed 112

Z

Zambia 4, 214
  nuclear energy expansion in 8, 211, **212–13**, 213, 239
  Twitter/X diplomacy of 90
Zaporizhzhia Nuclear Power Plant, Ukraine 214
Zene, Cherif Mahamat 98
Zenn, J. 111
Zhang, X. 24
Zimbabwe 96, 109, 143, 144, 230, 231
Zoomplomacy 94
Zuma, Jacob 24, 51, 91, 210